Harvard University

THE CAMPUS GUIDE

Harvard University

AN ARCHITECTURAL TOUR BY
Douglass Shand-Tucci

PHOTOGRAPHS BY
Richard Cheek

FOREWORD BY
Neil L. Rudenstine

Princeton Architectural Press
NEW YORK | *2001*

This book has been made possible through the generous support
of the Graham Foundation for Advanced Studies in the Fine Arts.

Published by Princeton Architectural Press
37 East 7th Street
New York, New York 10003

For a free catalog of books, call 1.800.722.6657.
Visit our web site at www.papress.com.

SERIES EDITOR: Jan Cigliano
SERIES CONCEPT: Dennis Looney
DESIGN: Sara E. Stemen
COPYEDITING: Heather Ewing
MAPS: Jane Garvie

SPECIAL THANKS TO: Nettie Aljian, Ann Alter, Amanda Atkins, Nicola Bednarek,
Janet Behning, Clare Jacobson, Mark Lamster, Nancy Eklund Later, Anne Nitschke,
Lottchen Shivers, Jennifer Thompson, and Deb Wood of Princeton Architectural Press
—Kevin C. Lippert, publisher

Cataloging-in-Publication Data is available from the Library of Congress.
ISBN 1-56898-280-1
PRINTED IN CHINA

CONTENTS

DINOCRATES

VITRVVIVS

MMHOLCONIIRVFVS
ETCELERCRYPTAMTRI
BVNALIATHEATRVMSP

Acknowledgments

There is perhaps no one thing, which the most Polite part of
Mankind have more universally agreed in; than the Vallue they have
ever set upon the Remains of distant Times. Nor amongst the
Severall kinds of those Antiquitys, are there any so much regarded,
as those of Buildings; Some for their Magnificence, or Curious
Workmanship; and others, as they move more lively and pleasing
Reflections (than History without their Aid can do) On the Persons
who have Inhabited them; On the Remarkable things which have
been transacted in them, Or the extraordinary Occasions of
Erecting them.

Sir John Vanbrugh (1709)

As for me, I distrust the commonplace;
Demand and am receiving marvels, signs,
Miracles wrought in air, acted in space
After imagination's own designs.
The lion and the tiger pace this way
As often as I call; the flight of wings
Surprises empty air, while out of clay
The golden-gourded vine unwatered springs.
I have inhaled impossibility,
And walk at such an angle, all the stars
Have hung their carnival chains of light for me:
There is a streetcar runs from here to Mars.
I shall be seeing you, my darling, there,
Or at the burning bush in Harvard Square.

Adrienne Rich

May we all keep that rendezvous. And if some there be (most?) who never
see Harvard as does Adrienne Rich, a notable graduate—and as I like to
think I do—this guide will be the more interesting to them for its attempt to
probe a little more deeply than is usual into the history and architecture of
this most ancient and storied of all the institutions of higher learning of the
New World.

This is in keeping with the overall design concept of Princeton
Architectural Press in this series of campus guides, all of which aim to offer
"an insider's view"; one that I have tried to disclose here of Harvard based on
the point Sir John Vanbrugh made so well three hundred years ago, when
Harvard was already in its second generation of college buildings: that there
can really be no effective demarcation between history and architecture, any

more than there can be in architecture itself between form and function. It is also the view, I believe, of at least one very great contemporary architect—Rafael Moneo—who with Tadao Ando may be the designer since Sir Edwin Lutyens whose work I most admire. Certainly Moneo seemed to urge this view in a speech of 1985, the year he became head of architecture at Harvard. *The New York Times* reported his words this way: "Ideas must be built in order to be called architecture." To this I agreed, but at once heard it, saw it, in my mind's eye, the other way around: *architecture is, must be, built ideas.*

Although I love the analysis of the formal aspects of architecture, and exalt the form giver above all, in no sense should all that ever claim any primacy over the underlying cultural or intellectual or social history of which architecture is the embodiment. Indeed, if humans be embodied souls, buildings for me are embodied ideas. Thus Harvard's history aside from its architecture is in a very real sense, invisible; while Harvard's architecture apart from the institution's history is hollow.

However, this conviction is easier to sustain in an architectural history than in a guidebook, where geographical and historical vectors will usually be in conflict. Harvard's most venerable history, evoked by its most ancient footprints and oldest buildings, is everywhere cheek by jowl, crowding its streets with its most modern buildings, shaped by its most recent history. And while most histories (and slide lectures) solve this problem by jumping from landmark to landmark as a crow may fly but no person could ever walk, most guides necessarily opt for geographical direction and sacrifice the underlying tale of historical development to a lengthy (and mostly unread) introduction. I made more than one such effort in the early drafts of this book, all of which fell far short of what I felt needed to be done. So, instead, I have tried here to use geography, so to speak, to address time, the interconnection of which, each with the other, today and throughout Harvard's nearly four centuries of development, I have made a key underlying theme of this book.

Thereby I have taken sides—evident to me as I write this acknowledgment (as most such are written, after writing the book)—in an issue of our own day, which most at Harvard in the past would have disagreed with me about, an issue raised insightfully by Sarah Boxer, a critic for *The New York Times*. Recently in that journal she wrote: "A little war against time has begun. As Jed Perl, an American art critic, put it in *The New Republic*, 'Chronology, that backbone of the historical sense, has been collapsed into some kind of postmodern time warp.'" Why, we may well ask? Because, Boxer insists, increasingly it is seen that "chronology and time are only surface issues." *Yes.* My view exactly. Now this is not so new an idea as it seems. Isabella Stewart Gardner, the great American collector, mentor, and designer, whose biographer I am, knew this a century ago—as the Picasso-like collage of her famous museum, with no chronology and not even much of themes, shows so well. But Gardner was a very unusual person, far ahead of her times in more than one way. Most still, today, would argue for the objective reality of chronology and time. Not in this book, the reader should be warned; though the result, I believe, is a much clearer reading of Harvard's history and architecture. That said, my debt to the massive published scholarship of Harvard's tercentenary historian, Samuel Eliot Morison, is enormous. Also of use was Bainbridge Bunting's Harvard architectural history, completed by my old friend, the late Margaret Henderson Floyd, and the several volumes of the Cambridge Historical Commission's *Survey of Cambridge Architecture*, one of the authors of which, Robert Bell Rettig, has kindly read this manuscript and given me the benefit of his many years of knowledge of the subject.

Two Harvard professor-architects, Rodolfo Machado and Jorge Silvetti, the second of whom succeeded Rafael Moneo as head of architecture at Harvard's Graduate School of Design, are in a very real sense the men I owe my first acknowledgment to, however, for it was Rodolfo and Jorge who suggested to Jan Cigliano of Princeton Architectural Press, who conceived this excellent series of campus guides, that I was the person to write the Harvard volumes. I am thus in each man's debt, and Jan's too, for the opportunity. I would also like to thank Harvard's twenty-sixth president, Neil Rudenstine, who advised me to accept the challenge, and offered to write an introductory essay. Though, truth to tell, that's not the half of it, for Neil subsequently agreed to serve as a reader and has committed a great deal more of his time than I had any right to expect. And his critical eye has been so dependable I have felt able to risk going the extra mile more than once here to produce what I feel is some of my best work. That cause has also been well served by a superb copyeditor, Heather Ewing, for whose work on the manuscript I am deeply grateful.

To these primary acknowledgments I must add several lesser but still important ones. Dean Archie T. Epps III, though we do not always agree, is always worth engaging, for he and Harvard go way back, and he and I not a little way too. Three heads of Houses who were my chief mentors at Harvard when I was an undergraduate in 1969–72 and a tutor in Eliot House in 1980–86 also deserve mention: Elliott Perkins, the master of Lowell House, Tom Crooks of Dudley, and Alan Heimert of Eliot. All three sought for me to stay at Harvard, but in ways that proved not possible; each would, I think, be happy with this guide, in which after all I have made a contribution they would each have valued, I believe.

A multitude of other acknowledgments also come pleasantly to mind: Dr. Oglesby Paul of the Medical School; Scott Levitan, Director of University and Commercial Real Estate; James Cuno, Director of the University Art Museums; Charles Sullivan, executive director of the Cambridge Historical Commission; Harley Holden, university archivist;

Upton Bradey, my agent; and for a miscellany of good deeds, Peter Kadzis, B. Hughes Morris, H. A. Crosby Forbes, Dennis Sheehan, Robin Bledsoe, Tim O'Donnell, Bill Fowler, Chris Lydon, Mark Pasnick, Diane and Stuart Myers, Luke Rogers, Nicholas Holder, Peter Davison, Peter Forbes, Paul Robertson, Beverly Sullivan, and Gifford Combs, co-founder with me of the Eliot House Architecture Table. Richard Cheek, whose extraordinary photographs bring a unique vision to the book, made a considerable accommodation to make all this possible, for which I am grateful. His eye and mine are different, and he has illustrated my text as much as I have verbalized his pictures. Each vision brings something valuable to subjects I chose and Richard then shot in his own inimitable manner. Only Rawson and Bessie Wood, in a different way, made a comparable contribution to my being able to write this book. Finally, as always: to one only will I tell it.

D. S.-T.
Boston Athenaeum 2000

How to Use This Book

This guide is intended for visitors, alumni, and students who wish to have an insider's look at the most historic and significant buildings on Harvard's several campuses, from the ancient seventeenth- and eighteenth-century precincts of the Old Yard and the Old Burying Ground to the most recent plans for expansion along Charlesbank Harvard.

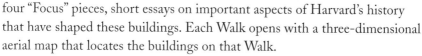

    The book is divided into twelve Walks; interspersed among them are four "Focus" pieces, short essays on important aspects of Harvard's history that have shaped these buildings. Each Walk opens with a three-dimensional aerial map that locates the buildings on that Walk.

    In addition to historic Harvard College and the Graduate School of Arts and Sciences, each of Harvard's ten famous graduate professional schools is included—Law, Design, Business, Education, Divinity, Medicine, Dental Medicine, Public Health, Government, and Continuing Education.

Visitors are welcome to tour Harvard Yard and the Harvard University campus.

Public Tours Harvard Events & Information Center, Holyoke Center, 1350 Massachusetts Avenue, Cambridge, 45 minutes. Free. (617) 495-1573

Prospective Student Tours Harvard Admissions Office, Byerly Hall, 8 Garden Street, Cambridge. Free. (617) 495-1551

Museum of Cultural and National History (617) 496-6972

Harvard University Art Museums include Busch-Reisinger Museum and Fogg Art Museum, 32 Quincy Street; Arthur M. Sackler Museum, 485 Broadway. Open Monday–Saturday 10am to 5 pm, Sunday 1pm–5pm. Admission $5 adult, $4 senior, $3 student. www.artmuseums.harvard.edu. (617) 495-9400

Carpenter Center for the Visual Arts 24 Quincy Street. Open Monday- Saturday 9am to 12 midnight, Saturday–Sunday 12 noon to midnight. (617) 495-3251

Arnold Arboretum Arborway, Jamaica Plain.www.arboretum.harvard.edu. (617) 524-1718

Harvard University Library http://hul.harvard.edu/libinfo. (617) 495-2411

This is as stimulating and refreshing a volume on university architecture and design as we are likely to discover. Douglass Shand-Tucci's eye is always on the alert for every minor or major inflection in architectural style, and his formalist—or more broadly aesthetic—observations always illuminate. He understands how clusters (sometimes apparently random clusters) of dissimilar buildings and their spaces can surprisingly "cohere" (or fail to cohere). He knows what it means to walk through the shifting scenes of a collegiate landscape and cityscape, attuned to the ways in which everything that is historical is in constant play with all that is contemporary.

Perhaps most distinctively, this volume is a rich and variegated essay in social and institutional history. As such, it tells us a very great deal about the particular motives and energies that helped to shape the forms, functions, and indeed the accoutrements not only of individual Harvard buildings, but also of the university's ambitious building campaigns in different eras.

Why were the so-called "Gold Coast" dormitories developed, and who lived in them? What accounted for the successive structural and "decorative" transformations of any number of Harvard's buildings? What unexpected convergence of temperaments—as well as intellectual and aesthetic fields of force—led to the swift appearance of Le Corbusier's Carpenter Center on so unlikely a site as Quincy Street?

These and many other questions are not only asked but answered in a style and manner that are always engaging and vivacious, often witty, sometimes provocative, and unfailingly informative. Documentation and anecdote—combined with fine expatiation—recreate dramatically the successive human and social contexts in which the university's various educational purposes have been translated into equally various architectural and spatial forms. The result is a book that is in many respects a vivid, animated, selective biography of Harvard, viewed through the perspective of the university's "built environment" as that environment was actually created and shaped over the course of several centuries.

It is obvious that the Harvard environment differs significantly from that of the paradigmatic idea of an American college or university campus. The concept of a campus implies—however imperfectly it may be realized—something that is delimited: a special space, somewhat apart, with its own confines; its own form of "wholeness" or visible unity and coherence; its own discernible scale; and its own overarching design in which landscape and architecture, communal purposes and special purposes, symbolic characteristics and functional characteristics are all interwoven in such a way as to represent something that can be "seen" and described recognizably as (for example) "the University of Virginia," or Amherst College, or Princeton, or Stanford, or Smith College.

Viewed from this vantage point, Harvard clearly has a number of identifiable precincts where several of the features of a campus are predominant. But while each of these has a strong sense of identity, it is also the case that these interludes tend to be episodic. Harvard Yard and the region of Quincy Street across to Memorial Hall form a kind of campus (as does the Business School, or the area around the River Houses). But as soon as we move beyond Memorial Hall, approaching the nearby spaces that encompass the School of Design, Busch Hall, and William James Hall—or further beyond, to the Law School and its neighboring engineering buildings—then we quickly recognize that we are somewhere "outside" the strict campus, and we must begin to think in rather different conceptual terms, with reference to a rather different aesthetic.

Moreover, if we leave the Yard, not via Quincy Street, but through the Johnston gate, then the differences are even more immediately striking. Harvard Square—with shops, automobiles, street-music, the subway, and much else that is urban—suddenly declares that the university is not so much something set apart, as it is an adjacency, where one kind of spatial "edge" is thrust directly against another. Even this formulation, however, must take into account the fact that the boundary line—or edge—is really much less sharp than might first appear. The Yard is—after all—very porous. There are *many* gates, not simply one. The Square is visible (and audible) from within the campus, just as the inviting quietude of the campus can be sensed from the Square. So the movement from Yard to Square (and back) ultimately has the feel of an anticipated extension and continuation of one's natural living space, rather than as an abrupt or disconcerting breakpoint. Campus and city interpenetrate—not everywhere, and not always with the same effect. But they do so in our consciousness, if not always visually and acoustically: we experience them as parts of a single larger "place" whose unity includes very different forms of experience.

If we ask what—if anything—can help us account for (and define) the unusual characteristics of Harvard's environment, there are obviously several reasons—including the comparatively decentralized nature of the university, as well as its evolution over a long period of time (through many happy and unhappy changes in architectural style and taste). I am persuaded, however, that a considerable part of the answer also lies in the way the university has always defined its basic educational purposes. In this respect, Harvard has been engaged in a longstanding, continuing institutional effort to include and reconcile what is relatively "inward"—or cloistered—and what is far-reaching or "open." Part of the university's orientation has always been strongly collegiate and campus-based, after the manner of the Oxford and Cambridge residential colleges. But the university has also been—from quite early times—committed to a dynamic role in public life, in public leadership, in the professions, and in professional education on a national and, increasingly, an international scale.

In this sense, Harvard has by tradition been open to the world, engaged with "practice," and "educationally designed" to be outside the perimeter of its campus as much as inside. So, it should not be surprising, perhaps, to discover that the terrain of the university as a whole includes different kinds of precincts, different textures and tonalities, with some sharp juxtapositions, some softer transitions, ample stylistic discordances, many elegant or harmonious passages, and a great number of unanticipated epiphanies when startling incidents of architectural grace or gravity suddenly confront one, and appear to embody in a single architectural master-stroke so many of the concatenated energies, the depth, and the aspirations of the university in its totality.

Strangely enough, this idiosyncratic pattern appears to work. And if the final result is not easy to describe, neither is it so elusive as to lack identity or the sense of being recognizable. The underlying geometry is complex. One assimilates it only gradually, over time. But the variety of Harvard's architectural and spatial clusterings wear well. And its "built environment" must ultimately be viewed as something that has arisen from the energy, movement, and power of its expansive intellectual environment—including the special tension between the university's commitment to the values of a residential campus community, and its equally strong desire to reach beyond the campus in order to engage energetically with the larger world outside.

Neil L. Rudenstine
January 2001

TOP: *Holworthy Hall, Memorial Hall, and Thayer Hall*
BOTTOM: *Massachusetts Hall, First Church, and Harvard Hall*

HARVARD YARD AND HARVARD SQUARE

Seventeenth- and Eighteenth-Century Harvard College: Harvard Yard and Harvard Square

Ralph Waldo Emerson had once an almost cinematic vision of Harvard Yard, a vision worthy of the famous early twentieth-century filmmaker, Sergei Eisenstein. Attending in 1836 the bicentennial of the college's founding, Emerson admitted that after two hundred years the Yard "at any time is full of ghosts." But on the day of the jubilee it was all, he felt, so much more intensified: "The anointed eye saw the crowd of spirits that mingled with the procession in the vacant spaces, year by year, as the classes proceeded," he confided to his journal; "and then the far longer train of ghosts that followed the company. . .the long and winding train reaching back into eternity." It is a vision no one should ever lose track of in Harvard Yard, even the least romantic of natives, the most practical of visitors. For here are no dreaming spires nor sylvan riverbanks of Oxbridge; nor elegant colonnades after the fashion of Mr. Jefferson's University at Virginia. Instead, spare Yankee rectangles mostly, red brick, not without grace, but certainly plainspoken. Which is why Emerson's vision is the right place to start; had better be, if there is to be any understanding at all of Harvard, in whose Yard, storied as it is, there is little enough reward without thought. Emerson's "winding train reaching back" is a visualization of history insightful in more than one sense; the unchanging backdrop equally as thoughtful a visualization of architecture. And all at once the observer may well feel like posing the question the learned professor famously asked the puzzled Spanish stationmaster on the train platform: "What time does Madrid get to this train?" Such is the nature of linear time. Though its seeming suspension can pull us back, in a second, as it did Emerson, so can it also, just as quickly, project us forward, a thing the Yard does all the time. Witness the twentieth-century poet, David McCord, musing on the bronze statue of John Harvard (aka Sherman Hoar; no one really knows what John looked like). McCord thought the statue, which presides over the Yard, seemed once to catch his eye: "Is that you John Harvard?" he thought. "Aye," the poet heard replied, "and after you're gone."

"First Flower of Their Wilderness":
The Collegiate Way and the Residential College Building Type

A century after the bicentennial Emerson attended, Harvard's president and fellows, in 1936, announced the college's tercentenary to the world in words that recounted Harvard's origins succinctly and beautifully:

> GREETING:
> It having pleased GOD to inspire the love of Learning amongst the first settlers of the Colony of Massachusetts Bay and, in the infancy of their

community, to direct their labors towards the well-being of Church and State through the establishment of foundations for the increase of knowledge and the education of youth, it is meet and proper that this Society of Scholars, founded in the Year of Our Lord one thousand six hundred and thirty-six, by Act of a Great and General Court of the Company of Massachusetts Bay convened in Boston the 8th/eighteenth of September of that year, should celebrate in the company of friends and benefactors the THREE HNDREDTH ANNIVERSARY of its foundation.

1636. The thirteenth year of the reign of Charles I, that most absolutist of Stuart monarchs (after whom the river Harvard presides over is named to this day), and only a few years into the great Puritan emigration to the New World of many of the King's most troublesome subjects. Several of them the next year were to be found on the College's newly established governing board—the Reverend and Honorable Board of Overseers. That august body, originally twelve Boston area ministers and magistrates, was quick "to take order" that very year, purchasing in 1637 a house owned by one William Peyntree and a sliver of land, one lot among many in Newtowne, each a house and a yard—a cow yard—hence Harvard Yard then, and still today, though the cows are mercifully long gone and the sliver has meanwhile grown some. (The Peyntree house, too, is long gone, torn down in 1644. But you can find the location if you are nimble enough: brass plates marking its front corners are set into the pavement in the middle of Massachusetts Avenue in Harvard Square.) Then, in 1638, the year the first freshmen arrived, came the providential benefaction (all his library and half his estate) of an otherwise anonymous Charlestown minister, John Harvard. In consequence of that stroke of good fortune the Great and General Court the year following "ordered that the colledge . . . to be built at Cambridge shall be called Harvard Colledge," Newtowne itself having been renamed in honor of the English university so many of the colony's leaders were graduates of. Thus there came finally and fully into being the first, and it may be still the foremost, of American institutions of higher learning.

The circumstances which account for all this proceeded from the policy goals of the Colony's leadership: "Harvard College was the acme of a series of cultural efforts in the 1630's and 1640's . . . [including] common schools, compulsory education laws, grammar schools such as Boston Latin," Samuel Eliot Morison wrote in *Three Centuries of Harvard*, and in each case the effort evidenced the famously tenacious Puritan purpose: "Yeoman for the most part, and artisans, [the Puritans] included a sprinkling of gentlefolk and (by 1640) over a hundred alumni of Oxford and Cambridge. . . . Enthusiasm for education was one aspect of that desire to know and do the will of God that bound the puritans together, and led them to brave the sea, the wilderness and the New England climate." Harvard's university historian continued: "New Englanders were no less English for being puritans. A firm determination to transplant English civilization as a whole was bound up with their desire to purify it." Today, nearly four centuries later, few would argue either with Morison's conclusion that if "learning was one of the by-products of English Puritanism that came over in the Winthrop fleet [it is] a by-product which we have come in time to value more than the leading article." But it is a measure of how important education was to them also that in 1635 the sum the Legislature voted for the new college was more than half the whole tax levy for the entire colony that year. Nor was fundraising in England neglected, and as early as in 1643 Harvard was endowed with its first scholarship fund, the gift of Lady Ann (Radcliffe) Moulson. (Such was the importance of this first endowment to Harvard College, that more than two centuries later when Harvard endorsed the education of women Radcliffe College was named almost inevitably after this early benefactor, whose own coat of arms, not her husband's, was chosen as Radcliffe's arms.) Striking too how apt this seventeenth-century tale seems to the twenty-first-century institution that has now grown up from those small beginnings, grown up into one of the most honored of all the great universities of the world. Was it not arrogance—at best it was courage to the point of foolhardiness—for European settlers to found a college as they saw it *in sylvestribus et incutis locis*, on the verge of the western wilderness? Certainly there is evident in so precipitate an action (as it must have seemed to many then) a supreme self-assurance in a cause, however noble, however idealistic, that was equally perhaps evidence of Puritan self-doubt, a cause Harvard's founders articulated in words admittedly by now well worn but surely still thrilling: their aim, they declared at a time when bare survival in the New World was still an issue, was "to advance learning and perpetuate it to posterity."

The United States of America, of course, and the evolution of its various state and local governments no less than Harvard, would suffer as much perhaps as benefit from this New World Puritanism. And still does today. For example, not only do town meetings regularly convene in one Colonial village-long-since-become-big-city-suburb after another throughout Greater Boston—a problematic way to govern America's seventh largest metropolis, Harvard's home base—but within memory there have been Harvard graduate schools hardly on nodding terms with other Harvard graduate schools; in its own realm quite as deliberate a polity, mind you, as town meeting government. It even has a sort of name, a mantra, heard for years in Cambridge, "every tub on its own bottom." Never mind. The best fruits of Puritan—what shall we call it? boldness?—have more than proved worth the trouble. Their determination to be "English, but purified," for instance, seems both father and mother to a paradox at the center of the Harvard experience to this day, the strong attachment to traditional values and ancient customs, coupled with a profoundly self-critical conviction that it is just the most ancient and sacred things that most often will stand in the greatest need of reform. Though even that virtuous enough conviction has its shadow side; no one is more intolerant than a Harvard liberal—hence all the jokes about "the Kremlin on the Charles" and "the People's Republic of Cambridge," the reference being to the so often relentlessly lefty politics of the modern day municipality of Greater Boston in which the historic heart of the university is located. But the sometimes perverse hardheadedness of town meeting (or university bureaucracy), even a pervasive hubris and self-righteousness, are surely in Harvard's case what the French so brilliantly call the weaknesses of strengths, in this case the strengths of the Puritan legacy.

Talk of hubris! Not withstanding new president's lodgings that in 1644 replaced the Peyntree house and another modest dwelling nearby bought in 1651 and rechristened (grandly enough) Goffe College, Harvard in its earliest days, though it might be in the middle of nowhere and hardly up and running at all, was by no means content with what might have been thought reasonable architecture. Despite perilous financial straits the college erected almost at once in the late 1630s a splendid collegiate building, the first Harvard College, Harvard Hall I or Old College—called familiarly "the House" after the English fashion—triumphantly completed by Henry Dunster, the college's earliest president, in time for the first commencement in 1642. Altogether a brash enough business all around. The award of academic degrees, a jealously guarded prerogative then of kings, popes, and emperors, was certainly nowhere granted in the legislative acts founding Harvard. Nor would this power be anywhere alluded to in the college's first charter of 1650, which set up under the Board of Overseers a self-perpetuating corporation—today the oldest in the Western Hemisphere—that still directs Harvard's affairs today. "The powers of a university," in Harvard historian Bernard Bailyn's words, "were simply assumed"; academic degrees forthwith were granted. By 1654 they were, in fact, acknowledged by Oxford and Cambridge. Until then, however, degrees were granted rather arrogantly on no authority whatsoever, except Harvard's own.

Equally outrageous was Old College. The "House" many of the citizenry of the colony saw for the first time at that 1642 commencement stood just about where Grays Hall is to be found today in Harvard Yard. It was a wooden structure that accommodated only about fifty students (more or less the maximum at Harvard throughout the seventeenth-century) and a number of tutors, assistant teachers who aided the president (there were not yet, nor would be for some years, professors). There were doubles, triples, and four-man rooms, and a Long Chamber that slept fifteen, probably for freshmen, on the second floor, arrangements primitive sounding now but comparable to those of the same period at Gonville and Caius College, for example, at Oxford. Similarly with the principal communal rooms in Old College. There were two. There was a passable rustic facsimile on the ground floor of the historic centerpiece of the Oxbridge college, the Hall, with adjoining Buttery (Dining Hall and Pantry we would call them today). The Hall was a great hall—"very faire and comely" it was called—where president and fellows, tutors, and students met day in and day out at meals, prayers, and classes. Behind it was a large kitchen. And although there was no chapel (the college worshipped daily in Hall and on Sunday in the town meeting house established by 1651 in Harvard Square), the other great necessity of the Oxford and Cambridge tradition, the College Library, took up a large part of the second floor.

Sensible enough it may sound, and given its wooden construction and folk-Gothic character (steep medieval gables, second floor overhangs and mullioned casement windows), modest enough too. But in its time Harvard's first House was the largest and most imposing building by far in the English colonies, approached in scale and presence by no other structure, governmental or ecclesiastical. And roundly criticized: it was, said many, "too gorgeous for a wilderness." A criticism they doubtless repeated about Harvard Hall II when Harvard Hall I, having not stood up very well to the New England climate, was replaced in 1677 by a new building on the site of the present Harvard Hall III. Harvard Hall II, still medieval in style, was an even more splendid building for its time and place, the pride of New England in 1677, and until the erection of the Wren Building in 1698 at the College of William and Mary in Virginia, by far the grandest architecture in the colonies—criticism of the "gorgeousness" of each building was understandable. But from the very beginning, the values and priorities of Harvard College were very different and much more ambitious than most probably appreciated. "The founders of Harvard insisted," wrote Morison, "that Harvard be a real college, in the English sense of the word; a society of scholars, where teachers and students lived in the same building . . . associating not only in lecture rooms but at meals, in chambers, at prayers and in recreation," easier to do in an age when all undergraduates undertook a uniform course of study at the same pace, but expensive, given the extensive dormitories required.

This distinctive educational concept originated in the twelfth and thirteenth centuries at Oxford and Cambridge, which although modeled on the University of Paris generally rejected almost at once the continental custom of what we would today call off-campus housing—students living independently on their own and connecting with their teachers only at lectures. Instead, Oxbridge evolved the residential college building type, derived from monastic prototypes, and designed to encourage hour by hour interaction between faculty and students in close quarters. The historic prototypes are two Oxford colleges, Merton College of 1264 and, most important, New College, founded in 1379, the latter the first to emphasize undergraduate education. Evolved to its height by the late sixteenth and early seventeenth

Massachusetts Hall and First Church

centuries, this concept energized Puritans as much in New England as in Old England. Familiar from their stay in Holland with the continental European university tradition, which also prevailed in Scotland, New England Puritans would have nothing to do with it, despite the fact that in Cambridge it would have been far less costly to have used the local meeting house for recitations and disputations and boarded the students out in the village. But "the Government of *New England*," Cotton Mather, a leading

Boston divine, declared, "was for having their students brought up in a more *Collegiate* Way of Living." And in all probability in more than one college, furthermore; surely the reason why Harvard, so eager to establish the full Oxbridge collegiate experience, so conspicuously avoided at first emulating Oxbridge's traditional architectural expression of that experience—linked, cloistered quadrangular buildings. Instead, Harvard by the mid-seventeenth century created a landscape in its slowly enlarging precincts of entirely separate structures. And neither the danger of fire, nor the natural enough Puritan dislike of the monastic ethos that fathered enclosed quads, nor the small lot sizes, nor even any sort of response to the vastness of the New World landscape, seems sufficient (all have been advanced plausibly) to explain what has been called this "momentous departure at Harvard," momentous because it influenced all American college design subsequently, to abandon the venerable English architectural model of an educational model Harvard's founders were determined to perpetuate.

Most likely, suggests the Stanford architectural historian, Paul Turner, in his now classic study *Campus*, the mindset involved is revealed by Harvard's habit, really inexplicable otherwise, of calling all its earliest buildings "Colleges." Take the Indian College of 1655, for instance. Idealistic enough then but difficult for us to understand today because of the implied attempt to "de-Indianize" (and now chiefly notable for its pioneering printing press, which brought out John Eliot's Algonquin-language bible, the first bible printed in the New World, in 1663). Of the Indian College Turner wrote: "It is possible that the Harvard authorities actually thought of it as a separate college in the English sense, for it had its own teachers and the Indian students were supposed to live together in the building. . . . In this sense, Harvard was more like a university than simply one college. . . . In the realm of architectural planning, Harvard's self-image as a near-university could have been expressed by the separation of buildings and by their designation as 'colleges.'" (Turner adds, "the original motive was no doubt forgotten, but the peculiar use of the word *college* persisted at Harvard, as shown in the engraving made by William Burgis in 1726, entitled 'A Prospect of the Colledges in Cambridge in New England.'") Overambitious as it turned out; resources hardly allowed for more than one college. But the ambitions of Harvard's founders are nonetheless important. Significantly, just as any idea of more than one college more or less passed away, so before long did Harvard's design concept of separate buildings, which soon enough began to be grouped quad-like. But the "Collegiate Way of Living" itself was far from abandoned. It remains to this day one of two key principles of the seventeenth-century college at the very center, historically, of Harvard's built environment.

An even more fundamental and enduring principle of the seventeenth-century college was that, in Morison's words, it was intended to be "a religious college, but emphatically not a 'divinity school'. . . . The difference was very nearly that between a Catholic university of today [1936] and a Catholic diocesan seminary. Harvard was founded, and in the seventeenth century supported, as a college of English university standards." It is an assertion that has sometimes been challenged. Certainly *Veritas*, Harvard's first seventeenth-century motto, was originally understood to mean *God*'s truth! But Harvard's more secular than religious foundations are now pretty widely accepted, set forth as they have been with considerable authority in the early twentieth century by a magisterial cohort of Harvard historians. Though Harvard in its earliest years was "not a modern liberal arts college . . . neither was it a divinity school," Bernard Bailyn has written, noting that the percentage of parsons among seventeenth-century alumni was only about fifty percent. From Harvard, Bailyn asserts, "the leadership of *church, state and trade* [emphasis added] was expected to emerge." And so it did, though not without a fight. Admittedly, there was never any religious oath or test at Harvard, but the issue was too nicely balanced in what was after all a Puritan commonwealth in a very narrowly religious era not to have caused contention. When perhaps the most eminent of Boston's Puritan divines, Increase Mather, was elected president of the college in 1685, the scales tipped one way; certainly he and his son, Cotton, argued forcefully for a "College of Divines" as they called it, in the face of the more liberal tradition championed by two legendary tutors of those days, John Leverett and William Brattle, who—when in 1708 Leverett was elected president—tipped the scales the other way, of course. Leverett was, in fact, the first Harvard president not a clergyman. Startlingly, he was scarcely much of a Puritan either. An ardent Tory, he was reputedly also a crypto-Anglican. Indeed, Leverett prevailed in the presidential election over the clerical Mathers chiefly because his friend, the governor of the day, did a deal in Leverett's behalf that Harvard absolutely could not turn down, virtually abdicating the royal prerogative of visitation in collegiate affairs as an inducement to the choice of tutor instead of cleric as president.

Leverett had an immense and immediate impact and on both large and small things. He on the one hand established the first professorial chair, for instance, the Hollis Professorship of Divinity. And on the other he seems also to have had a good effect on tutorial wit, even now hardly in short supply in Cambridge, but rooted then, perhaps, in more conviction. (My favorite Leverett-era example is the rejoinder of one Tutor Flynt to an orthodox visitor's disparagement of the teaching of a recently deceased Dr. Tillotson: "It is my opinion that Dr. Tillotson is in hell for his heresy," the visitor declared. To this Tutor Flynt replied: "It is my opinion that you will not meet him there.") Leverett also opened up the college to a somewhat more cosmopolitan religious tradition. When Christ Church was built across Cambridge Common from the college in 1760, students were permitted to attend the Anglican liturgy there with parental consent; thus for the first time being allowed to eschew the Puritan meeting house. It was a distinct contrast to the situation at Yale, founded in 1701 as a more orthodox alternative to a Harvard College more and more Puritans saw as deteriorating. In fact, *where* Yale was founded was as significant as *when* it was founded. Similarly, with what is now Princeton University, located in 1753 in a sequestered tiny country village, so as to avoid, in words expressing Puritan sentiments exactly by one of Princeton's founding trustees, "the various temptations attending a promiscuous converse with the world, that theatre of folly and dissipation."

Boston? At the end of the seventeenth-century? We are inclined to forget, as Bailyn points out in his *Massachusetts Shipping*, that already by the 1690s Boston was no inconsiderable capital. Its fleet of merchant ships ranked third, for instance, in the English-speaking world. Moreover, the royal authority—including that of the Anglican Church (hence new places of worship like Christ Church, Cambridge)—had been newly asserted in the 1680s. Even Boston's outlying environs were part of what was increasingly no longer a homogeneous Puritan capital. Thus Morison would write pointedly of Harvard's and Yale's situation when the latter was founded: "The distinct difference . . . between the two colleges was determined very largely by their respective communities. New Haven was a small place, and Connecticut a rural colony. . . at a time when Massachusetts was a royal province with a miniature viceregal court, and Boston a trading metropolis that aped the manners and reflected the fashions of England." Thus it was, for example, that in 1699 Renaissance architecture, no less, arrived at Harvard—late, but in some state. (It had also been late to arrive in England.) This at the bequest of the royal lieutenant governor William Stoughton, who although he certainly had his Gothic moments (Stoughton was notoriously the harshest of the Salem witchcraft trial judges) had also a more enlightened side. Whereas the Indian College of 1655, though Harvard's first brick building, was still medieval enough stylistically to have mullioned casement windows, and Harvard Hall II of 1677 had also still those same diamond-paned casements, and a whole parade of steep Gothic gables too, and only a few awkward attempts at classical detail, Stoughton College in 1699 was in its symmetrical composition, horizontal string courses and topmost cornice, and pedimented door frames a full fledged example of the Georgian mode of Renaissance Classicism. In fact, Stoughton, erected lengthwise to the street at right angles to Harvard Hall II, and set back so as to imply a court, was not only the first example of Renaissance Classicism at Harvard, but

Stoughton himself, the first individual donor of a building to an American college, was perhaps in his paradoxical repute a telling example of the fact that Boston was always going to be decidedly a mixed blessing for Harvard. So much so, even Morison would write that Boston and Harvard were ever a case of *non possum vivere sine te nec comte*, it is not possible to live with you or without you. Yet Morison was not unhappy with the result; nor to say, as others to this day might regret having to say, that "Leverett, in a word, founded the liberal tradition at Harvard University," only possible, of course, because of the influence of Boston's vice-regal court.

There was also, however, an influence traceable to the larger indigenous community of which the capstone was the legislature. Always more reflective of the Puritan point of view (certainly in a broadly cultural sense if less and less as time went on in the narrowly religious sense) the legislature perpetuated in rather a proprietorial way (the Massachusetts Bay Colony legislature, after all, not John Harvard, founded Harvard College) the long-standing Puritan attitude toward Harvard—irrespective of politics—as the common pride of the whole colony, with which there had grown up a continual interaction of town and gown; this was an interaction and a legacy, especially in the continuing dependence of the college on state grants, that yielded both a distinctive governance at Harvard, one which would reinforce the growth of the liberal tradition, and a distinctive architecture.

It had originally been assumed when Harvard's charter was promulgated, that after long-standing Oxbridge custom, the governing fellows of Harvard would be drawn from the resident tutors who assisted the president in teaching. But in the different conditions of the New World there was to grow up for a variety of reasons another and variant system: lay alumni fellows drawn from the community at large, only very loosely monitored by the Overseers. Beginning really in Leverett's era (it would take nearly a century for it to be established), this new system took root. Bailyn again: "Harvard was the progenitor of this form of governance for reasons that lay deep in the structure of American life. The pattern of external lay control . . . stemmed from the root impulse that accounted for the founding of [Harvard] in the first place. The pattern here was not that of medieval Europe, where masters and students came together to serve their guild needs," wrote the Harvard historian. Not at all. "In its inception Harvard was an artifact of the community as a whole, and the form of governance that developed allowed the community to retain control." And I think that "root impulse" of Bailyn's is what Paul Turner has called the "Puritan sense of the integrity of the whole community," which Turner, rightly, I think, sees as the formative principle of Harvard's evolving architecture in the late seventeenth and early eighteenth centuries. Whether or not Harvard's original predilection for separate rather than linked buildings reflected in some measure not just a tentative idea of a multi-college university but a more "Congregational" (i.e., more independent) design concept—as opposed to a more "Anglican"—design concept of buildings linked, in Ashton Willard's words, "like a group of Anglican communities under a bishop," an idea I think a bit of a stretch (or just the influence, perhaps, of lot divisions)—it is certainly the case that when Harvard's earliest architecture did begin in the 1670s to coalesce into the traditional Oxbridge quadrangular pattern after all, the form taken was that of the *open* court. This was an innovative idea that first vitalized the somewhat moribund Oxbridge quadrangular form at Gonville and Caius college in 1557. There it was that the traditional collegiate quad was first opened up, enclosed on only three sides by ranges of buildings, the fourth side marked only by a wall with a substantial gateway, thus introducing, in Turner's words, "a new Renaissance notion of planning [that created] . . . the possibility of focal points and axial organization not inherent in the closed, equilateral cloister [and] . . . suggest[ing] a more sympathetic and less defensive attitude to the world outside the college." It was an attitude that accorded very well with the Puritan idea of the community as a whole (encompassing both town and gown) which the Puritans sought to create in the New World, as well as with their sense of sentiment. One of the first open courts at Cambridge University after that of Gonville and Caius had been that of Emmanuel College in 1584, built just forty-five years before the advent of Harvard College, a large proportion of the founders of which were Emmanuel graduates. It is thus not altogether a surprise that Harvard Hall II and Stoughton College (as well as presidential lodgings) had been so placed vis-à-vis what is now Massachusetts Avenue that such an open court was created at Harvard as early as in the late seventeenth-century. Nor that in 1719, when President Leverett erected what is now Harvard's oldest building, Massachusetts Hall (on the site of the president's lodgings, replaced shortly thereafter by new lodgings elsewhere, today's Wadsworth House) he so placed Massachusetts as to achieve Harvard's first full-fledged brick three-sided open court. Behold again, in another connection, the famous Burgis view of 1726, where although each of the three buildings is still separate, they clearly are grouped to form what is really rather a grand courtyard for its time and place. Within a few years, furthermore, on the other side of Harvard Hall, another such court was developed.

Tory and Puritan. Betwixt and between Harvard ever was. If Harvard College at the end of the seventeenth and the beginning of the eighteenth centuries was deliberately reinforcing its openness to the larger New England community both in terms of government and architecture in accordance with a long-standing deep-seated Puritan sensibility, it was doing so still, however, in tension with the much more obviously liberal light cast by the powerful parallel influence of the royal governors' court, with perhaps not incompatible but distinctly different emphasis, intent as the royal governors were in endowing Harvard with more and more of Tory taste and vice-regal pomp (and

Holden Chapel and Stoughton Hall

crypto-Anglicanism, too, thought more than one Puritan). And seen in retrospect (though things by no means had to take the course they did, of course),
the underlying political tug of war of what turned out to be the period leading
to the American Revolution is very evident in Harvard's architecture. In fact,
it went back and forth right up to the eve of the revolution. The erection in
1744 of Holden Chapel, for instance, introduced to Harvard College, of all
improbable and astonishing things, a positively Baroque splendor. Though the
chapel would soon enough be one wing of a second open court, it became so
with striking royalist mien, its pediment blazoned with the Holden arms in a
sea of Baroque mantling. Its ceremonial interior was also very Anglican in
feeling: though the president's chair and reading desk replaced the high altar,
the congregational seating was longitudinal, facing inward, rising on tiers to
either side of a center aisle as in an Anglican college chapel. Hollis Hall of
1762 on the other hand, is plain to the point of being ungainly, a building as
much of Yankee mien as Harvard Hall and Holden Chapel are of royalist
mien, and one is not surprised to learn that Hollis' designer, Thomas Dawes,
was a native Colonial builder and subsequently a great patriot. Nor that the
pendulum swung back two years later, however, when the vice-regal court
clearly was the dominant influence in the design of the college's most distinguished building of the eighteenth century, Harvard Hall III.

Third in direct succession to Harvard's first "House" of 1638, Harvard
Hall III was made necessary by a catastrophic fire that in 1764 destroyed
Harvard Hall II; a catastrophe not least in that the loss included nearly all of
John Harvard's books. The fact that the provincial legislature was using the

building at the time placed the burden of its replacement unarguably on the government of the province, an opportunity quickly seized by the royal governor, Sir Francis Barnard, who himself was the architect of the new building, and in the design of which he introduced into Harvard College a quality best caught by Bainbridge Bunting's observation that Harvard Hall III was the "most sophisticated American college building before Bulfinch." Like the vice-regal court and all its Tory landmarks in and around the capital, from Province House overlooking the port of Boston to Christ Church across Cambridge Common and behind that the storied splendors of Tory Row (the parade of High Georgian mansions along Brattle Street), Harvard Hall III exuded unequivocally a distinctly royalist aura. It still does.

Particularly impressive within the new Harvard Hall were its College Hall and Library. The ten alcoves in the College Library were each blazoned above the shelving with donors' names in gold letters, just like Duke Humphrey's library at Oxford's Bodleian Library. The College Hall, moreover, was, according to Bunting, "the only American interior of the time where paintings, frames and architecture were planned to form a single decorative scheme." And a decidedly grand scheme it was, centered on the regal Copley portraits of King George III and Queen Charlotte that hung to either side of the great mantle piece behind the High Table dais from which at meals the president and tutors presided on state occasions—for which it is not too much to say Sir Francis surely designed Harvard Hall. Here it was, for instance, Morison recounts, that

> Harvard held the last great ceremony of the old regime [in honor of its then leading graduate, Thomas Hutchinson, newly invested Captain General and Governor-in-Chief of the Royal Province of Massachusetts Bay, when] his Excellency was pleased to visit the college. The cavalcade left the Province House [the Governor's official residence in the capital] with Governor Hutchinson and Lieutenant-Governor Andrew Oliver in their carriages, escorted by the troop of Horse Guards. . . . [in] their old-fashioned full wigs . . . great three-cornered hats bound with yellow braid, blue uniform coats with broad red lapels, red waistcoat and breeches, gorgeous saddles and caparisons, gold-edged royal standard, and trumpets with festoons of gold braid. . . . 'At the steps of Harvard Hall,' [a contemporary account reports,] 'his Excellency was received . . . by the President, Fellows, Professors and Tutors in their habits. [Within] he was met and welcomed by the Honorable and Reverend Overseers.
>
> The [interior accommodations] not being large enough [all went] in procession from Harvard Hall to the Meetinghouse [where] . . . the public exercises began with a handsome gratulatory Oration in Latin . . . To this his Excellency made an elegant reply in the

same language. . . . Then followed an Anthem . . . the Procession returned to the [Great] Hall where a genteel entertainment was provided. The whole was conducted with the greatest decorum and elegance.

If there is a whiff of a northern Williamsburg about Harvard Hall in this era there is something too of the aura of the Winter Palace, for Harvard Hall became on the eve of the Revolution a most conspicuous stage for the events of those dramatic days. It was to Harvard Hall, and Holden Chapel too, that the Massachusetts General Court retreated from the demanding uproar of the Boston mob, and it was there that were heard some of the great revolutionary speeches that heralded the Declaration of Independence of 1776. There too, within hardly two years of the royal governor's state visit to the college, a revolutionary mob stormed the College Hall and ripped the great royal portraits from their frames (alas—they were both Copleys), destroying them apparently on the spot. Indeed Harvard was deeply involved in the initial stages of the Revolutionary War. Washington not only planned the Siege of Boston at Harvard, in Wadsworth House, but some modern historians believe it was also there he took command of the new Continental Army in 1775. And though its facilities became so overtaxed by the revolutionary troops that the college actually moved for a season to Concord, Harvard's survival after the American victory was sure. No less than seven signers of the Declaration of Independence, including the most conspicuous, John Hancock, were Harvard graduates, and John Adams, another signer, would become the first of many Harvard men to become president of the United States.

However, a revolution may mean as much or as little, really, as one cares to make of it, whether socially, academically, or architecturally. At Harvard only the players seem to have changed. And those not much. When the first non-royal governor of Massachusetts, Hancock (than which, of course, there was no more famous patriot), first dined in hall at a feast given for Lafayette his behavior seemed vice-regal indeed. "The President sat at the head of high table, with the Marquis at his right, facing down the hall," Morison reports, "and the Governor opposite, with his back to the assembly. Hancock thought he should have had Lafayette's place." *Plus ça change. . .* And if the revolution did not much change Harvard's lifestyle, neither did the new Massachusetts constitution of 1779–80 alter anything more fundamental. It formally confirmed Harvard in all its privileges and, acknowledging long-standing ambitions, called it the "university at Cambridge." But the effect on Harvard's architecture was striking, and found almost immediate expression in the work of Charles Bulfinch, America's first native-born professional architect, and a Harvard graduate. By the time he left town to work in 1817 on the new national capitol in Washington, he had transformed Boston into a grand neoclassical city, and set the stage in Harvard Yard for what has been called the college's Augustan age, the presidency in 1810–28 of John Kirkland.

Sophisticated, free-thinking, committed to the intellectual quest—these are the values that time and time again arise in any discussion of Kirkland's Harvard, values that stand out in the galaxy of faculty and students of those days, the shortest list of which would include George Tichnor, Ralph Waldo Emerson, Edward Everett, Henry Thoreau, George Bancroft, Oliver Wendell Holmes, and Wendell Phillips. A scholar and a gentleman in the old phrase, a minister of Unitarian sympathies, Kirkland was an affable, kindly bachelor, both learned and logical in argument, and a wit as well (in fact, an eloquent speaker). To the faculty he appointed the first European-trained scholars and during his presidency no less than fifteen new professorships were founded; by the time of his departure from the stage Harvard was a university in fact as well as in name—not, to be sure, in the largest sense, but a university nonetheless. Kirkland founded Harvard Law School, for example, today the oldest existing law school in the United States. First, in 1815, came the Royall Professorship of Law, the gift of a loyalist, interestingly, many years after the revolution. Two years later the Law School itself was established. It was slow going for a while—professors who are also leaders in their professions are ever in danger of scanting one or another side of their life—but in 1829 the establishment of the Nathan Dane Chair allowed the appointment of Joseph Story, Associate Justice of the U.S. Supreme Court, who pioneered what Morison calls the "[Harvard] Law School tradition of studying jurisprudence as a science and a system of philosophy, the best groundwork for the sort of practice that would serve social ends rather than simply enrich the practitioner." All this, conducted mostly in rooms in the first College House in Harvard Square, achieved architectural expression in 1832 when the Dane Law College was built for the Law School just about where Matthews Hall now stands.

Similarly, Kirkland's spearheading of post-graduate education constituted a kind of re-founding of the Harvard Medical School, first founded in 1782 but none too securely established for many years. The Medical School's "cradle," of all unlikely places, had been Holden Chapel—the rising tiers of whose "choir stalls" made for a highly functional dissecting theater—and the Harvard Hall basement. In 1810, however, its first purpose-built structure, the Massachusetts Medical College in Boston proper, was built, Kirkland thereby endowing the Medical School with the same new life the Law School would achieve in the new Dane Law College. That first medical college was a part of an overall agitation for Harvard medicine, the other key aspect of which was the founding the very next year just after Kirkland became president of its new affiliated teaching hospital. "The daughter of the Harvard Medical School," as it has been aptly called by George Berry, "the founding of the Massachusetts General Hospital marked the passing of Harvard from its youth as a small provincial college to the greater maturity of a university. . . ." Concludes Berry, "had those early Harvard professors—John Warren, Benjamin Waterhouse, Aaron Dexter, John Collins Warren and James Jackson—been content to teach in the cradle of the Yard, there could have been no Harvard Medicine. It was soon vividly clear to them that. . .there would have to be a hospital." And within thirty-five years Harvard medicine more than fulfilled its promise when there took place at the M.G.H. what has been called (by Joseph Garland) "one of the greatest events in the history of medicine, and the first important, entirely American contribution to Medical science": the operation by Dr. Warren after which for the first time the medical world learned of the effective use of anesthesia at surgery.

Another professional school owed its founding to Kirkland, the Divinity School, which began life in 1819. Like law and medicine, theology had long been studied by students through the apprentice system of "reading law" or divinity or whatever under some master. Now this field too was given a full-fledged professional school, for which Kirkland built in 1825 a handsome Federalist building, Divinity Hall, the only one of these three original professional school structures to survive today. And in the case of divinity more immediately than in law or medicine, both of which had many ups and downs in the nineteenth century, the school's development was highly successful, and on a bigger stage by far than one might imagine today, marking as it did the triumph at Harvard of the "Boston religion," as M. A. Dewolfe Howe has called Unitarianism. A liberal religious strain, which was something of a counterweight to Federalism, the conservative political tendency of those days (when Harvard, as an ancient quasi-public institution that until 1823 still received a state subsidy, felt such things more keenly), Unitarianism was a key factor in generating the sunny era of good will that Kirkland cultivated. Unitarianism also had another effect, as George Phelps has explained: soon enough it was perceived that it had come to be that "New England was divided between the Boston enclave of liberal Christianity and the orthodox, Yale-oriented areas of western New England." It was a division reflected in the institution's governance. Since the advent of Kirkland, observed Walter Muir Whitehill, writing from the perspective of 1965, "the Fellows of Harvard College have been Bostonians—normally merchants, lawyers, or bankers, with an occasional clergyman, public figure, or man of letters. In the early nineteenth century they were generally . . . liberal in religion and conservative in politics. But they cared little for sectarianism or political expediency and chiefly sought excellence wherever they could find it." Whitehill goes on to instance three key families: the Lowells, the Eliots, and the Adamses. Judge John Lowell, a late eighteenth-century fellow of the college, inaugurated a Harvard dynasty of no less than seven generations dedicated to serving Harvard in every position, including the presidency; the Eliots, who would produce not only an exemplary treasurer but the university's greatest president; and John Quincy Adams and his son Charles Francis Adams, descendants of the patriot leader and second president of the United States, who were between them fellow and treasurer of Harvard for nearly half a century. Bostonians all. Now, of course, in Alfred North Whitehead's mid-twentieth-century words, "in so far as the world of learning today possesses a capital city, Boston, with its various neighboring institutions, approximates to the position that Paris occupied in the Middle Ages," rejoicing in a galaxy of universities and colleges. Harvard, though always preeminent if only because of its history, is but the first among equals. But in Kirkland's time, that galaxy in Harvard's wake had yet to be imagined. And Bostonians put all their eggs in the one basket: Harvard.

There was as always when the big-and-getting-bigger city was concerned another side to all this, more problematic. Long before subway or trolleys, when only stage coaches connected Harvard Square with urban pleasures (in fact, Boston proper had become its own city in 1822), so deeply invested were Harvard students in those pleasures, according to George Phelps, that "the forbidden city," became more and more an essential theme of the Harvard experience. It was in a period, moreover, when a highly regimented student body, whose entering age in Kirkland's period was about 15, regularly staged "rebellions" so raucous that after one such fully half the senior class was thrown out. More important, however, was the fact that the faculty found as many if different reasons to engage the larger community as Boston's first families found to engage Harvard. It was two of Kirkland's star professors, for instance, George Ticknor and Edward Everett, who were also the chief inspirers and founders of the Boston Public Library, the first municipally supported public library in the nation and the spearhead of the American public library movement. In the arts, among which by Kirkland's era architecture was coming to be counted in Boston (and not merely as a practical necessity that *might* be handsome as well), signs of vitality in this period were also widespread. The painter of choice was Washington Allston. And like Bulfinch, who would be the architect of choice, Allston was a Harvard graduate. Phelps wrote:

> [Boston] was rapidly becoming the intellectual capital of the country. . . . Letters, and to a lesser degree the arts, stirred perceptibly. . . . The *North American Review* . . . the Boston Athenaeum [an art gallery then as well as a library] . . . the Massachusetts Historical Society . . . were directed and supported by well-to-do Bostonians, most of whom had strong Harvard connections. These men were usually Federalists, and were, or became, mostly Unitarian. . . . [Old] Cambridge was the idyll, an Arcadian world adorned with splendid mansions . . . widespread lawns covered with wine glass elms and willows, with orchards [and] placid meadows to the river Charles.

Harvard Hall

Thus it is that Harvard's immediate Old Cambridge neighborhood (so called to distinguish it from the much larger suburban city of Cambridge it was by the nineteenth century a part of) also comes into mature focus here. Along with Brookline—its only rival—Old Cambridge was in Kirkland's era emerging as the premiere suburban face of a growing Boston. Was not Mount Auburn cemetery to be not only where all proper Bostonians went to their rest, but the ultimate proto-suburban American landscape? And the way Old Cambridge matters to Harvard has above all to do with architecture. The

matter has never been better analyzed in the Harvard context than by John
Coolidge, himself the scion of a great Boston family, a luminary of the
Harvard faculty and a life-long Cambridge resident. Old Cambridge,
Coolidge wrote, when Harvard was founded in the seventeenth century,
became "the earliest American example of . . . the corporation or one-industry
town. . . . But a century or so later it became the earliest (or one of the two or
three earliest) of yet another familiar type of American settlement, the fashionable suburb. This, too, it has remained." Noted Coolidge as well:
"Interplay between the suburban and university communities is in large part
responsible for the quality of Old Cambridge's architecture." And as an
example of how important, historically, that interplay has been, he adds:
"Harvard's immediate reaction to Tory Row and Christ Church was the vernacular ungainliness of Hollis." It was certainly a patrician and also a very
Anglophile point of view. But it is one that does go to the heart of the issue
we are approaching here, which pervaded in Kirkland's time so many aspects
of Harvard—an ancient semi-patrician institution in a nouveau riche post-
revolutionary era—the issue of (dreaded word) taste.

First, money. All those treasurers in Whitehill's catalogue of State
Street types on Harvard's Corporation point to another of Kirkland's gifts.
Wrote Morison: "a pattern of support for Harvard, the most popular of the
many good causes appealing to Boston, was firmly established." Second, taste,
as distinct from money. It is significant that Coolidge, in his hymn to Old
Cambridge, brought up the inadequacies of Hollis Hall, for example, whose
patriot or Yankee aesthetic, he felt, was somewhat lacking. George Santayana,
who also had a good eye, saw it, too, writing of Hollis: "it was the architecture
of sturdy poverty." Yet the much better Harvard Hall, Coolidge asserted, had
been a case of "official taste," his tactful way of alluding to the central fact of
art and architecture at Kirkland's Harvard, that when Boston's vice-regal
court was no more, and the State Street merchants came to the fore in the
post-revolutionary period, newcomers were much less sure of their taste than
the Tories had been upon whose taste a good deal of the Harvard tradition
had come to depend. Exactly how or why it was that he saw Old Cambridge
as saving the day is not clear. It was State Street, after all, that largely bought
up Tory Row! But in some way Coolidge seems to have felt Brattle Street's
more patrician precincts brought out in the new elite something State Street
moneymaking didn't. Certainly Coolidge felt that it was Harvard's Old
Cambridge "suburban neighbors who [would] effectively foster the appreciation and preservation of Harvard's architecture." And he was right.

All these vectors of Boston and Harvard at the nineteenth-century's
beginning met vividly in Charles Bulfinch. This gifted man, perhaps because
he was as much citizen of Boston and alumnus of Harvard as the leading
architect of both, gave brilliant architectural expression to the heightened
alliance of Kirkland's era between city and university. In fact, Kirkland was

hardly likely to have been interested in anyone else. Yet Bulfinch's debut at Harvard—the design in 1804 of Stoughton College II (or, as it has come to be called, Stoughton Hall)—was not auspicious. It is a building even the leading Bulfinch scholar, Harold Kirker, calls architecturally "insignificant," a judgment I do not protest. Nor would I argue either, however, with Coolidge's feeling that Hollis Hall's design is an example of "ungainliness"— which, in fact, explains Bulfinch's less than luminous first design at Harvard: the Corporation having instructed him in designing Stoughton to use Hollis as his model. Furthermore, Bulfinch's work had significance in another way not usually noticed; Stoughton was very likely, though the documentation is sparse, the pivotal building in the overall achievement of the design concept of what we call today the Old Yard.

Opinions on this matter have varied through the years. W. G. Lang, in the 1936 edition of the authoritative guide published by the president and fellows, asserted that when first built Stoughton *faced* not only outward to the street (to help form another open court on the north side of Holden Chapel as Hollis had done previously on the south side) but that Stoughton faced also *inward*, to what is now the Old Yard; that, in fact, Stoughton "was the first Harvard building to be entered both from the west and from the east . . . [and that] in the 1820s when [Bulfinch's] plan of the Yard had begun to take actual shape, the extra stairs of Stoughton were taken down and the east became its main facade." It had been a matter of Stoughton hedging its bets evidently as to the success of "Bulfinch's attempts to remedy the medieval clutter of college brewhouses, privies, and woodpiles which at the time distinguished Harvard Yard behind it," all this, according to Lang, in aid of "a plan for distributing new buildings on the borders of a rectangle, now the Old Yard . . . made at this time by Charles Bulfinch." Yet more recent scholarship has tended to associate Bulfinch's plans for the Yard not with the erection of Stoughton in 1804 but with his design of University Hall in 1812 for Kirkland, who had become president in 1810 and is always portrayed as taking the lead in the design of the Old Yard, planting elms, for instance, and laying out the pathways. More likely, Bulfinch, with his neo-classical-planner's eye, had first taken the measure of the problem in 1804 at Stoughton and had, however tentatively (recall the *front* entrances on either side), taken the lead himself, gaining the ally above all others he needed when Kirkland took office. Certainly the very next year, 1811, Holworthy College (now Hall) was built to the designs of Loammi Baldwin, an associate of Bulfinch (his agent, in fact, in the building of University Hall). Holworthy, itself progressive in that it was the first hall at Harvard to abandon the medieval plan of large bedchambers with small adjoining closet-like studies for study and prayer for the reverse modern arrangement of large study-sitting rooms with adjoining small bedrooms, was sited clearly with reference to Stoughton. It was placed at right angles to Stoughton, clearly implying a new courtyard of some sort *behind* Harvard's original streetfront open courts along today's Massachusetts Avenue. No less than on Beacon Hill (where it is also true Bulfinch designed relatively little himself, but set the tone in the wake of the Boston State House), Harvard Yard, what today we call the Old Yard, is as much the architectural creation of Charles Bulfinch as it was the academical creation of President Kirkland.

If the Old Yard seems not exactly what one might have expected from the foremost American neoclassical architect of the time, that is because Bulfinch no less than Kirkland dreamed of larger plans than the time was evidently ripe. Bulfinch's dreams were always large. A comparison of his Boston State House of 1795 with Jefferson's Virginia capitol of a decade earlier shows that whereas Jefferson was more radical politically (very anti-British) his architectural tastes (antique classicism really) were very conservative. Whereas Bulfinch, conservative politically (the Boston State House was very British) was much more a modernist architecturally, modeling the State House after the latest London fashion. At Harvard, too, Bulfinch was very up to date. He proposed a full professorship of architecture in 1816 to the corporation (which turned him down), and also suggested what is certainly the most striking bit of unbuilt Harvard ever: an elegantly neoclassical dormitory range of monumental sweep, 280 feet end to end, in the form of a semi-circle, with no less than nine entry doors and staircases, the whole range anchored at each end by two colonnaded halls. Inspired directly, no doubt, by Bulfinch's range of Boston townhouses of 1793, the Tontine Crescent, a seminal neoclassical work (even London had yet to boast such architecture); Paul Turner hardly exaggerates when he refers to Bulfinch's proposed Harvard designs as possessing "tremendous scale . . . [and] an impression of luxurious grandeur unheard of at American colleges" at that period. But while anyone with any imagination at all, could hardly not regret that Bulfinch's grand plan for Harvard Yard, which would have been comparable in magnificence to Thomas Jefferson's University of Virginia of the same period, was rejected, this is but the architectural face of a far deeper failure of nerve that finally enfeebled Kirkland's Harvard. Indeed, the objections doubtless urged against Bulfinch's splendid vision must have been very similar to those which undermined the larger educational reforms (which Bulfinch surely sought to express) of Kirkland's star faculty, George Ticknor and Edward Everett, who were in Phelps' words, "the two men who became the chief proponents of the modern university in America." Both, attempting to add to Harvard's curriculum the post-graduate training in academic subjects that had already been provided in the professions of law, medicine, and divinity, made proposals to Kirkland after a study trip to Europe in 1815 (during which they focused on the German universities and interviewed figures such as Byron, Goethe, Madame de Staël, and Sir Walter Scott), proposals would have made Harvard the pioneer of the highest academic education in America. Instead, though Everett and Ticknor made the trip with

Kirkland's blessing, inertia somehow triumphed. Indeed, Kirkland, faced with bad times economically and considerable internal opposition, had finally, in 1828, when ill, to confront an abusive interlocutor, and resigned. Bernard Bailyn has written: "Kirkland's failure—if it can be called that; he was eminently successful for over a decade—was a product of historical change he could not control. . . . Kirkland was caught in the middle."

Posterity, at least for a half century or so, was much less generous to Bulfinch, whose creation of a coherent architectural ensemble out of buildings of the Old Yard seemed to many hardly worthy of him. Anthony Trollope, the British novelist, visiting Harvard, railed against the Yard's "ugly red-brick houses," for instance, "standing here and there without order." Even the poet James Russell Lowell, Boston born and bred, would, according to Fiske Kimball, refer scathingly to the yard's halls as "factories to which nothing could lend even dignity, let alone beauty." Altogether reasonable by Victorian standards the tastes of those worthies were. But it would be very much to miss the point today critically to endorse them. Indeed, what now stands out about Bulfinch (as also about Kirkland) is his considerable achievement. Just as Kirkland did lay worthy foundations for the great university that would come in only a scant fifty years—a short time by Harvard's measure—so also did Bulfinch. Allowed as it turned out only one swift stroke—University Hall—it was enough to virtually create Harvard Yard in its first incarnation.

That noble structure—conceived as containing a new College Hall (a "Commons Hall," below, with a splendid two-story chapel above, and recitation and lecture rooms and the president's office to each side)—was placed astutely by Bulfinch. He sited it on axis with the old ceremonial way the royal governors had used to enter the college grounds, between Harvard and Massachusetts Halls. Bulfinch treated that old courtyard—the ancient footprint that is all that remains today of Harvard in the 1600s—as a forecourt to a huge new Yard dominated by University Hall, set way back as the new Yard's centerpiece. It was altogether a bravura performance, winning all the older buildings into allegiance so as to cohere finally in the larger idea; it was, as we would say today, a supremely contextual accomplishment but not in the usual red brick bland way of the 1980s and '90s. Indeed, in its gray and white palette and crisp Chelmsford granite neoclassicism University Hall could not have been more different than its older neighbors. Bulfinch, as ever, was a very modern architect in his day.

Yet what a long time ago it now seems. When University Hall was new Harvard was already almost 200 years old. Today, at the beginning of the twenty-first century, it has been nearly another 200 years since University Hall's erection. And as it approaches its fourth century, Harvard, its Old Yard, now storied beyond telling really, lives still chiefly because of the genius of Bulfinch, the first great shaping figure in Harvard architecture, who emerged from Harvard College to become more than that, indeed, one of the first great shaping figures in American architecture. He was, William Pierson has written, "one of the most creative architects of his time. . . . [Creating an architecture that] was rational, beautiful and workable. . . . Expressive of both Puritan primness and the earth-bound pragmatism of the New England temperament. . . . [in his work] for the first time in the development of the English-oriented architecture of New England the term 'American' as defining a quality decidedly un-English, become meaningful. . . . His older contemporary, Thomas Jefferson, who, like Bulfinch, was the most important native-born architect of his generation, achieved similar ends."

The accomplishment, it must be said, however, is more impressive today, when we know its issue and its effect so many years later. Then, when new, University Hall, nor even Harvard Yard, likely did not much impress Emerson, for example, the guide we took as our own at the start of this focus on seventeenth- and eighteenth-century Harvard College. Probably Bulfinch's Yard was too long coming and smacked too much, as the Sage of Concord saw it, of compromise—compromise University Hall did not redress. It was not the past—even the recent past—which interested Emerson but the future, the far future. Nor were primness or even earth-bound pragmatism Puritan virtues he saw a future for in the new country. More likely: boldness. Looking past the newly configured yard—where University hall was already being surrounded by the beginnings of those much loved wine-glass elms—Kirkland's most famous graduate, seeing at one and the same time the success of it and the failure of it, seems to me in good Harvard fashion to have been more interested in the failure, for much the same reason doubtless Tolstoi would pronounce unhappy families more interesting than happy ones! That at least is my reading of Emerson's still notable address at Harvard in 1837 to its Phi Beta Kappa chapter.

Oliver Wendell Holmes, who was there, remembered Emerson's speech fifty years later, calling it America's "intellectual Declaration of Independence." Robert D. Richardson, Jr., in his *Emerson: The Mind on Fire*, points out that the great man's intent that day, in an address entitled "The American Scholar," was to liberate, "not America . . . but the single person." Perhaps the nub of the matter is that Emerson was taking up, shaping even, what was to become a characteristic American stance.

Much more than architecture, of course, was on Emerson's mind that day as he mounted what was seen from the first as a biting assault on more or less everything in sight. ("His speech," writes Richardson, Emerson's most recent biographer, "had no praise for Harvard, no paean to the long tradition of scholarly learning that was even then silting up the rivers of thought.") But the Yard, in sight of which Emerson honed his attack, was a newly obvious expression of all he found majestic fault with. University Hall? Was there a nobler example in view, as Kirkland and Bulfinch had left it, of Man Learning? Yet what Emerson demanded was Man Thinking.

First Church, Burying Ground, Old Yard

Harvard Yard and Harvard Square

1. First Church/Unitarian, Old Burying Ground and Christ Church/Episcopal

First Church/Unitarian *Isaiah Rogers, 1833*
Old Burying Ground *Fenced 1635*
Christ Church/Presbyterian *Peter Harrison, 1760*

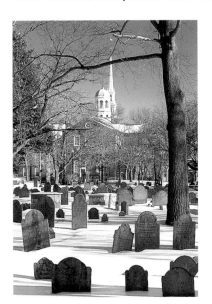

Old Burying Ground, Harvard Hall, and Memorial Church Steeple

The venerable First Church in which Emerson delivered his famously challenging speech of 1837, and the locale in times past of many Harvard commencements, still stands in Harvard Square. It is the primal landmark of Harvard. The visitor should take time to muse along the paths of the church's ancient burying ground. There was, of course, neither church nor square when Harvard College first put down roots here at what was in the 1630s barely a perceptible widening in what is Massachusetts Avenue today—then little more than a dirt road beaten hopefully through a wilderness.

This burying ground is all that is left in its original form, the only opportunity in Harvard Square now that holds out any hope at all of entering into the very different experience of those ancient times we must begin in. First fenced in 1635, it was to some extent the occasion of that dirt road beside which Harvard began, a road which connected the graveyard and Cambridge Common (with which the burying ground was originally contiguous) with the village center of Newetown-become-Cambridge on the other side of the present day Harvard Square, where what is now Dunster Street was in the 1630s projected as the village's "high street." The present church building was designed in 1833 by a local vernacular architect, Isaiah Rogers, its naive, rustic exterior—implausibly Gothic but charmingly "Gothick" (its buttresses, for example, so frankly of wood, buttress nothing)—is an apt backdrop for the Old Burying Ground, over which it lifts its stolid wooden tower protectively.

Best to see this burying ground on a wintry mid-day of bare tree limbs and slate sky, snow in the air, pale sun fading. Who was it who said—surely a Puritan, and surely of New England—fall is best, winter truest? So sleep the Puritans, forefathers and foremothers, long buried here and long storied among their number here many of Harvard's early presidents—including Henry Dunster and John Leverett, both of whose monuments are of interest. In fact, a most instructive approach is to study the monuments themselves—their form and style and ornament—fairly closely. They disclose, all in one place, and in miniature, many of the changing styles and fashions of architectural motifs to be encountered time and again on these Harvard walks. The death-heads of the Middle Ages, for instance, which appear on so many of the most ancient scallop-shouldered tombstones were contemporary with the equally medieval design of 1638 of Harvard Hall I. And while in Harvard Yard today the massive stone and brick Victorian dormitory (Grays Hall) which stands more or less on the site of the seventeenth-century Harvard Hall I is not at all likely to evoke the feeling of the long-gone ancient landmark, to muse among the oldest of these headstones—all of them "Folk Gothic" in style in just the way the contemporaneous Harvard Hall I was—can memorably evoke the anxious brittle, primitive seventeenth-century aesthetic shared by the long disappeared hall and the still extant tombstones. The old burying ground, more than the Yard (which has developed over the years into precincts far more gracious than Harvard's Puritan founders knew), is the place to think upon the life, bravely civilizing, of Harvard Hall I in the 1640s, the prototype in America of the residential college building type, which down through the centuries since has remained the key architectural vector at Harvard. Any description of seventeenth-century Harvard describes the life of people, after all, some of whom are buried here:

> The college day began at sunrise and followed a rigid schedule. At six were Morning Prayers . . . at seven, Morning Bever, when students lined up for their bread and mug of beer at the buttery hatch. At eight, nine and ten there were lectures for the different classes; dinner at eleven, when the College Silver was used at the high table. In the afternoon were Disputations in the Hall; Afternoon Bever at five; Supper at seven-thirty, with a fire blazing on the hearth in wintertime; and early to bed.

Among those who ended up here are not only college presidents and tutors, and one royal governor, Jonathan Belcher, but also students. Winslow Warren, for instance, who died aged only fifteen in 1747—"A Young Gentleman of Considerable Hopes"—his marker not only touches the heart, but reminds one of how very young undergraduates typically were in the eighteenth century. Here, too, are many of the fallen of the American Revolution, most notably fourteen "Minute Men" who died on that fateful April day of 1775 in skirmishes with British troops after Lexington and Concord. Two African-American Minute Men who survived those events are buried here too, Neptune Frost and Cato Stedman, both slaves and both interred in the tombs of their masters. (At least two early Harvard presidents had slaves.)

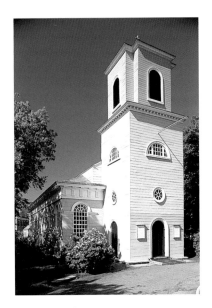

Christ Church

In artistic terms, the best of these old tombs are the oldest. The work here of the seventeenth-century Charlestown stone cutter Joseph Lamson, for example, has long stood out for its naturalistic and original detail; especially fine is his tombstone of 1642—that was the year of Harvard's first Commencement—for William Dickson. But there appear soon enough skillfully chiseled New World echoes of the distant Renaissance—the determinedly cheerful winged cherubs of the late seventeenth- and early and mid-eighteenth-century tombs; particularly impressive is the Vassal Tomb, a red-toned freestone slab supported by five fluted columns, erected in 1747. Although there are a few Victorian monuments (Richard Henry Dana, he of *Two Years Before the Mast*, and the painter Washington Allston), it is the late eighteenth- and early nineteenth-century neoclassical urn-and-willows designs that pretty much mark the culmination of this old graveyard. They reflect the increasing sophistication of the art and architecture of New England beginning to emerge by that era, an outstanding architectural example of which is the other church that guards the Old Burying Ground on its western flank: Christ Church/Episcopal. Erected in 1760, Christ Church is the epitome of the high Tory taste of Boston's vice-regal court, and was, in fact, inspired by the court's own place of worship in Boston proper, King's Chapel, where one may still see today the altar piece given by King William III and Queen Mary in 1698 as well as the royal governor's pew. Of course, these splendors were not duplicated at Christ Church, but King's Chapel's architect was also Christ Church's, and Peter Harrison combined here bold detailing and nice proportions to very stately, even monumental effect.

Finally, of unique significance is the tomb of Henry Dunster of 1659, Harvard's first president. Especially as the site of John Harvard's place of burial in nearby Charlestown is now lost, probably forever, how moving it is in the place of Dunster's final resting place to bring to mind the achievements of the man several historians have called Harvard's second founder. Born in England in 1609, a student at Magdalen College, Cambridge (at the same time John Harvard was at Emmanuel College), Dunster, a clergyman and schoolmaster, emigrated to Boston in 1640. Within three weeks, such was their eagerness, ten magistrates waited upon him and forthwith elected him president. Only thirty years old (the youngest Harvard president ever) and no great scholar, it is not clear why he so impressed. But the choice proved to be an inspired one. Dunster's presidency was stunningly success-ful. As teacher, inspirer, administrator, fund raiser, and as all but college steward too (presiding over good commons was not a president's least care then), Dunster exceeded all expectations. It was in his time that both Oxford and Cambridge came to acknowledge Harvard degrees; and it was Dunster who in 1650 secured the College Charter, still in force today. And it was entirely in character that when Dunster, acting very much against his practi-cal best interest, forswore (after long thought) orthodox Congregationalism and became a Baptist (comparable today would be President Rudenstine making a public profession of his faith in astrology), Dunster tendered his resignation and quietly retired without protest. Indeed, in all things he seems to have persevered gallantly. Harvard might well have floundered and died without Dunster. To stand before his tomb of 1659, letting the eye search out through the graveyard's trees the elegant eighteenth-century Harvard skyline across the square, a skyline Dunster never knew but must have dreamed of, is a thoughtful prologue to Harvard Yard, the main gate of which stands nearly always open across the street.

2. Johnston Gate *McKim, Mead and White, 1889–1890*

Harvard's two oldest eighteenth-century buildings, Massachusetts Hall and Harvard Hall III, flank what has been the principal ceremonial way into the precincts of Harvard College since the late 1660s, a way marked more than 200 years later by this splendid gate of 1889–1890, designed by Charles McKim. That halls and gate reflect the same stylistic vein may seem an attempt to obscure the fact that nearly two centuries intervene between their designs. But the gate was just as much stylistically a path breaker on the eve of the twentieth century as were the halls in the early and mid-eigh-teenth century—in the gate's case because of its place in the life and work of Charles McKim, who was perhaps the greatest American architect of the 1880s and '90s. The designer of many a palatial Renaissance landmark, McKim was equally interested in the Renaissance's eighteenth-century American derivative, the Georgian Colonial, particularly the severe, attenu-ated New England Federal mode after the fashion of Bulfinch. A genius, the wonderfully creative way in which McKim couched his work helped spark an historic change of taste in the late nineteenth century. And the Johnston Gate was, in the words of his biographer, Leland Roth, "one of the first such efforts in this mode of the period," an important landmark in the dawn of the American Colonial Revival, the background, in fact, to our great interest today in the architecture of the colonial period in the first place.

Johnston Gate

McKim's design relates to both of the eighteenth-century halls that flank the gates, and with the sensitivity to be expected of so distinguished a designer. A Harvard man himself (though only for a brief, not very successful year, in 1866) linked to Boston by many other and long-standing ties, including his marriage to Julia Appleton, McKim, though he practiced in New York, worked much in Boston. Indeed, it was of the staircase at his masterpiece, the Boston Public Library, that the critic Royal Cortissoz once said, McKim "deal[t] in marble as an artist deals in paint." Similarly in the Johnston Gate—where "Harvard brick," as it has since been called, was first used in aid of just that same devotion on McKim's part to texture, tone, and detail. Roth recounts that McKim was not too proud to make "the rounds of Boston brickyards, selecting blackened overburned clinkers and underfired brick in various buff, salmon, and reddish hues," which he then had laid in Flemish bond in a thick buff-colored mortar bed, achieving in Roth's words "just the variegated color and texture of the weathered walls of neighboring Massachusetts and Harvard Halls." The ironwork was handled after the same fashion: "standard machine-rolled bars, larger than necessary, were reheated and hammered down and made as true as possible by hand, giving the bars irregularities more in sympathy with eighteenth-century work." All, of course, very much more costly than first planned. But when McKim exceeded the budget and the university authorities protested, the architect's response was pointed: "our effort was to accomplish," the architect insisted, "always with a view to simplicity and economy, the most appropriate design we knew how to make, and not the most appropriate $10,000 design." The donor increased his gift and no one since has ever been sorry of it. Especially on Commencement Day. The Governor of Massachusetts, as successor to a line of royal governors reaching back to the 1680s, always entered the Yard for Commencement through this gate, until recently riding in the state carriage, with an escort of scarlet-clad mounted lancers, their now republican but still picturesque pennants fluttering grandly, the governor himself in morning dress and top hat. It was the sort of thing Americans go to England to see, but find it hard to sustain themselves, alas. Thus centuries of tradition were casually jettisoned when a "populist" gover- nor of the 1970s would not hear of such a thing and the university counted itself lucky he showed up at Commencement at all—by subway—in a raincoat.

3. Massachusetts Hall *possibly John Leverett, 1719*

Harvard's oldest building today, Massachusetts Hall, just to the right of the Johnston Gate, together with Harvard Hall III opposite, forms now a small and elegant eighteenth-century forecourt to the great expanse of nine- teenth-century Harvard Yard beyond. In 1721, however, when Massachusetts Hall was completed, today's forecourt—closed then by Stoughton Hall I where now the later and larger Yard opens out—was Harvard College, all there was, really, excepting the president's lodgings nearby. And to this stately ensemble, Massachusetts Hall brought then a more obvious contribution, perhaps, than it does to the forecourt of today. Though still medieval in plan—each bedchamber had attached to it after the

Massachusetts Hall and First Church

custom of the Middle Ages two small studies for prayer and study— Massachusetts Hall was in comparison then to the court's other two halls, a much grander and more stylish essay in the Colonial Georgian mode of Renaissance Classicism. Though Early Georgian in style—with a gambrel roof still somewhat medieval in its steepness—Massachusetts Hall fairly breathes Renaissance clarity even today; never was there a better example of how a simply conceived, plainspoken building of hardly any pretension can achieve a distinction that time and again eludes more elaborately contrived efforts. Notice its balustraded roof and twin-chimneyed gable end form, sure scale and pleasing proportions of varying window height, and simple brick detail—really just inset paneled chimney fronts and raised belt courses and water tables nicely laid in Flemish bond. Ornamental hoods originally surmounted the two original doors of the long facade, lending the building a more picturesque air, but their removal in 1790 and the introduction in 1939 of a simple off-center entrance on the end facade now facing into the Yard have had the good effect of emphasizing the simple dignity of the hall as built in 1719. The result of a grant of three thousand pounds that year from the royal province, Massachusetts Hall was a response to the college's urgent entreaty that because "the Numbers of Ye Sons of Ye Prophets are now so increased," further accommodation was clearly needed if the "collegiate way" was to be sustained. Sixty students and tutors on two staircases were provided for in the new dormitory, which brought the residential occupancy of the college up to about 140 in 1721, and it also provided for an entirely new collegiate facility to keep company with the hall and college library across the court in Harvard Hall: an "Apparatus Chamber." The precursor to all the vast Harvard laboratories of today, the Apparatus Chamber has been called the first experimental physics laboratory in America, evidence of the broadening curriculum of Leverett's time. A development of the "Philosophy Chamber," the Apparatus Chamber featured equipment procured by Benjamin Franklin himself. John Winthrop, Class of 1732, Harvard's first important scientist, presided over the Apparatus Chamber, the chief but not the only innovation in the new hall. Another, complementing the college bell in the cupola of Harvard Hall opposite, was the new college clock of 1725. It is only too easily missed today because (unlike the armorial display in Holden's pediment for instance) the clock was neither moved to nor reproduced on the other side of Massachusetts Hall when Bulfinch's new yard in the early 1800s made front facades of what were once back facades. A truly splendid decorative embellishment, the clock face is of a deep blue with elegant Roman numerals blazoned in gold.

Because it is so old, Massachusetts Hall's history just seems to go on and on, living more lives than anyone could have imagined when it was built. In the eighteenth century it survived (as Stoughton Hall I, only twenty

years older, did not) the ravages of use as a barracks for the patriot army
during the American Revolution. In the nineteenth century the building was
gutted to create large lecture rooms, and many a famous course has met
here over the last hundred and more years, including such fabled trysts with
the muses of the Italian Renaissance as Charles Eliot Norton's in the 1880s
and '90s. In the early twentieth century, George Pierce Baker taught here his
"47 Workshop," a course which is widely thought to have revolutionized
American drama, and which numbered among its students the playwright
Eugene O'Neill. Yet midst changes do continuities typically thrive at Harvard.
A Victorian-era undergraduate, for instance, observing his professor presiding over an examination being given in "Mass. Hall" (as everyone calls it),
pronounced himself struck by the likeness of the professor (who was Henry
Adams) to the full-length portrait of Adams' grandfather, U. S. President
John Quincy Adams, which hung in Massachusetts Hall then. Both, the stu-
dent felt, had "the same air of self-contained strength." So today does
Massachusetts Hall, which is now the domain of Harvard's president down-
stairs; upstairs, of freshmen. It is a typically Harvard arrangement.

4. Harvard Hall

Sir Francis Bernard, 1764; Richard Bond, 1842, addition; and Ware and Van Brunt, 1870, addition; Ashley, Myer Associates, interior remodeling, 1968

Historically—one might even say spiritually—this is Harvard's most important building. For here are to be found its earliest collegiate memories.
Since the seventeenth century Harvard Hall has stood at this site—first the
structure of 1677, and since 1766 the present structure. Bearing in mind the
controlling text I have chosen for these walks—Rafael Moneo's statement
that "an idea must be built..."—it is not too much to say that here at
Harvard Hall III is the first idea of Harvard first built, in direct continuity to
Harvard Hall I of 1638, the prototype of the residential college in America,
the first "House" and hearth of Harvard College. Equally, it is also true to
say that as it is now configured, Harvard Hall reminds me of Robert
Venturi's "Ghost House" in Philadelphia, contrived by that master more or
less out of thin air and unenclosed framing on the site where once stood
Benjamin Franklin's long since destroyed eighteenth-century house.
Harvard Hall today is different only in degree. Here the original and historic
exterior shell is intact, altered by a two-story pedimented addition of 1842
by Richard Bond and one story wings added in 1870 by Ware and Van Brunt
(who may even have used antique bricks in what was a century and more
ago a pioneering act of historic rehabilitation), while at Philadelphia, on the
other hand, the Franklin House exterior does not survive. However, twentieth-century spaces and systems now fill Harvard Hall's long since gutted

Harvard Hall

interior, creating the same sort of emptiness, really, out of modern interiors that Venturi created out of "framed air" in Philadelphia. Yet here as there the spaces are all the more charged with meaning for their emptiness; standing, for instance, in one of Harvard Hall's modern ground floor class-rooms, the usual unremarkable white plaster room with wall-to-wall carpet, metal furniture, and conspicuous audio-visual equipment, it can be startling to look up and out through one of its elegant arched windows—the one original eighteenth-century feature still evident inside—and realize you're enjoying much the same view Lafayette had as he dined in hall at high table here at the noon meal on such and such a day more than two centuries ago. Linear time again! The incongruity of space, setting, and view is stimulating and, after all, palpably ghostly. And the built idea of 1638 and 1677 and 1766 can still be felt here, despite the fact that of the great centerpieces of the Collegiate Way, the animating functional parts of the residential college as a building type—hall, chapel and library—there is now at Harvard Hall hardly any trace at all. Only some pieces of high table silver, a few paint-ings, and even fewer of John Harvard's books still survive. These last are a loss still felt, and a catastrophe it certainly seemed in 1764 when the library along with all of Harvard Hall II was burned to the ground in the middle of the night, out of term time, when few were at hand to fight a fierce winter storm such as still howls through Harvard Yard today.

Two and more centuries ago, as originally designed, the present building of 1766 gave ample evidence of the college's determination to recreate in Sir Francis Barnard's elegant new structure the historical

Oxbridge collegiate tripartite form with redoubled splendor. Moreover, because (unlike Harvard Halls I and II) the third and present structure did not include studies and chambers (these were provided in adjoining Massachusetts and Stoughton Hall I), Harvard Hall III, which may be justly accorded the accolade of being the first collegiate building in America erected for solely academic use, boasted examples of the traditional collegiate centerpieces much larger and more magnificent than their predecessors. Such was the splendor of the new hall and of the new chapel (now for the first time separate from the hall, each taking up half the full extent of the ground to either side of the entrance), and of the new college library on the second floor, that all these interiors have attracted the attention of more than one scholar of the period. The hall, particularly, was important to American architectural history for its seminal integration of architecture, décor, and paintings in a public building in the colonies, a reflection of the more sophisticated taste of Boston's vice-regal court. Indeed, Harvard Hall, historically, may be seen as something of a companion to Boston's old royal State House of 1712, also still standing. Like the old capitol at the head of State (then King) Street, Harvard Hall was designed for vice-regal as well as academical pomp—like the last state visit to Harvard of the final royal governor, described here already. The Great Hall of this building at that time is described by Morison in *Three Centuries of Harvard*:

> Finely proportioned...36 x 45 feet...on the east end [of the ground floor] was the college hall. Originally [on the Yard side today, where three arched windows have been inserted] it had no windows in the eastern end where the [high table] dais was; in the center was the hall fireplace, and on either side a niche where portraits of George III and Queen Charlotte hung....Even after commons were removed to University Hall in 1815, and until Memorial [Hall] was built in 1874, this hall remained *the* college hall, and was used for commencement dinners.

Actually the commencement feast for a time was transferred to University Hall. But by 1842 it was back at Harvard Hall, doubtless in part at least for just those reasons of continuity and sentiment to which Morison testified. Needless to say vice-regal pomp also has long since fled Harvard Hall. Though not from Harvard itself! Witness the appearance in the Yard of His Royal Highness the Prince of Wales in gold embroidered robes of sufficient gorgeousness as principal speaker at the college's 350th convocation in 1986. Of course, as is the case with Harvard's own academical pomp, such scenes are no longer enacted at Harvard Hall but in more recent and now much grander venues. But if there still is as I've suggested a whiff of a Northern Williamsburg in the air here—never mind as well of the Winter

Palace in the memory of the student mob storming Harvard Hall to tear
down the royal portraits in 1776—what sparks the imagination today at
Harvard Hall is the way the seemingly innate character of its design com-
municates still, mainly through the building's elegant lines, its graceful but
simple cupola, and its delicate stone cornices. The most sophisticated college building in America before Bulfinch, Harvard Hall is unique.

As at Massachusetts Hall traditional collegiate facilities at Harvard
Hall III kept company with newer ones. Teaching, for example, was no
longer after Harvard Hall III to be done solely in Hall. Classrooms were now
provided for alongside hall and chapel on the ground floor, according to
Morison "the first rooms ever built specially for lectures or recitations in
Harvard College." In one or another of them, Emerson recalled in his time
of Harvard Hall in the early nineteenth-century Professor Edward Everett
lecturing; "the novelty of the learning lost nothing in the skill and genius of
his relation," wrote Emerson, "and the rudest undergraduate found a new
morning opened to him in the lecture room of Harvard Hall."

5. Holden Quadrangle: Holden Chapel, Hollis, Mower, and Lionel Halls, and Phillips Brooks House

Holden Chapel *attributed to John Smibert 1742*
Hollis Hall *Thomas Dawes 1762*
Mower and Lionel Halls *Coolidge, Shepley, Bulfinch and Abbott 1925*
Phillips Brooks House *Longfellow, Alden & Harlow 1898*

Behind Harvard Hall is the oldest and one of the most evocative of all the
quads of Harvard College, a serene eddy of today's sometimes busy Yard.
Easily missed, because the closest access near Harvard Hall is barely a slit
between that building and Hollis (through which you almost feel you have
to slide sideways), this quad takes its name from its centerpiece, Holden
Chapel of 1742. The donor was Jane Holden, the widow of a Member of
Parliament and a friend of royal governor Thomas Hutchinson, who secured
this gift from the mother country. And Holden—even more in some ways
than that other landmark of another royal governor, Harvard Hall—fairly
radiates vice-regal authority and taste. Its architect, not content with the
sober elegance of Harvard Hall, lavished a great splendor of flamboyant
Baroque ornament across the tympanum of Holden's entrance pediment,
ornament that still enshrines the full achievement of the donor's arms, so
richly colored and detailed it must be accounted as brave a display as ever
was mounted in British North America. Worth noticing also is the fact that
those arms boldly declare the donor to have been a woman; more would
have recognized then than now that whereas a man's arms are emblazoned

Holden Chapel

on a shield, women's are traditionally emblazoned on a diamond-shaped lozenge, as at Holden. Within a generation, of course, such things would become after the Revolution as much *passé* in America generally as they were once the College's boast in 1742, but the survival of the Holden arms over the chapel's entrance these 300 years later suggests the Harvard royal governors had not labored entirely in vain. When new, Holden, the college's first experiment with a purpose-built free-standing chapel, contained the official pulpit or raised seat for the President, a formidable personage in this era, in whose presence any and all had to stand and uncover, deferring to him in every respect. Especially was this true in chapel or in hall where he was always the presiding and enabling presence. (Even today the ceremonial of the president's Great Chair endures at Harvard. At commencement the President is always enthroned in state in that august but reputedly very uncomfortable object, from which since at least the 1730s all Harvard's presidents have presided at those ceremonies, the choir meanwhile singing *Dominum salvum fac*/God save our president.)

No more remains of Holden's interior than of Harvard Hall's, and at Holden too the exterior has been somewhat altered. The original Baroque mantling has been reproduced on the Yard side, to which the entrance was moved and endowed with a new round-headed door surround in 1850. Seen from either vantage (the only important difference is that the pilasters of the Yard front lack the stone capitals of their mates on back, the original front) Holden is so fine a High Georgian work that it has—like the Wren Building of 1695 at the College of William and Mary in Virginia—long been thought to have been designed by a London architect (at Virginia the name of Sir Christopher Wren has surfaced). Hence the phrase so oft repeated in Harvard guidebooks that Holden is "a solitary English daisy in a field of Yankee dandelions." But this is all very unlikely, and is to underestimate seriously the gifts of Boston's designers of this period, especially of John Smibert, whose twin-pilaster and round-head window motif at Fanueil Hall in Boston proper some years before Holden is very like the Harvard Chapel, which has, in fact, been attributed to Smibert. It was a place of worship only

Hollis and Harvard Halls, Holden Chapel

until 1766, when a more commodious college chapel was fashioned as we've seen out of the east side of Harvard Hall III. Thereafter, however, Holden achieved no little renown (raised choir stalls making for a good dissecting theater!) as the "Cradle of the Harvard Medical School." Today, in yet another guise, it is the home of the Harvard Glee Club. Majestic in both scale and proportions, yet also elegant, even intimate, Holden, architecturally speaking, is arguably the glory of the Old Yard.

The quadrangle to which it gives its name is also well worth exploring in its own right, particularly the quad's southern half, between Holden and Harvard Hall. Holden Quadrangle is especially important because in the same way that the Old Burying Ground is now really the only place where the visitor can hope to penetrate the world of seventeenth-century Harvard, so also Holden Quad is now the only place set somewhat apart where the visitor has the opportunity to be quietly surrounded by the world of eighteenth-century Harvard.

It was a lively world, one in some respects Dickens might have recognized. It was in Holden Quad in the eighteenth century, for example, that the ceremonies of Class Day were held every year just before commencement. "It was in 1760 that the Seniors first selected an Orator to voice their farewell to College and Faculty," reports an old guide, which goes on under the heading "Holden Quadrangle: Site of the 'Class Day Tree'" to describe an event obviously both charming and ludicrous: "the farewell included iced punch for all comers. . . . Around the 'Tree,' while their Ladies looked on, crowds of Seniors used to struggle for the remnants of a wreath of flowers which encircled its trunk about 10 feet from the ground." Along not dissimilar lines hospitality of the most genial sort seems also to have thrived here then; in 1793 a student by name of Charles Angier (Class of 1793) got the bright idea of "holding a perpetual spread of punch and biscuits for his friends"— called by all his grateful pals "The Tavern," it flourished long, I'm sure. For if it was a lively world, it was also a pretty one. Closed and small—and very much on edge. Here one can see only a few feet apart the contrast between the austere elegance of the back facade of Harvard Hall, quite unaltered from 1766 and showing unmistakably the sophistication of the royal governor's taste, and the somewhat awkward hand of the colonial builder equally evident at Hollis Hall. (Never more so than in the elaborate Corinthian columns that flank Hollis' false center doorframe—which always framed tiny study windows—the capitals of which are overdone and more than a little at odds with the plainspoken facade. No such ostentation mars Harvard Hall, of course.) That the political tug of war noted earlier here had its cultural side on the eve of the American Revolution could not be clearer. And this, of course, is the magic of Holden Quad. Some of its buildings are relatively new; Lionel and Mower Halls, each faultlessly proportioned, are actually Colonial Revival structures of 1925. But most of Holden Quad's buildings are much older, and in the Quad's southern half you have only to stand in front of Lionel Hall facing Hollis Hall, with Holden Chapel on your left and Harvard Hall on your right, in order to suddenly realize you are completely surrounded on three sides by Harvard's only surviving intact eighteenth-century quad in just the way an entering freshman would have been in the 1700s, including Charles Bulfinch. America's soon to be first professional architect lived in Hollis, and it was during his time there as an undergraduate that he first perused the great folio sourcebooks of neoclassicism in Harvard's library across the quad, then located on the second floor of Harvard Hall, overlooking just the eighteenth-century scene you see today.

TOP: *Harvard Yard (Hollis, Stoughton, and Holworthy Halls)*
BOTTOM: *John Harvard Statue*

6. North Yard: Stoughton, Holworthy, Thayer and Canady Halls, and College Pump

Stoughton Hall *Charles Bulfinch, 1804*
Holworthy Hall *Laommi Baldwin, 1811*
College Pump *Restored 1936*
Thayer Hall *Ryder & Harris 1869*
Canady Hall *Ezra Ehrenkrantz 1973*

It is not often in architectural history one can move so easily—in a matter of seconds—from one of an architect's most formative environments as a student to one of his own mature designs. And in Charles Bulfinch's case it must be said that between his student years in Holden Quad and his conceiving of today's Old Yard there was also, of course, Paris, Jefferson, and Italy. But in the North of the Yard, where I believe his hand clearly ordered the overall design—a design that implied the design of the entire Yard, as already detailed here—one can see obvious resonances to Holden Quad. Indeed, two of the four landmarks of the Old Yard, Hollis Hall and Stoughton Hall II of 1804, are shared with quad and Yard. The later of these halls, the first designed by Bulfinch, is fully as dull as the earliest—no surprise as Stoughton was modeled after Hollis. But, a close comparison between the two halls nonetheless discloses not only the expected differences between a High Georgian and a Federal structure, but a few subtleties that betray the hand of the master; at Stoughton Bulfinch used white limestone lintels very suavely over the windows, eschewing the brick arches of Hollis, while both belt courses and a water table are likewise eliminated. The granite foundation of Bulfinch's hall is also beautifully flush with the facade's brick walls. Another instructive comparison, this one between Stoughton and Holworthy (designed eight years later by an associate of Bulfinch), is that Stoughton was the last Harvard dormitory built according to the medieval plan of a large bedchamber with two tiny attached studies or cubicles for prayer and study; Holworthy was the first to substitute the more modern plan of a large study-sitting room with two small bedrooms. Notice too at Holworthy that in that larger building, which has three, not just two staircases, the central doorframe, false at Hollis and also at Stoughton, is fully functional. Like all Holworthy's doors it is set off by robust granite rustication.*

    A sentimental and somewhat misleading feature in this part of the Yard between Hollis, Stoughton, Holworthy, and Thayer is the College Pump. It is misleading because visitors (and probably also present day stu-

---

* Hollis and Stoughton's roofs were rebuilt after fires in the 1870s, and a new roof was added to Holworthy in 1880 when the top floor was raised. All three dorms have heavier topmost cornices and overhangs than they should, particularly problematic in the case of late Georgian Stoughton and Holworthy.

dents and faculty) doubtless imagine eighteenth- and nineteenth-century tutors and students tumbling out in a genial, old-fashioned *Yankee Magazine* sort of way every morning to fetch their water midst much camaraderie. Its restoration by alumni attests to some of that. Yet, in fact, whereas other yard pumps have long since been mercifully covered over, this reconstruction is a memorializing of one left over from what was clearly an eighteenth-century wasteland of privies, pigsties, barns, breweries and such located here when this was the unappealing *back* yard of halls whose *front* courts opened on the street. President Kirkland, in developing today's Yard was more interested in his newly planted lawns and elm trees. But although the privies were replaced (with a long low structure discreetly shielded by pine trees), the pumps in the Old Yard necessarily remained until in the 1860s and '70s the Yard halls (starting with Grays) were endowed (in their basements only at first) with water taps. But even during that half century the idea of masculine ablutions around "ye olde pump" is more romantic than real, for more often than not it was the college porters who did the fetching for their young masters still abed. In the end, however, even Samuel Eliot Morison had joined the romanticists, imagining, somewhat tongue in cheek, the value in the late decades of the nineteenth-century Ralph Waldo Emerson "play[ing] Socrates for half a morning hour at the Yard pump." Not very likely. More characteristic of this period is the huge new Victorian dormitory, Thayer Hall, an Italianate design of 1869 across the Yard from the pump. Nothing of ye olde hall here—it stretches impressively for 213 feet. Yet it is carefully studied nonetheless so as to extend Bulfinch's scheme for the Yard. So, too, at a greater remove is a more recent dormitory, Canady Hall of 1973, behind Thayer, a much quieter design. Both dorms, the Victorian and the modern, play only supporting roles, but in architecture as well as in everything else there must be courtiers as well as stars.

7. University Hall *Charles Bulfinch, 1813*

Thwarted as we've seen in his plans for a great ellipse, Bulfinch nonetheless achieved in University Hall a noble building that as it turned out yielded something rather wonderful—the Old Yard as we know it today. Built in 1813–14, Bulfinch's design is very modernist for its day and very aggressive in its cool, gray Chelmsford granite stonework, so at variance with the Yard's red brick. Its scheme is a three-fold one, with a central section that boasts a full classical entablature according to the Ionic order, with large round-headed windows that focus attention on the central section, and smaller square-head windows below which tie the design to the flanking wings, whose only detail is such windows. The central section in turn is itself divided into three parts, the

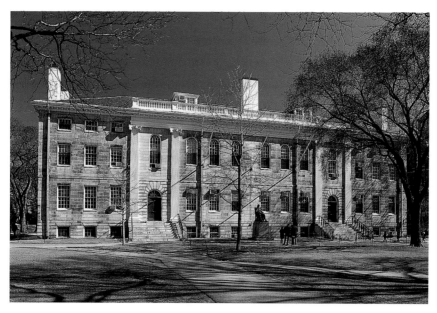

University Hall

emphasis adroitly shifted from the center to flanking entrance bays of boldly rusticated masonry that echoes the building's basement. This interpenetration on the facade of rusticated stonework with flush stonework and as well that of square and roundhead windows is very well done and gives the design a fine unity. There is also more than a hint of the coming Boston Granite Style in the superb stoniness that for all University Hall's refinement permeates the building, inside as well, where are magnificent cantilevered granite staircases. Noble as it is, University Hall is nonetheless a flawed design, doubtless reflecting the unsettled times of the War of 1812—which shadowed its construction, only finally begun after many delays in 1813. Bulfinch himself was during the war urgently preoccupied with various defensive fortifications intended to protect the port of Boston from British raiding parties. The Corporation, moreover, was no more inspiring a client in the case of University than with Stoughton Hall. At least two of Bulfinch's designs were rejected, including one that, while it would not have knit the old colonial halls together so suavely, was promising enough in itself to have later inspired the truly superb Bulfinch Pavilion, as it is now called, the architect erected at the Massachusetts General Hospital, the hospital founded in 1811 by two Harvard professors. Bulfinch's proposed cupola was also rejected for University Hall; the design later became the finale to Bulfinch's masterwork, Christ Church in Lancaster. On top of all that the Corporation forced on the architect an ungainly covered porch or colonnade that until finally removed in 1842 really ruined University Hall's facade. Nor did dormers, added in 1868, help.

It must also be said that most authorities agree Bulfinch's own eye went awry in the matter of the facade's central section; "as an academic performance," Bainbridge Bunting wrote, "the design suffers from the even number of bays of the middle zone and noticeably wider interval between windows at the exact center of the building." This was in the first place to provide space for chimney flues. And the location of the four first floor halls did require an even number of windows. But Bunting hardly exaggerated in thinking it "surprising that Bulfinch could not have devised a less awkward scheme." Four halls? An unprecedented form in Anglo-American collegiate design, the idea seems to have been Bulfinch's own. Certainly the original program for University Hall, as described by Harvard treasurer Ebenezer Storer (the father-in-law of Bulfinch's sister; Bostonians kept close company in those days), was in the grand collegiate tradition of library, hall and chapel—the idea having been that the library would stay on at Harvard Hall, much enlarged, while the new University Hall facing it across the recently laid out Yard was to be centered, in Storer's words, on "a convenient Hall in the middle, a Chapel over it." The capitalization and singular as opposed to plural nomenclature (there is nothing of "halls") can only mean that what was contemplated was the traditional Great Hall, Harvard College's fourth in succession to that of 1638–42. But perhaps because that architectural form by the early nineteenth century had ceased to be expressive or even functional (the president and faculty having apparently abandoned their role of presiding in hall), and because in the president's absence particularly the quality of Commons had greatly deteriorated both as to the food served and student behavior, the novel idea of four halls was proposed. The architect partitioned the first floor accordingly, intending one hall for each class (intending to discourage the food fights that had become common) while preserving a sense of the one Hall (with an eye to the traditional Commencement feast) by large open circular openings in the intervening partitions. Such a challenge to offer the high-spirited of those days—those oriels! Bulfinch of all people should have known better. In his own student days he had himself been fined forty shillings by the college authorities for making "an entertainment...which was introductory to great disorder." University Hall had been in use very few years before there occurred one fine Sunday night in 1818 the mother of all food fights, an altercation so fierce it was celebrated in verse heard still today:

> Nathan threw a piece of bread,
> And hit Abijah on the head.
> The wrathful Freshman, in a trice,
> Sent back another bigger slice;
> Which, being butter'd pretty well,
> Made greasy work where'er it fell.
> And thus arose a fearful battle;

The coffee-cups and saucers rattle;
The bread-bowls fly at woeful rate,
And break many a learned pate.

Many suspensions later, the fracas subsided. But Commons only went from
bad to worse, despite strenuous presidential efforts, including elegant new
Wedgwood china from England. By 1842 it had closed.

University Hall by then had for better reasons seen more than its
share of riotous days, most notably in 1834, when events took place, as
Morison recounted them in *Three Centuries of Harvard*, that strongly prefig-
ured a certain infamous late-twentieth-century occurrence in the same
building in 1969. Although Harvard histories often give the impression that
the student rebellions of the early nineteenth century—there were two chief
ones, in 1823 and 1834—were just rowdyism, that is not entirely true.
Noting that "the year 1823 is a convenient date to mark the passing away of
Massachusetts federalism as a political creed," E. Digby Baltzell, the
University of Pennsylvania historian, has written that

> ...at Harvard the 'great rebellion', in which John Quincy Adams'
> son was expelled along with many others of his class, took place in
> that transition year of 1823. That the students were in revolt against
> the authority of the Federalist establishment is indicated by the fol-
> lowing observations from a sympathetic faculty member of the
> time: 'our college is under the absolute direction of...the evil coun-
> cilor, the Ahithophel of the high Federal party.' Perhaps partly
> because of the rebellion Josiah Quincy was chosen president of
> Harvard in 1829, the year John Quincy Adams was defeated [for the
> presidency] by Andrew Jackson.

The 1834 rebellion, though it also ostensibly involved strictly collegiate politics—it has been suggested the problem was in requiring memorization of a
particularly vexatious Latin grammar—was again a case of, first, petitions
and then violence (a pattern only too tempting in the long wake of the
Boston Tea Party). To the student protests the Corporation made an altogether inappropriate response; "the power of the Commonwealth would be
invoked," in Morison's words, "[to] proceed against them by civil process."
In consequence, the university historian continued:

> Hell broke loose. Quincy had violated one of the oldest academic
> traditions: that the public authorities have no concern with what
> goes on inside a university, so long as the rights of outsiders are
> not infringed. The 'black flag of rebellion' was hung from the roof
> of Holworthy. Furniture and glass in the recitation rooms of

University [Hall] were smashed, and the fragments hurled out the windows. The juniors…voted to wear crepe on their arms, issued a handbill with an acute dissection of the President's character, and hanged his effigy to the Rebellion Tree. A terrific explosion took place in chapel….A printed senior's 'Circular', signed by a committee who were promptly deprived of their degrees, gave their version of the Rebellion in language so cogent that the Overseers issued a forty-seven page pamphlet by [President] Quincy to counteract it…two or three indictments [by a grand jury] were found [but] subsequently nol-prossed and the whole business fizzled out. [President] Quincy never recovered his popularity.

All that—in 1834. Of 1969, more later. Meanwhile, the old order passed away after all. And just as Harvard Hall I and II in the eighteenth century had been a centerpiece of the vice-regal court and a setting for the state visits of the royal governor, so too in the nineteenth century University Hall, in keeping with the era, would welcome several American presidents, including Jackson himself, who to the fury of Federal Boston was given an honorary degree in 1833. Usually such events were held in the second floor chapel. But that facility lasted not much longer than the Commons, closing in 1858 when a new freestanding chapel was built. But in the case of the University Hall chapel its increasingly inadequate size rather than its architectural character was the culprit, for Bulfinch engaged in no novelties of the sort he did in the first floor halls; nor was his design concept faulty. Somewhat reminiscent of the original Senate Chamber in his Boston State House, Bulfinch's chapel was elegantly conceived with floor to ceiling fluted ionic pilasters and surrounding paneling, as one may still see today, it having been restored in later years as a Faculty Room. The last of the building's original functions to survive was the President's office, which in 1939 was moved to the even more venerable Massachusetts Hall.

8. John Harvard Statue

Daniel Chester French, sculptor; C. Howard Walker, architect, 1884

The Minuteman guarding the historic green at Concord, Lincoln in his great temple at the foot of the Mall in Washington, John Harvard presiding over Harvard Yard—it fell to Daniel Chester French to create all these great figures of America's historical landscape. It was, in fact, the success of the Minuteman in 1874, and of a subsequent bust of Emerson, that earned French in 1884 the commission for the figure of John Harvard, who almost in the manner of a medieval saint "passes so briefly and mysteriously across the pages of our early history," in the words of French's daughter, Margaret Cresson. The sculptor's earliest interpreter, her's remains to my mind the best analysis of

John Harvard Statue

the Harvard figure. She noted firstly his "beautiful, wasted hand" (Harvard died of consumption; note also his scrawny calves) and how he is made to look up from his Bible and "forward with an abstract air, weaving a dream, perhaps...." One can hardly begrudge the sculptor that (or the sculptor's daughter). But in another place Cresson seems suddenly very much more acute; her father had given John Harvard "a countenance of strong intellectual mold"; yet he had also given him something else: "the hands," Cresson observed, "were thin and nervous."

French himself wrote while working on the figure: "I am sometimes scared by the importance of this work. It is a subject that one might not have in a lifetime and a failure would be inexcusable. As a general thing," he continued, "my model looks pretty well to me, but there are dark days." But that was surely apt; one of the reasons one studies the Puritan arrogance is the Puritan angst, and French caught both. As Michael Richman wrote: "in the *Harvard* [statue] French became a historical interpreter of Puritan America, as did...J. A. O. Ward in his *Pilgrim* (1882–85) in New York, and Augustus Saint-Gaudens in his *Deacon Chapin* (1882–87)...in Springfield [Massachusetts]. Each sculptor had to create an idealized portrait that embodied the spirit of seventeenth-century America." A task for a young man—perhaps only for a young man. But just as French, then only 24, had surprised everyone in 1875 with both the spirit of his minuteman—"so alert and so American," Lorado Taft had written there is about the Concord statue a distinctive "sense of action and its surface modeling...defines rather than hides the human form"—so the young sculptor proved in both respects again to intrigue with his Harvard figure even so austere an eye as President Eliot's, who was heard to say he thought it "very interesting. It moves one." Yet allegorical figures aside, it was only French's second major figure. Today, every man or woman in every commencement procession uncovers when passing it, doffing mortarboard or top hat or whatever; and the tip of the shoe of John Harvard's extended foot shines more brightly for the same reason St. Peter's does at the Vatican. Seniors especially, I'm told, are often seen to touch the founder's foot ere they commence. The founder?

So says the statue, certainly. "JOHN HARVARD • FOUNDER • 1638", words inscribed here by persons most learned. Yet chances are they're hardly read before some smartass guide breezily informs the unsuspecting visitor that this is, after all, the "Statue of Three Lies"—so very Harvard, right? But though it is in one sense an open question whether or not John Harvard was the founder of Harvard College, and though 1638 is certainly *not* the date of the college's founding, nor, in fact, the figure depicted John Harvard—the idea of the three lies is at best a fourth, and by far the greater falsehood. In truth, opinions differ greatly. Morison, who went into the matter exhaustively, notes that "the tradition that John Harvard founded the College was started in 1643 by *New England's First Fruits*," published that year. He also observes that in 1654 a widely known poetic eulogy by one John Wilson imputes the claim to Harvard himself. Finally, he records that the General Court of Massachusetts itself described John as the college's "principal founder" in 1661. All John Harvard's contemporaries thus seem quite unanimous in according to him this distinction. But (taking perhaps insufficient account of the political, even mercenary reasons the Harvard Corporation might have had for the assertion) Morison seizes on the Corporation's rather argumentative reply to the General Court: "Your Predecessors," they told the legislators in 1661, "were the *Founders* of the College." An irrefutable assertion. But distinctly an odd argument to be having all around; one influenced doubtless by the old truism that success has a thousand fathers, failures none, and at one time or another in its first years Harvard played both roles.

President Quincy in his Harvard history judged that the General Court "conferred upon [the College] the name of Harvard, thus acknowledging him as its founder." President Everett, on the other hand, refused even to use John Harvard's name; always referring to "the university at Cambridge." And still today there is no consensus. Witness Professor E. K. Rand in the twentieth century: "our ancestors knew what they were about in calling John Harvard *the* Founder of the college that bears his name." The only sure thing is that scholars will always be of two or more minds on the issue. Meanwhile, the inscription on the base of the statue does not call John Harvard the Founder—the quibbles of the centuries subside with a firm dignity in the simple word FOUNDER, which may be read (*pace* Morison) as *the* founder, or *a* founder, as the evidence convinces, one way or another. And Founder in one of those two senses John Harvard certainly was: as Cotton Mather put it, the Reverend Mr. Harvard certainly "laid the most significant stone in the Foundation." The College was founded in Boston, to be sure, by the legislature of the Puritan Colony. But the same colony self-evidently saw in John Harvard the personification and completion of the community's action—in 1838, the year rightly inscribed on the statue's base because it was the year of his benefaction. Finally, that Sherman Hoar modeled the statue for the sculptor, no likeness of John Harvard ever having been discovered, least of all makes it a lie. Unless in Picasso's sense that art is always a lie that tells the truth. Michelangelo himself, queried once about whether or not a portrait statue of Cosmo de Medici even vaguely resembled the sitter, impatiently retorted that in a hundred years it would. Was it not Michelangelo's vision that was wanted? And is now prized. So too with Daniel Chester French.

The figure was moved to this location in 1924 in no small measure to ameliorate the perceived design weakness of the midpoint of Bulfinch's University Hall facade. But the statue's placement on axis with the centuries old ceremonial entrance to the college could not be bettered, not least because it gives the figure itself a fair view, worth a visitor's long consideration. Follow John Harvard's gaze. Straight ahead the perspective goes, across the Old Yard to Johnston Gate. To the right, Harvard Hall; to the left Massachusetts Hall. But what the young Puritan minister is surely looking toward, looming up beyond the gate and across the square, is the tower of the First Church, stalwart seeming from this perspective in its grandeur of scale and terrific sense of weight and mass, for all its wooden awkwardness and naivete. It roots Harvard here, after all, the First Church, rising beside the old nineteenth-century burying ground where lie so many of those also entitled to be called Harvard's founders.

The only possible caption for this perspective would be from the sermon preached in 1630 by the first governor of the Massachusetts Bay Colony, John Winthrop, on board the *Arabella* in the bay before the settlers went ashore, on the eve of the New World, a sermon so powerful its memory is still deeply felt despite the conspicuous failure of both the original European settlers and their posterity to rise to it in coming years. Famously, Winthrop demanded:

Massachusetts Hall, First Church, and Harvard Hall

Weld Hall, top; *Matthews Hall, with Hollis and Stoughton Halls beyond*, bottom

We must entertain each other in brotherly affection; we must be willing to abridge ourselves of our superfluities, for the supply of others' necessities; we must uphold a familiar commerce together in all meekness, gentleness, patience and liberality. We must delight in each other, make each other's conditions our own, rejoice together, mourn together, labor and suffer together: always having before our eyes our commission.... For we must consider that we shall be like a city upon a hill, the eyes of all people are upon us.

Winthrop's sermon, Sean O'Connell has written, "defined the mix of idealism and anxiety which characterizes later conceptions of Boston," a place O'Connell aptly asserted was "imagined into being" by Winthrop in that shipboard homily in the face of the wilderness. And sustained in being still? It was Winthrop's words that three centuries later on the eve of his inauguration as President of the United States in 1961, John F. Kennedy would quote to the Great and General Court of Massachusetts of his day, whose predecessors I am far from denying were founders even before John Harvard of all you see here now! Look across the Yard to Harvard Hall III and consider that Governor Winthrop presided with President Dunster in Harvard Hall I at the college's first commencement in 1642. Extending your gaze leftwards to Weld Hall, a much more modern building of which more soon, consider that John F. Kennedy passed his freshman year there in the 1930s. It is in that sense that on great occasions at Harvard descendants of every imaginable race and religion find themselves doffing their hats, rubbing the tip of John Harvard's shoe, and cheerfully singing "*Fair* Harvard...Be the herald of Light, and the Bearer of Love/ Till the stock of the Puritans die."

9. South Yard Dormitories

Grays Hall *Nathaniel J. Bradlee, 1863*
Matthews Hall *Peabody and Stearns, 1872*
Weld Hall *Ware and Van Brunt, 1873*

Although the three dormitories that close the Yard to the south are all Victorian, they are really the progeny of early Federalist Harvard in that they are chiefly significant as completing the great rectangle of the Old Yard, the design concept of which arose out of Bulfinch's late eighteenth- and early nineteenth-century vision for Harvard. The first to be erected, Grays Hall, is a massive building made more massive still by its heavy granite trim and conspicuous mansard roof. A decade later followed Weld and Matthews, the first a dramatically picturesque work, very Queen Anne in feeling, with graceful Jacobean gables, and notable for its two rooftop clerestory towers, originally intended to light the stairwells. Matthews on the other hand represents quite another style entirely, though it is a work of only a year later. Vigorously Ruskin Gothic, with steep gables and picturesque Gothic porches, Matthews also rejoices in superb foliate stonecarving of a sort never before seen at Harvard. What each building has in common, however, is equally important: the facade of each is symmetrical and predominately brick, and each structure is more horizontal than vertical in feeling, at least at ground level. And although—just as Victorians in their day despaired of the colonial halls of the North Yard—these Victorian dorms of the South Yard have not always been admired (Weld, wrote Harvard's head of architecture, G. H. Edgell, in 1928, was "wholly ugly"), it would be hard to fault the designers of any of these buildings today. Each in his own voice, even discordantly with each other, had an eye for the needs of the Yard as a whole. And it is likely their own youthful college years informed their adult achievement. Just as Bulfinch brought his memories of college life in eighteenth-century Holden Quad to his design of the north and middle portions of the Old Yard, so did most of the architects of the Yard's south end bring to their work there their memory of college in Bulfinch's halls at the Yard's older end. Indeed, all the Victorian architects of the Yard's southern end except Bradlee (who did not go to college) were Harvard graduates, Ware in 1852, Van Brunt in '54, Stearns in '63, and Peabody in '66. For their gifts of reticence no less than their skills of design and planning American architecture owes them much—at a time when colonial work had fallen greatly out of favor, and was still a decade away from being rediscovered—for the manner of their completion of Old Harvard Yard.

10. Lehman, Strauss, and Wigglesworth Halls, Class of 1875 Gate and Class of 1857 Gate

Strauss Hall *Coolidge, Shepley, Bulfinch & Abbott, 1926*
Lehman Hall *Coolidge, Shepley, Bulfinch & Abbott, 1924*
Wigglesworth Hall *Coolidge, Shepley, Bulfinch & Abbott, 1931*
Class of 1875 Gate *McKim, Mead and White, 1900–01*
Class of 1857 Gate *McKim, Mead and White, 1900–01*

The south end of the Yard breaks down picturesquely behind Grays and Matthews and Weld into a series of small quads, rather like the apsidal chapels and ambulatories at the "altar end" of a great cathedral, the result of the twentieth-century cloistering of the Yard, which surrounds the regularity of the Yard's layout of buildings with the irregularity of boundary buildings that follow the lines of the surrounding streets. The resultant effect is wonderful, and all these spaces the central rectangular quad of the Yard leaks into are charming, worth more than the few moments most give them on their hurried way to and from Harvard Square. Most formal is Strauss Quad, formed when the hall of that name was given in 1926. Built opposite late nineteenth-century Matthews Hall and next to early eighteenth-century Massachusetts Hall, this quad is as fascinating an architectural exam as could be set at Harvard—"compare and contrast" over a range of three centuries: Matthews' late nineteenth-century Ruskin Gothic engages early eighteenth-century Georgian at Massachusetts Hall; Strauss' twentieth-century Georgian Revival engages not only the late nineteenth-century scale and Ruskin Gothic style of Matthews but the early eighteenth-century "original" of Massachusetts Hall. And that hardly exhausts the matter. It would be a long essay. Quite different is the adjoining triangular-shaped plaza dominated by Lehman Hall. Built in 1924, Lehman, designed as the university's business office, is now the social center of Dudley House, the only place where both graduate students and undergraduates can be members. Notable for its beautifully detailed main entrance, Lehman also boasts on both sides a heroic parade of pilasters, a bit overblown admittedly, but doubtless intended to mark the principal frontispiece, as Lehman is, of Yard to square. Indeed, to each side of this hall are what have come to be the busiest gates to Harvard Yard. On the Strauss Hall side of Lehman is the Class of 1875 Gate, built in 1900. Its inscription—"Open ye the gates that the righteous nation which keepeth the truth may enter in"—is from the Jewish scriptures, the words of the prophet Isaiah from the book (Isaiah xxvi: 2) of that name. On the other side of Lehman, at the Class of 1857 Gate, a more classical inspiration was preferred—in fact, the words of Horace (*Odes*: I, 13) "Thrice happy and more are they whom an unbroken bond unites, and when no sundering of love by wretched quarrels shall separate before life's dying day." Both gates, domestic Georgian style shading to imperial classical, are from the designs in 1900–01 of McKim, Mead and White, the success of whose Johnston Gate led to a series of walls and gates around the Yard.

Visible beyond Wadsworth House, of which more soon, is the third of the cloistering dorms of the Yard's south end, and surely the finest. Wigglesworth Hall, named in honor of a family whose service to Harvard reaches back to the days of Michael Wigglesworth, AB 1651, tutor, pastor, poet, and most famously now, diarist. Running from Wadsworth House to Lamont Library for virtually the entire length of Harvard Yard on south Massachusetts Avenue, Wigglesworth skillfully knits together all sorts of disparate architecture, transforming what would otherwise certainly be a very pedestrian part of the Yard into its most intimate and most picturesque precinct, brilliantly crowding, for example, much older buildings like Boylston Hall in a way no architect designing either Boylston or Wigglesworth *de novo* would dare to do now, but as a result creating as beautiful a built environment as exists anywhere, all the better for its very crowded medieval feeling. Even on the Massachusetts Avenue side the effect is striking, for here the yet further layering of fencing-

and-gates with the later ranges of halls is beautifully handled: for example the way the low arched entrance tunnel through the ground floor of Wigglesworth is aligned with the Class of 1889 Gate to Massachusetts Ave. But it is on the Yard side that the effect is so winning; the narrow perspective Wigglesworth forces from granite Boylston Hall to wood clapboard Wadsworth is an ideal vision of a New England village, which, of course, in one aspect Harvard Yard certainly is.

11. Wadsworth House *architect unknown, 1726; additions, 1783, 1810*

Harvard's fourth president's lodgings pull us back to 1726; Wadsworth House is now the second oldest building of the university, one happy result of the election of 1725, when Benjamin Wadsworth, the minister of Boston's First Church, was elected Harvard's president. A compromise candidate, a moderate acceptable to conservative and liberal alike, Wadsworth inspired so much confidence the General Court promptly voted a thousand pounds for new presidential lodgings. And though the designer of the house is unknown, the admirable issue of his labors nearly 300 years later is more than apparent despite the fact that the house has lost its once ample front lawn and garden to the wide and busy modern thoroughfare of Massachusetts Avenue. Two-and-a-half stories in height, its roof gambreled and with hipped dormers, its windows of twelve-over-twelve paned sash, Wadsworth House, in the unusual bracketing of the cornice formed around its boxed eaves, and in the curious lapping rather than mitering at the corners of its narrow clapboards, hand-planed to a beaded edge, shows pronounced local characteristics. The brick-ended kitchen wing to the rear of the house is an addition, built in 1810 and surrounds (with Grays and another hall) two sides of another small quad in the south of the Yard, in which it is hard not to be reminded again of Holden Quad in the Yard's northern precincts. Wadsworth House, however, like Harvard itself, presents at least two faces to the world. There is Harvard Yard and there is Harvard Square.

OPPOSITE: *Wigglesworth Hall, Wadsworth House, and Boylston Hall*

Church Street to Lower Brattle Street

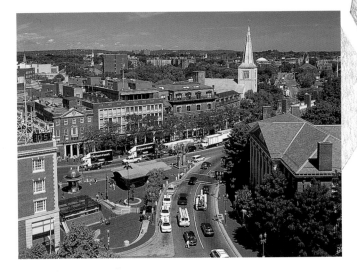

Harvard Yard and Harvard Square

11. Wadsworth House (Harvard Square facade)

1729; additions, 1783, 1810

The ancient, thoughtful Yard slows you down; the bustling modern square speeds you up. Thus do Harvard's conflicting constraints of chronology and geography immediately present themselves—confusingly but also usefully. For there is another way to experience historic architecture than thoughtfully musing over it as we have thus far here in evocative quads, a way somewhat unconventional, but, perhaps, more stimulating; a circumnavigation of Wadsworth House, overthrowing all the efforts of the Yard's cloistering, will disclose it at once. As Walter Benjamin put it in his study of the arcades of nineteenth-century Paris, we best gain access to the life of our ancestors by remembering that "the true method of making things present is to imagine [our ancestors] in our own space and not to imagine ourselves in their space." Holden Quad, even to some extent Wadsworth's cul-de-sac, is fundamentally *their* space. But to go from Wadsworth House's back door to its front door is to bring Wadsworth House into our own space—twenty-first-century Harvard Square.

What is the point to this other way of experiencing historical architecture? It is certainly not conducive to rumination. Benjamin again: "History is not a cumulative, additive narrative...from past to future, but rather a montage where any moment may enter into sudden adjacency with another. History as parataxis—time scattered through space like stars." Sudden adjacency could almost be said to be the overriding design concept, as it has turned out, of Harvard Square, where, for instance, history takes on a new intimacy, a new sharpness even, when you realize, waiting for the No. 1 bus (the "Harvard-Dudley" bus), that the only available shelter in the busy square within sprinting distance of the bus stop is the elegant Massachusetts Avenue front porch of Harvard's early eighteenth-century president's lodgings—Wadsworth House—which does as well today for waiting for a city bus as it surely did for any of our ancestors in the age of the stage coach two centuries ago. Waiting there myself on occasion I generally find myself musing on Josiah Quincy. When he became Harvard's fifteenth president in 1829, Quincy brought four daughters to live that year in Wadsworth House, and the journal of one, Miss Maria Quincy, describes many of the comings and goings through this portico at that year's commencement revels: "gentlemen and ladies began to pour in...arriving and departing till half past seven, ice-creams and coffee circulating all the time...[governor and staff and Lancers depart] in a tempest of drums and dust." Even grander entrances and exits come to mind; in Quincy's day Wadsworth House was already a century and more old. Sheltering on its front porch today, whether from a swirling snowstorm or a sudden July downpour, as another joins you on the tiny porch (there is hardly room for

Wadsworth House

more) that ordinary physical fact can itself be evocative. There is certainly no room for another to pass in and out—not even George Washington, who came and went just this way that long ago July of 1776 on the day he first took command of the Continental army, by any measure a world-changing event to share in some dimension of time and space with an old portico, waiting for the No. 1 bus.

A century or so after Washington, in the 1870s, the most arresting comings and goings from Wadsworth House are those of the young Henry Adams—via horse-drawn omnibus—and mostly to the Back Bay to woo his future wife (fateful choice). When in 1870 he began to teach at Harvard, he first took rooms in Wadsworth (two on the ground floor and a third on the second connected by a private staircase). Harvard Square, already more suburban than rural, as much brick as clapboard, was still too isolated for the city-loving, cosmopolitan Adams. Many concurred. So quiet was the square in 1865 that Artemus Ward observed not entirely in jest that "Harvard University was pleasantly and conveniently situated in the [downtown Boston] barroom of Parker's [the Parker House Hotel] in School Street." Fast forward to the 1900s, when T. S. Eliot lived across Massachusetts Avenue from Wadsworth House, just a few doors down Holyoke Street. The square was by then a much more urban scene. In Eliot's day it would have been an electric trolley one waited for on Wadsworth's front porch, whether he was bound for Beacon Hill (to canvass society: see "Portrait of a Lady"), or in search of much grittier urban locales (Eliot wrote both "Preludes in Roxbury" and "Caprices in North Cambridge" while a student at Harvard).

Or perhaps young Mr. Eliot was in his dress suit, headed for the Boston Opera House. (It was there about 1909 he first saw Wagner's *Tristan and Isolde*, an evening Igor Stravinsky inferred from Eliot's report was one of the seminal events in his life). Eliot, whether or not from Wadsworth's portico, surely cast a cold eye over all and missed little. Nor, surely, did Leonard Bernstein, equally as alive but in a different way to urban music, in his case in the late 1930s. Bernstein passed his freshman year in Wigglesworth Hall, adjoining Wadsworth House. By then, finally, the isolation—indeed, almost time itself—had been all but abolished by the subway (Madrid is getting closer and closer to our place of waiting), which in 1912 had reached Harvard Square: "8 minutes to Park Street" trumpeted the signage, Park Street Station being the downtown crossroads of the far flung Boston subway system. The "Red Line" (red for crimson, of course) extends today much beyond Harvard Square. *Nine* minutes! There were people alive in 1912 who could recall such a journey taking the better part of a working day. But if headed uptown rather than downtown, to Copley Square, say, rather than Park Street, Bernstein for one surely figured out soon enough that the "Harvard/Dudley" bus got you to Symphony Hall much faster.

Charming it would have been, I'm sure, to have waited in Wadsworth portico with "Lenny"; terrifying, I do not doubt, with Eliot; one hardly knows which with Adams; Washington, one imagines, just passed through, and hardly waited at all, that being presumably the office of his coachman. Yet for us today, drawn now to Harvard's historical architecture in the twenty-first century, to wait here at all, whether sheltering against wind or snow or just a spring shower, to muse here on any or all of the cast of Wadsworth House through the centuries, is not just to appropriate their space. But (it all being now in busy twenty-first-century Harvard Square) it is to imagine our predecessors here in what is fundamentally our space, a place *we've* made—and to share with them (never mind the New England climate) even Palladio himself, one modest issue of whose teachings Wadsworth's fine eighteenth-century portico is. "Sudden adjacencies." Is it not finally a great thing to have conjured in Harvard Square today a bus shelter by Andrea Palladio? Certainly it is a good example of what Benjamin argues we must do to understand any aspect of the past; that instead of positioning it as the place to which "the present must somehow return in order to recover or reconstruct it 'as it really was,'" what is really necessary is that "the historian must make it clear that if there is any knowledge of the past or present to be had, this can only result from the dialectical interchange that occurs when the two meet."

One could go further—as we will as we go further into the square; considering Wadsworth House, for example, not so much as an artifact of the past to be appropriated by ourselves in the present, but to consider what happens when such a landmark is forced by us into a present-day context that is potentially hostile, even destructive.

12. Holyoke Center and Forbes Plaza

Sert, Jackson & Gourley, 1960–1967

Holyoke Center

Old Cambridge, Boston's Left Bank today, though still retaining in some part those old elements John Coolidge focused on (of one-industry town and fashionable suburb), famously centers on Harvard Square. And hardly less so does the square center on Holyoke Center and Forbes Plaza, and the adjoining street spaces, where there thrives day in and day out a scene which, depending on how you take it, is picturesque, even fascinating or, on the other hand, alarming. In whichever event it is an ardent, anxious urban mix of town and gown, a mix perhaps without peer anywhere else in the western world. And Holyoke Center—a block wide and a block deep, conspicuously International Style, and towering ten stories high, right in Wadsworth House's face—offers a dramatic backdrop to the daily clash of culture and counterculture that is Harvard Square.

Holyoke Center, however, Harvard's main administration building and infirmary, is so adroitly massed that Wadsworth House really doesn't at all seem like an antique toy inadvertently left by the curb. And this despite the fact that grass has given way to pavement around Holyoke, the building is clumsily closed in at both ends and Forbes Plaza is as ever a sea of humanity gathered around cafe tables and stone chessboards, surrounded in turn by a street life that is part Paris cafe, part teenage mosh-pit, and part Middle Eastern bazaar, the whole engulfed by traffic only Boston drivers could generate. Cities thrive on congestion and excitement, of course. But do historic buildings? Susan Freeman has written: "the very agitation of modern life can work to enhance the experience of history. The skyscrapers that dwarf the Old Corner Bookstore building [in downtown Boston] also give it a real stature. The traffic roar in Harvard Square makes the hush of Longfellow's garden even deeper." She's right. Ditto Wadsworth House and Holyoke Center or the hush not just of Longfellow's garden, but of Harvard Yard itself. But this is a very modern view and cannot account, historically, for this raucous urban townscape of buildings and people in the square. How or why did all this come about? How on earth did Harvard University end up spawning Harvard Square?

But Harvard didn't spawn it. Boston spawned it. Mile by mile through the years, century by century, from the port of Boston and State Street, over Beacon Hill, through the Back Bay, across the Charles to engulf the Yard, the fleshpot Yale and Princeton were careful to stay clear of any version of; the "forbidden city" (as it was even by Kirkland's era) could not be stayed. And fundamentally for the same reason even late seventeenth- and early eighteenth-century Harvard found itself by Leverett's day committed on the one hand to Boston's vice-regal court and royal governor and what I've called here the Liberal Tradition on the other. Walls and dormitories might cloister the Yard's physical serenities, but that was only half the story. Recalling Artemus Ward's crack about Harvard and the Parker House bar in 1865, Lucius Beebe observed in his day in 1927, when Locke Ober's had replaced Parker's as Harvard's watering hole of choice near Park Street subway station (midway twixt State Street and Harvard Square) that in 62 years "the University [had moved] precisely four city blocks, where, of course, it again found itself in a saloon." There have, to be sure, been other points of view. Wrote David McCord in the 1950s: "The love and respect in which I hold my College and University is faintly shadowed by the dismal cloud which hangs over Harvard Square." McCord went on to affirm that "before and into the [nineteen] twenties, down to the first intimation of neon signs [do we even notice them now?]...the Square was not without its remnant of charm." But by 1958 the only way McCord could explain the Square's increasingly chaotic urban scene (as he saw it) and how Harvard tolerated it all was to compare the store-fronts particularly to *barnacles*: "people of the sea towns find a certain low-tide charm in the barnacles which grow on old wooden piles." Today some there are also who after the fashion of every generation have grown to treasure what McCord disparaged, and some who feel similarly gloomy about the present day square, which will, of course, doubtless be remembered fondly by the next generation. And so on. But it was always in the genes of the place that however it cherished the quiet of the Yard, Harvard would go out to meet the metropolis as it surged past to the western suburbs and now even to southern New Hampshire, insisting as Harvard always had from the very beginning with Boston on the importance of that "promiscuous conversation with the world." One immediate result of that conversation is present day Harvard Square.

If this hectic urban scene at Harvard's doorstep thus makes perfect sense historically, so does it offer untold riches architecturally. That dialectal interchange Benjamin spoke of that occurs when the present and the past meet up—very much a moving target, of course, as history unfolds—is everywhere present in the square's architecture. Think Proust, who conceived of the place where past and present meet as the place of "awakening," or as the effort (as Richard Sieburth explains it) of "a consciousness... to get its bearings in space and time as it hovers between past and present." The tension of the effort, that dialectical interchange, can tell us much about Harvard's architecture.

13. Harvard Square Station, Out-of-Town Newsstand, and "Omphalos"

Harvard Square Station *Skidmore, Owings and Merrill, 1981–85*
Out-of-Town Newsstand *1928*
"Omphalos" *Dmitri Hadzi, 1985*

All over the Square, in any lull of traffic, the attentive never miss the sound, the vibration (the one audible through the air grates in the sidewalk, the other *felt* at odd moments), of the subway. It runs mostly under Massachusetts Avenue, the surging traffic of which now sweeps past Wadsworth House. It is still, "Mass. Ave.," as everyone calls it, the principal transportation center to (and now through) Harvard Square from the West Boston (now Longfellow) Bridge. This was the route of the first stage coach service, and of the large horse-drawn omnibuses we imagined Henry Adams waiting for. Omnibus service was established between the square and downtown Boston in 1795; by 1826 it departed hourly. And it says much for how urgently Harvard Square and State Street felt the need to link up that it was, in Bainbridge Bunting's words, "apparently the first high-frequency transit route in America and one that appeared two years before the appearance of the omnibus in Paris, three before those in London." By 1860 horse-drawn trolley cars on rails were taking over; by 1890 electric trolleys; in 1912 when the subway arrived, so did the first architectural expression of all this—an elaborate oval-shaped brick and stone headhouse, now gone, replaced first by a steel-roofed modern headhouse in 1928, and most recently by the present mostly glass structure of 1985. The station below, by the same architects, is more interesting.

Designed around a huge underground lobby with rounded walls and deeply coffered cement ceilings and long sweeping ramps yielding dramatic four-story vistas, the station is highlighted by works of art like the spectacular stained glass busway mural by the celebrated Modernist artist, Gyorgy Kepes of MIT. Of the original subway station of 1912 little remains, but that little is charming: for example, the busway's glazed tile name panels—dark red, of course, the tiles laid not in the common bond of most of such panels in other stations, but in Flemish bond as in Harvard's eighteenth-century buildings in the Old Yard. The tunnels, of course, are also original, and if you peer carefully out of the train as it slowly pulls into the station, fugitive glimpses of underground Harvard Square are briefly but fascinatingly visible. The nineteenth-century cellars of Harvard's earliest buildings, discovered when the subway tunnel was dug (and commemorated by the brass markers outlining the buildings' corners in the middle of Mass. Ave.) are now so disrupted, of course, as to be beyond recognition again; but hardly less ghostly are the glimpses of now darkened station platforms, long abandoned. Indeed, there is a literary as well as an histori-

Harvard Square

cal aspect to this underground architecture, the most striking aspect of which arises from A. J. Deutsch's short story of 1950, "A Subway Named Mobius" (which picks up on the title of Tennessee Williams' *A Streetcar Named Desire*, published a few years previously). The culmination of the story comes when a Harvard mathematician commuting by subway between his Beacon Hill apartment and his office at Harvard—three stops apart, between Charles and Harvard stations—has a startling experience musing out the train window: the passengers he sees are all reading newspapers ten weeks old. For reasons too complicated to go into here this wild ride ends with "the train proceed[ing] to Harvard [where] the police took all passengers into protective custody." A literary fantasia published by Isaac Asimov in his anthology of 1971, *Where Do We Go From Here?*, the story is about a lost subway train in these old Boston Elevated Company tunnels that departs Park Street and never reaches Harvard Square. More specifically, it is about the Möbius strip, so called according to Asimov: "because its properties were first carefully analyzed by a German mathematician, August Ferdinand Möbius, in the mid-nineteenth century.... The properties of the Möbius strip are an example of the sort of thing studied in that branch of mathematics called topology.... Deutsch wrote the story [when] he was in the astronomy department at Harvard. Naturally, then, he wrote the story about the Boston subway system." This is, of course, science fiction. But the tunnels aren't. Especially if you are intrigued by what one character in the story calls "harebrained [Harvard] professors who thought that the whole subway trains could jump off [the track] into the fourth dimension."[*] Very pertinent, in other words, to the nature of Harvard Square—never mind underground, but also the street-life above. Where, by the way, the post–World War I subway kiosk is still here! It has been recycled into the Out-of-Town Newsstand and one's daily *Times* or *Globe* or *Crimson*—or *Paris Match*—is bought today under the flaring metal roof where yesterday you'd have plunged down incredibly steep stairs to the subway tunnels below. Harvard Square is like that. However, artistically considered, the Proustian moment between past and present, identified in the Yard by the poet—"Is that you, John Harvard?", David McCord asks—arises in the square out of the work instead of a sculptor, Dimitri Hadzi, whose huge 24-foot high sculpture, *Omphalos*, stands next to the old subway kiosk.

Hadzi's sculpture, Joseph Maschek writes, is "at once ancient and modern"—ancient in that "an 'omphalos' or world-navel was the ancient concrete civic marker of a spiritual center" (the most celebrated was that of Delphi, at the oracle site sacred to Apollo, "who personif[ied] all serenity of classical form and culture over and against barbarity. . ."); modern in how fitting it was for a place like Harvard Square and for a sculptor like Hadzi

> . . . embracing a paleoclassical aesthetic. . . [to] interject an utterly "civic" and Greek civically scaled, abstract Delphic "world navel" into the hubbub of the totally demythologized, and largely demodernized, 1980s. Putting it this way risks making *Omphalos* seem obscurantist—title, theme and all. Let's just say that culture itself has become in some degree inescapably Gnostic, or at least that a certain implicit intellectuality is not inappropriate at the gates of Harvard.

This, in the face of the First Church! But the provocation neither limits nor exhausts the meanings of this sculpture, the form of which suggests more than one aspect. "Revolutionary 'liberty tree'?" Certainly there was one in Harvard Yard in the years preceding 1776, around which patriot students gathered often and boisterously. "Memorializing abstract stand of doomed American elms?" These too once stood in the Yard until ravaged by Dutch Elm disease. Most grand of all is Maschek's last suggestion. Playing on the idea of Boston as the "Hub of the Universe"—words derived from those of Oliver Wendell Holmes in the nineteenth century but in our time credible only in Alfred North Whitehead's understanding of Boston as the intellectual capital of the West (and Harvard being by universal consent the crown jewel of Boston's galaxy of universities)—Maschek suggests that Hadzi's

---

[*] Architects take note: the three dimensions are length, breadth and thickness: a line has only length, one dimension; surface has length and breadth, two dimensions; a solid length, breadth and thickness, three dimensions.

Harvard Square sculpture "has the appropriate general aspect of a multidi-rectional sign at a New England crossroads, or the shifting vertical planes of the often sculpturesque weathervanes of Harvard, if not," Maschek con-cludes," . . . of Boston itself, that 'Hub' or omphalos 'of the Universe'."

Cynics might seize wryly on the crossroads idea, for more than one person has claimed one is as likely to find a Harvard professor on the Boston-Washington shuttle as in Harvard Yard, but for our purposes here the idea will point us instead across the street and down the first of the Square's storied side streets.

14. College House Block and Sumner Statue

Harvard Cooperative Society *Perry, Shaw & Hepburn, 1924*
College House *1845, 1859*
Charles Sumner Statue *Anne Whitney, sculptor, 1900*

"The Coop," as the *Harvard Cooperative Society* is universally known, was founded by Charles Kip, a Harvard undergraduate of uncommon enterprise, his purpose to offer his fellow students some alternative to the increasingly high prices (in 1882!) of Harvard Square. Although open to the general pub-lic, only members of the Harvard and MIT communities who pay a small fee receive an (equally small!) annual patronage rebate from the cooperative, run by a board of faculty and student directors. Primarily a bookstore today (operated by Barnes & Noble), its main ground floor bookroom, with its encircling Ionic columns, the grandest retail space in the square, was designed by the architects of the colonial Williamsburg restoration, and their facade for the Coop reflects that of the Yard dormitories opposite. It was in third-floor rooms above the Coop in the 1920s and '30s that the Harvard Society of Contemporary Art, a key shaping force in the history of modern art and architecture in this country, held the first exhibition any-where of the Bauhaus School of architecture. Intended to goad Boston's Museum of Fine Arts and Harvard's Fogg Art Museum toward modernism, the society—like the Coop a student-run enterprise—was founded by Lincoln Kirstein; the architect Philip Johnson was another early member during his student days at Harvard.

A few doors up from the Coop stands what was originally the cen-tral section of College House (or as it was first called, Graduates' Hall), built in 1845; beyond is the lower north section of 1859. A dormitory built and for many years operated by the University, College House, among whose notable residents was Richard T. Greener, the first African-American gradu-ate (in 1870) of Harvard College, is the second building of that name on this site. In the first building Harvard Law School was founded. Originally of uni-

Charles Sumner Statue

form height, the topmost story of the central section (as well as the Mansard roof throughout) was added in 1870. Notice that College House, though begun in 1832, was given not even a small yard in front or beside it and instead has always fronted directly on the street with provision for ground-story shops, underlying the increasing urban character of mid-nineteenth-century Harvard Square. College House at its fullest extent stretched for 260 feet along the square's southern edge. One might almost suspect that Harvard had in mind another, grander yard! Certainly with the dormitory's completion in 1860 the sense of collegiate enclosure of Harvard Square could not have been more complete on one of the two commercial sides of the triangular square of which Harvard Yard itself constitutes the third side. Whether or not it was ever envisaged, that grand enclosure never happened. Harvard eventually sold College House, which is today mostly business offices. Yet the collegiate character of the building still lingers; caught, so to speak, between worlds. College House is not your average office building, but is full of secrets and surprises and ambiguities, real and imagined. It is real enough, for example, that The Architects Collaborative, perhaps the most famous post–World War II architectural firm in America, was started in College House after the war by Walter Gropius and a group of younger colleagues on the Harvard Design Faculty. Equally real: the venerable and prestigious Medieval Academy of America, known the world over, is quietly headquartered today on an upper floor of College House, established here, of course, because of College House's proximity to the university, a pioneer since Henry Adams' day in the field of medieval studies in America. Entirely unreal on the other hand—though serious enough in the literary sense—is the secret society of the 1900s imagined here by John Reed. A journalist celebrated in his day for his eyewitness account of the Russian Revolution (and for being the only American who ended up buried at the foot of the Kremlin Wall in Moscow), Reed laid his only short story at Harvard, of which he was a graduate. His description of what happened to him in a building that can only be College House catches an aspect of Harvard Square in the 1900s that is not only very urban but very dark. Significantly, Reed's images are as architectural as Edith Wharton's much better known ones in her much lighter world. "Brodsky shuffled ahead past the Coop," Reed wrote at one point in his story, "and thrust open a door in the strange looking building next to it; and we began to mount interminable stairs. At the very top landing...Brodsky knocked five times, and with a click the door swung silently in and we entered a pitch-dark room. Behind our backs the door shut mysteriously and with an ominous sound...." Well it might have from Reed's point of view. His ethnic stereotypes grate on us today and much that was doubtless terrifying then now seems only over-wrought—he is confronted with a row of men drinking "deeply of greenish liquor," for example, from among whom a "Negro rose from his seat with a terrible look on his face, and thrusting a glass of liquor toward me, bade 'Drink'." But Reed imagined in College House nothing less than the Society of the Red Hand, before which in his tale both Beacon Street and University Hall shudder. And with good reason, argues the author, who achieves in his story a vivid penetration of the ugly ethnic and class bigotry of Harvard in the 1900s. Reed's is a tale of revenge that culminates in the explosion of a bomb in the office of a Harvard dean!

Finally, it is not only literary secrets that lie hidden in College House. An architectural secret (for anyone under fifty-something) is the huge movie and vaudeville house, the University Theater of 1925, which still lurks within and behind College House, all evidence of which on the historic dormitory's Massachusetts Avenue facade near Church Street is now covered over. Of this, more soon. Meanwhile, given Harvard Law School's connection with College House, it is appropriate that perhaps the best view of the seated bronze figure of Statue of Charles Sumner, one of the Law School's most illustrious graduates, is where College House turns the corner onto Church Street. A great abolitionist leader in the United States Senate in the 1850s and '60s, where he championed the emancipation of the slaves and free speech generally, Sumner took the liberal positions one might expect of a Massachusetts senator—views, however, very much at odds with the attitude of the commission which years after the Civil War set out to honor Sumner with a public memorial in 1875. In fact, the commissioners disqualified sculptor Anne Whitney when they found out she was a woman (wisely she had submitted her model anonymously) and gave the commission instead to Thomas Ball, whose figure of Sumner of 1878 still stands in the Boston Public Garden in the Back Bay. Whitney persisted, however, supported financially by friends, and completed this figure, her last major work, when she was nearly eighty.

15. Harvard Square Theater and Cambridge School of Architecture for Women

Harvard Square Theater *Mowll & Rand, 1925*
Club Passim Building *1857*
Poet's Theater Site *destroyed 1958*
Palmer Street *Moriece & Gary, 1964*
Cambridge School *1828; Eleanor Raymond, addition, 1928*

Palmer Street cobblestones

Church Street itself may be the best example of how, historically, the essence of Harvard Square has always tended to flourish best at about a block's remove from the square's center, down side streets at various odd corners and off alleys and in quiet cul-de-sacs. On Church are four such sites of the square's twentieth-century cultural (and countercultural!) life. The first, the Harvard Square Theater, is all that is left of the old University Theater, here emerging in new guise on College House's Church Street front. Although the "Uni," as everyone called the old movie house, had its serious side—many a bedazzled Harvard College freshman at orientation first heard the likes of Howard Mumford Jones or John Finley explaining Harvard in the University Theater—the old theater is most renowned in Harvard lore for events in musical history. Here Leonard Bernstein once delivered the Charles Eliot Norton lectures. Here, too, Bruce Springsteen, in the early years of his career, gave a performance at the Harvard Square Theater in 1974 so memorable it became a seminal event in rock history. After it critic Jon Landau famously wrote in the *Real Paper*: "I saw rock 'n' roll's future and its name is Bruce Springsteen." A decade later the theater had been divided up into smaller units, not very sensitively inside (bits of the old proscenium architectural have been spied in odd corners of the new cinemas), but more so on the exterior, where a tromp l'oeil mural of 1983 by two Harvard architecture students, Joshua Winer and Campari Knoepffler, endowed the new Church Street entrance with considerable faux elegance. If the history of rock is the key aspect in any account of the Harvard Square Theater, the history of American folk music is the chief interest attaching to another recycled old building—originally a carriage house factory, built in 1857—a few doors further along the same side of Church Street. On the corner of Palmer Street, an alley recycled by landscape architects in 1964 in a most picturesque way (cobblestones, etc.), the cellar of the old carriage factory has long been perhaps the most famous venue for live music in Harvard Square, the Club Passim; critic Scott Alarik called it "the Carnegie Hall of folk" in 1999, ascribing to this club most of the reasons why Boston became the folk music capital of the country. Originally the Club 47, a jazz club located on nearby Mount Auburn Street, the Passim (as it has been called for over three decades now) moved to Palmer Street in 1963 and except for a brief hiatus in 1968–70 has thrived here ever since. A veritable institution today, its 25th reunion was celebrated in 1985 by a three-night concert series at Boston's Symphony Hall! Joan Baez first became a national figure on the club's little stage. Another famous alumnus is Tom Rush, who also had his own show on WHRB, Harvard's student radio station.

Alas, the other notable bohemian cultural landmark of this Harvard Square alley, the Poets' Theater, which until it burned down in the late 1950s stood across the Passim, is now only a site (in search of a plaque?) The Poets' Theater was founded in 1951 by Donald Hall, Robert Bly, Frank O'Hara, Edmund St. John Gorey, Frank O'Hara, and John Ashbery—Harvardians all. A "tiny bandbox playhouse...in an old painting loft...at the top of a steep flight of stairs," as poet Peter Davison recalled in *The Fading Smile*, the Poets' Theater—though its celebrated readings by Osbert and Edith Sitwell and Dylan Thomas (including the first reading anywhere of *Under Milk Wood* by its author) were naturally held in grander precincts such as Harvard's Fogg Art Museum and Sanders Theater—was itself the scene of many now historic happenings. Poets Ted Hughes and Sylvia Plath, for example, gave a memorable joint reading at the Poets' Theater's little 50-seat garret playhouse in 1958; the same year Robert Lowell presided over an equally well-remembered reading by W. D. Snodgrass with Anne Sexton in attendance. Both events evidenced what has been called Boston's second poetic flowering in the 1950s, and such was the Poets' Theater's distinction that Harvard University Press published a special series of works performed there.

Further up Church and across the street, the stately yellow clapboarded house at no. 53 is very definitely a survivor. Like so many things around Harvard Square that never seem to be quite what they look like, this charming Federal house today lives a totally different life than would ever have been envisioned by its builder in 1827—it is home to the Tutorial Offices of Harvard's Government Department. It is most notable, however, for having been in the 1930s and '40s the home of the Cambridge School of Architecture and Landscape Architecture for Women, the first architectural school in the United States exclusively for women. Established in 1915 (when only men were admitted to Harvard's architecture school) by two progressive Harvard faculty members, professor of architecture Henry Atherton Frost and assistant professor of landscape architecture Bremer Pond, the Cambridge School, which established itself here in 1928, became in the 1930s a part of Smith College (which few realize ever had a presence in Harvard Square). As

53 and 53a Church Street

Smith's graduate school of architecture it awarded the master's degree both in architecture and in landscape architecture for studies here. Eventually, of course, Harvard relented (in 1942, during the war) and admitted women to architectural education, and the future of the Cambridge School became problematic. But in its day its faculty included so eminent a figure as Fletcher Steele, the leading American landscape designer of his generation, while its graduates numbered among them many important early women architects, including Eleanor Raymond, the architect in 1931 in nearby Belmont of one of the first International Style houses erected in the United States. Raymond also designed in 1928 the brick drafting building beside 53 Church, the only building at Harvard designed solely by a woman.

16. Brattle-Fuller House, Pratt House, Brattle Hall, and Chestnut Tree Memorial

Brattle-Fuller House *1727; entrance porch, 1890*
Pratt House (Window Shop) *1808*
Brattle Hall *A. W. Longfellow, 1889–90*
Chestnut Tree Memorial *Dimitri Gerakaris, 1989*

Interesting how many of the themes picked up on Church Street—architecture, women's studies, music, theater, and poetry—coalesce where Church Street culminates in the short stretch of Brattle Street to either side of Architects'

Corner. Here are a half dozen or so contiguous buildings spanning almost 250 years, ranging from Georgian of the 1720s to International Style of the 1960s. A tale it is of sometimes dense historical layering, not just of first and second but often of third and fourth acts, all these buildings having had many lives.

The earliest, beginning in 1727, was the William Brattle–Margaret Fuller House. William Brattle, the Major General of the colonial militias of the Royal Province of Massachusetts Bay before he was forced back to England when Boston was evacuated by the Crown at the start of the Revolution, was an influential and powerful figure of the vice-regal court and the son of a notable treasurer of Harvard College. The Brattles not only gave to Brattle Street its name—and in its residential parts further on at the street's lower end there is hardly a grander street in the country (see Walk 9)—but to Harvard the late seventeenth-century tutor who along with President Leverett so conspicuously and successfully thwarted the clerical Mathers and nurtured what I have called the Liberal Tradition at Harvard. In more spacious days the Brattle House was a showplace of Tory Row. This clapboarded, gambrel-roofed structure—entirely original except for new six-over-six sash and an enclosed entrance porch of 1891—was the centerpiece of a much more elaborate architectural and landscape ensemble, including formal gardens and elegant terraces and patteres—even an ornamental pool complete with exotic fish as the season allowed, picturesque bridges, and a splashing fountain, splendors well maintained, let it be said, by the residents of the post-revolutionary period. One such was Thomas Mifflin, Washington's Commissary-General, who lived here for a while; indeed, on his way to Philadelphia to sign the Declaration of Independence John Adams, the future president, stayed over with Mifflin to dine here one evening.

However, it is this house's third act that is the most interesting, and it is a measure of the role women played in Harvard's orbit in the nineteenth century that at the end of a short street, which began with Anne Whitney's controversial statue of Sumner and focused midway its length on the Cambridge School for women architects, we finally encounter, as the old house's most famous resident and Boston's foundational feminist, Margaret Fuller. It was Fuller's labors that made so many efforts like Whitney's and the Cambridge School possible. Famously the editor of the Transcendentalist journal, *The Dial*, and the author as well of *Women in the Nineteenth Century*, a pioneering feminist treatise, Fuller holds a unique place in American intellectual history, and is widely regarded today along with Henry Thoreau as preeminent among Emerson's collaborators. Here her time was brief—a little over a year and a half. Nor was it, largely because of family problems, happy; in fact, Fuller called this house her "gilded cage." But while living here on Christmas Day in 1834 she slipped away from church services she had been dragged to, "running out beyond the town limits into the bleak New England fields" and, exhausted, had the

Brattle Hall and Brattle–Fuller House

first of several key mystical insights: "that there was no self; that selfishness was folly," that she must school herself "to act in cooperation with the constraints of life." It was also while living here, in the post-Kirkland era at Harvard when studying German was newly the craze in order to keep up with the latest thought, that Fuller learned that language, reading Goethe particularly and even translating his work into English. Here too she made her first attempts at fiction. And for all her complaints about this period, when it came time for her to move to the country, she is known to have begged for "a few extra days," in her biographer's words, "so she would not miss the two great events of the Boston social season [in 1833]: the appearance at the Tremont Theater . . . [of] Fanny Kemble, the world renowned actress, in her role as Shakespeare's Juliet, and the thrilling display at the Boston Athenaeum of its collection of plaster casts . . . (including an Apollo Belvedere) for the first time at night, thanks to the installation of a recent innovation, the gas light"—a case study, if you will, of life in the Athens of America during and after Kirkland's presidency.

It was during the decade when Fuller lived for a year and more on Brattle Street that Henry Wadsworth Longfellow wrote of the Village Blacksmith ("under the spreading chestnut tree"). Only a few doors up the street from the Brattle House at No. 54 Brattle still stands the blacksmith's domicile, the Dexter Pratt House, a marvelous little two-story, hipped-roof, clapboarded Federal house of 1808 that like the Brattle house is in its present day life a vital part of the Cambridge Adult Education Center. A sculpture set against the brick wall facing the house commemorates blacksmith and tree alike; a forged, metal tree shelters the anvil and blacksmith's tools used to such good effect by sculptor Dimitri Gerakaris. The Dexter Pratt House is still today something of a literary shrine for the admirers of Longfellow (whose star has waxed and waned so dramatically he seems bound for a revival soon). If its first act as the blacksmith's original lair certainly remains its most prominent, here as at the Brattle-Fuller House there was to be a second act, and one characteristic of Harvard Square: the gentle recycling in the 1930s of this 1808 house into a fashionable tea room by a group of Cambridge ladies seeking to aid refugees from Nazi oppression with employment that would both be supportive financially and acclimate the refugees to American ways; best done, many doubtless thought, in an old New England house. The outgrowth of a one-room consignment shop that opened in 1939 above the corner of Church and Brattle, a shop named for that reason the Window Shop, the tea room and bakery that finally evolved came to rest at the Dexter-Pratt House in 1947. It not only acclimated European refugees to American ways, but at a time when doughnuts and apple pie were about it for Americans, the refugees themselves introduced such exotic fare as linzer torte and brioche—so successfully that Eleanor Roosevelt (in her "My Day" newspaper column) dwelt as much on the unusual cuisine of the Window Shop in describing her visit as on the refugee aspect. Moreover, entirely plausibly, legend has it that another noted devotee of this tea room, and drawn to this block because of it, was Walter Gropius, the founder of the Bauhaus, who himself fled Nazi Germany in 1937. Of all this more in a moment.

Meanwhile, there is more to say here of Longfellow before we get too far ahead of ourselves, for it was the poet's nephew, Alexander Wadsworth Longfellow, who was the architect of the third of the eighteenth- and nineteenth-century buildings of this short stretch of Brattle Street, the barn-like Brattle Hall of 1889–90 that stands beside the Brattle-Fuller House. A most picturesque playhouse is the Brattle, though shorn of its elegant original porte-cochere in 1907 (when the more urban brick front facade was added), and even today it brings to Brattle Street a touch of Edwardian high style. Though it does repeat the gambrel roof profile of the house, Brattle Hall attempts a much greater elegance 160 years later; notice, for instance, the stylishly elongated windows and the way what became dormers pierce the cornice line and rise into the lower slope of the roof. Called as often the Brattle Theater as Brattle Hall, it was the locale of several of the productions of George Pierce Baker's 47 Workshop. In fact, T. S. Eliot appeared once on the Brattle Stage playing the role of Lord Bantock in the season of 1912–13. (The very next year Emmeline Pankhurst, the leading British suffragist and a major force in the women's movement, spoke in 1914, after Harvard University refused her the use of a college hall.) The Brattle's subsequent history, furthermore, has been hardly less storied. Here the celebrated African-American actor and singer, Paul Robeson, played Othello in the American premiere of director Margaret Webster's production in 1942. And in the 1940s and '50s a resident repertory company, the Brattle Theater Group, performed numerous American and Boston premieres of works by Strindberg and Chekov, often headlined by visiting stars like Eva LeGallienne, Cyril Ritchard, Jessica Tandy, and Hermione Gingold, who made her U. S. debut at the Brattle in 1951. In the '60s, moreover, while Harvard president Nathan Pusey was battling Senator McCarthy's Permanent Committee on Investigations (then, un-American activities), the Brattle repertory company became a haven for blacklisted Hollywood stars such as Zero Mostel, Anne Revere, and Sam Jaffre.

As was the case with the Window Shop, Walter Gropius was also a great admirer of the Brattle company and in 1949 proposed a great three-level theater, office, and retail complex that only fell through at the last moment. Instead, after the end of live theater at the Brattle in the early 1950s, Bryan Haliday, a Harvard graduate student who had been impressed while studying in Paris with the interest of the French in film history, turned the Brattle into a pioneering American art film theater. He founded with Cyrus Harvey a company called Janus Films, which became the U.S. outlet for the most significant films of the era by Federico Fellini, Ingmar Bergman, and François Truffaut, all together perhaps the greatest work in film history. In addition to such cutting edge contemporary work, the Brattle also presented such classics, hardly ever screened then in America, as the films of Sergei Eisenstein. And in 1955 Haliday and Harvey challenged the blue laws over *Miss Julie*, a film adaptation of August Strindberg's sexually charged play, winning their appeal to the Massachusetts Supreme Judicial Court and thereby ending decades of film censorship in the state. At the Brattle too in the 1950s the ever sardonic but highly honorable character of Rick, played by Humphrey Bogart in the now classic 1942 film *Casablanca* (in which he co-starred with Ingrid Bergman), caught on with the Harvard students of that era to such an extent that it can fairly be said the "Bogie" cult began at the Brattle. Indeed, so pervasive and intense did that cult become at Harvard that it was not long before you could speak of "Bogie decor," even "Bogie architecture." Certainly you could have a drink in the concourse underneath Brattle Hall at the Club Casablanca, opened in 1955, or a cappuccino at the Blue Parrot. Still, today, the Casablanca's original "Bogie" murals, by the illustrator-cartoonist, David Omar White (who has taught for years at Boston's Museum of Fine Arts School) decorate the reconfigured Casablanca. A storied history indeed. As John Engstrom has written, the Brattle has been "a springboard for several major talents in the American theater, the setting for one of America's first regional theaters . . . an early home for art films, a shrine to a neglected movie star, and a battle-ground for the First Amendment." In short, very Harvard. No wonder the father of the Bauhaus was drawn here.

17. Architects' Corner

Gropius/TAC Building *Walter Gropius/TAC, 1966*
Design Research (now Crate & Barrel) *Benjamin Thompson & Assoc., 1969*
Sert Building (44 Brattle Street) *Sert, Jackson & Assoc., 1970*
Flansburgh Building (14 Story Street) *Earl R. Flansburgh and Assoc., 1970*

Though he was frustrated in his larger plans, Gropius was able in the 1960s, in company with the great Spanish master and friend of Le Corbusier, José Luis Sert, to enliven this historic eighteenth- and nineteenth-century Harvard Square townscape with the nucleus of a group of twentieth-century structures that surround a central inner courtyard opening off Brattle Street just opposite Church Street. To the left of the courtyard is the Sert Building of 1970–71, where Sert's own offices were located. To the court's right, its entrance well back in the court, is the Gropius Building, officially The Architects' Collaborative Building, where Gropius too had his own office. Beside it is the Flansburgh Building. Also opening off the court (still) is the Harvest restaurant.

The streetfront building on the corner of Story Street is the Design Research Building, the centerpiece of Architects' Corner, by TAC graduate Benjamin Thompson. A prismatic glass International Style fantasia, plain-spoken in the Boston-style modern manner, but stunningly seductive, especially at night, "DR," as it has always been called, marks "Architects' Corner" (at Brattle and Story Streets). This corner is so named not just because two eminent architects, one of whom introduced modernism to America, were

Sert Building, Design Research building, and Gropius/TAC Building

headquartered in this complex, but also because not a few of their disciples clustered about in the 1950s and '60s—Cambridge Seven, itself a firm of international distinction, Carl Koch, Earl Flansburgh, and others. Indeed, so pervasive was this aesthete Bauhaus group it yielded a residential companion complex to Architects' Corner, Six Moon Hill, in nearby Belmont (that "Harvard occupied suburb," in Peter Davison's apt phrase), another complex also dominated by Harvard faculty of the modernist persuasion. "DR" itself, of course, started what has been called "a national love affair" with modernism in the 1960s; so much so that in 1998 *New York Times* architecture critic Herbert Muschamp (writing nearly thirty years after he'd been a clerk in the New York branch of Design Research) could write of that branch as,

> Long famous as the only retail establishment in New York where you could buy the objects on view in the design collection of the Museum of Modern Art. Founded by Benjamin Thompson...who would later pioneer the concept of the festival marketplace in Boston, San Francisco and New York, the store stocked the classics of modern furniture by Thonet, Aalto, Mies van der Rohe, Breuer, Magistretti Hoffman and [Charles] Eames. It also introduced innovative work by young Italian designers like Joe Colombo....The store's esthetic embodied principles that began with Arts and Crafts and continued with the Bauhaus...functionality, truth to materials, simplicity of geometric form, the use of new material and methods.

Even today this legacy still dominates here in DR's mass-market successor, Crate and Barrel.

18. Upper Brattle Street

"Gateway to Knowledge" *Anne Norton, sculptor, 1979*
Origins and Tess Shopfronts *Peter Forbes, 1990s*
Abbot Building *Newhall & Blevins, 1909*
The Reed Block *1790–1820; W. R. and J. R. Richards, facade, 1896;*
   Symmes, Maini and McKee, entrance, 1999

Completing the loop around the College House Block to Architects' Corner and then back to Harvard Square proper illustrates only too well, alas, how exceptional is the short streetscape of Brattle Street just at the end of Church Street. The deadly monotony of American postmodernist design, especially in its "historically sensitive" and "contextual" mode could not be more apparent than in Brattle Square, the architecture of which is just one "safe," dispiriting, and banal brick monster after another, each arching around the intersection called Brattle Square so indifferently that even Anne Norton's "Gateway to Knowledge" at the intersection's center, in itself a fine work, seems finally just more brick, and all of it just too much to be borne. The only relief to the tired eye are two storefronts just about opposite each other at Palmer Street—"Origins" and "Tess"—by the award-winning Yale-trained Boston architect, Peter Forbes, where elegant minimalist modern glass fronts (set back in Origins' case from the marble pier of an older building) will likely if they survive 100 years be as prized then as some of Harvard Square's surviving nineteenth-century shopfronts are today (see Walk 4). Origins, in fact, is a prototype for the Harvard Square historic district projected by the Cambridge Historical Commission, a district in which meticulous restoration of historic architecture and imaginative modern design of high quality will, one hopes, go hand in hand.

The next and last corner of this Walk, the southeastern corner of Brattle and JFK Street in Harvard Square proper, is of more literary than architectural interest. At least at first glance. Overlooking this corner in the 1630s was the house of Simon Bradstreet, later Governor of the Massachusetts Bay Colony, whose wife, Anne Bradstreet, is often accounted the first "American" poet. Some of her work was printed at Harvard College's press. Thinking of her I recall the brilliant pairing of Bradstreet with the twentieth-century poet Anne Sexton by Paul Wright and Barbara Meil Hobson in their *Boston: A State of Mind* of 1977, where they contrasted Bradstreet's confrontation with the loneliness of the physical wilderness of seventeenth-century Harvard Square with Sexton's struggle (of which in the twentieth-century Harvard Square was part of the setting) with a wilderness that was hardly less real for being only "part of her psychic landscape." Whether or not Freud was right to declare that "there is no time in the unconscious," it may well be true of the *conscious* realm when it is experienced through layer upon layer of history in places like Harvard Yard and Harvard Square. Bradstreet's and Sexton's wilderness, finally, could be said to be very similar, and the pairing of the two poets together by scholars of a later period is fructifying not least because it does all but abolish time. All sorts of free-associating then becomes possible. Sexton was involved in the Poets' Theater, a part of that group Peter Davison has described as "mostly attend[ing] Harvard in its brilliant postwar [World War II] era...alerted to the theatrical tradition by excellent Brattle Theater Repertory productions." Which reminds me—riff on riff—that John Harvard's father, Robert, worshipped at the same parish church as William Shakespeare; that John's mother, Katherine, was a native of Stratford-on-Avon; that it has even been suggested Shakespeare introduced Harvard's parents; Conrad Edick Wright prudently calls this "an intriguing story, but the evidence is entirely circumstantial"—true about so much of what little we know of young John Harvard. Actually, Anne Bradstreet moved in the same close-knit circle of

Reed Block and Reed House

prominent settlers as did Harvard for his short time in the New World. She might well have known him. Sexton, of course, could not have. And neither poet could have known Shakespeare—except in another way, the way Paul Robeson at the Brattle did, through his work.

But to return to more solid ground, these riffs, these improvisations on history, all likely, each quite stimulating, like this walk around the block via just two of Harvard Square's side streets, certainly documents how intimate, how introverted, for nearly four hundred years now, has been the creative ferment of yard and square. And, you might say, how swiftly passed away; the Poets' Theater of Sexton's world as much as the more ancient landscape of Bradstreet's. Except that nothing in Harvard Square is ever quite what it appears to be, and this is certainly true at the corner of JFK and Brattle Streets. The rounded brick and stone flatiron building designed by Newhall and Blevins in 1909 is more than it seems. Here alone in Harvard Square proper, according to Cambridge Historical Commission records, the original street pattern of the first seventeenth-century settlement survives. Anne Bradstreet, in the loneliness of her years living across the street in the 1630s, must have known the footprint of the Abbot Building very well.

The corner opposite on Bradstreet's own side of the street, apparently just present-day stores, is worth notice as adding more than a little to this rumination on historical architecture and historical time. The Reed Block, two adjacent and quite commonplace commercial structures of the 1790s, wrapped in a continuous, curving wooden facade in the 1890s, engages at one end a brick house of the 1820s, Reed's own—all of them restored and imaginatively added to in the 1990s. And it may truthfully be said that the effect is far finer today than could ever really have been the case at any time in the last 200 years! The case of the Reed House interests particularly. If buildings have been known over the years in Harvard Square (as where not?) to disappear, here is one that has virtually reappeared, very much out of the mists of time. Certainly no one had ever really seen this house when, its facade restored, this all but unsuspected handsome brick Federal domicile emerged in 1999 to startle and delight Harvard Square. Best of all the restoration was a sophisticated one, and included a strikingly modern exposed steel entrance pavilion that sets off the old house with twenty-first-century elegance.

19. Nos. 90-95 Mount Auburn Street

Hans Hollein, design architect, Bruner/Cott, executive architects, 2000

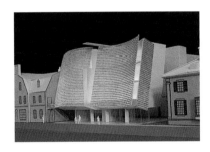

Nos. 90–95 Mount Auburn Street

At the end of the block begun by the Reed Buildings, at the corner of JFK Street and Mount Auburn, the visitor looking left across the street and down Mount Auburn will see—in between the two handsome Georgian Revival buildings at each end of the block (buildings to be touched on in the next Walk)—an old tenement and what amounts to a metal shack, eyesores which typically survive in even the most prosperous quarters because proper development is for some reason (a too small lot, for instance) difficult. Here it is that Harvard University, with an eye to introducing a much higher standard of modern design and urban amenity in an increasing scintillating Harvard Square (which is becoming, like Boston's Newbury Street, a showcase of fashion and retail style on the new "global" rialto) has proposed to build a truly wonderful new commercial structure. A building for the twenty-first century, as it were, it is high-style architecture indeed in comparison to other (mostly appalling) new building and so called "restoration" in the square—much of it safe, bland, and dated in concept and form and embarrassing to find in a place like Harvard Square. Seeing this proposed design at Nos. 90–95 Mount Auburn Street, one is reminded at once of the striking work for its time (and still today) only a block or two away, just discussed, of Gropius and Sert in the 1960s on Brattle at the end of Church Street, where they fused so well twentieth- and eighteenth-century work. Also comparable would be the building of the block-long brick

College House in 1845–59, which with its monumental urban scale and first floor shops introduced into the rustic wooden two-story square of those days a new style of urban design. Similarly, in 2001 Harvard's No. 90 Mount Auburn design is a great step forward for Harvard Square. The work of by any measure the most important architect to work in Harvard Square since the Coolidge and Perry offices in the 1920s, the Pritzker Prize-winning Hans Hollein has been characterized by John Smith as "typically Viennese in his extreme and often ironic sophistication, as shown in the small deluxe commercial buildings which made his name." Vienna, so similar to Boston in its demand for new design that meshes with fine old design without descending to imitation or mimicry, boasts many successful works by Hollein, who although he has done important large-scale architecture (such as his Museum of Modern Art in 1991 in Frankfurt), is celebrated for such small-scale work as the Schullin jewelry shop and the Austrian State Tourist Agency in Austria's capital. And it is that small scale work which doubtless suggested how right Hollein would be for Harvard Square, its streetscapes too often dull, commonplace, or even tawdry.

The "night model" reproduced here of Hollein's design shows how marvelously his structure would set off the two fine neo-Georgian structures on either side, in between which the Hollein building is set back in part so as to encourage access to the long overlooked ornamental backs of those structures, creating delightfully narrow, enclosed spaces—spaces, just as around the Brattle Theater, that are essentially urban. Beautifully recessed between the older structures, the four floors of the Hollein building murmur softly, so to speak, behind the glass facade and elegant metal screen. Indeed, the proposed new work is a brilliant foil to its older neighbors—a glowing, scintillating jewel set between them—its form surely inspired by that most historic seal to be found in Harvard's oldest seventeenth-century records: the open book. Hollein's design is exact, startling and lovely—and, finally, very serene, even thoughtful. An example of what John Vernon feels some writing accomplishes, this design, sensuous first, intellectual second, is on one level exciting and scintillating. Then comes (in architecture much the same way Vernon tracks it in writing) "the reflective inner drag and furrowing of thought." The book as lantern, glowing on Mount Auburn Street. Beautiful.

That Hollein's design is controversial is obvious, prompting critic Robert Campbell to point out that one important function of architecture is to be "playful because it's always seeking to surprise and delight us, and to make our world feel fresh and new," adding that "we should be wary of bad buildings, but never afraid of the new. A university, or a city, must maintain continuity with the past. But it also must look with optimism and daring—even with a sense of risk—toward the future. Maybe Nos. 90–95 Mount Auburn will shake up a Boston culture that's been getting a little tired in its architecture." Maybe.

Winthrop Square Park and the Gold Coast

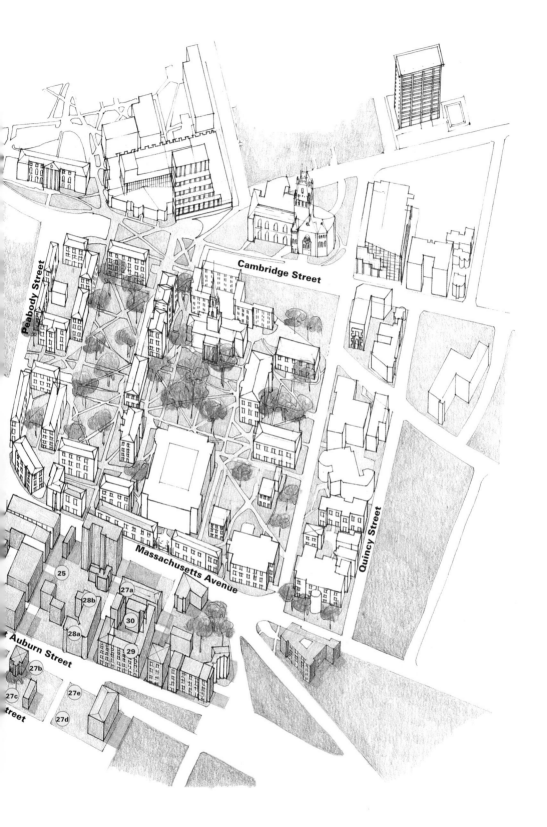

Peabody Street

Cambridge Street

Quincy Street

Massachusetts Avenue

Auburn Street

treet

25

28b

27a

30

28a

29

27b

27c

27e

27d

Harvard Yard and Harvard Square

20. Winthrop Square Park and "Quiet Stone"

Winthrop Square Park   *set aside 1631*

"Quiet Stone"   *Carlos Dorrien, sculptor, 1986*

Harvard Square has evolved through the centuries into five or six distinct quarters: Harvard Square proper and five smaller, satellite squares about a block away on all sides. To the west Brattle Square, just traversed, and Eliot Square adjoin each other; to the east Quincy Square and St. Paul's Square also adjoin; and to the south, a block down John F. Kennedy Street from the Reed Block, Winthrop Square centers on a rectangular park, the site of the original village marketplace of Old Cambridge in the mid-seventeenth century, and a particularly good place to consider the always shifting faces of history presented hereabouts. Of course these images are never entirely true. But they are never completely false either. "Quiet Stone," a marble sculpture in the park's center by the well-known Boston sculptor, Carlos Dorrien, is something else again. Marty Carlock has written of how Dorrien, a Wellesley College art professor, "likes to make 'imaginary remnants' in stone, objects that look as if they have a history. His sculpture here summarizes contemporary thinking about public art: thoroughly melded into its site, full of arcane references to the place, witty, a little puzzling, inviting interaction." Viewed from the park the work seems an authentic ruin, the lintel of the long-since destroyed market fallen to earth. Yet its opposite side looks like unworked stone, except that the sculptor has carved out steps for passersby to sit on. The stone lintel is, by the way, entirely imagined. There was a market, but not with cut stone detail like this.

"Quiet Stone"

21. University Lutheran Church *Arland Dirlam, 1950*

University Lutheran Church

Along the south side of Winthrop Square runs a street of the same name; eastward one block on the corner of Winthrop Street and Dunster stands this church, really the only example at Harvard of the Scandinavian Modern style, a style that in the Boston region flowered in the 1950s more at MIT, home to several major works by Alvar Aalto and Eero Saarinen. University Lutheran reflects the way that denomination made modernism its own in the immediate post–World War II period. Reminiscent of Saarinen's famous Christ Church, Minneapolis, also built in 1950, University Lutheran, with its beautifully detailed broad brick planes and nice proportions and massing, won the J. Harleston Parker Gold Medal in 1952 from the Boston Society of Architects for the region's most beautiful building of that year. Notice how the new handicapped-access ramp has been made an opportunity to enhance rather than harm this architecture.

22. Winthrop Street Houses and Drayton Hall

Freshman's Dean's House (53 Dunster Street)
  William Saunders and Stephen S. Bunker, housewrights, 1841
Pi Eta Clubhouse/Grendel's Den Restaurant *Putnam & Cox, 1908*
The House of Blues (106 Winthrop Street) *ca. 1799*
No. 98 Winthrop Street *ca. 1790*
Drayton Hall *George S. R. McLean, 1901*

Still eastward on Winthrop Street, on the other corner of Dunster is the freshmen dean's residence. Unusual for a Greek Revival house in its three-and-one-half-story stature, No. 53 Dunster Street has had a long and varied Harvard history; in years past it was the clubhouse of the Kappa Sigma Fraternity. Walking westward on Winthrop the old Pi Eta Clubhouse, perhaps the grandest relic of Harvard's once thriving nineteenth-century fraternity system, dominates. The Pi Eta lasted the longest of the major frats. But for whatever reason, perhaps because it was too democratic—interestingly,

Winthrop Street

only highly selective clubs have prospered at Harvard—the Pi Eta ultimately went under. Its handsome clubhouse was imaginatively recycled into a restaurant called Grendel's Den. Named doubtless by some ironically minded graduate of English I for the monster den Grendel and his mother shared in *Beowulf*, Grendel's is the only place in Harvard Square to offer its denizens a wood-burning fire, in an old oak paneled fireplace—in what was once a private Harvard 1900s student setting. Grendel's has become, over the last thirty years, something like Harvard's "front room" for the 100,000-or-so Boston-area college students who might not otherwise find themselves by an old Harvard fireplace. If *The New York Times* is correct that all these students, who "give Boston its youthful intellectual flavor...[and] make [it]...the college capital of the country," Harvard Square, inevitably the capital's collegiate heart, has found its own center in Grendel's.

Livelier still is the House of Blues across the street. This is the (carefully planned to be) original House of Blues, picturesquely conceived in a 200-year-old clapboarded house, a strange and perhaps even somewhat irreverent use of an historic structure. So too alley-like Winthrop Street is at odds with the increasingly slick, up-scale commercial character of Harvard Square. Actually, even more than the Brattle Hall/Casablanca complex (see Walk Two), this slightly seedy-seeming scene on Winthrop Street (and a carefully cultivated seediness it is, of course) is the closest thing now left in the area to a cherished local tradition—the Harvard Square dive—which is like no other dive for reasons both historical and architectural. The tradition reaches back hundreds of years to the taverns of the seventeenth century.

Cambridge's most celebrated public house then, the Blue Anchor Tavern, which opened in 1652, stood on the northwest corner of today's Winthrop Square (where Crimson Travel now is), and through the centuries many more watering holes of a similar nature grew up, ranging from the raffish late eighteenth-century Moore's Tavern on the Yard's northern fringe to the much lamented Cronin's of the 1950s on the Yard's southern edge. It is a tradition, the Harvard Square dive, one that compasses such well remembered locales as the Square's Depression-era cafeterias (decor by Edward Hopper)—the all-night Waldorf, Albiani's, and Hayes Bickford's of the 1940s, so full of minor beat poets by the 1960s. (All seemed "staffed" by the English Department! Poet Peter Davison could write, for instance, of "Frank O'Hara who sat around Harvard Square saloons from January to June chatting emphatically about movies.")

In the late nineteenth century, among similar hangouts, the most popular near here, found in all Victorian Harvard novels—was the Holly Tree Inn, which author Owen Wister (he of *The Virginian*), caused his two heroes, Bertie and Billy, to frequent faithfully and fruitfully. Nor was the Holly Tree by any means beneath even the Boylston Professor of Rhetoric and Oratory of the time (Mr. Fleetwood in Flandrau's *Diary of a Freshman*), for whom there was much deference indeed when he made "his entrance at a Harvard Square restaurant known as the Holly Tree." In real life the professor's name was Copeland—about whom see Walk Five—but the Holly Tree of the 1870s must have been quite similar in feeling to the House of Blues today. Lois Lilley Howe recalled in an article in the Cambridge Historical Society *Journal*: "The Holly Tree Inn on the east side of Brattle Street . . . [about where Tealuxe now is] was a picturesque story and a half house with the porch all across the front and yard all around it. . . . I have also been told that the best beer could be procured at the Holly Tree Inn." What an inviting image. With its gabled profile and front porch, the Holly Tree was, of course, an example of perhaps the first wave, historically, of adaptive reuse of old architecture—its original function (in this case residential) lost, but the image of which (genuine enough; hospitality) happily recycled for other uses. Similarly, with another of the Square's nineteenth-century dives, Allnutts, located in the top floor gable of one of the eighteenth-century wooden structures later enfolded into the Reed block. Daniel Gregory Mason, later a distinguished musician, recalled its character with much enthusiasm from his student days: "A dingy restaurant, Allnutts' by name, [existed] up a dark flight of wooden stairs, near the corner of Harvard Square. . . . Its nondescript clientele . . . was as depressing as its habitat; but its liver and bacon, to youth and in spring, could almost be exciting." Yet the House of Blues is more than a dive. It has become an institution for blues devotees something like what the Club Passim has long been for folk music types, and on any weekend night this circa 1799 house is a lively center of Harvard Square's nightlife.

Inspected by day the House of Blues (at 106 Winthrop) and the house next door to it (at 98 Winthrop) also constitute the only place in Harvard Square today where the seventeenth, eighteenth, and early nineteenth centuries come together, and in a streetscape I cherish, for it could not be more picturesque. No. 98 Winthrop is especially worth study. The house itself dates from about 1790, and the eight-foot high stone retaining wall that terraces the grade (once much steeper) is older still—and may be seventeenth century. To look up from that wall past the House of Blues toward the lofty bell tower of Harvard's Lowell House in the distance is to have one of the finest urban prospects in Cambridge. In a house very like one of these two (perhaps even in one of them) but certainly in a house also overlooking Winthrop Park lived Henry James as a student at Harvard in 1862–63. He described the house only as one where "everything in it [was] slanting and gaping and creaky," but he reveled in his youthful independence, writing here his first published work of criticism, a review of a play he saw, which appeared in Boston's *Traveler*. And it only adds to the dense historical layer here to also notice Drayton Hall (to the left of this perspective on the corner of Winthrop Street and J. F. Kennedy Street), a nineteenth-century red-brick apartment house complete with Harvard's seal cut into the entrance detail, an apartment house that through the years has slid rather into the genteel shabbiness of many streets such as this which in the pre-air-conditioned era of the 1920s became too noisy with traffic for any who could afford better. There is rather a Bohemian quality about Drayton Hall—recalling figures of its era like T. S. Eliot and John Reed in their student days, or even—in later times—Malcolm X, who in the 1950s led a burglary gang from another seedy red-brick Harvard Square apartment house quite like this (the old Ambassador on Cambridge Street, slated for demolition). Years later, after conviction, jail, self-education, and conversion to Islam, Malcolm (having risen from a life of crime to become perhaps the most dynamic and brilliant leader of black America of the period) found himself invited to speak in 1962 at Harvard: "I happened to glance through a window," he recalled. "Abruptly, I realized that I was looking in the direction of the apartment house that was my old burglary gang's hideout.... And there I stood, the invited speaker at Harvard."

In another house down an alley from Winthrop Park at 56 JFK Street—real not contrived—is Iruña, the restaurant to which in the 1960s Robert Lowell, perhaps America's leading poet then, used regularly to repair after his Harvard class. Asked recently in an interview in *Boston Magazine* if Lowell still haunted Iruña in the 2000s, Harvard president Neil Rudenstine replied, "definitely."

23. Fox Clubhouse *Guy Lowell, 1905*

Something there is about a cafe—or a tavern or a coffee house—that seems to beget a club. And if the House of Blues is a good example of the former, the Fox Clubhouse on the other side of Winthrop Square is an equally good example of the latter. Indeed, within a five-minute walk or a stone's throw of the House of Blues—or of the site of the old Holly Tree Inn—are over a dozen Harvard undergraduate clubhouses, all but three still used for their original purposes, and several of which are as well the work of architects of national repute.

The first clubs of interest at Harvard emerged in the era of President Leverett, in whose reign the editors of the "Telltale" of 1721, for example, rather a breezy periodical evidently, created the Spy Club, notable for debating such (still) timely subjects as "whether it be Fornication to lye with one's Sweetheart (after Contraction) before marriage." Also founded in the eighteenth century, in 1781, was Harvard's chapter, "Alpha of Massachusetts," of the famously academic Phi Beta Kappa (PBK). Similarly with Harvard's still extant Porcellian Club, which arose out of a legendary dinner of roast pig (hence the club's name) in 1794 at Moore's Tavern. Unlike PBK, the Porcellian's motto, *Dum Vivimus Vivamus*, indicates that they were not beguiled by concerns academical or even literary, but, rather by pure conviviality. It was a view some have always found wanting (William Ellery Channing, for example, thought the Porcellian "too frankly Epicurean"), but which many others have found among life's sweetest benefactions. And although Harvard's oldest club (indeed, the oldest club in

Fox Clubhouse

continuous existence under the same name in America according to an old university handbook) early earned the repute, in Morison's words, of including only "the most lively and convivial lads in the College—'The Bloods of Harvard'," it was not just in the Porcellian that good times have abounded over the years. Human nature being what it is, for good or ill, while the Harvard Poetry Club, and the Harvard Socialist Club and the Pierian Society and a host of other worthy groups have been left to do good deeds in basements and garret rooms beyond number (or finding) over the years, it is the ethos of the purely social clubs that has achieved the most picturesque architectural expression—mostly along Harvard's fabled "Gold Coast," as it has been called for over a century now, the main thoroughfare of which, Mount Auburn Street, opens off Winthrop Square. Thus, the handsome palazzo of the Fox Clubhouse.

Inspired by the great mansions of Tory Row, the Fox, unusual among Harvard's clubhouses in being of wood-frame construction (intelligently covered in aluminum, by the way, preserving all the architectural embellishment, although the central loggia has been glassed in), is the work of a Boston architect and Harvard graduate of wide repute in the early 1900s, Guy Lowell, the designer of Boston's Museum of Fine Arts and the New York County Courthouse in New York City. It is a sophisticated design, one that somehow combines qualities both patrician and Bohemian, appropriate for a club founded in 1898 in Boston's leading Italian cafe of the time, Marliaves. (Boston being Boston the restaurant is actually still there, just off Province Street, in the shadow of the Parker House, and though no longer very Bohemian, boasts still the original decor of the era when the founding foxes foregathered.) This was T. S. Eliot's club as a student—the first of many evidences of how closely intertwined, historically, have been the serious and the convivial side of things at Harvard. In fact, just on the next corner of Mount Auburn Street stood not only the early-seventeenth-century First Church but, next to it, Cambridge's very first tavern, opened in 1636, the proprietor of which, Thomas Chesholme, was not just Cambridge's first tavern keeper, but also the Church's Deacon. Significantly Chesholme was also the first Steward of Harvard College. Holy ground, so to speak: Harvard's first commencement took place here. Mostly, probably, in the meeting house. But I doubt the tavern was entirely overlooked.

24. J. Press (old D.U.) Building, Signet Society, and Society of Fellows

Old D. U. clubhouse / J. Press (45 Dunster Street)

> *Perry, Shaw & Hepburn, 1930*

Signet Society (46 Dunster Street)

> *Daniel Dascomb, housewright, 1820; Cram, Goodhue and Ferguson*
> *with Pierre LaRose, 1902*

Society of Fellows (78 Mount Auburn Street) *1839*

Now here's a cautionary tale. The club that in the early twentieth century commissioned perhaps the most refined of all the Mount Auburn Street clubhouses, begat at the end of that century a lifestyle so problematic its graduate members dissolved the club, merging it into another. So much for the moral effect of good architecture! Equally interesting, there is a sort of upstairs/downstairs aspect to the tale. For the tradition that has endured here, on the ground floor, is what many club members in 1930 doubtless regretted as a lamentable compromise (the introduction into the clubhouse's design of "trade")—J. Press, the men's clothier whose merchandise epitomizes the Ivy League look and has been here since the clubhouse's beginning. Not so old as La Flamme Barber Shop just up Dunster Street the other way at No. 21 (complete with rich oak woodwork, a mysterious 1890s wall frieze, and a glorious nickel-plated 100-and-more-year-old working cash register), J. Press has nonetheless serviced preppies at this corner for three quarters of a century, its only rival Charlie Davison's slightly hipper but still

Signet Society Clubhouse

discreet Andover Shop diagonally across Mount Auburn Street on Holyoke Street, itself an institution now, at its present location for nearly half a century. Around the corner on Mount Auburn itself, is the only other Gold Coast shop in the same league, the Tennis and Squash Shop, started here in the late 1920s. But J. Press, no doubt about it, has the best window displays—displays no less elegant than the shop windows themselves, so seamlessly are they keyed to the overall aesthete, stripy college scarves, "rep ties," and all. And if it seems a bit of Williamsburg in Cambridge, that's only to be expected. Superbly proportioned, soberly but elegantly detailed, clubhouse and shop front alike are the work of Perry, Shaw and Hepburn, the whole thing very much first cousin to many similar houses and shopfronts along their Duke of Gloucester Street in Virginia's old royal capital.

Curiously, this design by Boston's—indeed, America's—preeminent Georgian Revival architects of the early twentieth century faces the Signet Society Clubhouse, whose present appearance is the work of the other leading Boston firm of this sort, Cram, Goodhue and Ferguson, the country's preeminent Gothic Revival designers of the same period, master architects of Princeton, West Point, and such outstanding churches as New York's Cathedral of St. John the Divine and St. Thomas, Fifth Avenue. Curiouser still, given this firm's repute, Cram and Goodhue's work here is not Gothic at all. Why they of all people were asked to remodel an 1820 Federal style house is a mystery I may have answered in the Harvard College part of my *Boston Bohemia*. Sufficient in this context to note that Cram and Goodhue's work here, done in collaboration with heraldic artist Pierre LaRose, is in feeling wildly Baroque (of all things)—a welcome touch of flamboyance for what would otherwise have been rather a staid clubhouse for the Signet, since 1870 Harvard's leading artistic and literary social club. Interestingly, the graphic quality of the detail of Cram and Goodhue's and LaRose's new frontispiece is actually rather reminiscent of book design (not to mention the Palladianism of several Tory Row mansions), and centers on a two-story pedimented Ionic pavilion displaying the Signet arms: a signet ring circled by bees, surmounted by a forearm and hand holding a book inscribed Veritas. The Greek motto underneath is a quotation from Plato's *Phaedo*, and may be translated as "work and ply the Muses." The design concept—cavalier enough, but very successful—discloses another guise of history making in Harvard architecture: to "restore" the house, not as it originally was, but in LaRose's words, as it "ought to have been." Thus the architectural solecism of the two orders of the porch—the Doric columns and Ionic pilasters—was retained.

Very different from the Signet is No. 78 Mount Auburn Street, the building next door. An ordinary Greek Revival house of the sort that once abounded in this neighborhood a century and a half ago, it was previously the clubhouse of the long defunct Kex Club. Harvard's Society of Fellows is now based here. But the real story here is that although this is by far the most modest of all the houses of Mount Auburn Street, in 1961–63 (taking advantage of their proximity to the Holyoke Center across the street) the society, itself very prestigious, proposed on a street of many grand club dining rooms and banquet halls surely the grandest of them all—a Fellows Dining Room in a Holyoke Center penthouse to be adorned by a group of murals by no less than Mark Rothko. It was an historic commission for Harvard, and one that Rothko accepted with enthusiasm. Rothko's Harvard murals were the third in a series in which he tried to evoke the idea of meditative enclosure as architectural setting, an idea he had begun to explore in his 1958 project for Mies van der Rohe's Seagram Building, where his murals were planned to decorate Philip Johnson's Four Seasons restaurants." Like John Singer Sargent, whose Widener Library murals at Harvard were a part of a series of three last mural projects, Rothko's Harvard murals were also done in the last decade of the artist's life. And, like the Seagram Building murals, ill luck dogged them. A brilliant, glowing frieze around the fellows dining room, these paintings began where Rothko's first Seagram Building project left off. Alas, the artist's installation proved faulty and the murals, much deteriorated by too strong light, are now in storage, their future uncertain.

25. Hasty Pudding Clubhouse and Apley Court

Hasty Pudding Clubhouse *Peabody & Stearns, 1887*
Apley Court *John E. Howe, 1897*

Two landmarks, side by side, announce the two themes of the Gold Coast: the clubhouse and the private dormitory. First, the clubhouse—of the most famous of Harvard's clubs—the Hasty Pudding. Founded in 1795 and (by virtue of its amalgamation in the twentieth century with the Institute of 1770) claiming to be the oldest collegiate society of any kind in the United States, the Pudding began in Harvard Yard, where according to Morison, had you been an observer in the 1790s:

> ...on "Pudding" nights, when the bell tolled for the scanty evening commons, two members might be seen bearing on a pole an iron pot of steaming hasty-pudding from some near-by goodwife's kitchen to a member's room, where the brethren supped on that simple but filling fare, concluding their repast with "sacred music" which became less and less sacred as the years rolled by.... After 1800, when debates 'on questions of literature, morality and politics' were organized to follow supper, it became the largest of the college societies. Debates were followed by mock trials, one of the

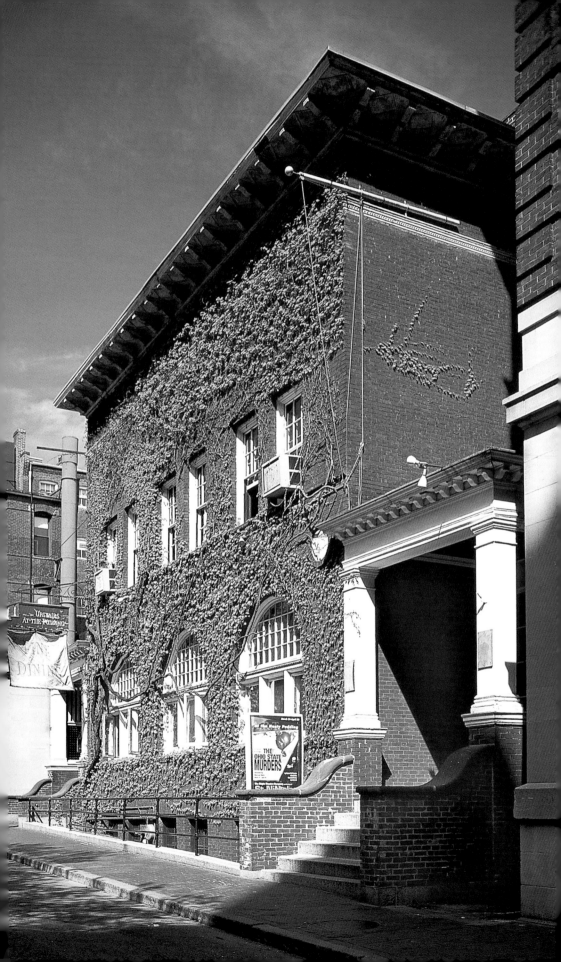

perennial cases being Dido vs. Aeneas for breach of promise. Every generation or so the 'Pudding' invented some new initiation or tomfoolery; it sought out the wits of each class.

The Pudding's most famous invention, its annual theatrical venture, began in 1844; *Bumbustes Furioso*, performed in the club's rooms on the third floor of Stoughton Hall, is the basis for the Pudding's claim to be the nation's oldest theatrical company. Then, in 1882, Owen Wister's brilliant *opéra bouffe*, *Dido and Aeneas* (music after the fashion of Sullivan and Offenbach) scored a huge success, and it is that production that has been called the first musical comedy ever performed in the United States. This is not the Pudding's only claim to fame in the history of the American musical theater—Pudding alumni have included in more recent years both Jack Lemmon and Alan Jay Lerner. But it was surely the success in 1882 of *Dido and Aeneas* that five years later stimulated the erection of this building. Peabody and Stearns, the leading Boston architects of the day, undertook the design, responding to the Pudding's exceptional architectural program with an unusual combination of playhouse (complete with stage house and lobbies and box office) and clubhouse (the usual amenities of which had if anything to be grander than the norm). The Holyoke Street front alone is full of interest. The boldness of its wide-flaring cornice, with its distinctive diamond-ornamented bracketed eaves, and the flamboyance of its large ground-floor round-arched windows lends the Pudding distinctly a theatrical quality. At the same time there is a stateliness about the building's dark brick facade, spare, but made gracious by the generous side porches—one for the "clubhouse," another (with box office) for the theater. Here it is that the annual Pudding shows are performed—drag shows characterized by excruciating puns and incredulous plots, the highlight of which traditionally is the all-male kickline of "chorus girls." (Think Jack Lemmon in *Some Like It Hot*.) The Pudding's club dining room is also notable for having become a superb restaurant, Upstairs at the Pudding. Though still used for (all the better) club dinners, it is otherwise open to the public, interesting especially for its wonderful décor of massed Pudding theatrical posters form the 1880s through the 1920s.

Apley Court, the one private dormitory next door, and one of the Gold Coast's most elegant, shows a similar face to Holyoke Street as the Pudding, but with a style of its own. Were ever neo-Georgian brick and limestone more sedate? But it is leavened by wrought-iron work Robert Bell Rettig was right to pronounce "almost rococo in feeling." T. S. Eliot lived here as a student.

OPPOSITE: *Hasty Pudding Clubhouse*

26. Spee Clubhouse (76 Mount Auburn Street)

William T. Aldrich, 1931

Many of the reasons purely social clubs and elite private dormitories developed at Harvard in the nineteenth century are forgotten now. First, with its tradition of the importance of residential living to education, as Harvard grew larger and larger, and the Yard more and more crowded (and commons less and less adequate), there was every encouragement for students and faculty (not to mention real estate developers) to address a highly unsatisfactory situation in the face of university inertia. Second, the surrounding Boston community, the cosmopolitan influence of which had proved so beneficial to Harvard's gathering liberal tradition in the seventeenth and eighteenth centuries, though it continued beneficial in the main in the nineteenth century (particularly in its ardent alumni support), became at the same time increasingly problematic socially. When George Santayana noted in the 1880s that "divisions of family and wealth [were] not made conspicuous at Yale as at Harvard," the reason is not hard to find; the domination of society in Boston by the great Brahmin families of the Back Bay and the North Shore, all closely linked to Harvard (the prestige of First Families and Harvard College fed off each other inevitably), had also the effect of imposing very narrow standards upon the Harvard community of who was and who was not, in Santayana's words, "socially presentable." The problem was compounded by the influence on Harvard of the elite New England Anglican prep schools founded in the second half of the nineteenth century. Itself a positive factor in many ways, for these splendid schools introduced much to America, their graduates, however, much prized by First Boston families, tended to form cliques which, while very supportive of Harvard, were welcoming only to fellow graduates, and otherwise rigidly exclusionary. By the 1900s the graduates of these elite St. Grottlesex schools—the names of St. Paul's, St. Mark's, Groton, and Middlesex Schools each contribute a syllable to the term—had placed even the graduates of older and themselves hardly unselective schools with long historic associations with Harvard (Exeter and Andover, for example, and Roxbury and Boston Latin) at an increasing disadvantage. Nor was the university alert to the negative effects of what was happening, emphasizing instead the positive effects. Samuel Eliot Morison, for example, Harvard's preeminent historian, insisted always not only on the historical importance of Harvard's final clubs but on the continuing value of these semi-independent institutions to the College. As to their importance, historically (and architecturally), it is significant that Cleveland Amory in his classic *The Proper Bostonians* devotes an entire chapter to Harvard's clubs. Their continuing value? "Education is not only book learning," Morison wrote, "but a decent place to dine," by which he meant the possibility of a glass of wine, even a tablecloth, and *not* going through a cafeteria line! Such clubs "maintain the

Spee Clubhouse

ancient ideal," Morison insisted, "preserving a valuable Harvard tradition."
Indeed, the Spee, as all the other clubhouses, may be said to be, whatever
else they are, the architecture of friendship.

The Spee is a particularly splendid example of that building type, in
style a kind of Moderne Georgian, its interior quite handsome—and
timely—including a hidden bar, an unusual architectural expression of the
Prohibition era. Its facade has been importantly altered (a bookshop having
been introduced into the first floor) but the result at the Spee is nonetheless
exemplary, and for more than one reason. The shop in question is
Schoenhof's, founded in downtown Boston in 1856, in Harvard Square
since 1939, and reputedly the oldest foreign language bookstore in America,
a revered institution of the sort that gives Harvard Square so much of its
unique character. Like all local shops, however, it has had to contend with
the increasing sheen of upscale-chain stores and their effect on rents
(Harvard Square having become an elite "display window" of the global
market place today), and it was a good deed widely appreciated for the presumably financially needful Spee to take in Schoehnof's—all the better for
the sensitive way the deed was done by adding a second pedimented door
frame in a quite nice relationship to the original club entrance on the left.
Harvard's clubs have often been identified with sports. It is good to see that
a club and a bookshop can keep such literate company architecturally.

27. Arts at Harvard Building and the Phoenix, Owl, Old Stylus, and Fly Clubhouses

Arts at Harvard Building (74 Mount Auburn) *Warren & Wetmore, 1916*
Phoenix S. K. Clubhouse (72 Mt. Auburn) *Coolidge & Shattuck, 1915*
Owl Clubhouse (130 Holyoke Street) *James Purdom, 1905*
Old Stylus Clubhouse (41 Winthrop) *ca. 1845*
Fly Clubhouse (2 Holyoke Place) *H. D. Hale, 1899*

The old Iroquois' club house just beyond the Spee is the centerpiece of a group of clubhouses, most of which face on to Mount Auburn Street, a group that itself forms the centerpiece of Mount Auburn's south side. Whereas the street's first clubhouses—even the rather grand Fox Club, but especially the old D. U. and the Signet—are very informal and American in architectural character (in two cases of wood frame construction), the clubhouses further along that form the group of which the old Iroquois is the centerpiece, are much more formal in feeling. Indeed the Spee, the old Iroquois and Phoenix, all in a row facing on to Mount Auburn Street, constitute a superb grouping of elaborate brick high-style Georgian Revival and Neo-Adamesque examples of the clubhouse, a building type never numerous or widespread in this country. There is no attempt to approach big city clubhouses of this era in magnificence. Instead, the older and smaller scale of the London clubs of St. James' prevails, and each of the Mount Auburn Street buildings achieves a just balance between expressing on the one hand the meant-to-be-distancing exterior pomp of the private Anglo-American club and, on the other hand, the

Phoenix Clubhouse and Arts at Harvard Building

Fly Clubhouse

welcoming if low-key domesticity of the home-away-from-home such a club must convey to welcome its members.

While the Phoenix Clubhouse is intact, alas, the old Iroquois is not, because, curiously, of an artistic, not a commercial, intrusion—a work of sculpture introduced into the archway over the chief facade window. Historically, it is yet another example (like the Signet) of a new group wanting to make its mark; this is now the Arts at Harvard Building. Most effective when seen in elevation, head on; the sculpture—the work of artist Richard Fleischner in 1997—is, however, less so in perspective, and overall, undermines the design of the facade. Such abstract modern insertions in classical or gothic architecture can be enlivening, but this one, although carefully considered (and by the exemplary Cambridge Historical Commission, which tries hard to strike the difficult balance between being too stuffy or too permissive), is highly problematic. In the first place, the designers of this clubhouse, Warren & Wetmore, were important American architects of their period of such landmarks as the recently restored Grand Central Station and the New York Yacht Club. The Iroquois is not a minor work, nor the detail removed unimportant, having been inspired by James Crunden's facade design in the Adam style in 1762 for Boodles Club on St. James' in London. In fact, the Iroquois clubhouse's shallow fluting around the big window, fluting now destroyed, was key to the evocation here of London's eighteenth-century clubland the architects' allusion to Crunden's Boodles facade was meant to convey. Moreover, the allusion is part of a spectacular design concept evident in the perspective eastward down Mount Auburn Street to the

Lampoon Castle, St. Paul's campanile rising behind it, one of the most splendid townscapes in the Boston area. One thinks at once of St. James', the principal thoroughfare of London's earlier eighteenth-century club-land—which in the nineteenth century would erupt in big city splendor on Pall Mall—a nice touch here as it was expected that nearly all the members of these clubs would eventually become members of the grand big city clubs (Pall Mall!) of Boston and New York. In this perspective, of course, the Lampoon castle plays the role of St. James' Palace gatehouse just as Mount Auburn Street's equivalent to White's, Brooks, and Boodles is the Spee-Iroquois-Phoenix group, itself a fine architectural development: the Phoenix vigorously, almost pompously, High Georgian Revival; the Iroquois—*cum* fluting—delicately Adamesque; the Spee a kind of modern Georgian, with its built-in balustrading and flat-roofed profile. Furthermore, behind the Iroquois and the Spee opposite each other across Holyoke Street, two other clubhouses buttress the effect: the Owl, an imposing dark red brick house designed by James Purdom, and—by way of older and homelier contrast—the old clubhouse (41 Winthrop Street) of the long defunct Stylus Club—a fine ca. 1845 wood-frame house where the likes of T. S. Eliot and George Santayana once talked the night away in the heyday of all these clubs in the late nineteenth and early twentieth centuries.

It was a heyday the cast of characters of which will surely endure forever. Freddy the coachman, for instance, the proprietor from the 1890s through the 1920s of a whole parade of horse-drawn vehicles according to the season: "the silver side lamps [of his cab] were an oriflamme of the night," Lucius Beebe recalled, never more so than on his closed winter coupe, a carriage with runners that made traveling over snow something Beebe never forgot: "to have been wafted home from a ball . . . amidst an early morning blizzard . . . the fine snow drifting in over the buffalo robe through the chinks in the door, and your last measure of S. S. Pierce's over-proof rum reserved as defense (for you and Freddy) against the elements while crossing the Harvard Bridge [between the Back Bay and Cambridge] is a lyric memory not to be ranked with any of the other exquisite souvenirs of this world." Freddy (who, rumor had it, taught Theodore Roosevelt how to box) "never missed . . . a club dinner on Mount Auburn Street," according to Beebe, who witnessed one of the gaffer's finer exploits the night the original Iroquois clubhouse burned down: "a very social fire it was too, what with the pompiers waited on by a liveried club steward with glasses of chilled champagne," wrote Beebe, who swore that "Freddy drove a fiacre load of top-hatted youths through the firelines and to a point of vantage just as the roof fell in."

What a scene! A much quieter one is the generous greensward—with the majestic Lowell House tower for background (see Walk 12)—that extends by a happy happenstance from the Phoenix clubhouse to that of the Fly Club, the oldest of these houses, designed in 1899 by H. D. Hale. The club itself is a good example of how all Harvard's clubs evolved, historically, from fraternity chapters to so-called "waiting clubs" and then into "final clubs" (meaning that one may belong to only one), and also how quietly but significantly they have helped to shape events far beyond Mount Auburn Street. Just as the Spee, for example, grew out of the Zeta Psi (one of whose presidents in the 1880s was William Randolph Hearst), so the Fly grew up out of Alpha Delta Phi. Indeed, Fly is an amalgamation of the "ph" from Alpha, the "l" from Delta and the "i" from Phi—hence "phli," pronounced Fly. The Harvard brothers adopted it as the club's formal name in 1916, having long since decided in the first place that they were far too grand to be just a local chapter of anything, and in the second place, that even serving as a Harvard waiting club—where prospective members of the august Porcellian and A. D. clubs were winnowed out—was not in keeping with their dignity. Dignity may not quite be the word, but the Fly claims as its most notable member, Franklin Delano Roosevelt, and it is through FDR that the club has left its deepest mark on the larger culture. An architectural mark actually—the mantelpiece of a ground story fireplace: a series of "fireside talks" at the club (on career choices) in FDR's student days having been Roosevelt's inspiration for—well, the rest is easily guessed, according to Dean Archie C. Epps III, an authoritative source if ever there was one of Harvard lore. Roosevelt's "fireside chats," be it said, have been called by one of FDR's biographers, James MacGregor Burns, the "most important link with the people" of the legendary president.

28. Claverly Hall and Senior House *George Fogerty, 1892*

On the other side of Mount Auburn Street from so many of the clubs is what is always in every sense the other side of Harvard's Gold Coast—the most elite of the private dormitories: Claverly, Randolph, and Westmorley Halls, one after the other, they march along, their splendor described by Owen Johnson with no little enthusiasm in an article in *Collier's Weekly* in 1912:

> an elevator obligingly saves [the residents] the agony of toiling up fatiguing flights of stairs...; when they rise in the morning they go down to their own private swimming pool...[only Westmorley's, on which Johnson dwelt in his article, survives today, as the Adams House Pool Theater, one of Harvard's most spectacular 1900s interiors]...with its marble surfaces and elaborate scheme of decorating, with gracefully distributed plants and twin fireplaces, with comfortable wicker chairs to lounge in....[Throughout it] has a Roman luxuriousness. Private squash courts...exist [some of

which also still survive].... Each dormitory has its uniformed servants on watch at the door—butlers ready to receive a card on a
tray or ready to run the minor annoying errands.

As Harvard became more and more prestigious, the demand for such
accommodations grew more and more insistent. Nor was it quite so unat-
tractive as it can be made to seem. Consider this report from the fall of 1912
of three men "walking down Mt. Auburn Street.... Dressed alike in white
pants and blue jackets, their faces browned from rowing with the crew, they
sauntered along the tree-lined street, their arms resting on each other's
shoulders.... They were not the men who made up the steady stream that
poured into dinner at Memorial Hall. Fine-shouldered lads with high cheek-
bones and healthy outdoor skin, they seemed to look out at the world from
an eminence of their own." Every Harvard novel eagerly devoured by the
American reading public in the 1890s and 1900s had a scene more or less
like this one, quoted by Doris Kearns Goodwin in *The Fitzgeralds and the
Kennedys*, and Claverly Hall was always at the novel's center. It was said to
have taken its name from Claverly Manor, the country seat of builder
Charles Wetmore. The biographer of an early resident, Ralph Lowell,
recalled just how exclusive the dormitory was: "Claverly Hall... started the
building boom on Mount Auburn Street.... At a time when many of the dormitories in Harvard Yard had no central heating and no plumbing above the
basement, Claverly and its neighbors offered suites with private baths and
steam heat. The great demand for these accommodations meant that a
freshman had to engage in a student-run election before he could get a
room." Monumental in scale, with immense rounded corner bays and windows of great sheets of Victorian plate glass, Claverly spoke to deeper
needs as well. In the courtyard behind it—which could be a marvelous garden but is instead today the dreariest of parking lots—there is a separate
building—Senior House—built for Claverly men in their senior year. It
bespeaks the attempt at collegiate community that underlay even the most
snobbish private dormitory.

29. Randolph Hall of Adams House *Coolidge & Wright, 1897*

Another such attempt—this time specifically by faculty—was this project
of the 1890s spearheaded by Archibald Carey Coolidge, a legendary
Harvard don and librarian and a nephew of no less than Isabella Stewart
Gardner. This dark brick Jacobean-gabled hall, built around Apthorp
House, an old Colonial-era mansion, of which more soon, was erected
some five years after Claverly, and achieves in a different style a similar
air of stoic luxury and a far greater architectural distinction. Laid out

around a spacious and elegant interior courtyard garden, still carefully tended today, Randolph Hall is one of Harvard's secret places, highly prized. Here, for example, is an old breakfast room, endowed with marvelous murals, at once traditional and Bohemian, by the artist of so many stylish 1890s *Harper's Magazine* covers, Edward Penfield. Historically, more was going on here than was at first apparent. As Wendell Garrett has written in "Apthorp College":

> In building Randolph Hall and buying Apthorp House, the Coolidge brothers had hoped to create in Harvard an American version of an English college, complete with interior courtyard and gardens. The addition of an athletic building and tennis court [with squash courts also and an indoor swimming pool] gave the new unit the requisite physical equipment except a library and a chapel.
>
> The two previous decades in Harvard's housing for undergraduates were a period of recurring calamities and almost unrelieved discontent. Rapid expansion, insufficient accommodation in the Yard...caused a crisis....With some thought of alleviating this shortage, Archibald Carey Coolidge conceived [his] plan.

There were not only the student rooms around the courtyard garden and the athletic facilities, but there were also, in effect, the Master's Lodgings to be expected in an English college; for Garrett also noted that Coolidge in his Bostonian way was doubly concerned with providing "his family with a financially sound real estate investment and himself with proctor's quarters rent free," in the event a spacious penthouse suite at the top of Randolph. In time other collegiate facilities emerged: the ground floor common room (a genuine *junior* common room, solely for students, complete with upright piano) came into being in the most natural way possible because so many undergraduates were drawn to Apthorp College. Continued Garrett: "the mists of distance have softened the outlines of the nineteen-twenties and the alumni of Apthorp College smile at the memory of those charming, crazy days. When George Weller published *Not to Eat, Not for Love*...he devoted one whole chapter to Apthorp....Since 1930 the history of Apthorp College has been absorbed into that of Adams House.... 'Apthorp College' has at last become a reality," Garrett concluded, and, indeed, when Harvard College came to be subdivided into smaller residential colleges called Houses in later years (See Walk 12), Coolidge's vision was seen as a significant part of the pre-history of the idea.

30. Apthorp House: Adams House Master's Lodgings

Peter Harrison, 1761

Picturesquely enfolded by the Jacobean style wings of old Randolph Hall, with which it once formed Apthorp College, is one of the great Tory mansions of the mid-eighteenth-century Royal Province of New England—Apthorp House—now the residence of the Master of Adams House. This mansion was built in 1761 by the Rev. East Apthorp, the son of Boston's wealthiest businessman, who after Boston Latin studied at Jesus College, Oxford, and, returning to Boston, married the sister of the Chief Justice of the Royal Province and was the founder and parish priest of Christ Church, the Episcopal Church on the other side of Harvard Square. Apthorp's residence became quickly notorious among the Puritan party in its day as the so-called "Bishop's Palace." To some extent this was because of Rector Apthorp's skirmishes in the *Boston Gazette* with the local Puritan clergy over the need for "an Episcopal Mission in Cambridge" and a plot real or imagined whereby Apthorp was seen as the spearhead of an attempt by the Archbishop of Canterbury (stoutly resisted by the Puritans) to send over a bishop and to found an Anglican see of Boston. (Certainly the controversy famously sparked in 1768 a satirical engraving, "An Attempt to Land a Bishop in America," featuring a conspicuous mitre and crosier on the deck of a transatlantic ship and a bystander shouting "No Lords Spiritual or Temporal in New England.") Actually, Rector Apthorp, whose sister, Susan, was the mother of Charles Bulfinch himself, needed no prelacy to justify his tastes in architecture, which were not only grand enough, but consciously Palladian. So much so that Wendell Garrett, a distinguished antiquarian, has pointed out that Apthorp's was "*not* a typical house in eighteenth-century New England," and should be seen as "part of an impressive American effort to carry out ideals bequeathed by the Palladians." And Garrett laid an equal stress on American as on Palladian in his study of Apthorp's palace: "the central pavilion, the colossal pilasters running through two stories, the high pedestals, the breaking of the entablature above them—all this derives from Palladio," he wrote. But he then goes on to note "the novel use of all these elements" by the architect, and concludes that Apthorp House is "a hybrid, a composite of alien and native elements, a medley fused into a sort of audacious unity." In other words, American.

The architect in question was almost surely Peter Harrison himself, designer of both Apthorp's parish church, Christ Church, and of downtown Boston's King's Chapel. Indeed, his house for Apthorp was sufficiently worthy to elicit from John Adams the observation that "a great house, at that time thought to be a splendid palace, was built by Mr. Apthorp at Cambridge." Built, but not long enjoyed. Forced back to England within four years as too controversial a figure, Apthorp sold his estate to a contemporary, another native New Englander, John Borland, Harvard Class of

Apthorp House

1748. It was this second owner, whose twelve children, two slaves, and numerous servants needed many chambers, who added the third story to the house—an addition more than one critic has thought worthy of the original. So fine a house did this seem to the Colonists that during the American Revolution, though it was briefly used as a barrack (and in consequence looted, particularly the wine cellar), Apthorp House was mostly utilized by the patriot leadership for themselves. In fact, it is thought that Sam and John Adams and John Hancock all visited here. It was also in the now enlarged Apthorp House that British General "Gentleman Johnny" Burgoyne was interned after his surrender at Saratoga in 1777 in a manner thought fitting to his high rank. Eventually the mansion passed as well out of the Borland family, but in 1897 when the Coolidges bought the front yard as the site for Randolph Hall and (four years later) the old house as well, it actually passed back to a branch of the Apthorps, the Coolidges being descendants of East Apthorp's sister, Susan Apthorp Bulfinch. Meanwhile the undergraduates resident in Apthorp's house itself in the 1920s found themselves being a good deal neater and more regular in their habits than they might have liked in the face of the architectural significance of their housing. So at least the *Boston Sunday Herald* reported in October 1920, when an article disclosed that "architects and designers come from all over the country to make sketches of [the house's first floor parlor mantle particularly]." So also did the Colonial Revival, of all unlikely places, come to the Gold Coast for inspiration.

The Environs of St. Paul's Square

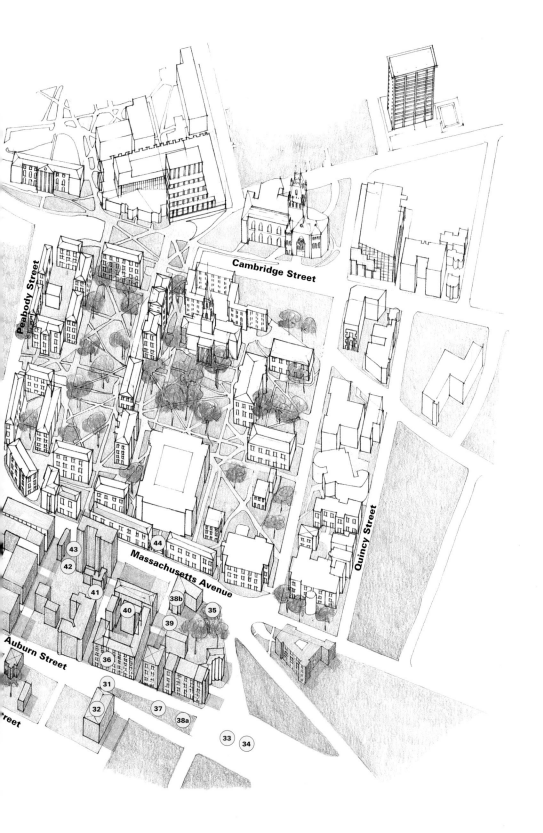

Harvard Yard and Harvard Square

31. Lampoon Castle *Wheelwright & Haven, 1909*

Presiding from its central island at the head of Mount Auburn Street over the length and breadth of that street is the flatiron-shaped Lampoon Castle, the picturesque culmination of this memorable townscape. It's a building it's safe to say is unique: a very animated, energizing design, the profile of which would not be out of place in Vermeer's *View of Delft*. The structure's most distinctive feature, on the other hand, its helmet-domed tower, is clearly derivative of the sixteenth-century Norman Manoir d'Ango in Varengeville, the country retreat of Francis I of France. Its progeny at Harvard is something else again; looked at head on it has, in John Updike's words, "a face—two round windows that look cross-eyed, a red lantern for a nose, and, above the bright bow-tie of its door, an exclamatory mouth of which the upper lip is so complex it might be a mustache. A copper hard-hat tasseled with a cage completes the apparition." What humor magazine could ask for more? This one, founded somewhat in imitation of *Punch* in 1876, and alive and well continuously since 1861, is still widely influential. Its parodies continue to stimulate and several of its graduates have gone on to be writers, for example, for "Saturday Night Live" ("the Harvard of comedy," as Chris Rock calls it). In 1969 several graduates also founded the *National Lampoon*, a commercial incarnation of the collegiate original, the income from which has funded a skillful restoration of the Lampoon's building, to say nothing of much "poonish" revelry. The interior, particularly its

LEFT: *Lampoon Castle and Rosovsky Hall*
RIGHT: *The Lampoon ibis*

two-story Great Hall, would appear to be a considerable incitement to same; its walls are lined with a dizzying seven thousand or so Delft tiles, thought to be the largest such architectural display in the world outside the Netherlands. The Lampoon's architect, Edmund March Wheelwright (he of the Boston Opera House, the Larz Anderson Bridge, and Jordan Hall at the New England Conservatory of Music), was also one of the Lampoon's founders, and though Wheelwright insisted the Lampoon is where it is because "he could get from [downtown] State Street to the bar in the Lampoon Building...and back to State Street again in half an hour," obviously much more thought than that went into it. And into the building's character. Indeed, Conan O'Brien, the Lampoon's sometime president, is not wrong to insist: "Of course, the building reflects us: we're all little mock Flemish castles." It also gives one pause to learn that some report none of the clocks inside keep time. Behind the Lampoon door, Andrew Pforzheimer writes, is "the Land that Time Forgot." The last word to Updike: "The gorgeous playful thing was put up as a civilized prank, by American wealth when it was untaxed and unconscience-stricken; it is a folly and a toy and a bastion, an outcropping, like the brick mass of Harvard itself, of that awful seismic force which has displaced nine-tenths of the world: WASP Power."

32. Harvard Hillel's Rosovsky Hall *Moshe Safdie, 1992*

Here is a new architecture come to Mount Auburn Street—but not very new—though if one sees architectural history as I do, as necessarily informed by social history, the idea behind the architecture of Harvard Hillel's Rosovsky Hall is pretty interesting, for its design concept—open, inviting, almost transparent—seems to celebrate *in*clusion, not *ex*clusion. And that is a quite exciting idea to bring to the heart of clubland, even if the architectural announcement of the idea is hardly riveting. Then again what *could* any architect do in the shadow of the Lampoon but sulk, or, worse, contrive gestures like transparent domes? Doubtless too there were good reasons for expressing so radical an idea as *in*clusion with so unthreatening an architecture. It was, after all, a long time coming, this idea.

How long is clear if one considers the career of Louis Brandeis, the first Jew to sit on the Supreme Court of the United States (after whom Brandeis University in the Boston suburb of Waltham is named) and the preeminent figure in the history of the Jewish community of Harvard. He was devoted to Harvard College (though he attended no college) and graduated first in his class from the Harvard Law School. Brought early under the influence of Boston's liberal German Jewish community in the nineteenth century, before the Brahmin social system ossified into a relentless anti-Semitism, the rising young Boston lawyer identified himself with the

philosophy of Emerson, who Brandeis revered, as he did the Puritans generally. Indeed, he saw their genius exemplified in the history of Harvard
College. In fact, he took as his partner in the practice of law a fellow Harvard
man, S. L. Warren, who was a Brahmin of the Brahmins. Brandeis was also
drawn to Harvard president Charles Eliot, who was something of a mentor,
and it was Eliot's enthusiasm for the founding at Harvard in 1907 of the
Menorah Society that first drew Brandeis's interest to that group. The
Menorah Society was, importantly, both cause and effect of Brandeis's
increasing interest in this period in Judaism generally and also in Zionism, of
which by World War I Brandeis was the leading figure in America. According
to the American Jewish Historical Society, "the Harvard Menorah Society
was Boston's first Jewish student organization. Subsequent Jewish student
activity has continued to expand through the establishment of college Hillel
societies." Harvard's, created in 1944, has been based since 1992 in Rosovsky
Hall, and before that in the old Iroquois clubhouse, which was not nearly the
irony many found it, for (though it is not too widely known) the Iroquois was
perhaps the first Harvard final club to accept—indeed, to seek out—Jewish
members, as Roger Prouty, sometime club president, recalls.

33. St. Paul's Church *Edward T. P. Graham, 1915*

Bow Street, looking toward St. Paul's

It is, perhaps, no coincidence that
Roman Catholics and Jews have ended
up based conspicuously within sight of
each other at the climax of the Gold
Coast, the very place where Harvard's
hostility to Jews and Catholics in the
late nineteenth and early twentieth
centuries was always most pronounced. St. Paul's came first. The earliest church of 1874–75, at the corner of
Mount Auburn and Holyoke, was augmented in 1893 by the Catholic Club,
which settled eventually in a now
destroyed clubhouse at Nos. 32–34
Mount Auburn, complete with a columned portico clearly intended to rival
the splendor of the older clubs. The present St. Paul's Church across the
street was built in 1915 and quickly became a Harvard Square landmark
because of its graceful tower, while the columnar marble high altar reredos
in the sanctuary of the upper church may be the handsomest in the Boston
archdiocese. It is also, however, the culmination of an overall decorative
scheme that, to put it nicely, was intended to be highly challenging to the

university. Most Harvard men undoubtedly heard the Angelus thrice daily from St. Paul's bell tower without murmuring *Aves*. Nor would a closer look at St. Paul's bells have made peace. The bells' inscription was from Isaiah: *Voxciamantis in deserto*/I am a voice crying in the wilderness—a worldview at some variance with Harvard's view of itself. (Recall the inscription on the Class of 1875 Gate built just fifteen years before St. Paul's erection in 1900, also from Isaiah; the one about Harvard as "the righteous nation which keepeth the truth.") Truth. *Veritas*—it was Harvard's motto of course, blazoned first in seventeenth-century corporation records and restored to Harvard's seal in the nineteenth century. But here again St. Paul's hurled defiance: carved into the architectural portal of the main facade is another biblical quote (this time from the Letter of Timothy): "The Church of the living God, the pillar and the ground of truth"—and as between the Church of Rome and the Church of the Puritans it leaves no doubt which was meant. Nor was that all. Lest anyone miss the point of this biblical war of words (and many still do) there was also the bas-relief inside St. Paul's of that great preacher preaching—to the pagan philosophers of Athens!

St. Paul's is spirited architecture—one riposte after another to Harvard—not least the prominent altar within dedicated to St. Patrick, for there was, of course, distinctly an ethnic edge to all this. Indeed, the church's architect, Edward T. P. Graham (a parishioner of St. Paul's who was also a Harvard graduate), sent another ethnic signal perhaps to the Harvard community in the church's overall architecture—Italian rather than Irish. But he may also have meant St. Paul's Italian Romanesque design, inspired by Verona's San Zeno Maggiore and the Torre del Commune to jog a few stolid heads; it was, after all, homage to a cultural heritage precious to Harvard, which had pioneered Italian studies in America through the work of such distinguished nineteenth-century Dante scholars as Henry Wadsworth Longfellow and Charles Eliot Norton, as well as through the latter's even more notable disciples, Bernard Berenson and Isabella Stewart Gardner. Moreover, however richly deserved St. Paul's rebuke to Harvard was in its era, everyone understood that it was only the democracy Harvard's Puritan tradition had played no small part in establishing that made such forceful rejoinder possible in the first place. The architecture of St. Paul's, at one and the same time, declared war and proposed the terms of peace. And, historically, there was reason enough for the ambiguity. Harvard had awarded its first degree to a Roman Catholic (Boston's French Consul) as far back as in 1799, and admitted its first Catholic undergraduate in 1808. (This before there was a Catholic church nearby to send him to, though Harvard's Corporation voted that young Joseph Lee, son of the Governor of Maryland, "who has been admitted in the Roman Catholic religion may be permitted to attend public worship at the Episcopal church in Cambridge.") By 1826 another student, Jerome Napoleon Bonaparte, a nephew of the Emperor Napoleon I,

St. Paul's Church

was even deputy marshal of the Porcellian Club, and things had gone so far that at mid-century Harvard University was paying pew rent for students at Boston's Roman Catholic cathedral; this was the predecessor to the "college pew" Harvard rented at St. Paul's after its founding, for Irish Catholics as well as French, by the way. When the Bishop of Boston, John Fitzpatrick, was given an honorary degree by Harvard in 1861, College Treasurer Amos Lawrence insisted it could never have happened "were it not for the loyalty shown by [Fitzpatrick] and by the Irish, who have offered themselves freely for the army" in the Civil War. It was not long before there was also a Roman Catholic Overseer of Harvard—Charles J. Bonaparte—in 1891.

There was as much to be said, however, on the other side of the matter; Harvard's welcome to Catholics was only part of the story. Read *The Last Puritan*, the best selling novel penned by George Santayana. Santayana wrote of how horrified the leading character, Boston Brahmin Nathaniel Alden, was to find himself seated in a trolley car next to an Irish Catholic priest. Alden, wrote Santayana, "had never actually *touched* a Catholic before." A telling observation, of the sort Catholics naturally keenly resented, nor always turned the other cheek to. The fact is that there were not more Catholics at Harvard in the late nineteenth century was as much because of the archdiocese of Boston as of Harvard. It was not only the future Rose Fitzgerald Kennedy, the daughter of Boston's mayor, who was forbidden by its archbishop, Cardinal O'Connell, from attending an Ivy League college—in her case Wellesley. The then president of Boston College, Thomas Gasson, was as censorious in print of "Godless" Harvard's

education as was Harvard's own president of Jesuit educational philosophy.
At one point (among Catholic schools) only credits from Georgetown—*not*
from Boston College—were deemed acceptable by Harvard Law School. On
the other hand the same Harvard president encouraged the forming of the
Catholic Club in the teeth of Mount Auburn Street bigotry. Perhaps this had
something to do with the fact St. Paul's Church itself gradually superseded
Boston College's Church of the Immaculate Conception as the cultural and
intellectual center of the Boston archdiocese. Thus today the Boston
Archdiosecan Choir School is based at St. Paul's, the superb music that has
turned more than one pagan into at least an aesthete. Today, too, Harvard's
president, Neil L. Rudenstine, is part Italian and part Jewish, while Bernard
Cardinal Law is a Harvard College graduate, Class of 1953.

34. St. Paul's School and Harvard Catholic Student Center (20 Arrow Street) *Koetter-Kim, 1986*

It is a measure of how things were changing at Harvard in the 1890s that J. D.
M. Ford, who earned not only his A.B. but his Ph.D. from Harvard in that
decade, should have been a founder of the Catholic Club, for in 1907 Ford, a
pioneer in the study of Latin American literature, was appointed the Smith
professor of French and Spanish languages in the department of romance languages and literature. This chair, which at that time had been vacant for over
thirty years, had been held previously by such figures as George Ticknor,
Henry Wadsworth Longfellow, and James Russell Lowell. And it was out of
the Catholic Club that the today's Harvard Catholic Student Center developed,
first in a building remodeled in 1960 by no less than José Luis Sert, a parishioner of St. Paul's. Today that structure is no more. It disappeared when in
1986 Koetter-Kim designed a new complex. Along with a new building for the
Archdiosecan Choir School and a hall for the parish, the student center is a
great success architecturally because of the way it is contextual. The overall
design is, in the first place, superbly urbanistic (in fact, very Italian). From the
street an elegant gateway gives on to a flight of stairs that leads down from
the street to a plaza between church and center. A playground, pedestrian
pathway, and parking lot are all one thing, really, a combination that works
because, depending on what time of day it is, each function gives way quite
naturally to the other, the overall design deferring more or less equally to
each. In the second place, Koetter-Kim's new work is deftly cast in terms both
historicist and modernist; not content to respond sensitively to the dark red
brick Romanesque Revival church, the architects also kept an eye on the magnificent proto-modernist apartment house (see below) across the street, the
severe stucco facade of which is reflected in the design of the new center as
much as the church's ornamental brick.

35. St. Paul's Square: No. 12 Bow Street, Longfellow Court, Westmorley Court

12 Bow Street *ca. 1825*
Longfellow Court *1916*
Westmorley Court *Warren & Wetmore, 1898, 1902*

Three buildings face St. Paul's Church and its auxiliary structures around a charming and picturesque square without equal throughout the Boston area. No. 12 Bow Street, the smallest of the three buildings, was erected originally in Harvard Square proper on the corner of Brattle Street next to the site of the present Harvard Coop about 1825. Russell's Store, as this simple gabled wood-frame building was then called, was moved away from there in 1847 to the corner of Massachusetts Avenue and Plimpton Street, and then moved again to this location in 1868. (Labor in those days was very cheap.) Blameless so far as is known throughout the subsequent development of St. Paul's Square, its history darkened in the 1950s, for (sad to say) the architecture of St. Paul's Square compasses, historically, not only the Catholic challenge to Harvard's ferocious anti-Catholic bigotry in the early twentieth century, but the equally vivid anti-Semitism of a small but conspicuous group of Roman Catholics of several generations later who notoriously found shelter in the 1950s in this little red clapboard house across from St. Paul's Church. It was, nonetheless, one of Harvard's leading Catholic students then, Robert Kennedy, '48, who rose to this provocation smartly enough. Kennedy biographer and Harvard historian Arthur Schlesinger, Jr., wrote: "Being an

12 Bow Street and Longfellow Court

Westmorley Court

Irish American, Henry James might have said, was a complicated fate." And never more so than in St. Paul's Square in the 1950s, when young Kennedy encountered Father Feeney's "anathematiz[ing of] Harvard as 'a pest-hole' of atheists and Jews." All this, Schlesinger continued, "vastly irritated [Kennedy], who put up an argument, angrily abandoned the center and shocked his mother by denouncing Fr. Feeney at the Kennedy dinner table." Whatever Rose Kennedy's feelings in the matter, Richard Cardinal Cushing, Boston's archbishop at the time, excommunicated Feeney in 1953, and today the little red clapboard house is a very different place. Where once old Mr. Russell's clerks or whoever traded their goods in the 1820s, and where a century and more later Bobby Kennedy contended with Feeney and company in hot debate, there is now Paul Robertson's superb Cambridge Architectural Bookstore, one of those small specialty bookstalls still unique to Harvard Square—and which gives it so much of its character. And in the cellar below, furthermore, Josefina Yangua, once the housekeeper of a Harvard refugee professor, conducts the Cafe Pamplona, perhaps the oldest and certainly the most picturesque of the square's coffeehouses.

Therein trade and debate continue, overwhelmed in both cases by that monumental stucco apartment house that dominates the side of St. Paul's Square facing the church. No city planner would ever contrive anything so brilliant as this streetscape. Longfellow Court, with its austere stucco wall surfaces and dramatic overhanging cornice, is surely a rare early twentieth-century example of an American building strongly influenced by the European modernist architecture of that era. Certainly the unknown architect hired in 1916 by the developer of this huge apartment block had seen the striking Looshaus of four years earlier in Vienna, designed by the modernist master, Adolf Loos. Longfellow Court's name, of course, honors the leading poet of the great era of New England poetry in the nineteenth century. But this apartment house was itself a locale of Boston's second poetic renaissance, which occurred in the 1950s—"one of the most vital milieux for poetry in the history of this country," in the words of Peter Davison, the poet and editor whose *The Fading Smile* deals with that milieu. Its leading lights included Robert Lowell and Richard Wilbur (of both more soon) and W. S. Merwin, Anne Sexton, Sylvia Plath, Adrienne

Rich, and Stanley Kunitz. It was the last named who moved into Longfellow Court in 1958, where he recalled that Plath and Ted Hughes that year "made a point of stopping by my apartment on a Thursday or Friday evening, and it became a sort of ritual.... It was serious talk about poetry."

The 1890s Gold Coast of Clubland—complete with ethnic tensions—and the literary Bohemia of the 1950s, by which time most if not all those tensions had abated, meet also in St. Paul's Square in Westmorley Court, another early twentieth-century apartment house, and now a dormitory of Adams House, one of Harvard's present day residential colleges. Originally a private dormitory, Westmorley Court set new standards of luxury for the Gold Coast when it was built, both inside and out. Certainly the exterior is splendid. A robustly modeled red brick Tudor Baroque extravaganza, it could not be more of a contrast to the severe Viennese modernism of Longfellow Court, or, indeed, to the dark Italian Romanesque of St. Paul's Church, all three together an expression certainly of architectural diversity worthy of the area's social history. But Westmorley Court works so well with those other buildings—and with the elegant plaza buildings of the Harvard Catholic Student Center—the result is perhaps the most picturesque quarter of Harvard Square. Only one thing is lacking: the Roman fountain the architect Gerhard Kallmann has often pointed out belongs here. Indeed, the exact design has been mooted: that of the Fontana delle Tartarughe of the Piazza Mattei, a little Roman square much like St. Paul's Square. Four young men there disport themselves with dolphins, which spout water into a shell, while turtles meanwhile climb into the bowl above. Already, there is one American replica—in front of Grace Cathedral in San Francisco. All this in front of Adams House is too appropriate. Church, bells (beautiful bells, newly restored), bookstore, cafe, and an American Looshaus: who will give the fountain?

36. Russell Hall of Adams House

Coolidge, Shepley, Bulfinch & Abbott, 1931

Adams House's commons building, staid enough Georgian Revival on the outside, is on the inside (with the possible exception of the Lampoon Castle—is this a Gold Coast tradition?) Harvard's most exotic building. But elaborate Moorish detail and gold-washed walls and enormous stone mantelpieces form an appropriate architectural setting for Adams House, where the bohemian and slightly raffish side of this part of Cambridge may be said ultimately to have flowered in the very different post-World War II bohemia of the 1950s. Witness Joan Baez's autobiography, where she recounts her "love affair with Michael and Harvard Square." Baez's first album, "Folksingers 'Round Harvard Square," caught very well the

Russell Hall of Adams House

flavor of the thing; so did her memories of Adams House on snowy nights: while Michael slept she would seek out the window and "watch the snowflakes go past in a ghostly cavalcade to cover the streets in silent blankets of white for the morning. I'd listen for the chiming of the Harvard bells in [the] tower [of St. Paul's Church a block away] and sit with a blanket wrapped around me, smiling like a bohemian Mona Lisa, at one with the snowflakes, with the tiny room, with Michael and myself."

Adams House also figured in the more intense bohemia of the 1960s which otherwise only brushed the Gold Coast. Edie Sedgwick, for instance, who would star in several of Andy Warhol's underground films until she turned instead toward Bob Dylan, was often to be seen in the early

'60s at Adams, where Sedgwick studied art with Lily Saarinen. Of Sedgwick at her most *outré* Truman Capote wrote: "Andy Warhol would like to have been Edie Sedgwick. He would like to have been a charming, well born debutante from Boston." High Society on the Gold Coast. Suddenly Russell Hall's gilded, multi-colored Moorish and Mediterranean interiors (hiding behind Georgian facades?) seem to make sense after all.

37. Old Harvard Advocate Building (on Plympton Street, between Bow Street and Mount Auburn)
circa 1900

Architecture in this part of the Gold Coast has always had the challenging task of facilitating the lifestyle of a quarter the two themes of which, historically, have been high society and literary life—ambiguous soulmates. Ambiguous architecture! Just astern of the Lampoon Castle, the old *Advocate* rooms, entered from No. 40 Bow Street just above a first floor shop called appropriately for years The Gold Coast Valeteria, endowed what started life as a down-at-heel 1900s-era tenement with a highly unusual character the building's remodelers are partially responsible for. Indeed, the building—like the Lampoon the edge of an island—is something of a case study in how picturesque, even smart, a walk-up tenement can be made to be with a little flair, surrounded as it came to be by the grand brick and limestone palaces of an area Harvard now dominates. Less than a block down Plympton Street from the *Crimson*, however, and across the street from the *Lampoon*, could hardly be bettered as a locale for Harvard's third great student literary bastion—as the *Advocate* still is today. The oldest continuously published college magazine in the country (the first journalistic and literary efforts at Harvard, including *Harvardiana* of the early 1800s, for which Thoreau wrote, have not survived), the *Advocate* boasts a fabled alumni roster going way back. The list, which includes Bernard Berenson, John Reed, and E. E. Cummings, was particularly strong in the first decade of the twentieth century, a time when Longfellow still reigned in home and even in academe across the country—but decidedly not at the *Advocate*, where T. S. Eliot, Wallace Stevens, and Conrad Aiken were "developing in the *Advocate* some of the techniques," in Jonathan Culler's words, "that would revitalize English and American poetry" soon enough. It was quite a spectrum. At a time when young Theodore Roosevelt held forth in the *Advocate* on college pacifists on the eve of World War I (of whom, of course, he did *not* approve), Conrad Aiken, Culler reports, published in the *Advocate* "poetry which he told the draft board was essential to the national defense." Though not as it turned out on the cutting edge when Eliot and company came into their own in the '20s, the *Advocate* was very much identified with the next poetic revolution of the 1950s, when Frank O'Hara and John Ashbery, two Harvard poets of the period, dominated its pages, and mid-twentieth-century habitués of its Bow Street "sanctum" included Norman Mailer, Adrienne Rich, and Robert Bly. In 1950 the *Advocate* decamped to a new building on South Street, but the old building still evokes the magazine: its steep staircase, for instance, off Bow Street. Here in 1942 there took place a Harvard literary party in honor of Somerset Maugham that is notorious still. As Norman Mailer remembered it, so many hundred people jammed into the *Advocate*'s rooms one late afternoon no one could move at all for an hour or more: "From time to time, word would pass like wind through grass that Maugham had just entered the building, Maugham was having trouble getting up the stairs, Maugham was through the door, Maugham was in the other room. We formed phalanxes to move into the other room; we did not budge.... About a half hour [later] the wind came through the grass again. Maugham, we heard, was at the door, Maugham was slowly going down the stair, Somerset Maugham was gone." Of course, as it turned out, Maugham had never been there in the first place! How many parties, how many years, in this half-gilded, half-tawdry quarter; it was after one, in 1909, that T. S. Eliot, a bit of a dandy and very much a party-goer as a student, stumbled out the street level door into the arms of Conrad Aiken, another young poet and fellow *Advocate* editor. "They actually first came together when Eliot," according to his biographer, "staggered, the worse for drink, out of the Lampoon Club and embraced Aiken ("reeled out of the door" was Aiken's memory). "And that," an acquaintance of Aiken told him, "if Tom remembers it tomorrow, will cause him to suffer agonies of shyness." Too true. But Eliot and Aiken became lifelong friends. The Gold Coast is like that. And it is curious what good architectural mates the exotic Lampoon Castle and the tarted up old *Advocate* tenement make still to this day.

Between Eliot and—a generation later—poet Robert Lowell things were more complicated. Lowell once interviewed for a position on the *Advocate* literary board. He "was asked to tack down a carpet in the sanctum and, when he had finished, told that he needn't come back anymore"—years later the embarrassed *Advocate* published in 1961 a special Lowell issue. Lowell in his early period at Harvard immersed himself in a study of Eliot's work, and in his notebooks Lowell records he and Eliot walking through Harvard Yard complaining about how much they hated to be compared with their Bostonian relatives (both Eliot and Lowell were related to the Harvard presidents of those names, Lowell also to the poet James Russell Lowell). Eliot in his day had lived, as we've seen, two streets up from Plympton, at Apley Court. There it was that he passed through his "spiritual crisis" of 1914, as Sean O'Connell calls it, when perhaps the greatest poet of religion in the twentieth century first began to write religious poetry. Lowell, decades later and a few blocks away, had more than one such crisis. In both cases O'Connell sees in both men "the Boston doubt", and, too, the "Boston dialectic," as he calls it, between Puritanism and Catholicism. Eliot and Lowell both, furthermore, remembered here in such urban contexts as Harvard's founders could hardly have imagined, disclose how vitalizing the Puritan legacy remains, never more so than when resisted. Wrote Lowell, famously not fond of Boston or Harvard: "New England also had for me some vibration of higher moral rectitude, of moral passion even, with its seventeenth-century Puritan self-scrutiny, its nineteenth-century literary 'flowering', its abolitionist righteousness, Colonel Shaw and his Black Civil War regiment depicted in granite on Boston Common." The architecture of these dark and narrow sidestreets between Harvard Square proper and Harvard's nineteenth-century Gold Coast, full of recesses and alleys and cul-de-sacs even darker, are apt mediators for such angst.

38. Starr Bookshop and Grollier Bookshop

Starr Bookshop (Lampoon Building rear) *E. M. Wheelwright, 1909*
Grollier Bookshop (1246–1260 Massachusetts Avenue) *Coolidge & Carlson, 1902*

Close urban contexts mediate these passions only very generally; more specifically over the years the task has fallen to the many odd and often used bookstores that have tended to frequent these side streets of the square. Listen to Robert Lowell as an undergraduate: "When I arrived [at Harvard], independent, fearful of advice, and with all the world before me, I began to rummage in Cambridge bookshops." One such, where I've found a few answers over the years, is Starr's, picturesquely located for nearly half a century now at the first floor rear of the Lampoon, a lovely example of how retail shopfronts can be integrated into more monumental architecture. Unusually, the Lampoon was designed with a front and a rear facade equally interesting and useful.

Yet another bookish landmark is on Plympton Street, a street of special interest to the Harvard Square milieu because, historically, it is a place where authors themselves have been known to lodge over or nearby the bookstores they depended on. In the 1940s, for example, poet Richard Wilbur lived in an old eighteenth-century house at No. 22 Plympton, since torn down, where he is said to have completed his first collection of poems. At No. 8 lived poet and novelist Conrad Aiken, in a flat where the English novelist Malcolm Lowry wrote his first novel in 1929. Aiken's—later Lowry's—apartment was just over the Grollier Book Shop, founded here in 1927. (Next to it today is the Harvard Bookstore, itself founded in Harvard Square in 1932 and now probably the best bookstore in Greater Boston.)

Grollier Bookshop

The Grollier, which specializes in poetry and gives excellent readings cosponsored by Adams House or the Fogg Art Museum, is in a category all its own now. It has been for three quarters of a century a positively cherished part of the Harvard Square literary scene, one of a number of area booksellers through the years tucked away in odd places, whose independent (i.e., modernist) proclivities have tested and thus nurtured American intellectual freedom in the face of "Banned in Boston" and worse. In 1929, for example, the noted Harvard scholar F. O. Matthiesen rallied to the side of the proprietor of the Dunster Bookshop (then on the street of that name) when he was fined $800 and sentenced to four months in jail for selling a copy of *Lady Chatterley's Lover*—an offense characteristic of that bookshop. Lincoln Kirstein, a student then at Harvard, would write years later that the shop was to him a key part of Harvard Square in the 1920s, even "a predication of Bloomsbury." Later, moved to Mount Auburn, it continued to thrive. The lengths booksellers would go to in order to fund such controversial activities are also clear in a recollection of Francis Russell's also involving *Lady Chatterley's Lover*, this time at the Kelmscott, another long gone Harvard Square bookshop. Located like the Grollier, in Russell's words, "on one of the narrow side streets off Harvard Square," booklined and defiantly decorated with Picasso and Braque reproductions, the Kelmscott, Russell discovered, cheerfully financed itself through the sale of hard core pornography; the proprietor's stock was secreted away in the back of the shop's roll-top desk, which could be swung away from the wall to disclose its illicit treasure.

Though Dunster and Kelmscott both passed away long ago, the Grollier survives—not only the most long lived, but atmospherically all that one might wish, and as much architecture, really, as décor, because of the heavy stone Beaux-Arts style of its building, and above all the gloriously flamboyant fin-de-siecle ironwork lantern at its entrance, a lantern of enormous presence—a lantern very much of Gertrude Stein's Paris or James Joyce's Dublin. Appropriately. The Grollier itself was reputedly the first bookstore in Harvard Square (which may mean in the United States) to sell both the work of Stein and Joyce; certainly in 1934 it was the first to offer *Ulysses* for sale. Similarly, in the 1950s only at Grollier could a Harvard student find Allan Ginsberg's *Howl*. For Plympton Street in the '50s participated in the poetic foment of Eliot and company with much more vigor than it urged them on in the 1920s. ("Must all successful rebels grow/From toreador to Sacred Cow?" wrote Peter Viereck in 1952; "Aging eagles know/That 1912 was long ago/ Today the women come and go/ Talking of T. S. Eliot.") And *Advocate* poets like John O'Hara and John Ashbery are only the best known today of many writers who hung out at the Grollier, sometimes before their books made them celebrities. And more often, of course, when they didn't. (The short list would include Delmore Schwartz, John Ashbery, Robert Bly, John O'Hara, and, of course, Aiken, when he wasn't at work upstairs.) Edward Gorey, the writer-illustrator, creator of a world, Edmund Wilson thought, "equally amusing and somber, nostalgic and claustrophobic, at the same time poetic and 'poisoned,'" also was well known at the Grollier. He roomed with Frank O'Hara then, adopting a persona that included wearing capes and innumerable rings. Very Plympton Street.

So was another of its denizens in the late 1940s and thereafter, whose first book of poems was on sale at the Grollier before she graduated, Adrienne Rich. It was still the era when Rich, because she was a woman, was not allowed access to the poetry room in Harvard's Lamont Library (see Walk Five) and had to have recourse to a secret staircase to use it. (This according to Peter Davison, to whom another poet, W. S. Merwin wrote: "People met at the Grollier Book Store.... [Adrienne] was the person to tell me that I could deduct typewriters and things, as a business [expense].")

39. Harvard Crimson Building (24 Plympton Street)

Jardine, Hill & Murdoch, 1915

Scribble, scribble, scribble. It never stops on Plympton Street, least of all next door to the Grollier at the Harvard *Crimson*. Unlike the *Lampoon* or the *Advocate*, however, the *Crimson* struck out, architecturally. Founded in 1873 as the *Magenta* (it adopted its present name three years later when Harvard's teams adopted Crimson), the *Crimson* takes itself very seriously. But not architecturally. Truth to tell, however—never mind Ben Bradlee, the publisher who directed the *Washington Post*'s Watergate coverage, and star reporter David Halberstam, both *Crimson* old boys—Harvard has, indeed, produced (despite *no*, repeat *no*, school of journalism) just a few of the twentieth-century's preeminent newspapermen. Theodore White comes to mind, Joseph Alsop, and, of course, Walter Lippmann, who is said to have failed the *Crimson*'s famously rigorous entrance competition. (Three times.) But despite the *Crimson*'s worthy journalistic repute (its editors have included Franklin Roosevelt, John F. Kennedy, and David Rockefeller), its muse failed in 1915 when its present building was commissioned. Stolid, institutional, and boring, it is all the things the *Crimson* isn't.

Harvard Crimson Building

40. A. D. Clubhouse (corner of Plympton Street and 1268-1278 Massachusetts Avenue)

Cummings & Parker, 1899

The architecture of friendship? More likely of bull must have been the response of more than one wit when this clubhouse opened, with its huge and robustly carved sculptural relief of that animal sporting itself above the entrance on Plympton Street. Of course the classical pagan pomp of the A. D.'s building lends itself to protuberant bulls of hearty mien (head lowered, naturally, because charging), much more than does the innately delicate neo-Georgian style of the Mount Auburn Street clubhouses. Still the A.D., the name of which derives from that of a once fleet college boat of long ago and far away, Hai-Dee, was convivial from the beginning. How convivial, and how important, historically, to Harvard, is clear, for example, in Mark Gelfand's biography of Ralph Lowell of the Class of 1912: The A.D., wrote Gelfand, "was the club of [Lowell's] father, his grandfather, and his brother Jack. The A. D.'s building . . . with its pool table, smoking room, and dining and bar services, would be the center of Ralph's active social life during his last two years of college." Nor did it end there. Ten, twenty, thirty and more years later, continued Gelfand, it was only at such places (at annual alumni dinners) that "Proper Bostonians usually [as adults] cast off their inhibitions." To which it is only necessary to add that so enormous were Ralph Lowell's services to Harvard that the university in 1952 gave him a much coveted honorary degree, 231 years after the first Lowell had been

A. D. Club bull

given a Harvard degree in 1721. Harvard has reaped untold and not only architectural rewards from such clubmen as Lowell, whose dedication to Harvard was fueled above all by club associations. (Nor is this only a tale of hoary old Brahmins. Microsoft founder Bill Gates was a member of the first club touched on here, the Fox.) But those associations have also run the gamut from very good to very bad. A part of the literary life of Plympton Street after all, the A. D.'s roster also included Harry Crosby, the Boston Brahmin editor in post-World War I Paris of the important avant-garde journal, *Transitions*, and owner of the Black Sun Press. As such Crosby published important work of James Joyce and D. H. Lawrence. On the other hand, Crosby, who led a pretty dissolute existence at Harvard in the 1920s—wild parties and high speed chases in Stutz roundabouts—opens a window for us as well onto the darker side of the heyday of Harvard's social clubs. Crosby's proper Boston father (according to his son's biographer) never tired of reminding Harry that the whole "point of his college enterprise was election to the A.D." In fact, once that was achieved, he let his son quit Harvard. Between Ralph Lowell and Harry Crosby is a wide gulf.

41. Delphic (Gas) Clubhouse (9 Linden Street)

James Purdom, 1902

The second of the three historic clubhouses that adorn the Massachusetts Avenue blocks that front on Harvard Yard, the Delphic—which stands on Linden Street just beside the corner building—is in many ways the most storied of them all, for despite its dark red brick Georgian reticence it too is the house that Morgan built, and not the lesser one. That's J. Pierpont Morgan, the moving spirit, historically, of the Delphic. Although it is nowhere absolutely documented that Morgan was one of the five undergraduates (all of whom "had not 'made' a club," according to Morison, and each of whom "wanted one badly") who in 1885 organized the Delphic's beginnings, certainly its "success was assured," in Morison's words, when Morgan became known as a member. And the depth of his loyalty to the Delphic—in which even in the days of his greatest fame he was heavily invested, serving as Graduate President of the Board of Managers and Treasurer (a post he also held as an undergraduate)—is strong testimony not only to how attached Morgan became to the Delphic but to his ill feeling over his rejection (so goes the Delphic's oral history) by the Porcellian Club. And this despite the problematic nature of the new club, made clear by its nickname, the "Gas House." It was actually one of the first buildings in the area to be lighted entirely by electricity, which members were apt to flaunt dramatically on dark Cambridge evenings when their clubhouse would suddenly "switch on" and blaze up. Joel Porte explains: "So novel and striking a method of illumination did not

Delphic Club (Claverly Hall in background)

pass unnoticed, and inspired Harvard wits, resorting to the classically approved principle of *lucus a non lucendo*, soon dubbed Delta Phi the 'Gas House'—quite simply because there was a glaring lack of gas." Brightness from the not very bright? It was a sharp wit, and its pointedness certainly documents the ridicule visited upon Morgan and his friends. Moreover, the fact that the Delphic invested in the latest dazzling technology of the day, shows more than spirit; electricity become a telling rejoinder to rejection, in which one surely sees Morgan's hand—and deep pockets. It is not surprising, therefore, that such a cohort, as Porte also writes, found its clubhouse "more substantially illuminated in a few years by the frequent presence of one of its first honorary [i.e., graduate] members, a brilliant and elegant young instructor in philosophy...George Santayana." Writing eloquently of same-sex association in those days, Porte continues:

> Here Santayana was able to enjoy convivial dinners surrounded by the gifted young men whose sprightly conversation evidently pleased him much more than that of his colleagues. And here at the "Gas House," moreover, Santayana was to form friendships of lasting importance: [including]...with Warwick Potter, the "WP" of [Santayana's] sonnets, whose premature death in 1893 contributed substantially to the "metanoia" [of] Santayana.

A souvenir of those heady days at the Delphic is the dedicatory poem the philosopher wrote for the inaugural dinner of the present clubhouse in 1902, partly addressed to the Delphic's architect, James Purdom. Santayana reminds him that his dreams and visions "would be but vistas in thy airy head/Were fleshly Morgans not in generous mood/Nor Forbes' infinite in multitude." Parts of the poem strike a little deeper: "Half the soul clutches what the world can give," the philosopher pines, "and remains where youth and beauty live."

42. Porcellian Clubhouse (1320–1324 Massachusetts Avenue) *W. Y. Peters, 1890*

Patrician (or is it Puritan) reserve, of the sort this facade exhibits, does not come amiss at the climax of this peregrination of Harvard's Victorian clubland. The architecture of friendship, rather extroverted on Mount Auburn Street was seen here by contrast as more introverted. And more intense. Historically, what Victorian club life was all about at Harvard is nowhere better documented than at the "Porc." Two case studies. First, Oliver Wendell Holmes, in later life a justice of the U. S. Supreme Court, for whom club life was not just the most important aspect of his years at Harvard, but really the chief way this considerable figure in the history of the period arrived at self-definition as a man. Courage, courtesy and good blood lines were, in his mind, the values the club celebrated; flawed values one might say today, having in mind the last particularly; but still we like well enough the ends Holmes thought they worked toward—not unrelated either to the Porcellian's architecture. These values, he thought, "restrained … needless display" and encouraged "dignity and weight." The Porcellian's facade exactly! A second case, Theodore Roosevelt, may seem at first glance more superficial: "there is a billiard table, magnificent library, punch room, etc.," "TR" wrote home, but added "my best friends are in it." There was a distinctly sybaritic air about it all; soon enough young Roosevelt was enjoying partridge suppers served by liveried workers. He also kept his own horse in Cambridge. Now it only fair to add that Roosevelt also taught Sunday School—in the poorest

Porcellian Clubhouse, with Leavitt & Pierce at left

section of Cambridge—while he was an undergraduate. But there is no doubt he set the pace on Harvard's Gold Coast. Nor that the future president's first lasting male friendship outside his family, and one with important political consequences, was with Henry Cabot Lodge—a fellow Porcellian man.

If this most famous of Harvard's final clubs casts the architecture of friendship in boldest relief, so too it sheds the strongest light on what was also the architecture of exclusion, the expression of a system established to thrive on what John Updike, writing of his own Harvard club life, called "the delicious immensity of the excluded." Others saw something else entirely, including one young man, President Kennedy's father, Joe Sr., who long before he became the controversial and problematic figure of his later years, found himself one evening in 1910, in Doris Kearns Goodwin's words, standing across the street from this elegant facade, and thinking very long thoughts; "drawn like a moth to the lighted windows above, he tried to imagine what it was like inside." Writes Goodwin: "Not a single one of his Catholic friends had been asked to join a final club. . . . It was a moment of high emotion, a moment he would remember all his life. . . . While his great common sense precluded . . . rebellion or withdrawal, Harvard had . . . ripped something out of him that night; never again would he experience loyalty to any institution. . . . In the place of that loyalty, resentment had crystallized out hard as rock; whether he knew it or not his siege against the world had already begun." That, of course, is the conclusion of his biographer. Kennedy was not a writer.

But Walter Lippmann, a Jewish classmate of Kennedy's, was. His article on Harvard in *The New Republic* in 1916 (an article Lippmann's biographer, Robert Steel, frankly calls Lippmann's "revenge") documents very well that just as the included (like Ralph Lowell), never forgot, so too the excluded didn't either. Lippman, in fact, did more than write about it and before he left Harvard, Steel recounts: "buoyed by the liberal spirit of their studies, a group of social rejects . . . began to act instead like sophisticated secessionists. They were led by Walter Lippmann. . . . Barred from the clubs by anti-Semitism, the Harvard . . . rebels formed a Socialist Club, which became the flagship chapter of the Intercollegiate Socialist Society. . . . In 1912, while one contingent from Harvard motored out to a bitter textile workers' strike in Lawrence, Massachusetts, to serve in the state militia . . . the socialists organized a demonstration to support the strikers." John Reed, whose anarchist-thriller writings were touched on in Walk One, was also involved in this group. And when he graduated it was, according to Robert Rosenstone, to his version of "an annex of Harvard Yard"—New York's Greenwich Village, the influence of which in the late 1910s and 1920s, particularly in the renaissance of American drama, was fueled immeasurably by the Class of 1910 in association with Eugene O'Neill. That class's advanced cohort included in addition to Reed and Lippmann, Edward Eyre

Hunt (founder of the Harvard Dramatic Club), Robert Edward Jones (founder with Reed of the Provincetown Players), drama critic Heywood Broun, and poets T. S. Eliot and Alan Seger. And in the Village "even as rebels, heralds of a new dawn," Reed and his friends had, however, "the confidence and authority of their old school ties. As Harvard has always wielded authority in New York, a secret cell of Boston influence, so they tended to position themselves nicely. . . . While they broke with Harvard power and privilege, they nonetheless arrived in New York fully costumed and prepared . . . leaders of the new age." Conversely, clubland could trouble even patricians. FDR, as has been noted, made the Fly and made much of it. But perhaps because cousin Teddy had been a "Porc" man, young Franklin called his exclusion by the Porcellian the "biggest disappointment of his life," a rejection as Goodwin points out with just a few consequences for the ruling classes of his day when he became president during the Great Depression.

Of course, privilege may mean many things. In the narrowest sense: Joe Kennedy's son, John, the future U. S. president, would be elected to the Spee. More to the point here, in the larger sense we are concerned with, it is, historically, one of the duties of privilege, however much it may deaden the imagination of some or the critical self-awareness of others, that it exemplify a high standard of taste. And in this respect, the architecture of Harvard's Victorian clubland does not disappoint. Especially does W. Y. Peters not disappoint. The Porcellian's architect, who after Harvard studied at the Atelier Guadet in Paris and in Boston under Sturgis and Brigham, designed a clubhouse the brown brick facade of which is not only restrained, it is refined—very spare and elegant. Peters, himself a Porcellian man, whose government work in Washington (for which he became best known) is not exceptional, here rose to the occasion superbly, even to the ground floor shopfront of J. August's clothing store. Not the least gift of clubland to Harvard Square, it is carefully maintained to this day.

43. The Fairfax and Leavitt & Pierce

The Fairfax (1300–1316 Massachusetts Avenue) *1869–85*
Gnomon Copy (1304 Massachusetts Avenue) *Coolidge & Carlson, 1907*
Leavitt & Pierce (1316 Massachusetts Avenue) *1883*

Just opposite Harvard Yard, in an enormous dormitory complex called the Fairfax—built at Nos. 1300–1316 Massachusetts Avenue in 1869–86 (next to the Porcellian Clubhouse today)—are two more shopfronts comparable in age to J. August's that are unique in the Boston region and would be unusual anywhere. The first is Gnomon Copy, an Art Nouveau front so extraordinary it is protected by deed covenants that insure, were it ever to

McKean Gate

be threatened, that the front would be given to Boston's Museum of Fine Arts. The second is in rather a different way hardly less important, for Leavitt & Pierce, its shopfront designed in 1883, is today the oldest shop in Harvard Square in its original location. Its front is by far the most historic in the area. Indeed, it is not every shop whose history has been recounted (and under "Education") in *Time Magazine*, but in the issue of August 4, 1958, that fate befell Leavitt & Pierce, when a 75th anniversary anthology was published. This historic and fragrant tobacconist of old still today is decorated with team pictures and other Harvardiana—certainly a masculine décor if not architecture—that offer a unique window into the Harvard College of a century and more ago. Perhaps Paul Hollister, Class of 1913, put it best when he wrote that Leavitt was once "Harvard's most universal and democratic club."

44. Porcellian Clubhouse Gate, New Yard

McKim, Mead and White, 1901

This grandiose architectural link between the Gold Coast and Harvard Yard, across the street from the Porcellian Clubhouse, memorializes its founder, Joseph McKean. (Notice the prominent boar's head above.) It points as well to a more personal architectural link between mid-nineteenth-century club-land and the college yard: the life and work of Henry Hobson Richardson, who graduated from Harvard in 1857, and whose disciples and draftsmen (McKim, Mead and White) this gate's designers were. A Porcellian member himself, in what Phillips Brooks called Richardson's student "days of care-lessness and plenty" at Harvard, young Henry had been very much the svelte dandy. At that time, in the 1850s, he was chiefly interested in music, when, that is, he was not being penalized for missing chapel or cutting classes or initiating disturbances in the Yard. Not perhaps what one expects of the Greatest American Architect of the nineteenth century. But that was later, after Richardson—a Southerner who after Harvard passed the Civil War in postgraduate study in Paris—returned not to the South, but to the triumphant North to practice architecture. Indeed, at the end of the nine-teenth century, he would create a new Harvard chapter in that field that would equal Bulfinch's own at the century's start. So does the Porcellian Gate announce the centerpiece of Victorian Harvard, the New Yard.

BOSSUET

Nineteenth- and Twentieth-Century Harvard and the Graduate School of Arts and Sciences

As the architecture of Harvard's Gold Coast documents so well, late nineteenth-century alumni apt to be well known to us today—Oliver Wendell Holmes, for example, or J. Pierpont Morgan or William Randolph Hearst—whether a forthcoming president such as Theodore Roosevelt, or a budding architect like Henry Hobson Richardson—tended to find their most important experience of Harvard south of the Yard, because they were usually a part of the elite ten or twenty percent of the College then who were clubmen. But the role of the Old Yard remained important to the life of the Harvard community throughout the Victorian period. So much so that, beginning in the mid-nineteenth century and culminating at the same time the Gold Coast was being developed at century's end, there came into being right next to the Old Yard a more modern one. Once through the Porcellian Gate this is immediately evident; to the gate's right Boylston Hall—bold granite Victorian knowing nothing of delicate eighteenth-century brick—forcefully announces what came to be called the New Yard. It was, however, a long time coming, its development as halting as the results were architecturally puzzling.

Of Harvard's history generally after Kirkland in the mid-nineteenth century there is little to tell. His successor, Josiah Quincy, upheld the liberal tradition, defending Professor Henry Ware, for example, president of Cambridge's Anti-Slavery Society, in an era when abolitionist sentiment was distinctly a minority view. Quincy also mounted a vigorous overall defense of academic freedom, writing in his 1840 Harvard history of "learning as an independent interest of the community," one that should have "no precarious dependence for existence on subservience to particular views in politics or religion." His defense of that tradition was so striking Samuel Eliot Morison thought it the most fundamental strength that undergirded and ultimately explained Harvard's eventual preeminence in American education by century's end. Quincy, no doubt about it, was gifted. Before becoming Harvard's president, he had shown himself to be a reforming mayor of Boston—"an unlikely populist," in Matthew Crocker's words; Quincy's "rebellion against the reigning Federalist party [in the early 1820s] not only altered the political landscape of Boston but also signaled the advent of the Jacksonian Age." As Harvard's leader, however, though Quincy did well enough, perhaps, in what might be called the university's "external" affairs—of no little importance admittedly in an era when Harvard was still formally linked to the Great and General Court of Massachusetts, which did not abdicate its role in university governance until 1865. In the university's internal affairs he was much less successful. Jackson's controversial visitation to Harvard in 1833, as it turned out, heralded student disturbances in the Yard the next year. Indeed, all Quincy's political skills, and even his brave declarations about professorial freedom (a principle not unrelated to the ancient custom of collegiate independence, which implies—does it not?—a certain student independence) seemed to collapse upon themselves in the president's utter ineptitude in dealing with undergraduates who approached him in any other than the most subservient guise. On this central aspect of college life he was, fatally for his presidency, at a complete loss.

Still more so, if that was possible, was his successor. It is true that Edward Everett, who succeeded to the presidency in 1846, has also been hailed for the way—this time in racial matters—he too defended Harvard's liberal tradition. According to Everett's biographer, P. R. Frothingham, when it was widely believed that a young African American boy, Beverly Williams, who had tutored Everett's son and was anxious to attend Harvard, would nevertheless not be allowed to enter whether or not he passed the entrance examinations, Everett, in his biographer's words, stoutly declared: "If this boy passes the examinations, he will be admitted; and if the white students choose to withdraw, all the income of the college will be devoted to his education." A ringing declaration indeed. Alas, university archivist Harley Holden, who has made a study of the matter, reports that no such statement by Everett can be verified. Still, letters of Everett that are extant do verify that he did support the admission of Williams vigorously. There is even a report (in Jonathan Messerli's *Horace Mann*) that "he resigned from the presidency of Harvard in protest against the Harvard Corporation, which had refused to admit a qualified black applicant." It was not until 1865 that blacks were allowed to proceed to graduation. However, if Emerson among others is to be believed, Everett was a better man and better scholar than leader. He was, in fact, so bad a president he scarcely stayed the course at all, resigning the office after three years; the first of many such disappointments.

So lackluster was the subsequent parade of presidents even the little good they did seemed almost to melt away before it was done. For instance, in an effort to move forward in the sciences, Harvard established in 1847 the Lawrence Scientific School on the model of the other graduate schools of Medicine, Law, and Divinity. Yet for a variety of reasons, mostly because donor, faculty, and administration worked steadily at cross purposes to each other in the matter, the Scientific School, though the idea was timely, seemed never to wax, but always to be waning; certainly it never stood any chance at all after the founding, fifteen years later, of the Massachusetts Institute of Technology in the Back Bay. Indeed, it was the case, wrote Morison, that by the 1860s, "Harvard College was hidebound, the Harvard Law School senescent, the Medical School ineffective, the Lawrence Scientific School the resort of shirks and stragglers. . . . The foundation," Morison concluded, "for a great university was there;" but another twenty years of the same inertia, he argued, would have reduced venerable Harvard to an institution "merely quaint."

No wonder the development of the New Yard was halting in its initial stages. Harvard itself languished. Not only were the New Yard's first landmarks slow to appear, but it hardly surprises that the first two were massive and costly failures; the earliest, a new library of 1838, Gore Hall; the second, built in 1858, Appleton Chapel; the former Gothic in style—a singularly awkward and clumsy attempt to recall the glories of King's College, Cambridge—and the latter, of a kind of Romanesque Classicism, even less felicitous. Though both were large and elaborate stone buildings meant to last ages, both were eventually torn down. Their significance, really, was their failure. And the day was only really saved in the long run by the skill with which Bulfinch and Kirkland, back in the early 1800s, had sited University Hall in the first place, upon which masterstroke later twentieth-century planners could build. Theirs is the credit that today, if one declines Boylston's invitation to bear right just inside the Porcellian Gate into the New Yard, and instead bears left towards Wadsworth House and the Old Yard, only moving into the New Yard from the midst of the old one at some later point, theirs is the credit that one is apt to feel that the two precincts have cohered forever.

It is by no means clear that was the goal when the development of what is now the New Yard was begun, so profound was the attachment to what we now call the Old Yard, the seventeenth- and eighteenth-century Old Yard, as we call it now. For Harvard continued to depend in some fundamental, almost spiritual way, on the by then well-worn antiquity of the Old Yard, and what it had come to stand for, with all its memories of idealist Puritans and royal governors and revolutionary speeches and Emersonian visions. Harvard's title deeds were enshrined there, as somehow they seem still. Even though its physical plant was, in fact, dating alarmingly (no Yard dormitory before the Civil War had even basement plumbing), the Old Yard, more and more an icon, was never meant in any sense to be superseded by the new one. Or so, I suspect, people told themselves. Change in New England is always fraught, even change manifestly for the better (as this one must seem to us now, with the benefit of historical hindsight). And visionaries are often in short supply; witness Harvard's uninspiring mid-century leaders. But one prophet there was at mid-century: Emerson. And from our perspective today, in order to catch hold of some of the advanced thought of this time, with which the New Yard ultimately would be related, we cannot do better than to revisit the writings of Harvard's then most famous graduate. I have in mind those remarks of Emerson where, notwithstanding the shortcomings he found in his time of his alma mater, he seemed more than sanguine about Harvard, after all, holding its position well enough in mid-nineteenth-century America. Sean O'Connell has perhaps best caught the discourse I have reference to when he writes:

Emerson proudly proclaimed that 'Boston commands the attention as the town which was appointed in the destiny of nations to lead the civilization of North America'... No one shone more brightly than Emerson...[but] Henry Thoreau followed his Concord neighbor to Cambridge... [where] Harvard nurtured the seedcorn of its nineteenth-century greatness.... Beginning around 1820 the school served as a laboratory for America's most creative intellects.... The sage of Concord, invited to address the Phi Beta Kappa exercises at his alma mater, [rose] to the occasion memorably with 'The American Scholar', his homeland's intellectual declaration of independence.... Boston provided in the first half of the nineteenth century a worthy setting for such jabs at the status quo.

What O'Connell is detailing, really, is a scenario in two acts. President Kirkland's Boston crown jewel in the first half of the nineteenth century, for all its failure of nerve in the matter of university curricular reform, had, all things considered, not only led very effectively the first stage of Boston's late eighteenth- and early to mid-nineteenth-century institutional growth (the American Academy of Arts and Sciences, the Boston Athenaeum, the Massachusetts Historical Society, the Perkins Institute for the Blind, the Massachusetts General Hospital, and the Boston Public Library), but would sufficiently nurture its seedcorn so as to achieve the much greater burst of energy at century's end—the Harvard (after 1870) of Charles W. Eliot, finally a full fledged university, which would so brilliantly cultivate and reap the harvest. This is the context of the New Yard's halting struggle to come into being: what in more strictly architectural terms Lewis Mumford meant when he pointed out that "it is not by accident that Harvard's rejuvenation in science and scholarship under Charles Eliot coincided with the constructive enterprises of the Back Bay in the generation between 1870 and 1900." Certainly Commonwealth Avenue, Back Bay's centerpiece, the first of the grandest boulevards in America, has much more in common with the New Yard than with the Old Yard, which would find its city center companion in Bulfinch's Beacon Hill. And was it surprising that the New Yard as it finally developed would be hardly less grandiose architecturally than Commonwealth Avenue, or of the many new Boston area institutions of the fifty years between 1870 and 1920? Boston's Museum of Fine Arts, the Massachusetts Institute of Technology, Boston Symphony Hall, the Peter Bent Brigham or Children's Hospitals, and so on, all reflected each other's gathering pomp and purposes—late-nineteenth- or very early twentieth-century institutions with close affiliations to Harvard, which within itself, moreover, would yield university institutions of comparable stature like Harvard's Medical, Law and Business Schools, the architecture of which (see

Walks 10, 8, and 11 respectively) was every bit as grandiose as that, finally, of the New Yard. Notice that John Singer Sargent, probably then the greatest painter in the grand manner, would paint murals in the 1890–1925 period (ranging from glorious to banal; alas, Harvard was at the losing end, artistically, of that continuum) in no less than three of Boston's late nineteenth-century imperial landmarks, the Boston Public Library, the Museum of Fine Arts, and the Widener Library that Harvard was to build in the New Yard. On every side, indeed, the stakes would rise dramatically as all these new institutions, within and without Harvard, bid for world rank—as Boston, in Howard Mumford Jones' and Bessie Zaban Jones' words, came increasingly to be seen by 1900 in the intellectual and academic sense as "the cultural capital of the United States." The New Yard, when finally it was achieved, stood not for Harvard languishing, but for Harvard triumphant. Which is to say after Eliot's ascent to the presidency in 1869.

The equal as a doer, if the distinction is admitted, of Emerson as a thinker, Charles William Eliot was the practical visionary Harvard needed. The son of a notable Mayor of Boston and U. S. congressman, though he had had no easy time of it at Harvard, either as student or teacher (his gifts those of neither), Eliot was a man, to say the least, of insistent conviction. He was dynamic, liberal (a disciple, indeed, of Emerson), an unrepentant individualist. There was in Eliot, it would seem, very little humor, not even very much tact. And no charm. But much character. He was as much a puritan in his sense of work and dedication as he was a progressive in his

Widener Library

thought and belief. And for all that he could be tiresome, as only an Olympian (or a saint) may be, he was a born fighter, notable for tenacity. He needed to be, for Eliot was what James McGregor Burns has called a "transformational leader."

Not very successful until his presidency, he had been passed over for the chair he sought at Harvard, and left soon thereafter (to take up a post at M.I.T.). Even after his election as president he was never very popular. Indeed, he was not Harvard's first choice, and one only elected because the front runner, Charles Francis Adams, Henry's brother, declined, and the only alternative was a minister. (In Donald Fleming's apt phrase, Eliot became Harvard's president chiefly because his adversaries "preferred a bad scientist to a good clergyman.") Moreover, as president, Eliot "was disliked by the patricians, partly because of his policy of making Harvard democratic, and he was unpopular with the masses, partly because he was a natural aristocrat. . . . He always spoke out. . . . His stern and lofty bearing set him apart from his own faculty and students. He sat alone in Appleton Chapel every morning and alone he strode across the Yard." In fact, it would seem many were afraid of Eliot. And with good reason. Certainly he turned Harvard upside down, and in its wake American education itself. Ever since the time of Periclean Athens the definition of an educated person had been based on some constellation of requirements; vary though they might and change dramatically as they did through the centuries, always *certain* things had to be known to be educated. This Eliot utterly repudiated. He began by sweeping away the classical curriculum; no less than eight college presidents, led by Yale's, unsuccessfully entreated the Board of Overseers to challenge Eliot so that Harvard not drop Greek as a required subject. Greek! Eliot vanquished more than that. In not very many years the *only* requirements left for a Harvard A. B. were English composition and modern language.

Freedom was the new president's primary thesis. Eliot's famously elective curriculum no less than his more diverse student body, as he saw it, was the simple application of democracy to education. And he was in these convictions utterly ruthless. An unabashed elitist, he was also a believer, not in inherited privilege, but in meritocracy. Challenged about the effect of his revolution at Harvard on the average student particularly, Eliot was indifferent: "in vain was the dunce Hellenized," he replied, "in vain the drone Latinized." Insisting that it really didn't "make much difference what these unawakened minds dawdle with," his only concern was for "an elite of intellect and character recruited from all levels of society but smoothed and polished," in Fleming's words, "by the distinctively Harvard infusion of young aristocrats that had been recurring at Harvard for a century or more." Eliot was resolute that "the community does not owe superior education to all children, but only to the *elite*." He added, however: "the process of preparing to enter college under the difficulty which poverty entails is just such a test of worthiness," and he once declared forthrightly, "the more Italian immigrants who come to the U.S. the better." He was also the mentor of Harvard's leading Jew—Louis Brandeis (see Walk 8), who he invited to teach at Harvard. Eliot also supported Brandeis' nomination to the U.S. Supreme Court.

Eliot's idea of freedom, moreover, encompassed not just students, but faculty. On the principle that only two kinds of people make good teachers—"young men and men who never grow old" and that students should choose *professors*, not courses, Eliot freed up the faculty as much as the student body; under Eliot they needed to lecture only in their field, they had much more time for their own scholarship. And though he was no feminist—(he wondered aloud more than once about "woman's role")—Eliot nonetheless worked assiduously to help Elizabeth Cary Agassiz and company with the establishment in 1879 of the so-called "Harvard Annex," out of which in Eliot's reign developed Radcliffe College (see Walk 9), in some sense, after all, in response to Eliot's own outstanding vision of the importance and role of education. Certainly Eliot's educational philosophy almost universally came to be seen as exhilarating. Thomas W. Lamont, Class of 1892, for example, cited the "sense of freedom" of those days: it was the "vast stores of learning and thought" newly available to him as a student on every side that he never forgot. Indeed, in 1886, even compulsory chapel was abolished. What the Mathers might have thought does not bear thinking. Under Eliot, as Fleming put it, even "God became an elective at Harvard."

Still, the New Yard did not keep pace with the new Harvard, straining toward new stature. The Old Yard was still prized. In fact, the overall "will to power," if you will, of Eliot's Harvard, was cleverly if not exactly deliberately softened and over the long run—right into the twentieth century—made perhaps less threatening than many at first must have found it, precisely because of the successful fusion of the New Yard (whose fate was to be so grandiose) with the historic, more human-scaled Old Yard. One thinks of Henry James' discomfiture at the bustling, booming, immigrant filled metropolis of the 1890s and 1900s encroaching on old Beacon Hill (where, in fact, he found that his youthful home had been torn down). What happened to Bulfinch's Beacon Hill did not happen, however, to Bulfinch's Old Yard. Certainly nothing of eighteenth-century origin in the Yard was destroyed. At most a few alterations occurred. And as time went on, and the trees grew taller and fuller (notwithstanding the much lamented demise of the Yard elms at the turn of the twentieth century) the two yards, as, indeed, they came to be seen more and more as one, found almost iconic focus on the oldest and most historic halls—in the Old Yard.

It was an image which may be said to have been most tellingly accomplished by the man who came to be by the twentieth century arguably the poet of the Yard, David McCord. Artists like engraver Thomas Nason and photographer Samuel Chamberlain helped. (Chamberlain's *Fair Harvard* may be the most distinguished photographic essay on Harvard of the twentieth century). Perhaps because McCord's daily experience so completely encompassed both new and old (he of the mid-twentieth century, in his early eighteenth-century Wadsworth House study, his view that of late-nineteenth-century Gray's Hall), McCord took the longest possible view, growing rhapsodic, for instance, over the trees that "scarcely tremble for a blizzard . . . howling the bitter north into the chimney pots of Gray's and Matthew." He made the Yard sound like a Colonial village, which, of course, in some sense it still is even today! With an eye no architectural historian would disdain, nor any naturalist either, McCord reported regularly to alumni (for he was fundraiser as well as poet, and good at both), on the Yard's daily life, not excluding either flora or fauna! One day, coming home on a winter night, he found himself wondering about "the light in Hollis [Hall that] burns mysteriously from dark to dawn." His readers wondered too. He had a way of melding bricks and chimney pots and trees and landscape and even huge classical columns too, into a mid-twentieth-century perspective that defined the feel of Harvard Yard: "Leaves raked and gathered . . . the last of ivy leaf burned red and ruined on so many ancient walls; the smoke of student fires rising thinly from old brick chimneys; a clear cut of November blue to the deepening sky; a jug of cider sighted on an isolated window ledge; elm and oak and bush gone bare; sparrows and starlings in forage at the south side of Grays . . . the long eternal business of life and learning steadied to the pulse of youthful blood." Then, too, there was his ear, as well as his eye; his historian's ear (his poet's ear too), for McCord missed very little, and, certainly not the voices:

> Late at night in Wadsworth House. . . . Emerson, of course, spoke of Cambridge at any time as being full of ghosts—but he failed to mention the voices. . . . Thoreau comes in well on warm spring nights, about the time when the snapping turtle begins to be restless out toward Walden. ("Surely, men love darkness rather than light.") But the voice for summer's end is the querying voice of Henry Adams. He speaks, you will remember, in the third person.
>
> Far back in childhood, among its earliest memories, Henry Adams could recall his first visit to Harvard College. He must have been nine years old when on one of the singularly gloomy winter afternoons . . . his mother drove him out to visit his aunt, Mrs. Everett. Edward Everett was then President of the college and lived in the old President's House on Harvard Square. The boy remembered the drawing-room, on the left of the hall door, in which Mrs. Everett received them. He remembered a marble greyhound in the corner. The house had an air of colonial self-respect that impressed even a nine-year-old child.

Many years later in 1870, when he was hired as a professor—Henry Adams would become a great luminary of Eliot's Harvard—young Adams, who would always remember so much, also remembered old Wadsworth House. And after his interview with the president, Adams walked across the Yard and in turn hired rooms for himself in the old house, by then a sort of college lodging house. And here he spent much of his Boston decade. Mostly this was all right. (Witness Henry James to Adams, January 13, 1877: "Your picture of Boston with its gorgeous Turner and its frescoed churches [a reference to Trinity Church in the Back Bay] is really glowing, and I feel like hurrying home, to become the Vasari of such a Florence, where didn't I advise you to remain and become the Machiavelli.") However, nothing seemed able to reconcile either man to Puritan shortcomings. Wrote Adams later, not just of academia: "Harvard College remained a tie, but a tie a little stronger than Beacon Street [the realm of society], and not so strong as State Street [the financial realm]." Indeed, he complained pointedly of Harvard particularly no less than of Boston generally that "Boston is well up in all things European, but it is no place for American news." Still, he courted and married his wife, Clover, while on the Harvard faculty. He even bought a proper town house in the Back Bay, on Marlborough Street. But he still kept his rooms in Wadsworth for work, of which there was always enough after he became editor-in-chief of the *North American Review*.

As Adams lived and worked in Wadsworth House, so he taught in another of the eighteenth-century buildings of the Old Yard, Massachusetts, where the reader will recall the story already told here in Walk One how during an examination in Adams' course, one of his students found irresistible the urge to compare Henry Adams with the full-length portrait of the wall of his grandfather, U. S. President John Quincy Adams. Henry himself, the undergraduate thought, was "robust and virile . . . original, unexpected, and even explosive. . . . His method of attack was direct, not subtle. . . . [He had] a genius for starting men to think. . . . He was so stimulating . . . that he conveyed to one unconsciously the true concept of education as the power to think in a subject. That was something of a miracle. . . ." Adams' laugh, this student recounted, was "infectious. . . . It might often be ironical, of course, but always good humored. His manner was animated and brusque, but kindly." The course, "U. S. History, 1789–1840," is still spoken of a century and more later. Whether or not it is too much to say Adams introduced the graduate seminar of the German university to America, his was certainly a course of instruction famously diverse. Indeed, he talked the president into dividing it in two, writing that one of his leading colleagues "being a federalist and conservative" and his [Adams'] views 'tend[ing] to democracy, and radicalism, it made sense to offer *both* courses: "the clash of opinions can hardly fail to stimulate inquiry among the students." Only Henry Adams then would have been likely to make such a suggestion. And probably only at the

Houghton Library reflected in the window of Lamont Hall

Harvard of those days, where two courses were duly offered in 1877–78, would Adams' idea have had a ghost of a chance of being acted upon.

Exciting times. New visions. Yet Eliot in University Hall, Adams in Wadsworth and Massachusetts Hall—the architectural setting seems wanting, more a case of recycling the old yard than creating a new one. Indeed, many of the stars of Eliot's era seemed to thrive in the Old Yard. George Lyman Kittredge ("Kitty" to generations), Harvard's great Shakespearean scholar, became so identified with old Harvard Hall, TK recalled, "undergraduates with vivid imaginations made sketches of the old building on the point of blowing up, with zigzag electric fragments of Shakespeare shooting from windows and roof, whenever 'Kitty' held forth. To many of them for a lifetime the total meaning of Harvard Hall was 'Kitty.'"

But what of the New Yard? In fact, its development took forever. However telling an expression it would finally be of Eliot's vision, the physical expression of that vision always lagged in Eliot's time—in no small part because the president's laissez-faire attitude worked less well in architecture than in education. Laissez-faire? Consider just the three Victorian dorms of 1869–71 he added to the Old Yard: Thayer, Weld, and Matthews. Though built within three years and within sight of each other in clear relation to age-old landmarks, the three dorms are respectively Italianate, Queen Anne, and Ruskin Gothic in style. Nor was the New Yard itself, which may be said to have achieved very loosely its first state in the 1850s when Boylston Hall, Appleton Chapel, and Gore Hall stood, not at all quad-like or ordered in any sense. Instead, all three buildings seem to have been isolated landmarks in something of a sylvan country park attached to the Old Yard, more like Mount Auburn Cemetery than a college quadrangle. Nor was Eliot solely at fault. Faculty ambitions in this regard seem to have been as diverse and episodic as the president's architectural tastes were lackadaisical. For example, Louis Agassiz. The famous Swiss scientist, whose advent on the Harvard faculty helped waken Americans to the importance of science, set heart and mind on building *his own* edifice (the great Museum of Comparative Zoology, erected as it turned out just north of the Old Yard—see Walk 8). Another unhelpful luminary, Charles Eliot Norton, in a different way, though a friend and mentor to the English critic, John Ruskin, and virtually the father in America of a whole new architectural style—Ruskin Gothic—was hardly enthusiastic about Harvard's development in any style. Of most new architecture at Harvard he seemed invariably regretful. And very loudly. The holder of America's first professorship in the Fine Arts, prophet, sage, and seer of all matters architectural in America, and perhaps the most respected critic in the land, at Harvard Norton never got beyond being a naysayer. A great teacher he certainly was. But insofar as Harvard's architecture was concerned, his nagging approached the pathological. President Eliot must have shaken his head more than once. Undergraduates were more cynical. They told how Charles Eliot Norton died and went to heaven. The story is told by Ernest Samuels in his biography of Bernard Berenson. Once there, Norton grew very upset: "So overdone! So garish! So Renaissance!" Norton hated Appleton Chapel, for instance. In his defense, it was pretty awful; while Norton did not live to see it torn down, Berenson, his leading student, did, and one can only hope he enjoyed its destruction as much as would have his old mentor.

Berenson is a salutary reminder that the Yard—which became under Eliot the setting of Harvard's legendary "golden age"—was a matter of good students as well as good professors. Berenson himself seems to have been drawn to Harvard more than anything else by Norton, both of whose courses on medieval and Renaissance art he took. Norton's work on Dante particularly dazzled the brilliant young Lithuanian Jewish immigrant, "in appearance . . . a strayed fawn from arcady," his biographer recounted, known throughout the college for his alert mind, extravagant personality, and luxuriant, Pre-Raphaelite curls, to say nothing of his ardent womanizing and literary skill. His delicate and sedate gait as he crossed the Yard was well remembered. Often he read as he walked, and once, perusing Walter Pater's *Studies in the History of the Renaissance* ("to burn always with the hard, gemlike flame, to maintain this ecstasy, is success in life"), he all but ran into Norton, to whom he lent the book only to suffer the rebuke: "My boy, it won't do." Sensuality above morality? Never.

Berenson's Harvard career also discloses that all of the great influences of the nineteenth-century Yard were not professors and students—one was a pastor (who briefly converted Berenson), although he was also an alumnus and Harvard overseer: Phillips Brooks. Episcopal bishop of Massachusetts, Brooks was so great a personality and so formidable a spiritual force in Boston and at Harvard especially (he is now in the calendar of saints and heroes of the Episcopal Church) that on his death a building to his honor was erected in Harvard Yard. And, significantly, Phillips Brooks House, the center of all sorts of social service programs for the community— it was said J. F. K. modeled the Peace Corps after a Brooks House program—was built, not in the emerging New Yard, but in the northwest corner of the Old Yard. Furthermore, as opposed to the modern stone mid-nineteenth-century landmarks that had inaugurated the New Yard, Brooks House, erected in 1898, followed McKim's lead of a decade earlier at the Johnston Gate; Brooks House's architect, A. W. Longfellow, cast his design very much in the High Georgian mode of eighteenth-century Holden Chapel and Harvard Hall nearby. Indeed, Brooks was the very first building in Harvard Yard that echoed—not just in its brick exterior but in its Colonial Revival style—the old eighteenth-century halls.

Victorians for many years found little good to say of those halls. We have seen how Anthony Trollope, visiting Harvard in 1861, cited Massachusetts, Stoughton and Holworthy, for example, as "very ugly." He added that he found it "almost astonishing that buildings so ugly should have been erected." Even James Russell Lowell, native born and loyal son of Harvard that he was, would protest according to Fiske Kimball against the old halls of the Yard as "factories to which nothing could lend even dignity, let alone beauty." But to some American eyes in the late nineteenth-century these halls were beginning to be of interest, even to gather some historic charm. In *The Bostonians*, for example, Henry James, fond of the Old Yard as he was of Beacon Hill, recounts how his protagonist "admired [the old halls], and thought several of them exceedingly quaint and venerable." The "rectangular structures of old red brick," wrote James, "especially gratified his eye: . . . they were an expression of scholastic quietude, and exhaled . . . a tradition, an antiquity." And one that late Victorian dons were quick to cultivate.

The most famous in all the long history of Harvard Yard undoubtedly was an overdelicate, sharp tongued old don named Charles Townsend Copeland—"Copey"—no scholar, but a wonderful tutor in the classic Oxbridge-Harvard tradition, for whom in Walter Lippmann's words, teaching was "not the handing down of knowledge from a platform to an anonymous mass of notetakers, but . . . the personal encounter of two individuals." Copeland, for more decades than anyone can remember the resident of the corner study on the top floor of Hollis Hall overlooking Harvard Hall, held weekly open house for students, the constituents of which custom describe perhaps better than anything else the life of Harvard Yard in its golden era. One student's biographer recounted that at about ten o'clock in the evening (even today Harvard tutors keep late hours) the undergraduate invitee would climb the south stairway of Hollis Hall [to a] room overflowing with "athletes, editors of college papers, Socialists, atheists, gentlemen, social stars and ... lesser orbs," so much so he "looked for a seat and often had to settle for a small patch of floor."

> The atmosphere was congenial and warm—the walls lined from floor to ceiling with books, a dim light emanating from a coal fire and a single candle on the mantelpiece. Presiding from an armchair, Copey led a conversation in which everybody talked 'of the thing nearest his heart' and managed to sound 'alert, quick, almost brilliant'. A magic time of closeness, such an evening in the shadowy room with voices rambling through philosophic systems, recent books, travels, drinking parties and political movements made life seem rich and beautiful. . . .

In another corner of Hollis in the 1890s lived Santayana himself, who was—unusually—both an important and productive scholar and a legendary don. And as aesthete, he was able without recourse to stylistic labels to describe just the quality of the Old Yard dorms as late Victorians began to see them and that dons like himself liked: it was "the red-brick lodging, tavern and stable-yard Bohemia of Dickens or Thackeray," as Santayana put it, that drew him to the Old Yard in the 1890s. In that era, when he was not at the Gas House, Santayana was invariably to be found in his rooms in Hollis, where he rejoiced, in his own words, in his "cheerful fire, that made solitude genial," a fire, the philosopher recalled, that attracted many a friend, including one or two who loved "to sit by it with me, not rejecting in addition a drink and a little poetry."

A productive scholar as well as a dedicated don, Santayana did extend his sway into the New Yard where—finally—in 1878 was built the first of its landmarks that would endure to our own day as an undoubted masterwork, Sever Hall—the first purpose-built classroom and lecture hall building erected in Harvard Yard, the magnificent work of Richardson himself. It was, remembered one of Santayana's students, the setting of one of the philosopher's most celebrated seminars, where the undergraduate recalled "we all sat about a long table in a room in Sever Hall [discussing first] existing systems, and then ... [Santayana's] own, as it crystallized a year or so later in his book, *The Sense of Beauty*. I usually sat at his left and next or very near him, savoring the clear intelligence of his gleaming dark eyes, the rich repose and ease of his manner, the accuracy and vividness of his analyses, but at the same time involuntarily on guard against what seemed to me the coldness, not to say cruelty, of his wit."

A more welcoming side of Santayana is evident in his relationship with perhaps the most notable of all his students, W.E.B. DuBois, the locale of whose relationship with the philosopher, interestingly, was as much

Otto Hall

Hollis, as Sever. In later years the pre-eminent black protest leader during the first half of the twentieth century, DuBois in 1890 graduated from Harvard with an A.B.; thereafter he was the first African American to earn a doctorate at Harvard. He thrived on the most demanding courses, famously declaring of one, on English composition: "I believe, foolishly perhaps but sincerely, that I have something to say to the world and I have taken English 12 in order to say it well." Although he was rejected by the Glee Club, and there was no warmth and elegance of club life open to him (he lived in a garret room at No. 20 Flagg St., just behind present day Mather House, very far then from the college world), DuBois made history at Harvard. He was, for example, one of six student orators in 1890 at Commencement. From the faculty, in fact, he encountered some small welcome, as he remembered it. Not, certainly, from Professor Agassiz, who was very racist in his thinking, and keen on skull measurements as relating to brain size (he would supply much ammunition to the eugenics movement), but from Professor Shaler, who actually expelled from his class a white southerner who had objected to DuBois' presence. And from Santayana there was even the offer of a certain intimacy. Sean O'Connell catches its likely meaning best:

> It was Santayana's hint of decadence and his disengaged and stylish approach that won students. . . . The cold, brilliant, skeptical young instructor with a 'curious Latin beauty about him physically' (he was not yet bald . . .) excited interest, loyalty, and the titillating, cerebral homoeroticism often just below the surface in all-male environments.
>
> Well connected socially, but not an authentic Puritan, the snobbish, swarthy Santayana, though infinitely more at home in the Cambridge milieu than it was possible for DuBois to be, was still subtly, slightly an outsider. . . . When DuBois and Santayana read [Kant's] *Critique of Pure Reason* together ("he and I alone, in an upstairs room") as undergraduate and graduate scholars, the undergraduate's lifelong memory of that experience may have been enhanced by a fleeting moment when each man recognized in the other something of his own anomalous situation.

Santayana's students particularly included many fascinating figures destined to become important in the twentieth century. Nor was DuBois the only African American among their number. There was also Alain LeRoy Locke. The first American black Rhodes scholar at Oxford, Locke became a critic of international repute, his *New Negro* of 1925 very much "the landmark," in Michael Winston's words, "of the Negro Renaissance of the 1920's," which is to carry old Santayana's influence, so little suspected today, to another country indeed.

Curious, the different report of each generation about the same thing really. Consider again Harvard's old hearth, so to speak, Harvard Hall of 1764, only the third of that name since the 1630s, by 1900 first among equals so to speak, even after the creation of Sever, almost immediately so magnificent a landmark. One building; many generations; as many reports. Never mind Lafayette. Or John Hancock. Think just of teachers. Remember how Emerson wrote in his time that such was Edward Everett's "genius" (he will be remembered as a good teacher long after he has been forgotten as a bad president) that when Everett lectured the rudest undergraduate found "a new morning opened to him in the lecture room of Harvard Hall." At that century's end it was George Lyman Kittredge that inspired; recall that "to many of them ... the total meaning of Harvard Hall was 'Kitty.'" Another century—the twentieth this time—another report; Jill Ker Conway, later president of Smith, a student here after World War II, wrote: "Bernard Bailyn taught colonial history as though it were a totally new subject. ... I found myself practically dancing out of the staid setting of Harvard Hall because of the excitement unleashed." Bailyn's history may have set a new standard but it was a kind of history Harvard Hall had long known at first hand. One building, several centuries, as many teachers, one report. Another—in our own time—comes from John Updike:

> Trying to picture an especially happy self, I came up with a Harvard student ... attending the first day of Professor Hyder Rollin's course in the later Romantic poets. ... As I settled into the first lecture, in my one-armed chair, my heart was beating like that of a boy with a pocket heavy with nickels as he walks through the door (which has a bell, to alert the kindly old lady dozing behind the counter) of a candy shop. It would be bliss, I think I thought, to go on forever like this, filling in one's ignorance of English literature slot by slot, poet by poet, under the guidance of tenured wizards, in classrooms dating from the colonial era, while the down-drooping golden-leafed elm branches shivered in the sunlight outside in the Yard.

New Yard and Memorial Hall

Peabody Str

Kirkland Street

Cambridge Street

Quincy Street

Massachusetts Avenue

50

53

48

54

49

47

51

52

45

55a

55b

55c

46

Harvard Yard and Harvard Square

45. Boylston Hall

Schulze and Schoen, 1857–1858; Peabody and Stearns, addition, 1871; The Architects Collaborative (TAC), remodeling, 1959

This superb granite building is the work of a young German immigrant architect, Paul Schulze; in fact, it is one of his earliest American buildings, and even with its third floor addition of 1871, one of the best works of its time at Harvard. It is also an example of the effect good design *can* have on youth, even the lively youth of the nineteenth-century Yard, among whom we must count Henry Hobson Richardson, who, in James O'Gorman's words, though he "came to Cambridge intending to draw upon his mathematical training to become an engineer...ultimately decided on a career in architecture. While we do not know why, it seems reasonable to assume he became interested in the profession by watching new buildings rising in Boston and at Harvard." Including Boylston Hall? So O'Gorman suggests when he writes: "architecture in Boston during the first half of the nineteenth-century was marked by the use of a local stone...Quincy granite....The Boston Granite Style as it was called even in its own day was exemplified [by the group] of granite warehouses along the harbor....Richardson later in life expressed his admiration for this stringent Granite Style in buildings...such as Edward Cabot's Boston Athenaeum... [and] new buildings rising at Harvard from the designs of Paul Schulze." Then only thirty, Schulze was also personally known to Richardson as a student through the Pierian Sodality, a college musical society, of which both

Boylston Hall

were members. O'Gorman thought Schulze's Harvard work some of the finest examples of the Boston Granite Style, "some of the finest, quietest, and most massive, lithic architecture in America"—adjectives he points out are applicable to the best of Richardson's work as well. Meanwhile, Boylston Hall, the first chemistry laboratory in America originally, endures very well, itself massive and lithic in its effect, and all the better for its remodeling by The Architects Collaborative in 1959. Originally the building had rather clumsy Italianate window tracery. TAC substituted great sheets of glass, just the sort of sophisticated opposition of materials—glass and granite (very Milan, that)—always likely to dramatize the underlying character of old architecture.

Boylston Hall's original role as one of the heralds of the New Yard when it was built emerges in Catherine Drinker Bowen's *Yankee from Olympus*, where Oliver Wendell Holmes' biographer gives an excellent picture of mid-nineteenth-century Harvard, awakening to its future. Already, Bowen writes, there were "dangerous new men on the teaching staff," men only too ready to liven things up. She cites above all, a group of scientists, one of whom rather blatantly disregarded the old Puritan statutes against public smoking: "On Thursday mornings, Louis Agassiz strolled through the College Yard, smoking his cigar in sublime disregard of law and order." Then there was Benjamin Pierce. "In the classroom Pierce was brief and impatient," she wrote. "Stupid students were terrified of him, the brilliant greeted him with joy." Another scientific luminary was Asa Gray, his field natural history, among his friends Charles Darwin himself. And then there was Josiah Parsons Cooke, Class of 1848, professor of chemistry. He it was who may be accounted the progenitor of Boylston Hall, the first building at Harvard dedicated to the physical sciences, home to what some have called the first chemistry laboratory in America.

46. Gore Hall Pinnacles

Richard Bond, 1838–1841; Ware and Van Brunt, addition, 1874–1876

On the plinths to either side of the ground story entrance of Widener Library on Massachusetts Avenue are two splendiferous granite pinnacles, all that is left today of Gore Hall, the first long since demolished landmark of the New Yard. But if the library itself, built in 1838, was distinctly a failure, its stack wing addition of 1874–76 by Robert Ware and Henry Van Brunt (both Harvard graduates, respectively of the Classes of 1852 and 1854) was on the other hand a great success. Indeed, it was evidence that notwithstanding President Eliot's rather laissez-faire attitude to architectural style, the buildings he caused to be erected sometimes made considerably more sense in other and perhaps more practical ways. Thus Donald Fleming relates

Harvard architecture in Eliot's reign very specifically to his educational reforms. These were, in Fleming's analysis, fourfold: there was, first, the elective system, which supposed, second, a growing honors program in order to drive student achievement, and, third, required the establishment of academic departments in the modern sense, departments that themselves formulated educational programs—all this necessitating many new classrooms and such—the whole structure dependent, fourth, on "a new conception of university libraries, both as physical structures," in Fleming's words, "and as human environments." Traditional libraries had hitherto been divided into alcoves for different categories of books around immense reading rooms, funneling people very jerkily. Some way had to be found to break the bottleneck. Declares Fleming:

> The solution to this was one of the notable inventions of the nineteenth century, first brought to perfection in recognizably modern form in the addition to Gore Hall in 1876—the bookstack, a narrow-aisled system of free-standing iron uprights which transferred weight to the foundations through the steel stack [rather than the frame of the building], extending uninterruptedly from the foundations to the top floor, adapted to bearing adjustable shelves. . . .
>
> Doubts were felt about the stability of a bookstack with six floors, and Eliot deserves credit for authorizing its construction. The gamble paid off in the most flexible, compact, and accessible form of shelving books that had ever been known. This pointed to the revolutionary principle that 'books should be used to the largest extent possible and with the least trouble,' heralding the opening of the stacks to students.

These two flamboyant pinnacles thus mark an important turning point not just in Harvard's history, but in the evolution of the American library and its architectural expression. Ware, moreover, though not perhaps a designer as eminent as other Harvard figures who have taken up architecture—Bulfinch or Richardson or McKim—nonetheless may be said to have found his own and high enough place in Western architectural history as the creator of the first American school of architecture in 1865 at M.I.T. (He also started the second, at Columbia University in New York City, twenty-three years later.)

47. Chinese Stele *Ch'ing Dynasty, 1796–1820*

What does one make of an elaborately sculpted Chinese stele in Harvard Yard? Originally the gift of a Chinese emperor to a provincial governor, it was the gift of the Harvard Club of Shanghai on behalf of all the alumni in China at the college's tercentenary in 1936. The dragon form in front represents power and happiness, the tortoise form in the rear is symbolic of long life. The inscription is twentieth century; carved just prior to its gift to Harvard entirely in classic Chinese script, it extols the university's stature at great length. Harvard's increasingly global perspective today is not the only possible justification for the stele's presence in the Yard. I think of a train of thought David McCord once essayed:

> An old friend and classmate, an intuitive scholar speaking Mandarin and honored still for a mind like a flawless piece of jade, once explained to me in simple English that "A Buddha is what you do to it." Since his death in 1960 these words have taken on a wider meaning every time I say them over. For example, who can fail to regret that a student *at* Harvard is not equally and always a student *of* Harvard, since Harvard, like the Buddha, is what you do to it? The Cambridge port of entry, if you ask me, is too wide. The freshman arrives, dragging his civilization with him: an instinctive act, no doubt, but nevertheless encumbering. Not so with a certain Oriental, as I have noticed him in the Square, his saffron robe accented by a pair of Argyll socks. He walks like a rainbow, but he is more than that: he is perceptively *of* Harvard. He brought no baggage with him.

He knows that "any Lhasa is what you do to it," writes McCord, as he thought, in fact, Thoreau did, and of Harvard too. "Thoreau lived to do more to Harvard—of which he feigned to disapprove—than it did to him." His "extension courses," concluded McCord, included pupils like Mahatma Gandhi: "As I walk these familiar paths, diagonals most of them to sanctuaries beyond my layman's reach of understanding, the mind goes [to the fact that]... to be a student of Harvard requires almost an abrogation of the temporal, a long walk late at night with accredited ghosts of the place, the stab of loneliness right through a multitude of dons. Even so, the revelation may not come." A worthy meditation, and a just retort to those who think the bustling countercultural square makes no contribution to the peaceful, ruminative yard.

48. University Hall (New Yard façade)

Charles Bulfinch, 1813; New Yard steps, 1917

University Hall, the Bulfinch-designed building (see Walk 1) whose placement virtually created the Old Yard at the start of the nineteenth century, is
unusual in having two front facades. And at century's end the facade facing
the New Yard played an equally important role in shaping that new space:
an old story in Harvard Yard. Because it has grown *backward* and inward
over the centuries (from the original street facing buildings and open
courts of the seventeenth and eighteenth centuries), it's been a case of
abandoning one front facade after another—Holden Chapel, for instance;
Hollis Hall is another—to ennoble what were once back facades so as to
make them worthy of their new role. Who guesses today that the stately
exterior granite staircases on the New Yard side of University Hall (the
same design, of course, as the staircases on the Old Yard side) were not
erected until over a hundred years after the building was completed? But
the really crucial element added to University Hall in the Victorian period is
only expressed on the exterior by the four original double-height arched
windows of the second and third floors. For Victorians in Harvard Yard
these tall arched windows—originally the windows of Bulfinch's chapel
space, a place of worship rendered superfluous by the erection of the now
destroyed Appleton Chapel—meant something very different; after a short
period subdivided into two floors of lecture rooms, what was the old
chapel was "restored" as the Faculty Room of the new Faculty of Arts and
Sciences, the centerpiece reform of Eliot's of Harvard, in which he combined the faculty of Harvard College and the new Graduate School of Arts
and Sciences he'd started in 1872. The crowning achievement of his presidency, that graduate school (together with Johns Hopkins in Baltimore)
introduced to the United States the advanced scholarly training in the
major fields of learning that Tichnor, the originator of the university idea in
America, had failed to achieve at Harvard in Kirkland's reign. (The first
Harvard Ph.D.—in mathematics—was given in 1873.) In the words of the
great classicist and sometime master of Eliot House, John Finley, Eliot it
was who thus "created here the new model of the American university college. The European universities [as the projected new Johns Hopkins
University] lacked colleges. Oxford and Cambridge lacked graduate
schools. By superimposing the continental higher learning on the college
transplanted from Britain by the early college, he gave rise to Harvard's
glory and endless demand. We run with the hares and hunt with the
hounds, forever seeking to combine the best of colleges with the best of
graduate schools."

Today University Hall is a veritable hive of deans. Here the Dean of
the Faculty pours sherry and then some for young scholars and their part-
ners, all the while repeating the dean's traditional recruitment speech

("Harvard is special, perhaps unique. It is a place where scholars can grow, offering the finest colleagues and students. I have never regretted moving to Harvard and neither will you. The Boston area is exciting, etc.") Here the Dean of the College opines on the importance of needs-blind admission or, to students, the importance of taking honors; similarly the Dean of the Graduate School speaks of keeping up doctoral standards or the need for more graduate housing. In fact, in some cases over the last 100 years, University Hall's deans endure as much for their deaning as for their teaching; of legendary figures like Le Baron Russell Briggs, who not only taught English, but was Dean of the College at the end of the nineteenth century, the poet Robert Hillier memorably wrote: "His head thrown back, his amiable walk/Time equally to progress or to talk . . ./These I remember, and remembering, see/The Dean walk home toward immortality." Here too, because the New Yard used to be a back yard, archaeology has made its contribution. In 1926, for example a cache of broken eighteenth-century Staffordshire china originally commissioned by President Quincy for Commons in the 1830s was unearthed. Later Kenneth Conant of the Architecture School used their design for the borders of his design for the new twentieth-century Harvard china.

49. Sever Hall *Henry Hobson Richardson, 1878*

Notwithstanding University Hall's contribution to the layout of the whole of Harvard Yard, both Old and New, what that hall was to the formation of the Old Yard in 1815 Sever Hall was to the development of the New Yard in 1878. The first successful building as we've observed to be built there, Sever began to define, as the older mid-nineteenth-century landmarks had not, a great central quadrangle on the other side of University Hall that would ultimately become the center of the New Yard. Alike in their architectural effect, it is perhaps no surprise that each hall constitutes creative work of the highest order by the two greatest architects to work in Harvard Yard over the centuries. Richardson, like Bulfinch before him, more than did his college proud. Similarly, and perhaps for some more challenging, Sever was also alike to University in the manner of architect selection. Just as Bulfinch, when he came back from Europe to start his practice in Boston, was given his chance by the old boy network of his student days in Harvard College, so also when Richardson returned from Paris to take up the practice of architecture, not a few of his important clients were Harvard friends. His first great work was Phillips Brooks' Trinity Church on Copley Square. In 1878 Richardson's most influential friend on the Harvard scene was Ned Hooper, Harvard's treasurer. And it was through a very small committee indeed—Hooper and John Quincy

Sever Hall

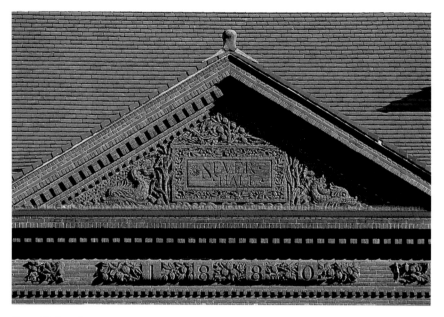

Sever Hall, pediment over west entrance

Adams (another old boy, the founder in 1840 of the increasingly influential Harvard Alumni Association)—that Richardson received the commission to design Sever.

Erected as the result of a fixed bequest, as opposed to the much
more flexible budget provided for Richardson's other Harvard work of some
years later, Austin Hall at the Law School, is interesting that while
O'Gorman concludes that Austin's design is "formulaic, as if the architect
were copying himself rather than giving the work the benefit of fresh
thought," this is not true of Sever. Indeed, if the "cronyism," as we would
call it, and nepotism of Sever's architect selection is a problem for us today,
so is O'Gorman's conclusion that "Austin [Hall] proves that a larger budget
does not necessarily a better building make." It is Sever that is a masterwork of American architecture. For although Sever defers very much to the
eighteenth-century brick rectangles of the Old Yard, it is entirely "free of historical cant" (O'Gorman again). It is all the more subtle and masterful a
work for its dark, medieval character—the first time, certainly, the low-
sprung, exotic Syrian architectural arch (at its entrance) was seen at
Harvard. A very picturesque building, generally, it is nonetheless disciplined
by an almost classical gravity of mien and serenity of mass. Bainbridge
Bunting believed that "in Sever Hall Richardson combined lavish ornamen-
tation with monumentality in a way no other nineteenth-century designer
(save his admirer Louis Sullivan) could." The craft here, moreover, is as
amazing as the design. The cut and molded brickwork, of a distinctive dark
hue, is worthy of the closest study. The carved-brick foliate work is a revela-

tion. Indeed, Rafael Moneo, the distinguished modern architect, has written of how he feels that at Sever "Richardson wanted to demonstrate that ornament is not something aggregated or applied, but instead is capable of sharing in the substance—the very matter—of the building itself," an insight only perhaps a designer of Moneo's stature could capture. The Spanish master concluded: "I love to see the hall's carved brick.... We are touched by the white joints of mortar running through the eyes of the owl.... A phantom appears, almost lost in the mass of gently carved bricks: the shield of Harvard, to which Richardson seems to have dedicated this work." It is work, finally, that should be studied by all architects sworn to so-called contextualism, which comes in all flavors, so to speak, and at all learning levels, from kindergarten to graduate school. And Sever Hall abides in solitude, to be sure, but in no sense in isolation.

50. Memorial Hall

Ware and Van Brunt, 1866–1878; Venturi, Scott-Brown Assoc. withBruner/Cott (Robert Venturi, architect in charge), Loker Commons interior, 1992–1996; Robert G. Neiley, Architects, restoration, 1992–1996

Notwithstanding the importance of Gore Hall's stack wing to Eliot's great reforms, nor that Sever Hall is the one inspired masterpiece of the period at Harvard, Memorial Hall in some way very nearly spiritual transcends both buildings and everything else at Harvard to this day. It is unarguably the great landmark of Victorian Harvard. Riding the Delta on the Yard's northern border, its magnificent and for so long sorely missed tower now splendidly restored by the Rudenstine administration in all its glory, this great work of architecture makes itself felt even at a considerable distance. Indeed, Memorial is one of two works of architecture that I see as representing in the largest possible sense the culmination of Boston in the age of Ralph Waldo Emerson; more broadly, too, of American architecture in the second half of the nineteenth century. There would be, twenty years later, McKim, Mead and White's Boston Public Library building, the first truly magisterial union in America of art and architecture for a cause worthy of such splendor: the first free big-city public library in the world supported by taxation, in the establishment of which as we have seen, Harvard played a crucial founding role. But, first, there was Memorial Hall, the great symbol of Boston's commitment to the Unionist cause and the abolitionist movement in America which also crested in the Civil War, a war Harvard took up with almost a religious fervor. Memorial Hall, which memorializes the sacrifices made by Harvard's Union dead, is in fact, really, only understandable as Unionist triumphalism merged, historically, with the equal fervor of abolitionist triumphalism. The only thing anywhere in this country in the same

Memorial Hall

league is the Shaw sculpture on Boston Common. Indeed, Memorial Hall stands today—its only rival is the Lincoln Memorial in Washington—as the pre-eminent architectural symbol in this country of the triumph of the anti-slavery crusade, a crucial defining moment in the evolution of American democracy in the nineteenth century.

That Memorial Hall does this so effectively testifies to the quality of its design. Its style (Ruskin Gothic) is called such after John Ruskin, the English critic and friend of Charles Eliot Norton, who though he disliked this building too in the end (because it was of brick, not stone), certainly inspired Memorial Hall's style. It achieved its apogee in Britain in the 1860s, the decade during which, in 1865, Robert Ware and Henry Van Brunt won the design competition for Memorial Hall and developed their plans. The time lag between the European genesis of the style and its most notable American expression was thus close enough that for the first time Harvard architecture could be said to have been, if not cutting edge, then absolutely contemporary with the forefront of Western design thought. For just that reason, no doubt, within only a generation or two Memorial Hall was felt to be old-fashioned. Witness the wonderful story told by Walter Kilham in *Boston After Bulfinch* of the day in the 1920s when President Lowell conducted a noted French architectural critic on a tour of Harvard, Lowell "proudly pointing out the cherished square brick boxes, Hollis, Stoughton, and the rest, Duquesne bowing and saying 'Ah, oui,' 'très chic,' 'c'est charmant,' and so forth, and Lowell dreading the moment when they should come to Memorial Hall. Finally they turned a corner and Memorial appeared, all its pinnacles shining in the sun, and the clock striking like a band coming up the street. Duquesne stopped short, gesticulated, and exclaimed, 'Ah, voila, quelque chose.'" Indeed. That in Memorial Hall, at last, Harvard had something to show must have astonished Lowell—no tastemaker he. The aggressive massing, dynamic silhouette, and polychromatic wall and roof surfaces, all characteristic of the Ruskin Gothic style—of which Memorial Hall today is universally regarded as the greatest American landmark—had long been out of favor with those who *were* tastemakers. But Duquesne, a sophisticate who clearly understood that *every* style has its successes and its failures, was quick to rise to the architectural zest of Ware and Van Brunt's masterwork, whatever he thought of its high Victorian style.

In its day, Memorial Hall dazzled. Henry James described it in *The Bostonians* through the eyes of a Southern and presumably unsympathetic visitor, in words of high praise:

> The ornate, overtopping structure...was the finest piece of architecture he had ever seen....He thought there was rather too much brick about it [Norton doubtless had a word with James on the subject], but it was buttressed, cloistered, turreted, dedicated, superscribed, as he had never seen anything; though it didn't look old, it looked significant; it covered a large area, and it sprang majestic into the winter air.

The building's design concept, whether deliberate or not, is that of a vast Gothic secular cathedral, the nave of which, now called Annenberg Hall, was especially important as representing an attempt to restore the old Hall of Harvard College. The third incarnation of the old Hall in the present Harvard Hall (Harvard Hall III) had expired in various makeshift arrangements, including the ill-fated University Hall commons of 1815, and was finally abandoned in the 1840s entirely. No one missed commons, though that too was revived at Memorial, but the commencement banquet, a dearly loved institution dating back to the 1600s, was in great need of a worthy setting. Which Annenberg Hall certainly provides: 176 feet long and 59 feet wide, it is comparable, in fact, to London's fourteenth-century Westminster Hall, the largest surviving medieval trussed hall in the world, the trusses of which are only nine feet greater in length than Memorial's. Used today primarily for first-year students, introducing them at once to the glories of collegiate Harvard, the Hall is still used for great occasions. At such times, with the seventeenth-century state silver arrayed at high table, it could be said still to function as the Hall of the entire university. (Today, a basement alternative to the Hall has been provided in Loker Commons, the interior of which was designed by Robert Venturi and Denise Scott Brown using a variety of electronic features,

West entrance loggia to Memorial Hall

including colored fluorescent tubing on the ceiling marking the major circulation route and a "frieze" of always moving images along and over the food counter. "Electronics," Venturi explains, "succeeds revivalist craft.")

The crossing and transepts are in one sense the heart of the design. Ennobled by glorious stained glass (there is work here by John LaFarge and Sarah Wyman Whitman), the staircase volumes to each side are alone worth attending any event to see, while the Memorial Transept, as it is called, is the sort of place most people would want to take their hat off in; "a chamber high, dim and severe, consecrated to the sons of the university who fell," wrote Henry James, who added: "the effect of the place is singularly noble and solemn, and it is impossible to feel it without a lifting of the heart."

Finally, there is the apse, and here the secular quality of the building would seem triumphant in Sanders Theater, a Gothic variant of Christopher Wren's Baroque Sheldonian Theater of 1664–68 at Oxford, and not least because of its superb acoustics, one of the Boston area's premiere concert halls. Sanders was intended for rhetoric as much as for music, and the seven sculptured heads that adorn the exterior—of which Desmosthenes, Cicero, Chrysostom, and Webster stand out, orators all, express the fact that Sanders' dedication was also conceived as lofty enough. Yet the real-life historical figures that have spoken and performed here are now the greater roster: Theodore Roosevelt, Winston Churchill, Leonard Bernstein, Martin Luther King, Jr., Arnold Schoenberg, E. E. Cummings. Nor is this to forget more regular but nonetheless cherished

Gargoyle, Memorial Hall

moments like the breathtaking effect of John Finley, the great classics scholar, pacing the stage before a thousand students, discoursing on Thucydides with perhaps one small index card in his hand to guide him. (Ben Bradlee once declared that "Finley made classical Greek literature and thought as incandescent as a five-alarm fire.") Nor is this to overlook all those, famous and not, who graduated from Harvard in Sanders, where commencement itself was moved after it had exceeded the First Church's capacity in 1873.

One commencement has particular reference to our theme in this Walk of the interface between professors and students, which all these buildings were designed as settings for in this era. The commencement I have in mind is that of 1915, quite on the cusp between the Victorian and modern eras. That year one of the speakers, a rising senior, was E. E. Cummings. In a brilliant talk, entitled "The New Art," he was, it is true, persuaded by his father not to refer to Marcel Duchamp-Villon's nude as a "phallic fantasy"! But of the work of Amy Lowell and of Gertrude Stein, two Harvard figures then very controversial, Cummings talked freely enough—a subject not at all welcome to Harvard's then president, Abbott Lawrence Lowell, Amy's brother. Enthroned in state in the president's Tudor chair, he was observed carefully by one and all as he "turned to brick" during Cummings' address. It was a deliciously Harvard collegiate event, herald of a significant variation on our theme (somewhat idealistic, of course) of great teachers in the Yard's legendary lecture halls shaping eager, devoted students. For Cummings, like Berenson and Eliot, would themselves of course, in later years, turn the tables. Cummings, in the wake of Eliot and Pound and Joyce, may be said to have revolutionized literary experience in English generally in the twentieth century. Now during his time at Harvard Cummings was in full Oedipal revolt against family and Harvard and Boston. A "spree-drinking, girl-chasing" undergraduate much given to gin-fizzes at the Copley Plaza's fashionable Back Bay hotel nightspot, to say nothing of fast automobiles, dances at Brattle Hall, and moonlight drives around Fresh Pond (Harvard's "lovers' lane" of those days), Cummings nonetheless took much away from the Yard. It was there that faculty mentors Harvard's president had appointed introduced him to Stein's and Amy Lowell's work in the first

place, as well as to Picasso and to Stravinsky. The same mentors brought
him to the Armory Show when it visited Boston (where Cummings became
ecstatic over Brancusi), urging on him also the writings of Pound and
Joyce. (Not only did the Armory Show come to *Boston*, but one of Charles
Eliot Norton's most ardent disciples, Isabella Stewart Gardner, was one of
the show's twelve honorary sponsors.) Yet all the while, one of the greatest
influences, of all unlikely people, on Cummings, was beloved old Dean
Briggs, who would never care much for free verse but also didn't think anyone could actually be taught to write, only guided, closely and critically,
and encouraged to do what they did best. In Cummings' case, it hardly
mattered that he went beyond Amy Lowell's Imagism into more or less
Cubism. The truth was, as R. S. Kennedy noted, that year after year Briggs'
course drew not just Cummings, but "the most interesting young men at
Harvard." And the result was predictable. In 1916 at year's end it was
widely felt that so much good poetry had been written therein—and published regularly in Harvard's literary magazine—that some of it at least
should be brought out in book form. Thus *Eight Harvard Poets*. Most
Harvard courses, even in the Yard's golden era, did not yield a book. And in
most cases those written were, like Santayana's, by faculty. *Eight Harvard
Poets* was written by the students.

51. Emerson Hall *Guy Lowell, 1900*

The other great landmark, after Memorial Hall, that dominates the New Yard, is
Widener Library—which bluntly trumpets Eliot's triumph. But before Widener
there was Emerson, a building that not only heralds Widener, but in some
sense may be Widener's better self. Emerson's heroic columns are the first
example in the New Yard, as Widener's are the grandest, of what John
Coolidge used to call "Imperial Harvard." And though Emerson too has been
called bombastic that is simply to decline what Baroque has to offer. Emerson
is not bombastic. Emerson is grand. And because it was built for the
Philosophy Department—the pride of Harvard's golden era at the end of the
nineteenth century (remember that one of Eliot's four goals was to endow
Harvard with strong academic departments)—Emerson's architectural pomp
was immediately upheld by that department's intellectual pomp so as to create
a kind of seamless Wagnerian setting and action. The hall's very name and
dedication was a valediction, though not without irony. Across the yard, it was
built, Emerson Hall, across from old University Hall, in and out of which on various errands as young Waldo had once been seen to dash, day in and day out
in years past. That there should arise in that place twenty-odd years after his
death a great becolumned temple of learning proudly labeled on its frieze,
"Philosophy," and named "Emerson," was, if not surprising, then astonishing.

Emerson Hall

Though how great a loss Harvard had sustained in ignoring Emerson (who was not only a great thinker, but who possessed just the mind of a great Oxbridge or Harvard tutor) is not in doubt. It comes through, for example, in the quality of his informal guidance of Oliver Wendell Holmes as an undergraduate. Asked, not only because of his erudition but because Emerson was, in Holmes' experience, never patronizing or condescending to a student and dealt "man to man," to be reader for a critical paper on Plato that Holmes thought to publish or, perhaps, submit for a prize, Emerson did so, carefully, in front of Holmes, only to hand the paper back with a shake of the head and the famous rejoinder: "When you shoot at a king you must kill him." To which Holmes did not respond with youth's usual insecurities. Instead he promptly tore the paper up and did it over. But what is equally important from our point of view is Emerson's further advice to Holmes: "Hold Plato at arm's length as you've been doing," he advised him. "That's good. But say to yourself, 'Plato—you have pleased the world for two thousand years. Now let's see if you can please *me*.'" The much better paper that resulted was Emerson's as well as Holmes'! As Morison wrote in Harvard's tercentenary history: "The unforgivable sin of the University was her failure to find Emerson the chair of Rhetoric that he craved, or to provide something to keep him in Cambridge, even if he did nothing more than play Socrates for half a morning hour at the Yard pump." By 1900, of course, scholars around the globe would have been lining up, and would not have disdained that pump. And that of course was the great thing about Emerson Hall. It needed to be grand. It was about America's Plato, as it were—about Emerson, perhaps even more about William James. It represented finally much more than Harvard making up for past omissions. I have in mind the view Richard Rorty has attributed in our day to Harold Bloom, that "America truly begins only when Emersonian self-reliance replaces Calvinist guilt. No real American takes himself to be younger than God." Grand indeed. Emerson Hall's dedication was serious business. And getting more serious. Recently Robert Coles wrote: "No American has matched William James in the breadth and depth of his psychological studies.... Freud attracted Freudians, Jung gathered around him Jungians, but there weren't—there aren't—Jamesians.... Yet today.... Freudians and Jungians become, more and more, Jamesians—though James would laugh at the word." Indeed he would have. Not that he was in his day at all a shy figure in the Yard. One student remembered how James "lingered with the fertile-minded ones after class. He invited them to walk homeward with him to finish the discussion—and to one who passed them on Kirkland Street it was difficult to say whether student or professor had more of the eagerness of youth." Emerson Hall breathes its subject. It has over the years been a place of great teaching. Berkeley professor Jacob Lowenberg (who taught there for some forty years) during a fellowship year at Harvard wrote of Emerson that it was a hallowed place, hallowed by unseen but living spirits." And in a very real sense it was designed to be, however absurd the concept, or, perhaps, my own idea of it. In a very real sense, Emerson Hall's program is disclosed by Margaret Henderson Floyd: "the great brick columns rising to the Ionic capitals and ebullient inscribed entablature of terra cotta—from Psalm 8: 'WHAT IS MAN THAT THOU ART MINDFUL OF HIM'—provide the ultimate synthesis of the design. For if man is clay, then the man-fired ornament that is embedded in the structure of Emerson Hall embodies the philosophical ideals of its inhabitant."

52. Widener Library *Horace Trumbauer 1913–1915*

Although Widener was built in 1913–15, three or more years into the reign of Eliot's successor, Bainbridge Bunting has pointed out that it in both "scale and style was an extension of the Imperial Harvard of the late Eliot years." Extension and apotheosis! Coolidge's term "Imperial Harvard" was never more apt. Widener, by any measure monumental (some would say elephantine), is the most conspicuous example of the style at Harvard, its only rival being Langdell Hall at the Law School or perhaps, though it is more generously sited, the Medical School quadrangle. Yet the record would seem to indicate that its grandeur was more the donor's vision than Harvard's, to which according to your point of view either praise or blame attaches; in an age when the deference shown such a donor precluded plain speaking, certainly in print, more than a hint of criticism is surely conveyed in the way Harvard's then president tried to disarm the project's

Harvard Yard in fall with Widener Library in distance

opponents in his annual report—the donor, he insisted "does not give the university the money to build the library, but has offered to build a library satisfactory in external appearance *to herself* [emphasis added]....The exterior was her own choice, and she has decided architectural opinions." He might have added that she also insisted upon the architect, Horace Trumbauer of Philadelphia. It was just the sort of donor independence Eliot encouraged, and which his successor put a stop to after Widener. But it must be admitted in retrospect that while it is a monster, no denying it, subsequent architecture has played so well off Widener—Wigglesworth Hall has already been discussed in Walk One—that the library's hugeness became in the long run almost a virtue. It has turned out to be both an anchor (to a congregation of disparate buildings that are now seen to cluster around it) and a provocation forever challenging other architects to interesting response. Moreover, although self-importance, indeed, pomposity, is never attractive, there is a certain blunt logic (very *un*-Harvard and therefore the more fascinating here) in the way the design concept refuses subterfuge or even tact, and insists on the building looking frankly like what it is—"unambiguously the greatest university library in the world," in library director Sidney Verba's words. Certainly that is the impression of a stone and brick mass 250 feet by 200 feet, 80 feet high throughout, and colonnaded on its front by immense pillars with elaborate Corinthian capitals, all of which stand at the head of a flight of stairs that would not

OPPOSITE: *Widener Library*

Widener Library

disgrace the capitol in Washington. (Midst all this the fifteenth-century printer's marks over the central door seem a pale salute indeed to the realm of the book. But they are beautifully done nonetheless.) Then there is the palatial interior—though here it must be said that acres of yellow-gray Bottinco marble of imperious hue and fatal mien are enlivened only a very little by architectural murals by John Singer Sargent. But here too history has had its way, leavening even the effect of the main reading room. A confident enough space, 42 feet wide and nearly 200 feet long under a vault 44 feet high, it is not only a stage set without peer of human vanity and idiosyncrasy, thus redeeming its inhuman scale, but this huge room exemplifies in a very real sense what Thomas Wolfe, when he was a Harvard graduate student, wrote of in his notebook—"the lust for knowledge and recognition," which Wolfe noted significantly in the same breath as "the books in the Widener Library" and of how they roused him "to want to know all things." (After Wolfe's death, his editor, Maxwell Perkins, confirmed that "Wolfe had loved the reading room of [Widener] Library, where, as he so often told me, he discovered his hundreds of books and spent most of his Harvard years.")

There are, in truth, many sides to Widener, above all the turf of the undergraduate student, whose world can be a particularly brutal one at Harvard, as Jill Ker Conway has noted: "The Ph.D. system was a European import, grafted onto American undergraduate studies in the late nineteenth century." It was particularly problematic at Harvard, she continued, "for the puritanical inheritors of New England's founding culture...the Ph.D. system cast a blight more powerful than phylloxera or the Irish potato wilt." And she illustrates her point by touching on just that cold, impersonal, institutional quality of Widener's architecture that can seem so soul destroying in its daily demand. "Each morning as Widener opened," Conway recalled, "white-faced young men" went in only to emerge "grey of face but determined" at twilight, "as the sun set on the Yard...clutching the precious thesis notes...." A "Kafkaesque" world, Widener, Conway recalls. Yet, especially in the stacks, one that has its charms. The Widener stacks, a legacy as we've seen of what is distinctly a triumph of Harvard's own architectural history, focuses on two environments. In her *Library: The Drama Within* (1996) Diane Asseo Griliches cites examples of both. One is the life of the isolated, often unsuspected faculty study—where, buried in the deepest, densest stack areas, much seminal scholarship is done. Another example, the stacks themselves, hardly less private, is certainly more fun. Griliches, remarking on how "the stacks seem like such a natural place to bring heart and mind together," quotes Perry Viles on the subject of this traditional trysting place: "She [wife to be] was a senior, and we had access to the stacks. Study breaks and cuddling breaks (French History Section), then alternated. To this day I have marks on my knees from crawling on marble floors." Other loves, and a few lusts, thrive in other Widener locales, including an oddly purer love Verba highlights when he recounts how he "fell in love with Widener my freshman year.... The odor of the Widener stacks is something you never forget.... The first time I went in... it was like one of those movies where you see a miser with a large box of gold coins that he's throwing in the air just for the physical presence of them. I was knocked over by having that many books there, by the physical presence of that much knowledge."

Both points of view capture aspects of Widener few would quarrel with. But there is another overall view, more extreme (more religious almost) reasonable seeming, but one John F. Kennedy, persuasively argued against:

> Professor George Lyman Kittredge is supposed to have stopped in the Harvard Yard one day, pointed to the Widener Library, and remarked that every other building could burn to the ground, but if the Library continued to stand "we should still have a University."
>
> I share Professor Kittredge's admiration for the Library. But I am inclined to think that even the Library could be devoured in a general conflagration and the essence of Harvard would endure if teachers like Kittredge and his fellows survived.... The teachers, not the Library, serve as the organ of memory, distilling the knowledge of the past... showing the enchantment of thought to young men who, in this springtime of their youth, were more enchanted with life itself.

He went on to speak of his own master, government professor Arthur Holcombe, who like so many faculty doubtless did some of his best work buried in an out of the way study deep in Widener, unsuspected unless one is invited therein. However, Holcombe's "greatest impact was not in his erudition," said Kennedy, "but in his personality and character," which Kennedy, a Harvard College man who never went on to graduate school, thought "dispassionate, reserved, self-restrained, without illusions yet persistently idealistic." Not unlike what drew a whole generation across party and class lines to the sixth president Harvard has given to the United States.

53. Memorial Church *Coolidge, Shepley, Bulfinch, and Abbott, 1931*

To turn from Widener Library to Memorial Church is not just to make a physical about-face. It is to turn an important page in Harvard's history, and to confront the blunt architectural rejoinder of Abbott Lawrence Lowell, who became president in 1909, to his legendary predecessor, Charles William Eliot. It was not that Lowell, every bit as much a Boston Brahmin as Eliot, valued a chapel more than a library; Lowell was a distinguished scholar and author in his own field, Anglo-American government. Nor was Lowell more religious than Eliot; Memorial Church has always been a place more of academic ceremony than Christian worship, and today is open for use to all religions and none; not even among Christians does it claim any primacy—as only First Church could, historically—among the many churches of all faiths that minister to the Harvard community. Rather, the signal Lowell meant to send with Memorial Church touched less on libraries or chapels and more, much more, on his theories of education.

The new president was just opposite of Eliot. Lowell, for example, was vice-president of the Immigration Restriction League, and raised more than a few eyebrows when he signed a petition protesting Brandeis' nomination to the U. S. Supreme Court on character grounds. Hardly less troubling is the fact that he also sought over the years to restrict Jews at Harvard to a fixed quota and enthusiastically chaired the committee that validated the court proceedings and death penalty in the Sacco-Vanzetti case; shameful acts, most of us would say today, all of them. Lowell was also widely reputed to have denied Madame Curie an honorary degree because of her sex. But in other respects he was, confusingly, for his time quite liberal. Lowell, despite vigorous opposition, appointed the first Roman Catholic to the Harvard Corporation. Above all, he was a staunch defender of academic freedom. When a socialist faculty member, Harold Laski, supported the strikers in the Boston Police Strike of 1919 and was hauled before the senior governing board—within a year, recall, of the Communist Revolution in Russia; Americans had reason to be nervous—Lowell, no socialist he, nonetheless

Memorial Church

forthrightly declared: "If the Overseers ask for Laski's resignation, they will get mine." Similarly, when Felix Frankfurter, the highly liberal law school professor and Zionist who favored American recognition of the new Soviet government in Russia, signed a petition of one of his colleagues, Zechariah Chafee, protesting the controversial results of a case brought under the Espionage Act, asking for executive clemency and thereby arousing the ire of more than

Memorial Church

one law school donor, Lowell came to the defense of Chafee, pilloried as the instigator of the petition. When Chafee's dismissal was demanded and the law school visiting committee convened at the Harvard Club of Boston to settle the matter, Lowell himself appeared and conducted Chafee's defense. Not surprisingly, Chafee dedicated his book, *Free Speech in the United States* (1941), to the president. Lowell was alternately hero and villain, or so it seems to us today.

Nowhere was he more the hero, more the progressive, than in education itself. Lowell's major book in this field was entitled *At War With Academic Tradition in America* (1934). And, hardly less than his predecessor, Lowell worked to make a revolution at Harvard, one that proceeded from his core belief, in the words of a student of his thought, that "certain powerful, non-intellectual currents in American culture had come to exert a baleful influence on...academic communities," communities whose "superior intellectual achievement" Lowell thought essential for the construction of a good society, especially a democratic American society. And while he well knew that, historically, for Americans the things of the mind had never come first, Lowell thought Harvard—for America's sake as well as its own—had better steer by a better compass, rejecting the philistinism Lowell thought had corrupted and undermined Eliot's vision, and the elective system itself, with its liberating ethos and innovative curricula, which Lowell respected, but thought had gone too far, much too far. One can hear Lowell's view loud and clear, for instance, in a letter of 1929 he wrote to an alumnus about Memorial Church: "The policy [at Harvard] in the past . . . has been very vocational and materialistic. We are now striving to make it more cultural and spiritual.... All but the younger alumni were hatched in a materialistic temperature and it is not always easy to persuade them that there is something in life more important than athletic victories." Hence Memorial Church, which confronted Widener Library, not because Lowell quarreled with the elective system itself, but with the effect a materialistic society gave to it. Although he was no more against sports as such than had President Eliot been (Eliot had been a rower, Lowell a runner), Lowell simply argued for putting first things first. Above all he wanted students to value the pursuit of intellectual interests, and in the context of a challenging but supportive common collegiate life, free of those factors that divided and polarized the college—in the way, for instance, rich students thrived on the Gold Coast, while poor ones were relegated to sleazy rooming houses. Eliot, the architectural liberal, seems to have thought such disparities were the way of the world, from which it was no business of Harvard's to shelter students. Lowell, almost reactionary in comparison to Eliot, insisted Harvard could not tolerate such disparities.

Lowell's overall plan, so revolutionary he only very slowly unfolded it between 1909 and 1933, was fourfold. First, so as to bring more order and coherence to the students' experience of the vast new curriculum Eliot had achieved, Lowell persuaded the Faculty of Arts and Sciences in 1904–1905 to require that all undergraduates should be required both to "concentrate" and to "distribute" their coursework; that is, to declare for a field of concentration in the sophomore year (what elsewhere has come to be called a "major") and to distribute their other courses in certain broad categories of knowledge; to know a lot about something, a little about everything. Second, so that the A.B. degree amounted to more than just passing courses, whichever were chosen, all seniors were required to take "Generals," comprehensive examinations in their field of concentration. Third, to prepare students for those "generals" and to guide them closely, and to encourage taking honors the role of tutor—though not the rank; Lowell envisaged even full-tenured professors serving also as tutors—was revived at twentieth-century Harvard, firstly in the trend-setting and highly rigorous field of History and Literature, a founder of which Lowell had been, and ultimately in nearly all departments. Fourth, the capstone, would come when Lowell—taking a leaf not just out of experiences like Apthorp College (see Walk 3)—but out of Harvard's own history, subdivided Harvard College into smaller residential colleges (called Houses after the nickname of Harvard's first seventeenth-century Old College or Harvard Hall I).

In each new residential college he would re-create a modern version of the Old Yard (an achievement whose architecture along Charlesbank Harvard will be explored at length in Walk 12). Here, at Memorial Church, is the Harvard Yard side of the signal, as it were, at the heart of the University. Just as seventeenth-century Harvard College had laid stress on two of the three great collegiate functions, Hall and Library—at first enfolding the third but (at Harvard) secondary one, the Chapel, into the Hall—so Lowell provided for elaborate halls and libraries in all the new residential colleges, but no chapels. Modern Harvard, even less than Colonial Harvard, had no need of such as chapels, he reasoned. Instead, there would be one chapel: Memorial Church in Harvard Yard, a war memorial that would also be a suitable backdrop for ceremonial events for all the Houses and graduate schools as well.

Architecture was key to Lowell's plans. All the new Houses were entirely Colonial/Georgian in style after the Old Yard. Similarly, here in the center of the New Yard (and with all the pomp of Imperial Harvard) Lowell built—a Colonial meeting house! Actually, he and his designers endowed

Memorial Church with much of the Anglican elegance that once, at Christ Church, Harvard Square, in the late eighteenth century had so infuriated the Puritans. Harvard, grown now to national stature, needed a very grand meeting house! That said, it must also be noted that Memorial Church was itself a new and hybrid building type. As at Memorial Hall the historic Catholic plan was adapted to other uses. The nave was treated as a meeting house and was broad enough to seem so. The transept ("certainly without historical precedent," as J. D. Forbes observed in a 1958 article on the subject in *The Journal of the Society of Architectural Historians*) was treated as a memorial room and entrance vestibule with portico attached. What would have been the high altar chancel was walled off to a certain height from the nave by an elaborate almost impenetrable screen, behind which, accessible outside the church by its own separate entrance, was a chapel for weekday prayers, in plan replicating the old Puritan-Anglican compromise of Holden Chapel: the pews, choir-like, facing inward to either side of the central aisle, the president's chair at the east end. Today, when the chancel-screen doorway has been walled up, a communion table placed in front of it on the nave side, and the president's chair at the east end of the chancel usurped by an organ, the architects' achievement has, alas, been entirely overthrown. But in 1930–31, when most Protestants were abandoning the meeting house—what William Pierson in *The Colonial and Neo-Classical Styles* has called "the only original architectural invention of the English colonies"—in favor of Gothic Revival pseudo-Catholic cathedrals (the Duke University Chapel, for example, or Riverside Church in New York), Harvard not only tore down its Gothic chapel but built a new university "meeting house" without equal in the history of Protestant church architecture in this country. I hope one day it can all be restored, though I fear it would be as controversial a second or third act as Memorial Church's first act, when "all Hell broke loose," in Paul Hollister's words, at the very idea of Memorial Church, that "Dormitory of the Immortals, with its stout Doric ankles and its tiara of stars," as Hollister described it. Emily Dickinson above, Howard Mumford Jones used to say, but pure Mae West below!

In one sense, Lowell's idea, considered only as a war memorial, was the reverse of timely. "Godless Harvard," the first American college to abandon compulsory daily chapel, had had no religious revival; moreover, "the very idea of such a suggestion [for a new chapel]," declared the editors of the *Crimson* in 1923, "would have seemed sentimental and not a little ironic to the men whom it is intended to honor." To say nothing of those it might not honor, for there was the problem of what to do about those Harvard men who died in the First World War in the German Army. Harvard by the 1920s was a very different place than it had been after the Civil War. None of the 64 Harvard men who had died for the Confederacy had been commemorated in Memorial Hall (or anywhere else). But in 1931 even

Memorial Church

President Lowell admitted that though he "had every reason to suppose [Fritz Daur, Konrad Delbrock, Kurt Peters, and Max Schneider, all Harvard men who had died for Germany] were as brave and conscientious as anyone else," and that if any of them had asked him at the time he "should have told them to fight for their own country," he still felt bound to argue for the difference a "just cause" made; otherwise, he wrote, one ran the danger of saying "like barbarians, that all war is glorious." With beautiful tact the Germans were commemorated in a very fine plaque—in Latin. (After World War II the deed was done again, and in English—though this time the words "enemy casualty" were added after the name.) Nor were the first plans auspicious. In contrast to the transepts of Memorial Hall, which even today compel respect, the memorial transept at Memorial Church turned out, in fact, to be worse than sentimental. Despite excellently crafted architectural detail by Joseph Colletti, this memorial transept, all marble and gilt bronze, is coldly disappointing, and not just in its triumphalism. *Alma Mater*, typically, is shown bearing the torch of wisdom, for example. Which torch was that, one wonders, and turns away. There is none of the greatness of Lutyens' war memorials here, and the tone is oddly much more pagan than Christian. And perhaps for that reason, the centerpiece, *The Sacrifice*, probably the chief work of the sculptor Malvina Hoffman, seems rather out of place, and is reluctantly engaged—one feels in this work the danger is greatest: to add sentimentality to triumphalism must be fatal. And so it is, though in its own terms—outdated even then—the work is a fine one. In all this one hears, behind all the controversy at Harvard about the form its war memorial should take, Siegfried Sassoon's harsh, withering judgment of another memorial: that "pile of peace-complacent stone," he wrote of the Ypres memorial. "Well might the Dead who struggled in the slime/Rise and deride this sepulchre of crime." Still, Hoffman's sentimentality has, in fact, worn better than Coletti's triumphalism.

If the Memorial Transept is Memorial Church's great failure, Appleton Chapel is the church's singular success. Similarly it is the religious services of the chapel today that have the most significance; Morning Prayers here every morning—with a short homily now by a wide ranging group of speakers of all faiths and none—is perhaps the thing John Harvard would identify with most today in the Yard; that and the ancient psalm Harvard has made its own, the 78th. *Attendite, popule*: "Give ear O my people to my law: incline your ears unto the words of my mouth./ I will open my mouth in a parable: I will utter dark sayings of old which we have heard and known, and our fathers have told us." Morning Prayers can be one's first experience at Harvard of the dead who are ever present. On the outside the great bell in the steeple speaks its Amen at prayers' end and signals still the first class of the day.

And what a steeple is. Modeled on that of the Old North Church of Paul Revere fame in Boston's North End, Harvard's steeple is, strictly speaking, too lofty perhaps. But it was meant to also be seen from the Harvard riverfront and in its sharp loftiness to lighten Widener's ponderous mass and to counterbalance the main body of the church, which is distinctly low-lying and outspread, reaching out to shape a landscape that would otherwise seem much less ordered. Charles Coolidge, let it be said, was the senior designing partner of H. H. Richardson's successor firm, and he more than most must also have despaired of the effect on the Yard of Widener. Thus he made perhaps his masterwork, as Bainbridge Bunting and Robert H. Nylander assert: "How infinitely better is the design, placement, and scale of [Memorial Church] than was that of [the nineteenth-century chapel]...on the same site.... The tower with the portico at its base on axis with Widener serves to define the limits of the quadrangle, and together they form the 'scena' and 'cavea' of a great unroofed theater.... The enormous Doric portico...is wisely scaled to the ponderous colonnade of Widener."

More private moments of so many crowd about here as well, never to be known probably, unless the person achieves great distinction. One such experience—which at one and the same time conveys a sense of the grandeur, albeit homely in some ways, of the New Yard, and how it can influence those who think on it—happened to a young man in the 1960s; doubtless observed by no one, nor meant to be, we only know it now because decades later that young man became Harvard's president. Neil Rudenstine was once moved to tell an alumni gathering about it:

> The first time I really *saw* Harvard was in September, 1960. I arrived as a graduate student on a brilliant autumn day, ready to study Renaissance literature [after military service]. I sat more or less motionless for two or three hours, perched on the edge of one of those high parapets that flank the front steps of Widener, looking out over Sever Hall, Memorial Church, University Hall, and the buildings beyond. Those hours on Widener's parapet began my own romance with Harvard [a romance that started] as a form of intoxication, [but] also contained the sense of something inevitable.... I realized that if I failed to keep a rendezvous with this University, I would always feel as if I had been unwilling to test myself against the very best.

54. Tercentenary Theater

This natural theater—called the Tercentenary Theater because the 1936 ceremonies marking Harvard's 300th anniversary were held here—has succeeded Memorial Hall and Sever Quadrangle as the site in modern times of commencement. It is an impressive spectacle. There are famous faces, often surprising ones—degree recipients over the years have included Walt Disney (1938) and Benny Goodman (1984), as well as more expected worthies such as Booker T. Washington (1896) and Helen Keller (1904). There is ancient ceremony; the exercises begin, for example, with the University Marshall's age-old charge: "Mr. Sheriff, pray give us order," to which that top-hatted official responds in the correct antique manner; thrice pounding the stage with his sword, he announces: "The meeting will be in order." The president is then seated, presiding throughout the ceremonies from what Morison calls "the ancient Tudor chair." (Its exact date is unknown.) There is still a student salutary oration in Latin (a written translation is provided) and two English "parts" or addresses by other students, and no celebrity speaker at all. *Domine Salvum fac* (O Lord, make safe [our president]), Harvard's equivalent of *God Save the Queen*, is the first of several invarying musical selections. Another is a gorgeous *Alleluia* written by Randall Thompson for the Boston Symphony. And, of course, Psalm 78 ("Give ear, ye children, to my law") is sung, as it has been at every Harvard Commencement for more than 200 years and in the form in which it was first published in 1755. Most impressively, the graduating students form a

Tercentenary Theater

gowned corridor through which passes the procession of the alumni, whose day this really is, a fact made clear at the Alumni Association meeting the afternoon of commencement day, when the alumni march past Widener, class by class and to the lonely end of time, really, as we know it. In 1913 Rupert Brooke observed memorably: "Harvard, Boston, New England, it is impossible to say how much they are interwoven, and how much they have influenced America. I saw Harvard in 'Commencement'.... Class by class [the alumni] paraded.... I wonder if English nerves could stand it. It seems to bring the passage of time so very presently and vividly to the mind.... In five minutes fifty years of America, of so much of America, go past one.... And through the whole appearance runs some continuity, which is Harvard."

Although commencement is the chief event held in this theater, in the three quarters of a century since the Tercentenary Theater and Memorial Church were contrived as stage and backdrop, other historical events have occurred here. The most notable? In great secrecy, at the height of World War II, Winston Churchill came to Harvard to be given an honorary degree. After the ceremonies in Sanders Theater, contemporary accounts record that Churchill walked from the south door of Memorial Hall to the south porch of Memorial Church, where he was greeted by eleven or twelve students, faculty, alumni, guests, and employees. That day Harvard's state silver from the seventeenth-century High Table (its centerpiece, the Great Salt of 1650, set before the president) was used to honor Churchill at the formal meal which followed. It was also in Tercentenary Theater that three years later General George C. Marshall announced the Marshall Plan for the reconstruction of wartorn Europe.

55. Pusey, Houghton, and Lamont Libraries, and the Calder and Moore Sculptures

Pusey Library *Hugh Stubbins, 1973*
"Onion" *Alexander Calder, 1965*
Houghton Library *Perry, Shaw & Hepburn, 1941*
Lamont Library *CSBA, 1947*
"Large Four-Piece Reclining Figure" *Henry Moore, 1972*

Mostly underground Pusey Library, its entrance under a kind of protruding deck continuous with the elevated knoll behind it at the Yard's most north-east corner, now forms (or at least its roof does) a kind of plateau, continu-ous with the flat of the knoll, set back on which are two older libraries. At Pusey's entrance is "Onion," one of the "stabiles" that became after World War II the chief work of Alexander Calder, whose earlier "mobiles" played so vital a role in the life of the Harvard Society of Contemporary Art in the

Houghton Library

1920s. Houghton Library is Harvard's treasure house. Here are stored wonders ranging from a 1608 Shakespeare quarto to a rare copy of the first book printed from movable type, the fifteenth-century Bible published by Johannes Gutenberg at Mainz. Similarly, manuscripts. There is the one of *The House of the Seven Gables* Nathaniel Hawthorne sent to his printer, as well as many manuscripts of Emily Dickinson she sent no one, only discovered after her death. Her writing desk is here too, and the bureau in which hundreds of her lyrics were found. Not a few treasures relate to Harvard's own history. There are volumes from John Harvard's library, a copy of John Milton's *Paradise Lost* owned by Phillis Wheatley, as well as a seventeenth-century woodcut portrait by John Foster of Richard Mather, a portrait printed in Cambridge at the only American press of that era in 1669. Hard for any architecture to live up to. That Houghton may is a reflection of the skill of the gifted librarian and planner who led the project, Keyes Metcalf, and the library's principal designer, Robert C. Dean, an excellent and too often overlooked Boston architect of his era. A Memphis native, trained at M.I.T., where he later taught design, Dean worked on the firm's signature architecture at Williamsburg, and was well grounded in Georgian classicism. He was also, at the time he was working on Houghton, beginning a long if intermittent association with Alvar Aalto, for whom Perry, Shaw & Hepburn served as executive architects in the design of M.I.T.'s Baker House in 1946–49. Dean may have been involved as well with Aalto's Harvard work; be that as it may the spare elegance of Houghton seems not unrelated to Aalto's influence, though it is not hard to see the more dominant

Lamont Library

Georgian sources, like the late Georgian windows whose elongated shape and stylish pediments were clearly inspired by those of Bulfinch's third Otis House on Beacon Hill. Inside, the splendid South Gallery, with its floor to ceiling paneling, has been called the handsomest room at Harvard. The building as a whole won the Parker Gold Medal from the Boston Society of Architects in 1943. Thirty-four years later, moreover, when the Johnson Room was created in the attic, original molds were used of Robert Adam, who directly inspired Bulfinch, for the new room's ceiling.

What a difference four years makes, or so it seems looking at neighboring Lamont, which forms two sides of a quad with Houghton. With Lamont's design—which was erected in 1947, after World War II—the change one sees beginning rather tentatively with Houghton comes now with a rush; this time there is much more "modern" than "Georgian," making the shift at Harvard from neo-Georgian forms to the International Style, "reflecting," as Bainbridge Bunting put it, the "egalitarian and scientific educational concepts" of James Bryant Conant, who succeeded Lowell as Harvard's twenty-fourth president in 1933.

"Science and Puritanism merged in Jim Conant," wrote John Finley perceptively of Harvard's 23rd president: "his scientific rigor replaced the puritan vision." According to Richard Norton Smith, within twenty-four hours of his ascent to the presidency in 1933, Conant, a chemist and native Bostonian of old Puritan stock but from a much less haute bourgeois background than Lowell, had done two things his predecessor would never have done: talk informally to reporters and ride the subway, both typical of "a hardheaded prophet preaching the glories of a classless society." Conant, however, became president in the roseate afterglow of Harvard's tercentenary in the 1930s, for which Lowell's Georgian provided so incomparable a setting it tended to hold back change, certainly architectural change. Conant, moreover, was not a man of tremendous political skills. Then came World War II, which changed everyone's focus and further muted Conant's effect. Still, his legacy is considerable. He strove with varying degrees of success to make the student body truly national (forty percent of incoming freshmen in 1933 still came from Massachusetts) and to expand the pool Harvard's governors were drawn from (the first member of the Corporation not from Boston or New York was appointed at his urging). He achieved his most enduring success in his famous "up or out" policy and the ad hoc committee for appointments. Disparaging tutorial (the chemistry department had led in opposing Lowell in the matter), and also with less thought, his enemies said, for teaching (especially in the humanities) than research, Conant proposed (and in the end all agreed) that after a certain number of years a faculty member must either be promoted or let go, and that vacancies as they occurred in a department would be filled by the president with the consent of the governing boards on the advice of an ad hoc committee, mostly of Harvard specialists in that field, but including also outside, non-Harvard specialists and one or two from altogether different fields and from the private sector. Although it ended the president's absolute power of appointment, this new policy insured the president's continuing and pivotal role in all faculty appointments, even as the new policy preserved the consent of the governing boards while making sure that the advice acted upon would be of a high professional order. Conant it was who decreed (albeit at the expense of some important old collegiate values perhaps) that *the faculty that taught Harvard undergraduates as well as graduate students* (there was the gain, of course, that stilled argument) *must be the best in the world.* And it was a view given added credence by the fact that Conant continued himself to teach after he ascended to the presidency. (On the other hand he was seldom if ever seen at Harvard football games.) His best known initiative was his postwar General Education program. In an age when the G.I. Bill was at last creating the socio-economic diversity in the student body Conant wanted, and teaching too was changing (the dramatics of Roger Merriman were giving way to the dryer verities of Arthur Schlesinger, Sr., which is to say biography was receding, economics and statistics advancing), the General Education program renewed the idea of a liberal arts education and perpetuated it for another generation.

Lamont (like the now destroyed Burr Lecture Hall) was distinctly related to these ideals when it opened in 1946–49. Sidney Verba recalls that when he came to Harvard as a freshman in 1949 Lamont was "the first stand-alone undergraduate library in the country." The philosophy behind

Lamont was that it would contain the basic readings that undergraduates needed for their instruction, while graduate students and faculty would use the in-depth research collection in Widener. Subsequently, as Verba also notes, it turns out that half the users of Widener are undergraduates. This has to do with the specialization of knowledge. But that is today. Yesterday, and certainly architecturally, Lamont was for Harvard distinctly a revelation, the herald, in fact, albeit a quiet and relatively conservative herald, of a whole new kind of architecture marked by perhaps the most striking appointment of Conant's presidency, Walter Gropius, the founder of the Bauhaus. Not that the revolution in American architecture Gropius led achieved any great apotheosis in Lamont. That came in Gropius' own house in the Boston suburb of Lincoln a decade before Lamont; its principal university landmark was the Harkness Center (see Walk Eight). But Lamont, though it perpetuated the red brick and white trim of Georgian Harvard, did introduce into Harvard Yard, albeit conservatively, the radical new ideas of the International Style. Its extremely spare exterior, moreover, enfolds a much more blatantly modern interior of much glass and blond wood, the highlight of which is the Poetry Room, the first in America with recording and listening equipment, its handsome design by no less than Alvar Aalto.

Twenty-five years later came the installation in front of Lamont of Henry Moore's "Large Four-Piece Reclining Figure." A blatant and wondrous appeal to our sense of touch, our need to caress, the warmly rounded forms and luminous bronze patina of this reclining figure (the most enduring theme of this sculptor's work) is beyond praise. Conceived by Moore, perhaps the preeminent sculptor of the twentieth century, on a gigantic scale, it is a group of independent but connected segments, the idea is to encourage the mind to fill in the intervening spaces. In *Celebrating Moore* John Read writes of this work that it is "one of Moore's most abstract inventions and almost Surrealistic in its effects. There is a wonderful tension between the tangible and the intangible.... I remember sitting with him one evening in the garden of an Italian hotel enjoying an aperitif. He wanted to explain...his reasons for working with multiple forms. He reached out for a plate of potato crisps. In a few moments they had been arranged into a variety of intriguing compositions. In a similar way I have watched him working with his assistants on the crest of a hill, trying out the separate parts of his multiple sculptures." Superbly sited on the greensward in front of Lamont's main entrance, the Moore sculpture ennobles everything around it, creating by its own resonance the most lyrical passage in Harvard Yard, highlighting this elevated knoll in the northeast corner of the Yard, now appearing as something of a man-made plateau or deck that extends out from the knoll's highest grade.

From this deck, especially from the top of the staircase that leads down to Tercentenary Theater, the elevation is just enough that one gets a real sense of the mature Yard, here brought to completion three and more centuries after it was begun in the 1630s. What stands out, interestingly enough, are not so much the buildings as the landscape; above all what my eye dwells on are the paths—which the historian's mind's eye fills at once, of course, with people long gone. Musing again, as we have been in the Yard, on the great teachers of its golden era, I think for instance of Professor Edward Kennard Rand, whose career extended into the 1920s, and who wrote, referring to Harvard's oldest English collegiate tradition, that "the crown of a professor's activities is his teaching.... Administration or scholarly research...matter little if they are not caught up into character—*abeunt studia in mores*—and insensibly translated to students. If the teacher gives himself to them, they furnish part of his education. While he is maturing them," continued Rand, echoing a point made by President Eliot, "they are keeping him young." A later Harvard luminary of the mid- and late twentieth century, John H. Finley, Jr., himself a legendary teacher, in a biographical sketch of Rand, noted that if Rand's "words express the teacher's code, they were in no conflict with the scholar's." In turn, W. Bentinck-Smith thought Finley's evocation so good that he believed Rand, long after his death, still "walks briskly in spirit along the paths of the Yard."

Paths? So long a way from architecture one might say. But not really. No less than Le Corbusier found his inspiration for his Harvard work (see Walk Six) glancing casually out a window, his attention arrested by figures just like Rand's, or Eliot's, or yours or mine, figures moving constantly along the crisscrossing pathways of Harvard Yard, dare I say crisscrossing time as well. I am reminded of Emerson's more traditional, more ceremonial vision of the early nineteenth century of the long line of graduates. Le Corbusier's glance was at first much less considered, typically brief, discontinuous and modern. But his was a mid-twentieth-century vision nonetheless of the New Yard not more farseeing than Emerson's in the Old Yard, but perhaps more intimate. Paths. Architectural paths.

Arts Area: Dana Hill to the Delta

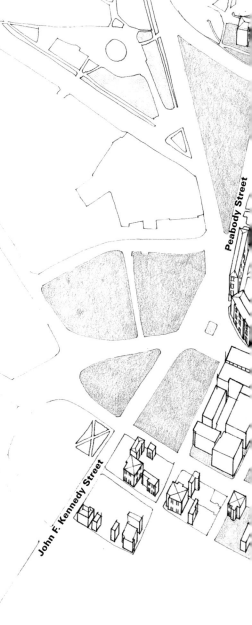

Mid-Cambridge Campus

56. Dana Palmer House _1822_

Dana Palmer House

Emerging from the Yard onto Quincy Street, its western boundary, an unexpected vista discloses, almost like a flashback, what this area looked like about 200 years ago; across the street is a very stately Federal house of 1822, behind it a hardly less striking similar structure—elegant reminders on this approach to the western slope of Dana Hill of the early nineteenth-century suburban subdivision by the Dana family. The residential parallel to the growth of mercantile Harvard Square on the Yard's other side, this and adjoining subdivisions became the Victorian suburb of Mid Cambridge, a reflection of the fact, in the words of one contemporary, that Dana Hill was as the mid-nineteenth century saw such things "a comfortable walk's distance from [downtown] Boston." (By 1849, according to Cambridge Historical Commission records, more than thirty percent of residents worked in downtown Boston.) As the name of the largest of these two houses suggests, some of the Danas remained and took up residence in one of the new suburban houses, a particularly handsome one which used to stand where Lamont Library now is just across the street. The house's most notable associations are with Martha Dana, who went on to marry the first distinguished painter to graduate from Harvard, Washington Allston, and Richard Henry Dana, Class of 1808, poet and essayist and father of the author of _Two Years Before the Mast_. In later years, the first Harvard observatory was established in this house, a cupola or revolving turret having been at the time attached to it.

It has been said that in the late twentieth century the memoir became what the novel was in the nineteenth century: "the primary means," in John Vernon's words, "by which we try, yet fail, to make a captive of time." Architecturally, the means of choice has now become the historic house museum, which the Dana-Palmer House (the university guesthouse) and Warren House (no. 57) distinctly are not, and all the better for it. The discontinuity between original architecture and present day use is a constantly thought-provoking foil, each to the other.

57. Barker Center for the Humanities

Goody, Clancy & Assoc., remodeling, 1995

Harvard Union *McKim, Mead and White, 1901*
Burr Hall *Thomas Mott Shaw, 1911*
Warren House *1833*

Approaching the Barker Center, with Houghton and Lamont immediately behind, the Inn at Harvard to the far right, Loeb House and the Faculty Club to the left, and the old Harvard Union directly across the street, these six buildings can be seen to compass the whole history of the American Georgian Revival from the 1890s to the 1980s. It is a confusing scenario. Like the young toddler on the Potomac tourist boat who exclaimed when first Mount Vernon came into view: "Look, Mother, a Howard Johnson's on the river," this collection of Harvard buildings is not only puzzling but in some ways distressing. Compare, for example, Barker's main building, the earliest, with the nearby Inn, the latest. The Barker's main building, the old Harvard Union, is convincing and handsome work; by contrast, the Inn at Harvard is a mere postcard of a building. In between these two extremes, however, is an interesting story— for the robust antiquarian 1900s-era Loeb House and the more imaginatively conceived 1930s-era Faculty Club are, according to your tastes in Georgian design, the yin and yang of a tradition of which Houghton is the last and perhaps the best (though not very astringent) exemplar, and Lamont the palest of receding shadows—all of it generated by Charles McKim's Harvard Union, now the central building of the Barker Center.

Barker Center for the Humanities

In the wake of his crucially important "Harvard brick" Johnston Gate of 1889–90, McKim was the formative influence in Harvard architecture in the 1900s, in the same way Bulfinch and Richardson were to in previous eras. And McKim's legacy to Harvard, though it included no individual masterworks like Richardson, was in many ways far more important. Such was the success of his neo-Colonial aesthetic, not just in his 1889 Johnston Gate, but in the subsequent and equally elaborate gates of his design that quickly followed (Meyer and McKean), that McKim persuaded the Corporation to sponsor a dramatic sequence of many such architectural extravagances of stone and brick, erected between 1900 and 1906. While McKim's Colonial Revival aesthetic attracted within a decade of Johnston Gate other architects to follow his lead (the Coolidge office at Conant and Perkins Hall in 1893 and A. W. Longfellow at Brooks House in 1898), McKim himself—though in 1898 he did the Radcliffe Gymnasium and continued with the gates around Harvard Yard—was only commissioned to design one entire building near Harvard Yard in 1899–1900: the Union. The climax of this formative episode in Harvard's architectural history, McKim's design here established Harvard's iconic image.

Given in an effort to provide a large democratic "clubhouse" or "student union" as we'd say today for clubless undergraduates, the Union, was also intended to memorialize the eleven Harvard men (including Sherman Hoar, the model for the John Harvard statue in front of University Hall) who had died in the controversial Spanish-American War of 1898. Appropriately enough, Theodore Roosevelt donated the antler chandeliers, one of which hangs now in the entrance hall today, all that is left of reputedly more than thirty trophy heads of animals mounted and displayed in the new building. (No one, mercifully, knows if Roosevelt shot them all, or, indeed, any of them.) The Union's Great Hall, a noble room, was designed by McKim on the scale of his Harvard Hall of 1900–02 at the Harvard Club of New York, and until Boston's Harvard Club (with its similar great hall) was built in 1910 it was without peer in the Harvard context. One of the finest interiors of the College, about which both Henry James and George Santayana exulted, its remodeling and division recently caused great controversy. The idea of the Barker Center for the Humanities (including once scattered activities like the English Department, the German Department, and History and Literature) did not, however, much needed as it was. The center opened in 1997.

Two of Barker's other buildings are Burr Hall, designed originally for the Varsity Club in 1911, and the house behind the Dana-Palmer House, the Beck-Warren House of 1833, moved here from the site of the new Union in 1900. A late Federal-going-Greek Revival yellow-clapboard house, it is usually just called the Warren House, because it was the gift to Harvard of Professor Henry Clarke Warren, a famous scholar of Buddhism, who long lived there. The original house (the two ells are later) is most interesting, for its first occupant, Latin professor Charles Beck, and its most important architectural feature undoubtedly dates from Beck's occupancy here, probably a reflection of the fact that the professor was an ardent abolitionist in the years before the Civil War. This feature (rediscovered during modern renovations) is an old first floor trap door leading through to an also secret room in the cellar, a room only four by four feet. It suggests that this house was a stop on the "underground railroad" for fugitive slaves. As the DuBois Institute (named for the African American graduate student touched on in Walk Five) and the Afro-American Studies Department both are housed within the Barker Center today this is all very well—history, so to speak, catching up with history, and where better than overlooking Harvard Yard.

58. Faculty Club and Loeb House

Faculty Club *CSBA, 1929–1931*
Loeb House *Guy Lowell, 1912*

Faculty Club

Although the Faculty Club, through deft landscaping—including even a delightful fountain—has been nicely integrated with the Barker Center and the Dana Palmer House, it is more closely related architecturally with Loeb House, across the street, for both are variations on a theme of "Lowell Georgian," one dating from the early years of President Lowell's reign, in 1912, the other from his last years in 1931. The sixth president's lodgings built in the Yard since the 1630s, much has happened in this house over the years. Perhaps most interesting is the rather unexpected role it has played in the history of television! In fact it is the birthplace—at a 1946 luncheon hosted by President Conant—of what has since become the national leader in educational broadcasting in America, Boston's PBS station, WGBH. The call letters stand for Great Blue Hill (in the southern Boston suburb of Milton, site of the station's original antenna atop a Harvard weather station)—or, as one Cambridge wit had it, God Bless Harvard, which, in fact, gave Channel 2 the land in Allston on which its present studio stands.

Today, the president's lodgings are the headquarters of Harvard's two governing boards. The president now lives at Elmwood (Walk Nine); understandably, as it offers a much greater degree of privacy for family life. Still the

Loeb House

president's departure from the Yard has left a perceptible vacuum that surrogates cannot fill, however dedicated or however grand. Shades of Abbott Lawrence Lowell chatting with students at tea still linger, though it is only fair to add it was sometimes the case that the college more than its president appreciated what was always inevitably something of a fishbowl. Certainly that was the view of President Conant, who was glad of the chance during World War II to move to more modest presidential lodgings in the Dana Palmer House!

59. Carpenter Center for the Visual Arts *Le Corbusier, 1959–61*

In 1953 Nathan Marsh Pusey, a Midwesterner who had already been the president of Lawrence College, a Classics scholar and a graduate not only of Harvard College but of Fine Arts 1, became Harvard's twenty-fifth president, succeeding Conant, who stepped down earlier than might have been expected to enter government service—to which Conant, who despite considerable achievements as president was never entirely a success in that office, had grown more and more committed during the course of World War II. Naturally, the new Harvard president had many ambitions: none, not his prodigious fundraising, nor even his able defense of the university in the McCarthy era, was he more keen in pursing than the arts. Pusey was quick, therefore, to appoint the committee which in 1956 recommended the creation of a visual arts center, an idea so radical in the Harvard context it was felt it "merit[ed] symbolic expression" at the highest level; in the event by Frank Lloyd Wright's only rival as the most famous architect of the world at that time—Le Corbusier.

Today most would call the French master the most influential figure in the history of architecture in the twentieth century, and the Carpenter Center itself now ranks as one of his major works. Indeed, almost a half-century after its erection, it is still an astonishing sight to see overlooking venerable Harvard Yard. To be sure, the appointment by Conant in 1937 of Walter Gropius, who was, in James Stevens Curl's words, "probably the most influential architectural pedagogue of all time," had made Harvard the spearhead of the modern movement in architecture in America and had long since led (a decade before Carpenter) to the erection of perhaps the chief collegiate landmark of the modern movement in this country, the Gropius-designed Harkness Commons and Graduate Center (see Walk Eight). Moreover, not only in Cambridge, but in several Boston suburbs there were by the 1950s quite a number of modernist houses (equaled in distinction elsewhere in the country only on the West Coast), including several by Gropius and Marcel Breuer and including Philip Johnson's own house (see Walk 9), designed while he was a student at Harvard's Design School; and several developments of many houses by Gropius and TAC and Carl Koch in Belmont and Concord, developments dominated by (indeed, almost restricted to) Harvard faculty. There was also landmark modernist work by Eero Saarinen and Alvar Aalto at M.I.T. But these were episodic pockets in a world still very unfriendly to the Modern Movement when Carpenter began to rise on the verge of Harvard Yard in 1961. The strange new building, crowding ivy-clad neo-Georgian imperiously on all sides, caused widespread consternation and considerable disapproval. Indeed, as a student in the late 1960s and early '70s, I always thought Carpenter must envisage a future when the Faculty Club and the Fogg Art Museum would have moved away to other and perhaps more spacious quarters, their locales and Quincy Street itself meanwhile having become a gracious greensward. (Do not mock: the street Quincy empties into now runs under a grassy overpass, while on Quincy Street itself only one of many structures which stood there in 1900 were still there in 2000. Who can know what 2100 will look like?)

Le Corbusier himself, confronted with the notion that the rectangular red brick buildings of Quincy Street constituted a sacrosanct design concept, would have none of it. A supreme contextualist in his way, he was never quite so simple minded as most present day contextualists and would have maddened today's preservationists in the same way as does Frank Lloyd Wright's Guggenheim Museum in New York. Le Corbusier was determined the Carpenter Center would be "a threat to the old Quincy Street.... He was intent on producing a manifesto," according to William Curtis, who observed that the master referred to "the curve jutting out over

Carpenter Center for the Visual Arts

Quincy Street as the 'coup de poing'—a term which might be interpreted . . . literally as a 'punch.'" Interestingly, the manifesto is felt both within and without
Le Corbusier's building. Consider the way the building's great asymmetrical, dynamic sandy colored concrete volumes are pierced by an ascending ramp; of which Curtis writes: "The ramp is a fantasy . . . involving the fulfillment of a primordial dream of the Modern Movement in painting and sculpture: projection of the spectator into the heart of the work. . . . This fantasy is the more alluring since it is on such a large scale. . . . "

Yet it is just here where the building, so "inward" in every way, looks outward most notably. Curtis again: "What most fascinated the architect about the Yard was the way the fixed rectangular buildings defined a grid through which the paths of circulation flowed. Once during his stay he was discussing the program . . . in an office in Thayer Hall. . . . Outside the bells sounded. . . . Le Corbusier's attention was riveted to the Yard below him . . . crossed by lines of people approaching one another under the trees along the paths. . . . When he turned back he remarked on the beauty of what he had just seen." We have already observed the importance of these Yard paths as the chief influence on the design of the Carpenter Center; now in the way the Center "captures the diagonals of the Yard" the other side of the thing becomes evident. And not just the ramp. Curtis goes so far, in fact, as to claim that at the Carpenter Center "the pilotis are like trees with clearings."

If it was all—still is, even in the age of Frank Gehry's Guggenheim Bilbao—revolutionary, and was doubtless made possible only by the ardent support of the new president who chose the site and among several insisted upon it, Le Corbusier was disappointed with how cramped it was. "Such a small commission from such a large country," he is reported to have said. Yet he was just the designer to bring to life architecturally this radical curricular reform at Harvard (studio art!), where he was eager because of the historical legacy of Gropius and company at Harvard to show what he could do. French intellectual that he was, he carried the premise forward to its logical conclusion: a building dedicated to studio art, to the visual arts, must be itself, he felt, constantly generative, no less at all, in fact, than an exultant, utterly freeing experience of creative power. This the Carpenter is. Bainbridge Bunting, by no means uncritical in his approach to modernism, well called the Carpenter "a promethean symbol of creativity." And so it has seemed—midst the usual practical complaints of clients and workers everywhere—to more than one denizen over the years of the Department of Visual Environment Studies, which has lived there ever since.

The whole design turns, in fact, on exactly the relationship "between the hand and the head," celebrating a fusion still suspect to many academics with enough success to influence the argument. For it is as forceful and sculptural an architectural form as it means to be a dynamic and fructifying as a learning environment. In fact, Le Corbusier's last major work has seemed to most observers to deliberately recapitulate his life's work. It is, Curtis has said, a sort of "diary of life-long themes," and in Reaburn and Wilson's *Le Corbusier, Architect of the Century*, Tim Benton writes that what is interesting here is that "Le Corbusier seems to have self-consciously anthologized his own architectural development. The building can be read as a sort of dictionary of Corbusian discoveries...a lifetime's restless *recherche patiente*. Perhaps because he was keenly aware that he was being employed as an 'old master'...Perhaps because he responded warmly to his old friend [Luis] Sert...possibly even because he was 'teaching' the young Jullian de la Fuente, the design of the Carpenter Center became explicitly self-referential." For an academic building, and the only one of his designs in the country he wished to influence above all, this all makes very good sense. Sigfried Giedeon, however, said more, surely, when he acknowledged the mysteriousness of it all: "The Carpenter Center," he wrote, "is an attempt to penetrate the unknown." Walk the "ramp path," not only Le Corbusier's three-dimensional response to the paths of Harvard Yard, but his response to its underlying purposes. The Carpenter Center seems to float above the landscape, an architecture of freely formed libertarian space, flowing with the ramp through it, with its views into the studios, making the disciplines of the creative process an actual part of the building's own design. The building also seems to hint at the fact that as modernists see it, the visual arts do not only portray the external world, but a vastly altered universe of perception—psychology again; even a little William James. One is never far from the past here. The James' family house stood in the nineteenth century on the site of today's Faculty Club, right next to the Carpenter Center. And it is by no means unlikely Le Corbusier had read James. Certainly he understood him. Certainly, too, the effect of all this on Harvard—never mind on the architecture of the Boston region and on the country generally—was electrifying. "At Boston's Logan International Airport the exact time of his arrival [in November of 1959] had not been announced," Sigfried Gideon remembered; "nevertheless the entire [Harvard] School of Architecture was there to greet him." And when he returned the next year, in June of 1960, his final plans completed, one of President Pusey's deans wrote that the committee, having first seen those plans, could only be described as in a "state of euphoria."

Still today, of course, people love to make jokes (two elephants copulating, and so on) about Carpenter. Historically, only Memorial Hall among Harvard's great buildings has been more reviled. But that, surely, is a warning. If Memorial Hall had not been more or less sacrosanct as a war memorial, President Pusey, who then despised most things Victorian, would have torn it down. Never any secret was made of his desire to. It is a cautionary tale in view of how cherished as architecture Memorial Hall now is, splendidly restored in all its glory. And it's as well to recall that if Memorial Hall became very soon the brass band marching up the street of Victorian Harvard (much too loudly, perhaps, for its own good) so also Carpenter Center was (still is for some) a case of Stravinsky and Picasso and all the rest of "them" come to declare war on the venerable Yard. As recently as 1998 a Harvard-affiliated author wrote of the Littauer Center of 1978 at the new Kennedy School, not a great building, that "unlike so much University architecture of the 1960s this school was intended to look like Harvard." Poor Harvard! To think so little of it. Yet in that sense the Carpenter Center still does not look like Harvard. But, then again, which Harvard are we talking about. Neither had Memorial Hall when it was new. Yes, it was red brick, but with all its Gothic (Gothic!) pomps and additional gilded pinnacles of the 1890s it posed just the challenge then to the Harvard image that Carpenter would later pose. And in both cases, historically, the meaning was the same: each building did not "look like Harvard" because each building meant to herald a new Harvard. In both cases, indeed, what might be called the ongoing image of the Old Yard proved hard to displace. Yet, historically, the change each foretold was very real. In Memorial Hall's case, in addition to its significance for the abolitionist movement and the Union cause in the Civil War, the building's scale and splendor clearly sought both to inspire and to express the fast approaching reality of the small regional college become a great national university. And in Carpenter's case its meaning was also twofold, more just than the introduction into the curriculum of the studio arts. In commissioning the first and as it turned out the only building in the New World by the greatest twentieth-century architect of the Old World, Harvard was expressing a truly global reach.

Meanwhile, there abides at Carpenter a very special muse. Of the fifth-level artist studio with its breathtaking views of the Yard, William Curtis wrote of VAC BOS (Le Corbusier's codename for the project: VISUAL ARTS CENTER BOSTON) that "to open these doors is to step into an element of Le Corbusier's dream: he might have designed this place for himself."

60. Otto Hall and Busch-Reisinger Museum

Gwathmey, Siegal, 1990

Otto Hall

Treasure houses of old art for study and learning, side by side centers of new art-making like Carpenter, are characteristic of the Arts area. And if one traverses the Carpenter Center ramp through that building's heart at its end is a companion building designed with the Carpenter in mind that is just such a repository, the Busch-Reisinger Museum—a destination for the ramp after all, Carpenter's detractors insisted.

One of Harvard's several art museums, the Busch is most notable for the art of the 1900s Vienna Secessionist School, that of the 1920s constructivist school and, above all, of German Expressionist art, Harvard's collection of which is among the best in the world. Historically, because so much of this art was rescued by Harvard from the Nazis, who thought it "degenerate," one might say this museum (in this like the design school in Gropius' era) represents in Harvard's history the grander end of a continuum the other end of which is the Window Shop (See Walk Two). Indeed, Walter Gropius' archives are here too. Architecturally, however, Otto Hall's design understandably relates less to the Bauhaus than to the Carpenter Center, for Charles Gwathmey, Otto Hall's architect, confessed more than once that it was the proximity of the new hall to Le Corbusier's only work in the New World that attracted him to this project most keenly. What designer, indeed, would not have been captivated by the opportunity to dance with the Master.

61. Robinson Hall *McKim, Mead and White, 1904*

For just about a century now the visual arts at Harvard have been largely based at the northeast corner of the Yard, extending eventually fully half way up Quincy Street. Robinson Hall is the earliest of those first buildings of the 1890s and 1900s to survive the century—appropriately, given that the study of architecture at Harvard was first undertaken in the Fine Arts Department in 1874. The next year an independent Department of Architecture was started. Seven years later Harvard was the first American university to offer courses in landscape architecture. Then, in 1903, Charles McKim designed Robinson Hall as the home of architecture and company at Harvard, where in 1929 the country's first school of city planning was founded. In 1936, together with Architecture and Landscape Architecture, it was formed into a new Graduate School of Design.

Robinson Hall itself could scarcely have been better sited. Situated as it is to the east of Richardson's Sever Hall, then as now the masterpiece of the New Yard, Robinson and Sever were always more than neighbors. Through the field of architecture they established—albeit informally—the pattern of the contrasting combination of new artists being nurtured in the shade of old art being admired. Robinson also formed with Emerson an open court onto Quincy Street; fascinating the way, on what was still a quiet side street, Harvard here reverted to the original design concept of the seventeenth- and eighteenth-century college of street-facing courts. Then, when the present Fogg Museum was built in 1925 across Quincy Street facing Sever, the court became a quad, albeit one with a street running through it. A quad full of the history of architecture—not only Richardson and McKim, but Gropius and Le Corbusier—all of whom have played their part here, for it is Robinson Hall which is, historically, a shrine of the modernist movement in America. Does one speak of episodes? It was in McKim's great space in 1959 that design students threw a spontaneous party for Le Corbusier that delighted the usually retiring master (including the construction of a pair of huge cardboard glasses mimicking Le Corbusier's horn-rimmed spectacles). Or, perhaps, one speaks of the day-in and day-out transformation of American design? It was from Robinson Hall, in a very real sense, that Gropius fired what Ada Louise Huxtable called "the architectural shot heard 'round the world," the design in the Boston suburb of Lincoln of Gropius' own house, now a museum. It was a nice touch, that, on the New York critic's part, to ascribe such a thing to a Harvard professor; it having been on the other side of Harvard Yard some centuries earlier that some of the preliminaries of the first shot had taken place in 1775. As for the design of Robinson Hall itself, one of McKim's quieter works, as Leland Roth, the McKim scholar, points out, it was designed to be a "background building, defining spaces but not dominating them." McKim wisely left that role to Sever.

OPPOSITE: *Robinson Hall, with Memorial Hall in background*

62. Fogg Art Museum *Coolidge, Shepley, Bulfinch, and Abbott, 1925*

Holy ground—certainly insofar as the history of art is concerned. In the late nineteenth century the Fogg stood at a critical intersection of architects like H. H. Richardson and Charles McKim (whose work the museum now faces) and of several artists' circles as well. One was centered on John LaFarge, another on Sarah Wyman Whitman, and some of the best work of both adorns nearby Memorial Hall. Yet another such circle formed around William Morris Hunt, the painter, who introduced the Barbizon School to America. William was an undergraduate of Harvard, where his architect brother, Richard Morris Hunt, designed the Fogg's first building in 1893, of which this building is the successor. With this new building of 1925 the emphasis shifted. While artists were still important—John Singer Sargent, the first living artist whose work the Fogg added to its collection, left not only murals at Harvard but a living legacy at the new Fogg in disciples like Joseph Coletti—art historians and collectors now dominated. Neither had been unknown at the old Fogg, including perhaps the best known of all of them before World War I, Bernard Berenson, who revolutionized our understanding of the Italian Renaissance. But at the new Fogg the leading figures were men like Edward Waldo Forbes, who had introduced the work of Degas to America in the first exhibition in this country at the Fogg, and Paul Sachs, who for the new museum borrowed works from the Peabody Museum to install at the Fogg a gallery of Maya and other such art which was the first permanent installation in any museum anywhere of such "primitive" work, not as ethnographic artifact, but as art. Curators like this worked hand in glove with collectors. As a result, works by Monet and Bernini, by Ingres (the finest collection of his paintings outside France), by William Blake, and by Whistler and Beardsley (and now too by Picasso and Pollock) are to be found here, as well as one of America's finest collections of early Renaissance Italian pictures. Perhaps the best known collector celebrated at the Fogg is Grenville Winthrop. He left Harvard one of the great Pre-Raphaelite collections of the world. He also focuses our attention on the role of the undergraduate in the Fogg's history, which has been at least as important as that of the faculty—for Winthrop was a student in the 1890s, one of those (Isabella Stewart Gardner was another) who Charles Eliot Norton fired up to a lifelong passion for art. Holy ground. But a difficult program for architect Charles Coolidge when he set about the design of this building in the late 1920s.

Difficult in more than one way. The Fogg Museum's design is intimately related to the character of the institution, which more often than not is misunderstood. As James Cuno, the present director explains: "A teaching museum at a small liberal arts college in a provincial setting . . . will have a very different mission from one at a large research university in a major met-

Fogg Art Museum

ropolitan area. The former is likely to concentrate on assisting faculty in the general education of undergraduates and on providing cultural opportunities to... the surrounding community. The latter... is more likely to be an active agent in the specialized education of undergraduate and graduate students and in the professional education of future art museum curators, conservators, and directors." The Fogg, "obviously of the latter kind," does, however, Cuno continues, have a public role—that of "introducing that community into the particular academic culture of the research university through specialized exhibitions, lectures, symposia and publications" that complement the public art museum. Indeed, the Fogg from the beginning has always been an academic companion piece to Boston's Museum of Fine Arts in offering (Cuno again) "their common metropolitan audience a full range of educational programs." Thus the Fogg Museum is the architectural expression of the Department of the History of Art and Architecture in the same way Emerson Hall is of the Philosophy Department. This museum's curators are fundamentally instructors; exhibitions are as often jointly mounted by staff and students; and internships, whether curatorial or conservation-oriented, are internationally competitive even, of course, as are faculty positions.

How unusual the Fogg is may be seen in the fact that the establishment of MIT in 1865 as much as the founding of Boston's Museum of Fine Arts five years later (the first American art museum, followed within the same year by New York's Metropolitan Museum) shaped decisively the Fogg's purposes and goals. President Eliot, who had established the first art history professorial chair in America for Charles Eliot Norton in 1875, was no

Interior courtyard, Fogg Art Museum, showing Frank Stella painting

less in art than in other fields a proponent of the hands-on experience of the scientific laboratory. A chemist, Eliot saw the Fogg, in the words in 1895 of the *Harvard Graduates Magazine*, as "a well-fitted art laboratory." An odd way of putting it, but in an environment stiflingly conservative at the time it became a kind of charter for the Fogg. As Caroline A. Joners put it in *Modern Art at Harvard*: "counterpoised to [the] conservatism which lingered longer in Boston than in New York, was a powerful liberalizing force: the progressive laboratory ideal, in which a commitment to direct experience fostered an openness to experimentation.... From its inception [the Fogg] was ... an 'art laboratory', where art works could be analyzed and compared, rather than as a treasure house built to enshrine a cultural legacy."

Repercussions both pedagogical and architectural resulted. For example, the generalized liberal idea of an art laboratory certainly stimulated the design in this building of the first university-based research and conservation laboratory in the country. But that was only one part of what became really a unique and really world famous mission for the Fogg. The crown of the unusual partnership of Forbes (a Boston Brahmin, a grandson of Emerson) and Sachs (scion of the famous New York banking family of Goldman Sachs) was virtually to "define the role of the university art museum in America." Now jokes about how Harvard rules the world feed on this sort of thing, but it is perfectly true that directors of the Metropolitan Museum, the Philadelphia Museum, the National Gallery, the Art Institute of Chicago, the Museum of Modern Art, the New York Guggenheim, even the Los Angeles County Museum and the Fitzwilliam at Cambridge University have all received their training in the classrooms and halls of this Georgian Revival—sorry, Italian Renaissance, or is it something else?—building which is the architectural result of all this; one might say the architectural solution or, equally, the architectural problem.

The facade is a composition of many Georgian themes, from Boston's Old State House (the window trim and balconied consoles) and Westover, the Byrd mansion in Virginia (the entrance pediment, which is magnificently carved), and doubtless others yet undiscovered. The principal exhibition area, the Warburg Room, takes its character from a French sixteenth-century carved oak ceiling from Dijon. In the Naumberg Room the interior is English and of the seventeenth century. Theme upon theme. And each earns, as it were, compound interest. The court around which all revolves, accessed through the Georgian Revival facade, is a splendid four-fifths-scale travertine replica of the sixteenth-century Italian loggia of the canon's house at San Biagio at Montepulciano by Antonio da Sangallo. Totally unrelated stylistically to the flanking vaulted cloister, or, indeed, to the Fogg's exterior or to any or all of the other interiors, the court, like all of the Fogg, is, however, profoundly related in this sense. It is all an architec-ture of proposals, not evocations—one impeccable Eurocentric stage set after the other. And an architecture of proposals, not evocations, has this merit: it is likely to incite more proposals. Truly, it is not entirely wide off the mark to suggest that the Fogg Museum's design, less deliberately but per-haps no less inevitably than the Carpenter Center's, plays a real part in stim-ulating the creative mind. And not just to exhibitions. Consider just the Fogg's court, so apparently antique in orientation (Robert Bell Rettig calls it, quite properly in one sense, "reproduction" architecture), and consider it in relation even to modernism, and in conservative Boston's orbit to boot. In her *Modern Art at Harvard*, Caroline A. Jones relates how A. Everett "Chick" Austin of the Fogg, when he became director of the Wadsworth Atheneum in Hartford, Connecticut, not only mounted a ground-breaking Picasso exhi-bition as well as the world premiere of the Gertrude Stein/Virgil Thomson opera, *Four Saints in Three Acts*, both to mark the opening of a new wing, but that, "striving for the 'hovering horizontals' and smooth planes of the International Style, the new addition included an atrium that echoed—in a modern idiom—the Fogg's own Renaissance courtyard."

Similarly, a part of the background for Gropius' coming to Harvard, discussed earlier, were the activities of a group of undergraduates led by Lincoln Kirstein. Compare what he means by "possibility" about Harvard with what I mean by "proposal" about the Fogg's architecture; Kirstein wrote that what was "magical about Harvard was its whiff of limitless possi-bility. Identification with a society of living and thinking New England dynastic actors gave a security and assurance prompting freedom of action which I do not think anywhere else in America then offered. Wide worlds were open.... Backed by the functional services of the Fogg, a couple of classmates and I founded the Harvard Society for Contemporary Art, today credited as a forerunner of Manhattan's Museum of Modern Art...." Founded at a dinner party in 1928 at Shady Hill (Norton's old home, thus renewing those old ties too), the society declared its intent to be "to supple-ment the work being done by the Boston Museum of Fine Arts and the Fogg Museum of Art" in the field of modernism, which was very little if anything, of course, in the conservative Boston of the 1920s. Yet this undergraduate society was, in Nicholas Fox Weber's words, "the first organization in the country to devote itself to an ongoing program of changing exhibitions of recent art." Indeed, according to one of its student presidents, John Coolidge, the ambition of the society was nothing less than "to pick up the torch lit by the Armory Show of 1913 and to introduce younger Americans to the art of the twentieth century and of our own time." Alas, if Boston was the one place such a thing could happen because of Harvard, as Kirstein saw, the flowering of the idea (just as in the case of John Reed and his friends in Greenwich Village) had to come in New York—because of the inbred conservatism of Boston's Brahmin ruling class, which controlled both the Museum of Fine Arts and the Fogg with an iron hand. Indeed, Sachs favored the society chiefly as a way of keeping modernism at some distance from both institutions. Thus did conservative constraints and more liberal causes each well serve each other's purposes, architecture meanwhile playing into the institution's larger purposes very well.

Not least in the Harvard Society. Very soon after its invention, the society exhibited the now famous Dymaxion House (a portable dwelling so called from combining part of the words *dyn*amic and *max*imum) of the highly regarded architect-engineer (and philosopher), Buckminster Fuller. The descendent of eight generations of New England clergymen and lawyers, Fuller, born in the Boston suburb of Milton in 1895, entered Harvard College full of promise from Milton Academy, but in what other innovators (including Edwin Land and Bill Gates) were to make a grand Harvard tradition, never graduated. In fact, in Fuller's own words, he was expelled "officially for cutting classes, but actually for general irresponsibility." Today he is known everywhere for his development of the geodesic dome. Ambitious to say the least, it was this society that also mounted the first exhibition in America of the Bauhaus, six years ahead of Gropius' appointment to lead Harvard's architecture school.

63. Sackler Museum *James Stirling, 1981*

By the time, in our own era, the question of the expansion of the Fogg Art Museum arose, its design was bound to provoke dispute. There was no question of reverting to neo-Georgian. But if the modern movement had then written finis to that vector, modernism's own bright promise—exemplified at Harvard by the Carpenter Center—had by the late 1970s faded considerably. What to do? Harvard's response was that of American architecture generally, to try to have its cake and eat it too: postmodernism. A pretty much discredited mode today, even its successes were problematic. But Harvard landed one of the best of the postmodernists, James Stirling. Though he was certainly tactless enough in describing the surrounding area as an "architectural zoo," he was gifted enough to take a

Sackler Museum

chance on (declining a proposal, for instance, by Frank Gehry) tackling such a problem. This response was characteristically postmodernist: in Susan and Michael Southworth's words, each feature of his new building "borrowed one theme from each of his neighbors," tending to exaggerate in a striking but playful or at least irreverent way some visual aspect of each one of them. I like the Southworths' analysis. They see a memory of the columns of Gund Hall in the Sackler's entrance pylons (intended to support a connecting bridge to the Fogg, now unlikely to be built), and another memory, a monumental "Gibbs surround," in the facade behind the pylons, one which mimics the neo-Georgian of the old Fogg. This sort of thing may seem too highly speculative a criticism. But who could fail to notice that the Sackler's polychromatic striped facade unarguably echoes the only slightly more reserved stripes of Memorial Hall, stripes which account for why detractors of Ruskin Gothic were always quick to call it the "streaky bacon" style. The Sackler was, finally, too glib a response, only adding yet another theme to the zoo, and not the most distinguished.

But the interior confirmed the wisdom of choosing Stirling. Built to house Harvard's ancient, classical, pre-Colombian, Islamic, Indian, and Asian art collections (including what has been called the world's most important collection of Chinese jades and a notable collection of Byzantine coinage), the Sackler boasts an interior, exotic without being kitsch, that is spectacular—and very architecturally expressive of the history and art of these collections. Margaret Henderson Floyd's ecstatic description of the stair hall highlights the design's roots in the famous Harvard-Boston

Museum of Fine Arts Egyptian Expedition that in 1924 began the historic excavation of the royal cemetery of King Cheops (Khufu) near the Great Pyramid. Wrote Floyd of the Sackler:

> The enormous height of the flagstone entrance hall, lighted at night from behind its four megalithic columns, evokes...the Hypostyle Hall of the temple of Karnak.... On the staircase walls are embedded ancient sculptural reliefs.... One of the most creative elements of the building, this staircase slashed up the full height of the structure at a width of only seven feet, producing a sense of compression and movement equal to that of the grand gallery leading to the King's Chamber in the Pyramid of Cheops at Gizeh.... Stirling has produced a masterpiece in this interior."

The last word goes to Keith Morgan and Naomi Miller, who rightly call the Sackler's great stair nothing less than "an object of wonder."

64. Gund Hall *John Andrews, Anderson and Baldwin, 1969*

Never at Harvard are the constraints of chronology and geography more conflicting than here. Next to the 1980s postmodern Sackler a really dull modernist box of the 1960s would illustrate perfectly that however gaudy and tawdry the worst postmodernism could be there was good reason for the zest and wit of the best of it, when compared to the boring and tired cliches the modern movement in architecture had sunk to by the late 1960s. Instead, there is Gund Hall, an imaginative and brilliant modernist work that shows how much vitality the International Style still was capable of in 1969 in the hands of a designer like John Andrews. The elegantly stepped, glassed-in form of Gund is masterful both in mass and in its proportions, and very satisfying to the eye, while disclosing superbly the giant four-deck drafting room that itself expresses (and, like the Carpenter, generates) an experience of architectural study that encourages interaction both in and out of the studio. A splendid example of the form-giver's gift, although the design is very self-contained and supremely expressive, it also defers in the

LEFT: *Sackler Museum and Gund Hall*
RIGHT: *Gund Hall*

most remarkable ways to its neighbors. The form of "a giant staircase . . . overhanging the other side to create a huge colonnade is nothing short of astonishing," Bunting exclaimed—remarking on the fact that "the forward thrust of Gund as it overhangs its colonnade directs attention to [Memorial Hall, while] the diagonal of the overhang reinforc[es] the pyramidal massing of the older building." Nor was that the extent of Gund's virtues: "The monumental colonnade of Gund . . . directs one's eye surely toward William James Hall, a significant gesture which indicates the continuation of the Harvard 'campus' on Divinity Avenue beyond the little Gothic church." Truly, Gund Hall is a tour-de-force, a modernist masterpiece—even if its roof does leak, and even if the building marked a difficult time for Harvard, and what turned out to be the coda of the Pusey years. The hall's groundbreaking ceremonies in 1969 were marked by demonstrations protesting $10 million for architecture but no black faculty. Typical '60s: as if not building Gund, or, indeed, spending any number of million dollars could address that lack, a far more complicated issue. Yet how else to make a point that very much needed to be made.

65. Science Center and Tanner Fountain

Science Center *Sert, Jackson & Gourley, 1970–1972*
Tanner Fountain *Peter Walker and Joan Brigham, 1985*

Meyer Gate and Science Center

This is the gateway building to Harvard's Science Area (see Walk Eight)—on the other side of Memorial Hall from Gund Hall—but it could hardly be more intimately related to the adjacent Arts Area: for the Science Center is a major work of Harvard's great architectural luminary, who presided from Gund Hall as Dean of the Design School in the 1950s and '60s, José Luis Sert. The chief though then anonymous donor of the Science Center was also a Harvard notable, one of the inventors just alluded to who never graduated from Harvard, Edwin Land. The inventor of no end of things (he helped design the cameras, for example, of the U-2 spy plane), Land was also entrepreneur and philanthropist as well as the founder of the Polaroid Corporation. Of immigrant Jewish background, Land entered Harvard in 1926 at age seventeen, his field of concentration physics. He left at the end of his first term. But he returned in 1929 and (though he earned no degree) never left thereafter, in the sense that he and his wife would live

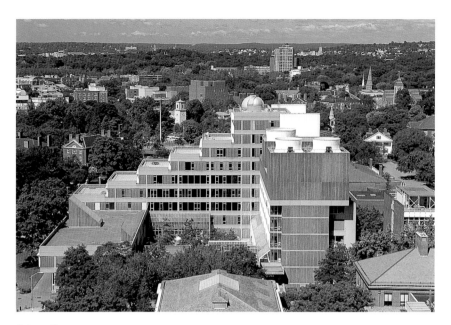

Science Center

in Cambridge for 60 years, until the late 1980s. As Sert also lived nearby, the Science Center was very much an "in-house" project and it had a vitally important Harvard subtext, as A. H. Dupree has pointed out: "Land was making a major statement with the Science Center that cannot be denied on the excuse of his choosing anonymity, especially in the troubled atmosphere of [the radical student disruptions of] 1972.... Housed within [the Science Center] was the Godfrey Lowell Cabot Science Library. Thomas D. Cabot, who described himself as a strong supporter of President Pusey, would be instrumental in developing the campus of science buildings heralded by Sert's architecture."

A major statement, indeed. The administration of Pusey—so brilliant in our context because so winning insofar as architecture at Harvard is concerned—and notable as well for many other fine advances in the life of the university, had by 1970–72 ended in disarray and tragedy. The angst of the anti-Vietnam protest movement in 1969 fueled a takeover by student radicals of University Hall, an act of aggression met by equally violent aggression by the Pusey administration. Having forgotten the lessons of the 1834 anti-Federalist student revolt in the Yard—and, indeed, of ancient statues claiming the Yard as sanctuary in most cases from civil authorities—Pusey on the advice of (predominantly graduate school) deans called the police to clear the building, afraid it would become a magnet for radical students all over the Boston area. A bloody eviction followed which shocked and to some extent radicalized the entire Harvard community, leading to a student "strike." The following year, 1970, Pusey announced he would take early retirement; that same year there occurred the famous Harvard Square riot—mayhem complete with massed state troopers battling rioters with tear gas and all the rest of it. I well recall as an undergraduate how the excavations proceeding for the Science Center seemed to assume almost heroic proportions. At a time when violent civil unrest engulfed the university, the fact that this huge multimillion dollar project funded by strong supporters of Harvard was going ahead had its effect; clearly, Land and Cabot and Sert, major figures at Harvard (and in the outside world), stayed steady in their purpose. As Dupree adds, each also took the long view: "It would be equally appropriate to call Cabot a strong supporter of President [Derek] Bok [who succeeded Pusey in 1971]. Land's gift as a part of that series [of buildings of the future science campus] was a guaranty of Harvard's strength in science to the end of the twentieth century and beyond." The election of Bok as Harvard's twenty-sixth president also restored confidence. A successful dean of the Law School who was more alert to the times (and more adept at the leadership skills they required), Bok, a Stanford graduate, and the first Harvard president drawn from the professional schools, was elected president just as the Science Center was nearing completion.

Sert's design was also confidence-building; though no one loved it, it was at once seen to be successful. To the north of Harvard Yard he did with the Science Center what he had done equally well to the south of the Yard with Holyoke Center; he connected the Yard adroitly with its environs; in the case of the Science Center "envisag[ing] the building as a staircase leading up from the old Harvard Yard and soaring in the direction of the new science campus of the future." The design concept of the new center, moreover, was also very expressive of the building's program: there at the center's front a low-rise science library and administrative center; to the left a spider-roofed form betokens the demonstration theaters; behind is the laboratory mass, high and long, while rising toward it in the building's center is the Science Center's heart, the terraced classroom section, stepped back six times, higher each time, seeming indeed to lead from the Yard to the Science Area beyond. Within, furthermore, adorning the entrance hall is a very effective "mural" by Constantino Nivola.

Like so many of the buildings of the Delta's "200," as Stirling called it, this building has long stimulated wits. It is not uncommon, for example, to hear students assert the Science Building is intended to resemble an early Polaroid camera. These are often the same students who believe Le Corbusier, when he first saw the Carpenter Center, exclaimed how much better it would have looked had it been built right-side up! Their fathers and mothers, moreover, doubtless told worse stories about Memorial Hall. Now, much more than fun is going on here. It was for the Science Center, in fact, that Pusey had wanted to tear down Memorial Hall.

As ever exhibiting the weaknesses of his strengths, Pusey, who disdained Victorian architecture as much as he loved modern architecture, could not see that both "styles" had their masterpieces and their missteps, and consequently he longed to be rid of Memorial. The alumni frustrated him, however. Doubtless today there are those who would tear down the Science Center. Thus do architectural tastes advance and recede. Like the surf. Speaking of which, do not fail to notice the Tanner Fountain in front of the Science Center, the work in 1985 of Peter Walker and Joan Brigham, very much stimulated by the new president's more expansive tastes. Seasonal timed cycles of clouds of low pressure steam (in winter) or of fine mists (in summer), play in each case on field boulders set casually in grass and asphalt, the whole intended as homage to the New England landscape. By all means sit on a rock. But be wary.

66. Paine Hall/Music Building

Music Building *John Mead* , *1913*
Loeb Library Wing *Stanley B. Parker, 1955*
Fanny Mason Wing *SBRA, 1970*
Addition *Wallace Floyd, 1997*

Paine Hall

"To charm, to strengthen and to teach: these are the three great chords of might." So says Longfellow (in *The Singers*) and so says the inscription on the chaste, pilastered Federal Revival facade of Harvard's Music Building. Located just behind the Science Center today at the western end of the Delta, somewhat removed from the main arts area at the eastern end, the Music building, was designed by John Mead in 1913. Since that time it has been the one place hereabouts where aural arts trump the visual arts. It's also a case of better music than architecture. Much better. No less than the Boston Symphony Orchestra was an outgrowth of the history of music at Harvard; it was the Harvard Musical Association that sponsored the first symphonic concerts in Boston, the joys and flaws of which prompted Henry Lee Higginson to found what is now a symphony orchestra of world rank. The same association, itself a Beacon Hill club of postgraduates, also helped provide the money for the university to engage as instructor in music in 1862 John Knowles Paine—for whom thirteen years later Harvard established the first academic chair in music in the United States. Paine was also the first major American composer in the larger forms, such as symphonies, masses, and oratorios. It is thus fitting that the concert hall that occupies the second and third floors of the original music building is named Paine Hall, designed by Mead in consultation with a pioneer in the study of acoustics (at Boston's Symphony Hall), Wallace Sabine. For all that, Leonard Bernstein used to complain you never heard a note in the Music Building; all the music, he protested, was on a blackboard or being endlessly talked about—yet another commentary on the fact that in music, no less than sculpture or drama or in any of the arts, Harvard was long wary of formal instruction involving studio or performance art, there being after all a distinguished tradition of spontaneous, extracurricular music making, a tradition still vital in Cambridge today. Bernstein, in fact, when he was an undergraduate music concentrator here, made his professional debut at Sanders Theater, a major Boston-area performance venue where the visual and the aural arts may be said to fuse at Harvard to unique and wonderful effect.

The training of composers, however (if not necessarily the performance of their work by faculty or students), has always been a part of the tradition here, in part doubtless because of the lead given by the Music Department's first professor. A certain logic suggests itself: Harvard, according to this theory should train composers, but not performers, just as it should train architects but not artists, though no one doubts, of course, a jerry-built building or an inept contractor or architectural sculptor could ruin the work of the greatest architect as easily as a slipshod performer could make a riot of the work of Bach. Thus Harvard has only recently produced performing artists of the stature of Yo Yo Ma, but since Paine's day has gifted the world with a half dozen major composers. Two who taught here stand out, both intimately associated with the Music Building: the Boston composer Walter Piston, he of elegant Pulitzer Prize-winning neoclassical symphonies, and New York composer Elliot Carter, Piston's student, who became a major figure in twentieth-century music because of his complex experiments in rhythm, speed, and such. Also significant was Archibald T. Davison, director of the Harvard Glee Club, the pioneering American scholar who laid the foundation for Boston becoming the world center of the early music movement in our own day. (Why Boston's proclivity for folk music, blues [see Walk 1] and early music? And why always at Harvard?)

Late twentieth-century additions to the Music Building include one quite striking modern work of more architectural interest by far than the original building. Designed by SBRA (James F. Clapp, Jr., architect-in-charge) in 1970, the Fanny Mason wing, a streamlined inverted pyramidal structure, is rather a sleek variation on a theme masterfully adumbrated some years previously at the Boston City Hall, where Kallmann, McKinnell and Knowles set the pace with the boldly projecting and gigantic cornice, from which plane after plane receded, seemingly infinitely. Interestingly, the city hall is often analyzed by reference to musical patterns by Igor Stravinsky.

67. Kirkland Street West

Lowell Lecture Hall *Guy Lowell, 1902*
Sparks House *William Saunders, builder, 1838*
Adolphus Busch Hall (Minda de Gunzberg Center for European Studies)
G. Bestelmeyer and Warren and Smith, 1914; Goody, Clancy & Associates, renovation, 1989

TOP: *Lowell Lecture Hall*
MIDDLE: *Sparks House*
BOTTOM: *Adolphus Busch Hall*

Here are three minor but interesting works that highlight variously aspects of the life of the university in the late nineteenth and early twentieth centuries. Lowell Lecture Hall, recently renovated, was the place Stravinsky, when he was Norton Professor at Harvard, delivered his series of lectures—in French and, after the fashion of the day, in white tie and tails. The cathedral of the lecture at Harvard, this hall originally seated 985 people in one auditorium—the strongest possible documentation that President Lowell, the donor, had nothing against lecture courses! An odd melange of Classical and Baroque architecture (rather unimaginatively decorated by the national, state, and university arms) this brick and limestone building nonetheless exudes a definite elegance, its proportions and materials lending much sympathy to neo-Georgian neighbors. Sparks House, on the other hand, sounds a very contrasting note; basically a Greek Revival house, this broad-pilastered mansion verges on being pompous, but is redeemed by a certain suaveness that seems Regency in feeling. The house makes no attempt at any dialogue architecturally with its neighbors. But how could it? It was moved here from Quincy Street; it used to stand where Gund Hall now is. Historically it is of interest as having been the residence of a mid-nineteenth-century Harvard president, from whom it takes its name. Busch Hall, its next door neighbor, an untimely essay in turn of the twentieth-century German romanticism (completed in 1917, the year the United States entered World War I against Germany) has survived to find new life as the Gunzberg Center for European Studies. It is also one building postmodernist remodeling has improved. One feels overwhelmingly the sense of having stumbled into some railroad station on the Orient Express. This seems oddly appropriate, as Busch Hall was built for the Busch-Reisinger Museum originally. In addition to dramatic life-size plaster casts, there is wrought ironwork of exceptional charm by Frank Koraleweski of Boston's Krasser Company in Renaissance Hall, and on the exterior sculpture carved by anonymous Italian immigrant carvers and modeled by Roger Noble Burnham and Johannes Kirchmayer. The latter artist, a German immigrant who became in the 1920s the preeminent architectural sculptor in this country, modeled all the Wagnerian figures (Wotan, Brunhilde, Siegfried, and Albrich) that sing their hymn to German culture above the windows overlooking the garden, and also both the head of the warrior on the west wing and the head of Apollo in the keystone over the front entrance. Notice also the carvings on the exterior walls—sayings like Schiller's wording of Immanuel Kant's categorical imperative (on the Divinity Hall side): *DU KANNST DENN DU SOLLST*/You can, for you should.

68. William James Hall *Minoru Yamasaki, 1963*

William James Hall and Church of New Jerusalem

Here is the finale that never quite happened—of modernist architecture as well as of student unrest (the Design School was equally home to both in the '60s), two themes of Pusey's Harvard becoming Bok's on this Walk in and around the Arts Area. Harvard's first skyscraper—and in that alone a serious provocation—William James Hall was another modernist work by a major architect, another triumph of Pusey's architectural program. But here Harvard's luck ran out. James Hall was so immediately disastrous in effect that when the blowing up of a Yamasaki building in St. Louis in 1972 made headlines across the country, aesthetes all over Greater Boston took heart. Might not the same fate befall James Hall? The early '70s were violent years after all. Student radicals (for reasons more political than aesthetic, of course) were rumored at varying times to be planning the destruction of everything from Widener Library (the Faculty mounted guard) to the Center for International Affairs, then located just behind James Hall. Mercifully, sanity prevailed. But so too did James Hall, still there now, as appalling as ever: the modern movement as its own worst enemy.

Divinity School and Shady Hill

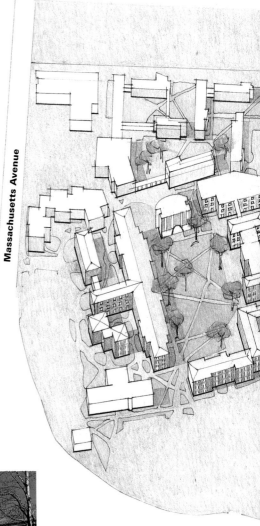

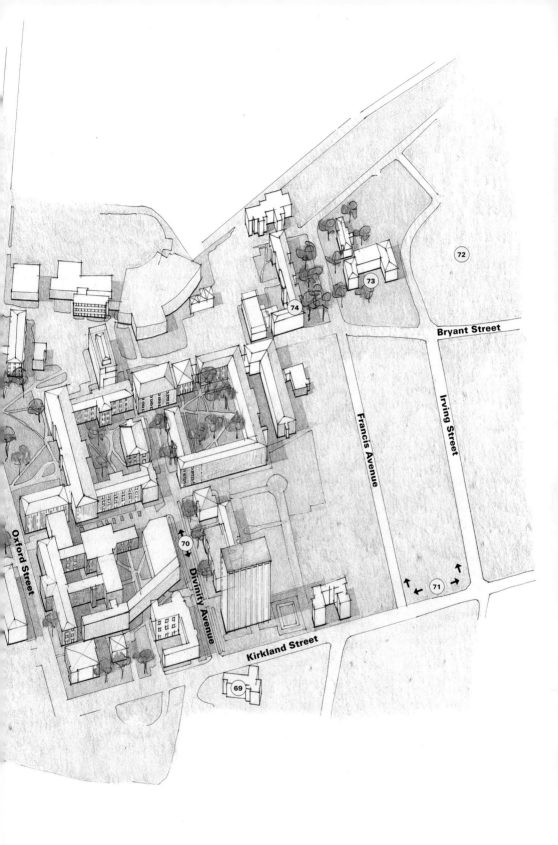

Bryant Street

Kirkland Street

Oxford Street

Divinity Avenue

Francis Avenue

Irving Street

72

73

74

70

71

69

Mid-Cambridge Campus

69. Church of the New Jerusalem *H. Langford Warren, 1903*

There is perhaps no more dramatic architectural contrast that speaks volumes for the university's growth in the last century than that of the sheer 1960s cliff-like skyscraper of William James Hall with the tiny little Gothic Revival church (the work in 1903 of the then head of Harvard architecture) at its foot across Kirkland Street. Yet the relationship between them amounts to more than their striking proximity and different scales. It is not just a good example of how the passage of time changes so much, but it also hints at one way to reduce to a more human scale Harvard's expanding physical plant in the twentieth century—which is to track specific individuals in the historical throng (both of people and buildings), trying to relate them to their specific locales. William James for instance: first met here in Walk Five where he taught, at Emerson Hall, and then on Kirkland Street heading home with the invariable student in tow (soon enough his old home will come into view), comes again to the fore at this small Swedenborgian church, where a hundred or so years ago he was to be found every Sunday morning in his pew, entirely unsuspecting, one may be sure, of what would one day be his towering university memorial across the street. The church itself, once part of a Swedenborgian theological school that before the School of Design built Gund Hall here occupied the whole Quincy Street frontage, is modest enough. Unlike another theological school drawn to Harvard's vicinity in the nineteenth century, the Episcopal Divinity School on Brattle Street, there is no shapely steeple. The Swedenborgians contented themselves with a diminutive bell-cote. But it gives the church an especially picturesque air. Thanks to neighborhood activists who rallied to its defense when yet another skyscraper was threatened here (decidedly not the place for one)—it endures into the twenty-first century.

70. Divinity Avenue Buildings

Divinity Hall *Solomon Willard, 1825*
Semitic Museum *A. W. Longfellow, 1902*
Harvard-Yenching Institute *Horace Trumbauer, 1930*

Three landmarks in a row: the oldest and most important (renovated in 2000 so as to restore it to full academic uses), one of the foundational buildings of Kirkland's Harvard in the early nineteenth century, is Divinity Hall. Built in 1825, this hall was the design—perhaps the very last design—of a leading Boston architect of those days, Solomon Willard. Best known as the architect of the Bunker Hill Monument in nearby Charlestown, Willard, at this time retiring from his downtown practice, seems to have turned over the commission to Thomas Sumner. But Willard's hand is evident. Though more elaborate than

Semitic Museum, left, *and Harvard–Yenching Institute,* right

Bunker Hill, especially in its broken massing, Divinity Hall is in character very austere and plainspoken, a quality that would have been all the more evident when it stood, as it first did, utterly alone, none of its present neighbors then built. Similar to University Hall in the Yard in its tripartite facade with two flanking entrances and central second floor chapel (marked by tall round-headed windows), Divinity, if it has none of University's elegance, discloses a much greater seriousness and dignity of bearing. Only the massed chimneys and graceful porticos (themselves so full of dignity) and, somewhat, the central pediment (though it is as plain as plain can be), articulate this sober, solid and commodious building. All very much in keeping with the program. Derek Brewer, Master of Emmanuel, John Harvard's old college at the English Cambridge, has observed that "the special character of early [i.e., seventeenth-century] New England . . . [was that] there was surely no more argumentative community in the whole world than the one which founded the many towns of New England." Nor, he insisted, was there ever a community of more "intensely rational, argumentative, and serious people who believed [emphasis added] *in getting it right.*" God knows to that end Harvard Divinity School has never been known to fail in the struggle, whatever one concludes about the result. Fittingly, its birthplace, exemplary architecturally, may be the most serious building at Harvard. Today used by the school only as a dormitory, it nonetheless remains sacred to Harvard as having been the scene in 1838 (a year after his more famous Harvard Phi Beta Kappa address at First Church) of Emerson's Divinity School Address, itself a memorable attack on New England's religious establishment.

When Paul Tillich, perhaps the most eminent theologian to lecture at the Divinity School, met his classes in the 1950s, he did so not in Divinity Hall itself but in the large lecture hall of the neighboring Semitic Museum. The headquarters today of Harvard's Department of Near Eastern Languages and Civilization, the museum sponsors teaching and publication as well as archaeological excavation, and may be credited with the discovery as well as the exhibiting of most of the 40,000 Near Eastern artifacts this building contains. Moreover, there was an underlying agenda to all this set by Jacob Schiff. A Jewish leader and Wall Street banker in the late nineteenth century (observant in the Reform tradition), Schiff made gifts to Harvard that are described by his biographer Naomi Cohen as "the first of its kind in the country," gifts President Eliot, Cohen recounts, believed would help reverse "the centuries-long antagonism of the Christian Church to the Jews," gifts centered on this museum. Its specific purpose was to bring together the study of all the lands of the Biblical Near East. Schiff's overall purpose seems to have been to combat anti-Semitism, an evil he was not wrong to think would get worse before it got better at Harvard— which two decades later, in fact, would be roiled by controversy over a supposed Jewish quota. Alas, the architecture does not live up to the cause.

Another minor work by an even more major architect adjoins it— what is now the Harvard-Yenching Institute. A different Horace Trumbauer entirely than the architect of Widener Library seems to have designed this structure at No. 2 Divinity Avenue, which Robert Bell Rettig could only call "placid" (which is certainly the *mot just*). Nevertheless, today its confusion of symbols requires explanation. The map of the world over the main entrance and the series of roundels and signs of the zodiac on the facade betoken the building's origins as the Institute of Geographical Exploration. The two guardian lions are, however, self-evidently from China. They announce the present use of the building, which houses a renowned library. Founded in 1928, the Institute, originally in Boylston Hall (hence the nearby stele), runs a program of visiting scholars and supports many Asian doctoral candidates.

71. Professors' Row

Lovering House (No. 38 Kirkland Street) *1839*
Lippmann House (No. 1 Francis Avenue) *1837*
James House (No. 95 Irving Street) *W. R. Emerson, 1889*
Cummings House (104A Irving Street) *Walker and Kimball, 1893*

The nickname, "Professors' Row," originally given at Harvard to a series of nineteenth-century houses on the south side of Kirkland Street, more or less where the Science Center now is, has been for the better part of a century more apt for the few houses now remaining on the opposite side of Kirkland and for the still predominantly residential streets off Kirkland, Francis Avenue and Irving Street. The oldest and handsomest of them all, both now dedicated to university use, are the Lovering House at No. 38 Kirkland notable for its splendid galleried Ionic portico, and the Walter Lippmann House on the corner of Kirkland and Francis Avenue; built in 1835, it is Greek Revival in origin but was "colonialized" in the last century. Its name recalls our exploration of the Gold Coast, for surely the final stage of privilege is a named memorial building at Harvard?—and the headquarters for Harvard's Nieman Foundation for Journalism does, indeed, honor the unsuccessful clubby of Walk Four, one of the great American journalists of the twentieth century. As interesting as the house, please note, is its handicapped access, proof positive (which some young fogies seem still to need) of what a good designer can do with this much maligned modern provision for access by the physically disabled. In this case the head of Northeastern University's architecture program George Thrush, and his partner in the Cambridge firm of Smart Architecture, Margaret Booz, achieved a design that is at once discreet (by careful attention to the grade they avoided the necessity of railings) and supremely elegant in the way the stylish curvilinear paths (ramps) sweep around one way and then another between garden gate and front door. Worthy of Jane Austen, this design is a gift to the fully-abled as much as to the disabled.

One block further, on Irving Street, beloved (like Francis) of the Harvard faculty for over a century now, stand the homes of two figures touched on here at some length. At No. 104 Irving is the E. E. Cummings House, where the poet grew up, and at No. 95 Irving William James' walk home (see Walk Five) has at

Lovering House (38 Kirkland Street)

last found it destination. The design of the most gifted of Boston's shingle style architects, William Ralph Emerson, a cousin of the philosopher, the elegant old James House, evokes an equally elegant old memory. Lucien Price, the writer and *Boston Globe* editor (author most notably of *Dialogues of Alfred North Whitehead*) recalled of his first days at Harvard as a seventeen-year-old newly arrived in Cambridge in 1903 from a small town in the Midwest: "After having gone to Concord and seen where Emerson and Hawthorne had lived,

I...walk[ed] around to see where William James lived. A college directory gave the street and number...." In fact, he encountered the great man himself, or, rather, spied him, in front of this house, sitting "in a lawn chair chatting with friends like an affable archangel." Why is it so hard to imagine? Because there is now only the house. Not even the lawn chair. I find myself wondering if a hundred years later students of spunk similar to Price will still arrive in Cambridge and track down their heroes. John Kenneth Galbraith lives nearby today, in a house made famous by years of post-commencement garden parties at which the great of the earth gather and, it being Cambridge, everyone tries not to gawk. Perhaps in every generation we reenact and reinvent the same professorial types to be sighted as one might sight a particular bird each spring. Is it wide off the mark to call Galbraith an "affable archangel" of our own day?

72. Charles Eliot Norton Estate: American Academy of Arts and Sciences Clubhouse (136 Irving Street)

Kallman, McKinnell & Wood, 1977–1981

No less than in the picturesque urban alleys of Harvard Square to the Yard's south, mostly a quite youthful venue, the intellectual and cultural life of the Harvard community also flowers in the quiet wooded hillsides to the Yard's north, mostly the domain of the older and very often quite famous. Many such, after lifetimes of achievement, may often be glimpsed in Norton's Woods, as the setting is often called of the Charles Eliot Norton estate from which comes the neighborhood's name now, Shady Hill. Alas, Norton's house is long gone, torn down by the university in what almost amounted to an act of vandalism, such were its memories of Victorian Harvard. The end result, however, shows that even with important buildings, preservation is not always the right answer. The magnificent site made available by the house's destruction attracted to Shady Hill no less than the American Academy of Arts and Sciences, which after years of moving, first here, then there (most recently in the Back Bay and then in Brookline) finally found in 1977 a permanent home on the site of Norton's house. One of Boston's most venerable intellectual institutions, founded in 1780 by John Hancock, John Adams, and James Bowdoin in those heady first days after the American Revolution, the Academy was conceived to "cultivate every art and science which may tend to advance the interest, honor, dignity and happiness of a free, independent and virtuous people." Today, its 400 or so fellows and honorary members, including no less than 173 Nobel laureates, give the Academy global stature (as does its scholarly journal, *Daedalus*) and when the decision was taken to settle in Shady Hill, they scored two considerable hits. The first came when (on the advice of the Fogg Museum's Agnes Mongan, a legendary curator of the time) Edwin

American Academy of Arts and Sciences Clubhouse

Land himself, only six years after his gift to Harvard of the Science Center, agreed to virtually fund the whole project; the second when they chose the architectural firm of Kallmann, McKinnell and Wood. Whether it be art or science, or both (or worse), one thing the Academy cannot be said to have neglected here is architecture.

Gerhard Kallmann, a German Jewish refugee first in Britain and then in America, and Michael McKinnell, his Manchester-born partner, had met in New York at Columbia, where there they formed a tentative partnership, hoping as architects just starting out do that they might win an open competition. In fact, they won the first they entered; their Brutalist style Boston City Hall of 1962 turned out to be one of the icons of twentieth-century American architecture. Forthwith, like Richardson nearly a century previously (after in his case winning the Trinity Church competition), Kallmann and McKinnell relocated to Boston, to which, again like Richardson, they were drawn in part by Harvard. Both Kallmann and McKinnell became members of the Harvard faculty of architecture. And it was their teaching, doubtless, that stabilized the post-City Hall practice in the 1970s when a rampaging postmodernism—*not* their style—became ascendant. Then it was that the Academy commission came. All the more attractive because it was, so to speak, just around the corner and up the street, it was nevertheless problematic perhaps in that the fellows by wide report insisted on no concrete, challenging Kallmann and McKinnell to eschew their Brutalist aesthetic. They did and they didn't, and with effects both good and bad. The academy's house they

designed is very fine and gracious. But it does not to my mind possess
the distinction of some of their Brutalist work like the Phillips Exeter
Gymnasium. Instead, marking a pivotal shift in their work (which, after
the Academy's house would include a whole series of distinguished buildings in what might be called their mature style, and very beautiful it is—
the Hynes Auditorium in the Back Bay, for instance), the Academy's
headquarters is very Wrightian in an Arts and Crafts way. (The plan, however, as Kallmann points out, is very similar after all to the City Hall.) In
the Cambridge context it is undoubtedly the most luxurious of clubhouses (the Academy *is* truly a final club), a fitting building type for
Shady Hill, one Norton would have approved of. If a bit too serene on the
outside, some of the interiors, however, are austerely magnificent.

73. José Luis Sert Buildings

Sert House (64 Francis Avenue) *José Luis Sert, 1957*
Center for the Study of World Religions *Sert, Jackson & Gourley, 1958*

Rather an intimate footnote to the distinguished and large scale body of
institutional work left at Harvard by José Luis Sert are these two very small
scale works in Shady Hill. The Sert House itself, designed by the architect of
the Science Center and Holyoke Center and so many other buildings at
Harvard and in the Boston area generally, over which Sert presided as the
reigning resident architectural master in the 1960s, stands at No. 64 Francis.

Sert House

Center for the Study of World Religions

Sert built it for himself four years after he became the dean of the Graduate School of Design, in the same year, 1953, that Nathan Pusey became Harvard's president. And it was in one of the three enclosed courts of this house one night in November of 1959 that no less than Le Corbusier himself, drinking Pernod, was discovered by incoming guests, including President Pusey. After dinner the party gathered around the model of the proposed Carpenter Le Corbusier had brought with him from Paris. No such drama has marked the history of Sert's other work here, but the *Center for the Study of World Religions*, best seen across the grass from Francis Avenue, shows that Sert was as comfortable working at small scale in a rather suburban setting as he was working at immense scale in a very urban or institutional setting. The center might well be mistaken for garden apartments in some outlying Boston suburb.

74. Divinity School Complex

Andover Hall *Allen & Collens, 1910*
Rockefeller Hall *Edward Larabee Barnes, 1970*
Andover Theological Library *Shepley, Bulfinch, Richardson & Abbott, 1960*

As this Walk began with the first Divinity School building of 1825 so it ends with the three most recent of the school's buildings, each erected on Francis Avenue at some distance from old Divinity Hall, now rather marooned among laboratories. The main Divinity School complex around Francis Avenue centers on Andover Hall, the only example at Harvard of the Collegiate Gothic style. Its architects, Allen and Collens (along with Maginnis and Walsh and in the wake of Henry Vaughan and Ralph Adams Cram and Bertram Grosvenor Goodhue), were leaders of the so-called Boston Gothicists, a group of architects who dominated this highly creative mode in the early twentieth century. Both the cloisters and Riverside Church in New York City were designed by Allen and Collens. Their Harvard work, though not inspired, is, however, handsome enough, and certainly deserved better in 1970 than Edward Larabee Barnes' Rockefeller Hall, built of the wrong colored brick entirely and very stridently massed—unless the point was to make a quite separable statement from Andover; if so, the statement seems unequal to its task. Far better is the Shepley Offices' Andover Theological Library on the other side of Andover Hall, where the very vertical fenestration actually comments nicely on Andover Hall's Gothic style though in a strikingly modern way. The quad thus begun behind these halls needs another side, but this is by now an old story. On suburban Francis Avenue in the twenty-first century, as 300 years before facing a wilderness crossroads, Harvard seems instinctively not to design self-centered quads (even where land ownership allows) but to build facing the streetside of the townscape, withdrawing to the inward centered quad only as necessity or experience (are they different?) urges again and again the value to academe of the introvert.

Andover Hall

Science Area and the Law School

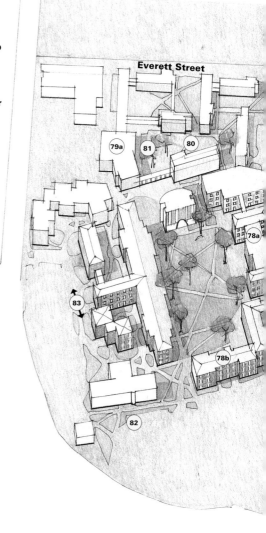

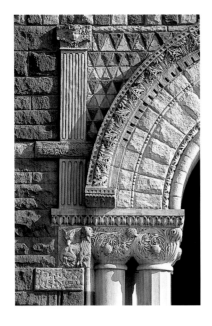

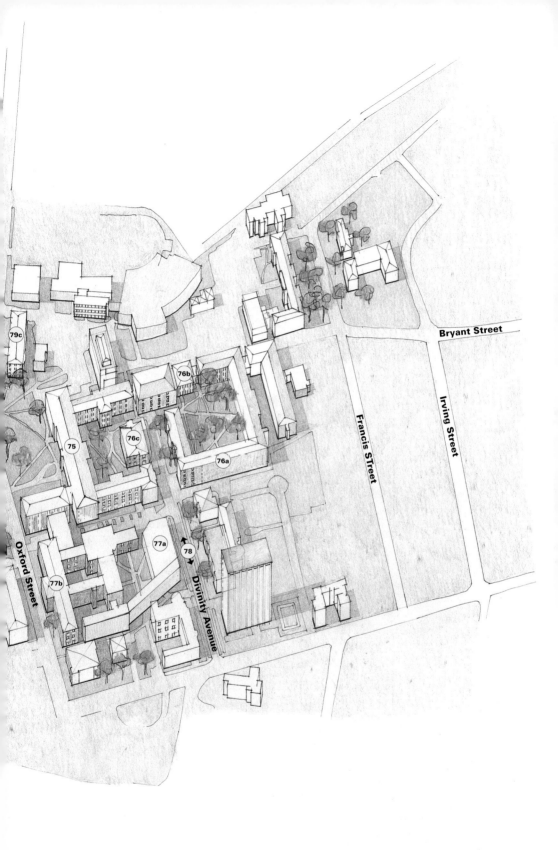

Mid-Cambridge Campus

75. The University Museum of Cultural and Natural History

Henry Greenough and George Snell, 1859, 1871; Robert H. Slack, 1876; George R. Shaw, 1880; Stone, Carpenter and Co., 1888; architects unknown, 1888–1889; Shaw & Hunnewell, 1900; architect unknown, 1906; Walter S. Burke, 1913

Those given to quoting Santayana's dicta that if we do not remember the past we condemn ourselves to repeat it are only too apt to overlook the countervailing truism that only forgetfulness sets one truly free. Harvard, in respect to the North Yard, is in a quandary today in either event. And one cannot help but feel President Eliot, were he still with us, would declare himself at once at least in one respect quite the opposite of Edith Piaf: regretting everything from one end of the North Yard to the other. However eloquently he argued for mercy, moreover, I doubt any architectural historian would even listen. It is that bad. And this despite the fact that development north of Harvard Yard was an important component of Eliot's reign and that he did not lack for advisors of considerable stature. One of them, an architect who did much work for Harvard, was the president's brother-in-law, Robert Peabody. Another, Charles W. Eliot, Jr., a distinguished landscape architect, was the president's son. Nor, at least by the 1890s, was Eliot Jr. retiring on the subject: "this permitting donors of buildings or gates to choose their sites is fatal," he railed; outside Harvard Yard itself the university risked becoming, he thought, a "jumble of badly placed buildings." He was right. So was Charles McKim who also spoke up in the '90s: "Some

The University Museum

The University Museum

plan," he protested, "is woefully needed at Harvard." By then, even Charles Francis Adams, Harvard's treasurer (and no aesthete), was dismayed, admitting later that planning in Eliot's administration had been a "disgrace." Today one can only speculate that in this as in all things Eliot believed in almost unbridled freedom. Thus the plans of individual architects at Harvard cohered more often by accident than design during Eliot's time. No better example of all this exists than the University Museum, opposite Divinity Hall.

Bunting aptly describes the effect of these two of only three buildings standing at the start of Eliot's presidency north of Harvard Yard as having "the aloof air of mansions of none too friendly millionaires attempting to ignore each other." The museum itself, begun in 1859 by an outside corporation using state funds and only ceded to Harvard in 1876, ultimately took over half a century to build. A fusion of the Harvard University of Natural History (itself a fusion of the Museum of Comparative Zoology, the Botanical Museum, and the Mineralogical and Geological Museum) and the George Peabody Museum of Anthropology and Ethnology, today even the names confuse, a case of too many words and then some. And the list of architects responsible for the eleven separate buildings of this huge U-shaped complex is not much shorter. Nor has it all been entirely a success. To be sure, on the academic and research side this is, for example, where Stephen Jay Gould has his office. But the museum side is more problematic. Notwithstanding the famous "glass flowers" exhibit—and even the famous twelve-foot-high "Harvard mastodon"—museum officials today continually lament that while traditionally there's a Museum Big Three in every metropolis: art, science, and natural history, that's not true today in Boston. Museum spokesman Kyle Roberts points out, "we are the major natural-history museum in Boston"; yet Harvard's museum attracts just a little over 100,000 visitors a year, much less than the 1.9 million that seek out the Museum of Science or the 1.7 million that visit the Museum of Fine Arts. Nor can one entirely discount the idea that the museum's architecture is part of the problem. There is a certain period feeling. The gloom can be overwhelming, despite a sort of stolid coherency. The most that can be said is that the museum is impressive; most would call it oppressive. A gigantic but not graceful building surrounding an open court, 364 feet by 269, the museum has been aptly called a "warehouse." Though one as well with a literary dimension! Absorbed here through the 1940s, in what he called "the tactile delights of precise delineation," was no less than Vladimir Nabokov, whose spirit still seems to haunt the place. Before he became professor of Russian literature (at Cornell) and while he was lecturing at Wellesley College, Nabokov was primarily a research fellow here in Entomology and curator of Lepidoptera. Nor did he at all resent his "day job." Butterflies fascinated him all his life. "The years at the Harvard Museum remain the most delightful and thrilling of my adult life," he wrote, rivaled perhaps only by his summer trips collecting butterflies. Writes Robert Pyle: "The astonishing bit of time travel at the end of chapter 6 in *Speak, Memory*—when he sets out on a morning's expedition...and ends up...some forty years later—expresses the magic of his passion as piquantly as anything he ever wrote."

76. Biological Laboratory and Herbarium and Tozzer Library

Biological Laboratory *Coolidge, Shepley, Bulfinch & Abbott, 1931*
Farlow Herbarium *Peabody and Stearns, 1910*
University Herbarium *Shelpley, Bulfinch, Richardson & Abbott, 1974*
Tozzer Library *Johnson & Hodvelt, 1974*

Eliot's posterity, which has endeavored to make more sense out of the North Yard, has here scored its greatest success. The Bio Labs were, in fact, sited in 1931 so as to form another large open court with the University Museum (the open arms of each reach toward each other), and when the two huge courts were eventually linked (in 1953 by the University Herbarium) they created a continuous 500 foot-long north wall of a huge quadrangle that remains today the organizing basis for almost the only part of the North Yard that makes visual sense. The Bio Lab itself, moreover, deftly incorporated two pre-existing and rather discordant buildings

Biological Laboratory

of Eliot's era. The handsome Divinity School Library of 1910 by Peabody and Stearns (now the Farlow Herbarium) was annexed to augment one arm of the Bio Lab's lovely sunken court, which also enfolds old Divinity Hall, at once setting it off as something of an antique jewel—shades of Harvard Square's Wadsworth House—but also putting it to good practical use in the complex as a whole as somewhat shielding the Bio Lab's court on its otherwise open side. It is a bravura performance (augmented in 1974 by Tozzer Library, which on the museum side of the street balances off Divinity Hall on the Bio Lab's side), in the face of which a building notable as the home base of Nobel laureates such as James D. Watson (the co-discoverer of DNA) seems almost more notable for its architectural design. This is all the more the case because the Bio Labs are not only brilliantly designed overall, but wonderfully detailed. Indeed, the ornament is so gorgeous many a medieval cathedral—even Chatres itself—might fairly be challenged to equal it. At Harvard only Sever Hall is in the same league.

In overall design and massing the Biological Laboratory, of brick and metal sash, is really very simple; indeed, this is where the Coolidge Office began the long process of introducing Harvard to the modern movement in architecture; the International Style hovers close here. But what stands out at once is the way the simplicity of the building is enlivened by the architectural sculpture of Katherine Lane Weems. A Boston artist, a student of Anna Hyatt Huntington, Weems was responsible for the designs (modeled in clay and then enlarged to stencils that were then incised into the brick by pneumatic drill), which she based on an overall scheme representing the several zoögeographic regions of the world. The centerpiece is a majestic grouping of seventeen African elephants—a relief 100 feet long and 10 feet high. Stylized as well as naturalistic (the composition is symmetrical, for instance, in contours), the elephants, furthermore, are on the move, led by a female, a baby marching beside its mother. This central frieze is flanked by individual animals, which also read well: the gorilla, the lion, the Cape buffalo, the ostrich—all are easily spotted, the point being to represent the animals of Africa south of the deserts. The Indo-Asiatic region is represented on the south wing, where are carved a number of exotic animals, of which, perhaps, the group of tigers (the furthest in from the corner)

Frieze, Biological Laboratory

stands out most forcefully, along with (fourth from the corner) the Indian leopard. Also on the south wing are representative animals of what is called the Holarctic region, which covers most of the northern temperate zone as well as the arctic; here are the polar bear, the Himalayan ibex, the timber wolf, the puma, the Rocky Mountain goat, Marco Polo sheep, the sea lion, and a group of buffalo. At the Divinity Avenue end is seen a group of pelicans in flight. On and on it goes, including a more sinister throng on the north wing, representing the neotropical region of South America: visible here are a boa constrictor, a giant anteater, a jaguar, and a wolf.

Hardly less intriguing are the flora and fauna of Lane's grillwork sculptures (all highly magnified representations) on the three pairs of entrance doors which are dedicated to the theme of sea, air, and earth—which is to say, shellfish, insects, and plants. The center doors symbolize the insects of the air: the praying mantis, the wasp, the queen ant, the beetle, the spider, the fly, the bee, and the butterfly are all shown. The left pair of doors stands for the sea, showing representatives (the starfish and the crab, for example) of several invertebrate groups, while the right two doors represent the earth—specifically, the rise of higher or flowering plants (shown at the tops of the doors) from the lower or non-flowering plants (shown at the bottom of the doors). These botanical subjects are exotic indeed, ranging from "the follicles of a sedge adapted to wind dispersal" to a "spikelet of a rough hair grass," but including also the flowers of the gingko tree and even common seaweed. It is a world and then some that this sculptor discloses to us, full of incident and edification, its greatest force and effect in the magnificent frieze of African elephants that dominates all high above the main doors. Not only is this an impeccable *architectural* design concept—this frieze is the decoration of a top story of necessarily windowless rooms of ventilating fans and other machinery—but the carvings themselves are very well done, cut into the brickwork with broad, slanting strokes, the line therefore always heightened by the way it catches and holds shadow. And though Weems excelled in the design of these reliefs, her more conventional work, entirely in the round on ground level plinths flanking the entrance doors, is equally hard to resist: two rhinoceros, named respectively Victoria (after an animal the sculptor had been alternately "fascinated and terrified" by at the Bronx Zoo) and Bess—names chosen by Weems as those of two queens she admired. They are blunt beasts, so to speak, with more heft and rump than grace. But they are not ugly.

77. Fairchild and Mallinckrodt Laboratories

Fairchild Laboratory *Payette Associates, 1979*
Mallinckrodt Laboratory *Coolidge, Shepley, Bulfinch & Abbott, 1927*

Fairchild Laboratory

Just a little way down Divinity Avenue behind Fairchild Laboratory is Mallinckrodt Laboratory, the grandest of the first generation of labs to be built in the North Yard in the early twentieth century, all red brick Georgian Revival, and in Mallinckrodt's case, boasting as well a lofty colonnade that now seems a bit passe in the face of so many newer later twentieth-century labs. The best of these is Fairchild Laboratory, a DNA research building. As Richard Dober in *Campus Architecture* notes: "beguiling and surprising open spaces, views, and pedestrian circulation, developed with a facade that invites passers-by to see and intuitively understand [the]

building's purpose; detailing that divides a large and complex building into harmonious parts; human in scale; materials that are reminiscent of other buildings but not diluted copy-cat architecture. Like many masterworks the building does not exhaust its subtlety, grace and beauty on first glance." The balconies here are actually for emergency refuge from the possible hazards of the labs, which also have "break-out" panels between them.

78. Oxford Street Physics Group

Pierce Hall *Shaw & Hunnewell, 1900*
Jefferson Lab *Shaw & Hunnewell, 1884*

Oxford Street, towards its center, where the west front of the University Museum stands across the street from Pierce Hall, centerpiece of the physics range opposite, is, just briefly, beautiful—in a very Victorian kind of way. Dignified, red-brick, industrial Harvard presides in Victorian sobriety on all sides, set back behind spacious lawns—where one can easily imagine frock-coated professors of long ago hurrying by in a sort of collegiate ballet. The oldest and most storied building in this range is the Jefferson Physical Laboratory of 1884, which even from the outside seems to conjure what Natalie Angier calls the "core moment of discovery that's so exciting in science," a moment caught so well by the twentieth-century surrealist painter, Remedios Varo; Varo realizes that "this central art of the imagination in science, this free play of the mind, is very similar to what artists do." Therein lies the magic of this rigorously academic structure, ordered handsomely by its brick pilasters on the outside, no less so within, where the exposed brick interiors positively evoke ethos of Victorian science. Here Percy Bridgeman did some of his Nobel Prize–winning work. Indeed, Jefferson Lab itself is historic, being one of the first purpose-built physics labs in America. Sixteen years later Jefferson's architects, in their design of Pierce Hall, essayed more elaborate limestone trim, but so ordered things that when minor connector buildings were later built into the physics range all fused nicely together.

79. Harkness Graduate Center, Perkins Hall, and Conant Hall

Harkness Graduate Center *Walter Gropius/TAC, 1948–1952*
Perkins Hall *Shepley, Rutan & Coolidge, 1893*
Conant Hall *Shepley, Rutan & Coolidge, 1893*

This elegant buff-colored brick ensemble of residence halls, low-slung, crisp and clean of line, grouped at the end of Oxford Street around open courts ("outdoor living rooms" their architect called them) connected by covered walkways, is an utterly pristine example of the International Style, and by no less than Gropius himself and The Architects Collaborative. Neglected today, the Harkness Graduate Center is a work of immense importance to American architectural history, the first major collegiate landmark of this

Harkness Graduate Center, left, *and Holmes Quadrangle West,* right

style in the country. Art integrated into the complex by Gropius includes works by Joseph Albers, Herbert Bayer, Joan Miro, Jean Arp, and Richard Lippold, the last of whom was the sculptor of "World Tree" in the central court yard. Yet Philip Johnson has recounted how President Bok wanted to tear Harkness down. Of course, it's Pusey and Memorial Hall all over again. Different building, different president, same situation. Today, one just holds one's breath, not at all sure that the historic preservation movement (code, really, for "traditional" Victorian usually) really can rise to the International Style! This major landmark is overdue not just for preservation, but for restoration. It was built to introduce some amenities of university life to graduate students. Though two of its residence halls, Child and Richards, are Graduate School of Arts and Sciences housing (as are two more older halls adjoining, Perkins and Conant of 1893 by the Shepley Office, their first Georgian Revival at Harvard), Harkness Center today is dominated by Harvard Law School, which houses virtually all its students in the remaining residence halls of Gropius' complex. The names of these halls, moreover, now celebrate the Law School's history; Story Hall, for instance, commemorates Justice Joseph Story, Class of 1798. He was a key early figure in legal education at Harvard, the Law School of which, though it is now the oldest in the country (deriving ultimately from the endowment of the Royall Professorship by Isaac Royall, who died in London in 1781), was only really firmly established after Kirkland's creation of a separate law faculty in 1817 and the appointment in 1829 of Story, a justice of the U. S. Supreme Court. Similarly, Dane Hall commemorates Nathan Dane, the donor of Dane Hall

Perkins Hall

(or Dane Legal College as it was originally called), erected in Harvard Yard in the southwest corner of the Old Yard overlooking Harvard Square in 1832. There it was that Rutherford B. Hayes, drawn even in 1843 to "the intellectual atmosphere of Boston," studied law. Although five graduates of Harvard College later became U.S. presidents, Hayes was the only graduate of one of Harvard's graduate professional schools to be elected chief executive of the United States until George Walker Bush, a Yale graduate with a Harvard MBA, became president in 2001. Interestingly both elections were very close and highly controversial.

80. Holmes Quadrangle North

Hauser Hall *Kallmann, McKinnell & Wood, 1993*
Maxwell-Dworkin Computation Center *Payette Associates, 1999*

Hauser Hall

Law School teaching and administration buildings dominate this quad, something of an oasis in the sea of parking lots throughout the North Yard. Newest and best is Hauser, which in both its plan and overall siting is wonderfully sensitive to Harkness Commons. Hauser's rounded back seems almost to be spooning with the elegant and shallow ellipse of the Commons. Otherwise, despite such striking contemporary touches as the very effective wide-flaring, space age cornice, Hauser is too obviously in bondage to Richardson's nearby Austin Hall (see No. 82, this Walk). Particularly problematic is Hauser's detail, which is at least misleading if not dishonest; the stone imposts of the window surrounds, for instance, are totally decorative in a non load-bearing brick skin.

Maxwell Dworkin Computational Center could not be more different in overall impression, with its aggressive New Age silhouette. The edge it presents to Oxford Street is as acute as the blade of a stiletto, the edge it offers staid Holmes Quadrangle only slightly less high tech. It is a building

OPPOSITE: *Maxwell–Dworkin Computational Center*

Maxwell-Dworkin Computational Center

that attempts to answer a question posed once by *Harvard Magazine*, that, while somewhat self-congratulatory, is of obvious pertinence to the university at the dawn of the twenty-first century: "How is it that a famous liberal-arts center like Harvard, home to what is arguably the world's first computer, could also be called the birthplace of the world's most successful software company? Are we sure we're not talking about MIT?" Various answers, each too smart, suggest themselves. And what Harvard has to fear in all this is as clear as what it has to gain. But the two simplest answers emerged from accounts heard at the building's dedication, where Steve Ballmer, Class of 1977, president of Microsoft, told the story of how it was this very site (in the old Aikens Computation Center of 1946–64) where his friend and classmate, William H. Gates III, wrote the code for the software that became the first product of Microsoft. The second answer came from Harvard President Neil L. Rudenstine, who observed that the new building, named after both men's mothers, was evidence that even Harvard and even in the computer age remained "a deeply human enterprise." It had been, said Rudenstine, "a day of families." And of architecture. No one will miss Aiken. But Payette Associates, whose earlier success with Fairchild has already been noticed, scored again here; by including generous public spaces, and such features as opposing open staircases, the architect designed the building to encourage interaction among the users.

81. Holmes Quadrangle West: Langdell Hall

Shepley, Rutan & Coolidge, 1906; Coolidge, Shepley, Bulfinch & Abbott, 1928

Of all the times at Harvard when buildings that were originally street-facing later turned their backs to the street to reorient rearward onto a later-developed quad, this is the biggest example and the worst failure. Holmes Field, so-called because the family home of the Autocrat of the Breakfast Table, Oliver Wendell Holmes, Sr., was located nearby in the nineteenth century, was by the 1890s the principal athletic field of the university, one of several north of Harvard Yard. Another was Jarvis Field, where Harkness Graduate Center now is, the site in 1874 of Harvard's first intercollegiate football game, with McGill. Today Holmes Quadrangle—as it really should be called now it's surrounded by large buildings—is, however, only half a quad, though the many trees somewhat obscure the fact, for its entire south and west ranges are the backs of the physics range that still fronts on Oxford Street.

It is on its east side that Holmes Quadrangle comes to life—in Langdell Hall. The seat and state of Harvard Law School for more or less a century now, with the exceptions of Widener Library and Harvard Medical School, Langdell is the most imposing building on any Harvard campus. A gigantic Ionic order of engaged columns—sixteen of them, count them—all in limestone, march heroically along; and on the central pediment above words attributed by Sir Edward Coke to Henry de Bracton at the conference between James I and the Judges of England—tremendous words: *Non sub homine sed sub Deo et lege*—Not under Man, but under God and the Law.

Langdell Hall

One is meant to be impressed, and one is. The building is named for Christopher C. Langdell, the now legendary dean that President Eliot personally plucked from obscurity in New York in 1870 and backed to the hilt in his radical reform of the by then moribund Law School. Langdell's reform challenged the whole Anglo-American professional tradition, for "Langdell regarded the law as a science to be mastered only by the investigation of its sources—decisions and opinions—and," in Morison's words, "he insisted on the students' learning the law as a growing organism, by studying cases." Students, who "wished to be told what the law was, not to search it out for themselves," liked Langdell's reforms even less than did the Bar, but in the end, despite the revival in the twentieth century of textbook and lecture and even of some of the original practical field work of the eighteenth-century legal apprentice tradition, Langdell (dean until 1895) is still seen to stand at the summit of legal education. Not only the father of the case method, an inductive method that emphasizes studying the details of specific cases rather than trying to derive specific law from general principles, Langdell was a great proponent of the Socratic method. Backing all this up is the principal interior feature of Langdell, the largest university law library in the world, housed on five floors of stacks below Langdell's second floor reading room.

Langdell itself, however, is flawed, architecturally, and will remain so as long as Holmes Quad survives in its present form. Because, by the time it was built, Harvard had used up all the sites in this area facing a street, Langdell had to be built so that "the principal walkway by which one approaches it," in Bunting's words, "forms so sharp an angle with the facade that it is impossible to comprehend. . . . All this grandeur is lost on a very large quadrangle." Holmes Quadrangle awaits a master planner perhaps not yet born. Meanwhile the university has just mounted a major restoration of Langdell's imposing interiors, which now again form a worthy setting for the great tradition of Harvard Law School, the modern development of which is explored in our discussion of Austin Hall.

82. Austin Hall Triangle

Littauer Center *Coolidge, Shepley, Bulfinch & Abbott, 1937*
Gannett House *circa 1838*
Austin Hall *Henry Hobson Richardson, 1881*

So chaotic is the North Yard, and so incoherent its architectural ensembles, it is more wishful thinking than anything else to use words like quadrangle or triangle of anything but the development of old Holmes Field, and even that use is a very free one not everyone would accept. At the North Yard's southernmost limit, just below Langdell, the Shepley Office's Littauer Center of 1937, for instance, the home of the Graduate School of Public Administration (now the Economics Department), is perhaps the most incongruously sited of all these buildings. Street facing, of course, it presides above the Cambridge Street overpass, entirely uninterested in the North Yard, its focus on dominating Massachusetts Avenue north of Harvard Square. The result in the North Yard is what has been called the most awkward public space in all of Harvard. All the more so because Littauer is another immense and immovable imperial landmark. It is also a kind of time warp. A re-study in 1937 of a rejected design of ca. 1810 for University Hall that was used for the Bulfinch Pavilion of the Massachusetts General Hospital, it was built of stone from the same Chelmsford quarries as University Hall. It was also a great provocation—erected the very year of Gropius' arrival at Harvard!

Adding to the confusion, moreover, is nearby Gannett House. Like the Dana Palmer House on Quincy Street, this small, handsome Greek

Gannett House

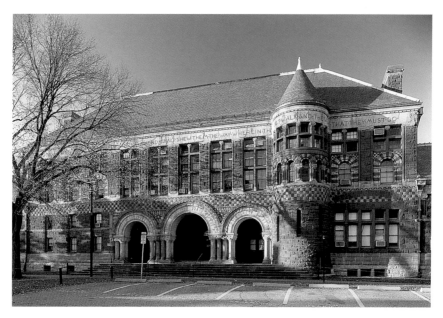

Austin Hall

Revival house is, however, priceless evidence of what this area looked like before the university's expansion into it. It is also a link with the past that, together with the triangular greensward it shares with Littauer and Austin Hall (on the site of which Gannett House once stood), gives a valuable human scale to the whole area. It is home to the prestigious *Harvard Law Review*, an elite student-run publication open to students according to their class rank and writing skills; and it also houses the Harvard Legal Aid Bureau, founded in 1913, the oldest student-run legal service in the United States.

On the third side of this triangle and facing on it is the Law School's most beautiful and venerable building—Austin Hall—not a masterpiece on the order of Sever Hall, but nonetheless one of Richardson's most moving and evocative works. Austin's massive, quarry-faced masonry, strong too with clustered entrance columns and rich capitals—even its orders of the day, every day, inscribed on the facade (from Exodus XVIII: 20—"And Thou shalt teach them ordinances and laws and shalt show them the way wherein they must walk and the work they must do")—all herald and express the revival of the Law School under its great dean, which Langdell Hall would celebrate so unequivocally decades later. A classroom building, Austin Hall's interiors can be moving, even intimidating as the layers of its history grow denser. As recently as 1977 Scott Turow wrote of a classroom in Austin: "Its seats and desks were in rows of yellowed oak, tiered steeply toward the rear. At its highest, the classroom was nearly forty feet, with long, heavy curtains on the windows and dark portraits of English judges, dressed in their wigs and robes, hanging in gilt frames high on the wall. It was an awesome setting." Austin Hall is also the sort of place where law professors like Sam Thorne entranced interlocutors like Jill Ker Conway. Thorne she recalled as "a white-haired figure striding into our lecture hall...to announce that we were to see ourselves as knights who had just paid tribute to our lord with a red rose at mid-summer." While this is admittedly an eccentric way to begin an academic discourse, Ker recounts thereafter Thorne "wandered absentmindedly about the small lecture room [leading] his listeners in successive lectures to a deeper and deeper understanding of this seemingly fanciful obligation."

Courtrooms as well as lecture halls and libraries figure, of course, in the life of a law school, and Austin Hall is the locale of the James Baur Ames Courtroom (originally the library). Here are held the famous Ames moot courts, over which U. S. Supreme Court justices have been known to preside in the competition's final round. The huge chamber rejoices in surely the most magnificent fireplace mantel and overmantel anywhere on any Harvard campus. It is a wonderful work of art, the great mantelpiece of the Ames Courtroom, and more than once I suspect it well may have sparked— not so much in the wandering as in the foraging mind, if a formal analysis is of its artistry or even a conscious notation of its virtues—perhaps a line of thought fructifying to what is sometimes called the legal mind. For the law is also about lawyering. And lawyering, like art dealing, is in Terry Teachout's words, "one of the equivocal professions." Admittedly, both occupations are at once "inescapable and indispensable," but the "very existence," he felt, of both was somehow unwelcome. The art dealer "reminds us that art is a business, a mundane reality that has never gone down smoothly." So is lawyering. Yet in the throes of weighing this or that disparate thing, the stuff of any trial, the Ames courtroom mantelpiece is not likely a neutral back-ground for counsel with an eye, achieving as this enormous work of art does so beautiful an equilibrium of nobility of form and elegance of presentation; of studied thought, of the play of the mind and the mind's eye; of precedent, of freedom; of justice, illusive goal—to start my own train of thought—and mercy. Behold, a meditation. But such will arise in the alert mind frequently here, for like the eighteenth-century halls of the Old Yard, like Widener, like parts of Brattle Street and the Plympton Street literary quarter or the Fogg or Memorial Hall (it is a lengthening list at the end of Harvard's fourth century), the Law School is yet another example of holy ground, as I have called it, in this case evoking the extraordinary intellectual tradition of possibly the most storied of the graduate schools, for the Law School has exerted an enor-mous influence even well beyond the profession it engages, in the social and political life of the nation.

At Austin Hall, of course, one's mind turns to the Law School of Victorian days that Henry James knew so well and liked so little; then very much a work in progress, it was in Austin Hall the school was rejuvenated in 1881 by President Eliot and his new dean. And a much needed rejuvena-

Austin Hall

tion it was! In James' day in the 1860s one was a law student at old Dane Hall, the building Austin replaced. Though he diligently attended all his law classes, he was probably not the first and assuredly not the last Harvard student (the list is long, right down to Bill Gates and Frank Gehry today) to feel a need to search out more arresting fare in other realms of the university. In James' case it was the entirely literary lectures in the Old Yard of the poet professor James Russell Lowell, which "glowed" in James' memory for years in a way the law certainly didn't. (James did not, however, escape participation in moot court, at which he was conspicuously a failure; ashamed, he wrote, the experience was like the "merciless fall of the curtain on some actor stricken and stammering.")

Vastly more important to the post–Civil War Law School was James' classmate, Oliver Wendell Holmes, Jr., and Holmes Quadrangle today (though actually named after the Autocrat, Holmes, Sr.) inevitably evokes the memory mostly of the younger Holmes, one of the founders of the Law School's august intellectual tradition in the modern period. Holmes entered the Law School from Harvard College in 1864, and whereas James had found nothing and dropped out, Holmes found the passion of his life, going on to become Chief Justice of Massachusetts and Associate Justice of the U. S. Supreme Court. Indeed, since his reappraisal by contemporary scholars, beginning in the 1970s, he has increasingly become recognized, in Richard A. Posner's words, as "the greatest figure in the history of American law."

It was an article published in *The Boston Globe Magazine*—an article rejected by the *Boston Bar Journal*—that sparked that important reappraisal, by focusing on Holmes' romantic life and revealing at last a multi-dimensional figure of engrossing interest. A clubby "sport" in college, thrice wounded (twice almost fatally) in the Civil War, a friend at varying times not just of Henry but of William James, and of Emerson too, and very much the ladies' man the *Globe* article celebrated, Holmes was bon vivant, scholar, and man of action, too. A Boston Brahmin conscious of his ethnic and class heritage, who had none of that caste's innate narrowness. Broadly liberal, he was, for example entirely without anti-Semitism, in an age in which it was pervasive. Equally, he was extremely egotistical, ambitious to a fault, and intellectually aloof. But as scholar and justice he more than made up for those flaws. In 1880, for example, Holmes gave in Boston a series of Lowell Lectures that—when they were published by Little, Brown the next year as *The Common Law*—were called "arguably the most original work of legal scholarship by an American." It is a vibrant work even today; "The life of the law," wrote Holmes, and his words resound still a century and more later, "has not been logic, it has been experience." An offer followed forthwith from Eliot to join the faculty of the Law School, where Holmes had already lectured on constitutional law between 1870 and 1873. Appointed to the Massachusetts Supreme Judicial Court the next year, his tenure there and (after 1902) on the U.S. Supreme Court amounted to nearly half a century, and encompassed many themes that have dominated twentieth-century law, including Holmes' stand in favor of Congressional regulation of the economy and the defense of free speech, what Holmes referred to as "free trade in ideas."

If Holmes, the sort of open-minded Boston Brahmin President Eliot himself was, dominates the Victorian period of the Law School's history, the period Austin Hall evokes so well, the kind of student nurtured at Eliot's Harvard exemplified in the life and work of Felix Frankfurter. An immigrant Austrian Jew who could not speak English when he arrived in the United States at age twelve in 1894, Frankfurter went on to Harvard Law School and graduated with highest honors in 1906, eventually blossoming into a jurist of great distinction, himself appointed to the U.S. Supreme Court in 1939. Harvard's preeminent law professor in the post–World War era—the evocative image has shifted back now to Langdell Hall—Frankfurter exercised a considerable national influence. Very much a liberal activist as a citizen, though he ever upheld professorial balance and judicial restraint professionally, Frankfurter helped launch the American Civil Liberties Union and *The New Republic* and famously defended Sacco and Vanzetti— defended them in the pages of the *Atlantic Monthly* too, and in the teeth of then President Lowell's opposition. (Lowell's objection to Frankfurter was rather obviously—and repugnantly to us today—the same as his objection to the Law School's other great Jewish luminary of the era, Brandeis, who also ascended to the U.S. Supreme Court; both, Lowell declared, possessed high intelligence but defective character!). Very much a disciple of Holmes, Frankfurter had not a few detractors at Harvard, who ridiculed his so-called "WASP patina," as if the characteristics and temperament of the highly refined Frankfurter could not as naturally arise among Jews as among WASPS, as if Jews had any monopoly among ethnic groups in the matter of ambition. Justice Holmes, by then something of a legend, would, of course, have none of it and mentored Frankfurter as President Eliot had Brandeis. And if all this is a measure of the Law School's growing national influence in the twentieth century, we should also fill in the windows between the columns of Langdell Hall with a figure of more recent years, who though he did not achieve the U.S. Supreme Court still has left an indelible legacy in Holmes Quad: Archibald Cox.

In modern times the Law School has more than once been the center of bitter controversy about its values and lifestyle. In the 1970s with new professors like Arthur Miller, Alan Dershowitz, and Lawrence Tribe appearing regularly on network television, books like John Jay Osborne, Jr.'s *The Paper Chase* and Scott Turow's *One L* probed closely into whether or not the Law School had become more of a "trade school," too intimately linked with Boston's and New York's prestigious corporate law firms. Now these are issues one can hardly engage too often in a world enamored with the bottom line. Someone has said that if you compared Business School students and Law School students, while it would likely be true that large numbers of both were chiefly after money, the difference was that at least the law students felt guilty about it. However, it's not that easy a call and things are, in fact, much more complicated than they seem: one thinks of Archibald MacLeish, the Pulitzer Prize–winning poet and playwright and later Librarian of Congress and a Harvard professor and great humanist who became Acting Master of Eliot House—all in the years after he left the corporate practice of law and absconded to Europe to write verse. Then there is the Boston law firm of Bingham, Dana and Gould's First Amendment work for the *Atlantic Monthly* and *The Boston Globe*, or the cast of characters, often admirable, even superlative, that have been conspicuous in the recent history of Harvard's own lawyers, Ropes and Gray, the Boston firm founded in 1865 and filled, of course, with Law School graduates. One thinks of Elliot Richardson's role in the Watergate investigation. Above all, one thinks of Archibald Cox.

Scion of an old New England family, a graduate of St. Paul's School, Concord, N.H., perhaps the preeminent American prep school, Cox was asked after a stint as a Boston lawyer to join the Law School faculty. By the 1950s a leading scholar of American labor law, he was also a "Boston Brahmin, a stiff fellow," all agreed; "Harvard tweeds, the sharp New England profile, the brisk walk on tall legs," all added up easily to a cold unfeeling stereotype too easily poked fun at, whether affectionately or maliciously. But if clarity and intellect were more Cox's forte than warmth and personality, he soon showed his worth in the Watergate scandal as Special Prosecutor. When President Nixon fired him, and Cox's onetime student Elliot Richardson resigned in protest, Cox emerged, in Phil Hyemann's words, as that rarest of things in our own era—"a permanent American hero." (He even made it into *The New York Times* crossword puzzle: three letters for "important figure in Saturday Night Massacre.") That morning Harvard president Derek Bok might have been Henry Dunster, when he brought to Morning Prayers in the Yard a special urgency, very much in the Puritan tradition, declaring from the president's stall in Appleton Chapel, that "Cox's actions exemplified "the truth embedded in Aristotle's *Ethics*: if you would understand virtue, observe the conduct of virtuous men."

83. The Griswold-Pound Axis

Griswold Hall *Benjamin Thompson Associates, 1967*
Hastings Hall *Cabot & Chandler, 1888*
Hemenway Gymnasium *Coolidge, Shepley, Bulfinch & Abbott, 1938*
Harvard-Epworth Church *A. P. Cutting, 1891*
Pound Hall *Benjamin Thompson Associates, 1968*

Sheltering behind the east side of Langdell Hall, between that building and Massachusetts Avenue, is a clustering of seven structures built at varying times over the last hundred years, and now forming a sort of long free-form grouping more or less divided into two quads, each very charming. The first quad emerged with Austin Hall as its south side and Hastings Hall as its east side. Hastings, a Queen Anne Style work of 1889 by Cabot and Chandler, though it achieved a certain notoriety as the "Little Jerusalem" of pre–World War I Harvard, when Jewish students were, by whatever informal means, segregated, has never been thought a success architecturally. Of tawny yellow brick, terracotta and brownstone trim, its character was not improved when the Shepley office designed the extremely bland adjacent Hemenway Gymnasium, forming now the southwest corner of this quad. The second gym of that name to be built here, red brick Hemenway ill meshes with Hasting's much more yellowish brick. What finally knits all this together effectively, however, is Griswold Hall, built in 1967. Similarly, the northern part of this axis—formed by Pound and Lewis Halls and the Harvard-Epworth Methodist Church (a work in the Richardsonian Romanesque style)—is given coherent form by Pound Hall, Griswold Hall's companion piece of the next year. Both Griswold and Pound are the design of one of the best of the architectural firms that evolved out of the Gropius/TAC circle, Benjamin Thompson Associates. Although best known for such extraordinary work as Boston's Fanueil Hall "festival marketplace," these gifted designers nowhere solved a more difficult problem than here at the Law School. By deft planning, including even hollowing out the terrain, and through clever design (plum-colored brick, for instance, in deference to Austin Hall and bush-hammered concrete resembling the limestone of Langdell), the Thompson firm created two lovely secluded quads that relate to each other very well. Bunting was correct to pronounce this long axis created by Ben Thompson of two quads—in the middle of which is the Center for International Legal Studies—"the most adroit example of design for a given environment provided at Harvard" in recent years.

It was from the faculty of the Law School, in the wake of the enormously disruptive student unrest President Pusey in 1969–70 seemed so at a loss to handle, that his successor was chosen. Derek Bok, the first president of Harvard ever to come from one of the professional schools, three of which—the Big Three: Medicine, Law and Business—have come in the twentieth century to rival (in distinction at least) the still pre-eminent liberal arts core of Harvard, exemplified by Harvard College and the university's central faculty of Arts and Sciences. Harvard's twenty-sixth president, Bok, though he had been dean of Harvard Law School, was the first president of the university not a graduate of the college. However, in his long reign of 20 years, collegiate affairs loomed very large; most notably Bok accomplished a seminal curricular reform in the college, a considerable refinement of Conant's "General Education," which Bok and his dean of the faculty of arts and sciences, Henry Rosovsky, called the "Core Curriculum," successfully insuring the integrity of the Harvard A.B. Bok also accomplished the key first stage of co-educational living that set Harvard and Radcliffe Colleges all but irretrievably on the course that would lead to their merger many years later. More at ease with the times than Pusey (Bok famously brought coffee and doughnuts to an all night sit-in demonstration at Langdell Hall he helped to resolve), he was able as president not only to successfully negotiate his way without violence through another building take-over (this time of Massachusetts Hall, where his own office was located), but he seriously engaged the political issues of the day—disinvestment in South Africa, for instance—an issue, incidentally, which provoked the only example I know of in Harvard's history of what might be called "protest architecture": African shanties, built in front of University Hall in the spring of 1986, flanked by a sixteen-foot ivory tower compliments of ever helpful students of the Graduate School of Design, and answered by conservative students with nearby "gulags." The Old Yard as street theater shocked many who had perhaps forgotten that within those venerable precincts students had once before helped to incite a revolution—on the eve of 1776.

Radcliffe Institute, Quad Houses, Upper Brattle Street, and School of Education

Cambridge North and Radcliffe Yard

Women's Education at Harvard

Pulitzer Prize-winning historian, Laurel Thatcher Ulrich, Phillips professor of early American history and director of Harvard's Charles Warren Center for Studies in American History, wrote for *Harvard Magazine* in 1999 a provocatively titled article: "Harvard's Womanless History." In that article Ulrich lamented how little is made of the brilliant but utterly thwarted women (Henry Adams' wife Clover, for instance, or William James' sister Alice) who might have made equally significant contributions to Harvard in a less sexist culture. She also protests that not very much more is made of those women in that period who did break out to achieve a great deal, including Elizabeth Cary Agassiz, Radcliffe's first president in 1882. Indeed many today are hardly aware that the history of higher education for women at Harvard began well over a century ago. In 1879 a group—led by historian Arthur Gilman and spearheaded by Abby Leach, a young woman who had successfully sought instruction on her own from three Harvard professors (and has forever after figured in Radcliffe history as "the nucleus")— formed and soon coalesced around the now legendary figure of Agassiz, creating a "collegiate society" for the instruction of women by Harvard faculty. Christened the "Harvard Annex," it became a corporation in 1882 and a college in 1894. Of course, a number of pioneering woman's colleges existed even in 1879—including Vassar (1861) and Smith (1871) and Wellesley (1875)—but none were established in such curricular relationship as Radcliffe was with an established and distinguished institution of higher learning like Harvard, much less a university such as President Eliot was fast creating, one with a faculty of increasingly national and international repute whose stars were often in fact the quickest to respond to the new idea. William James, for instance, signed on at once (at "not less than $4 an hour")—and so did Charles Eliot Norton. Indeed, thirty-eight Harvard professors agreed to the experiment, begun in rented rooms at No. 6 Appian Way (a house long since torn down) in September of 1879.

Not all would embrace the idea. We have Marion Schlesinger's word for it that historian Roger Bigelow Merriman, for instance, "would not have been caught dead teaching a Radcliffe class." And it is certainly true to say that in 1879 Harvard was not just wary of co-education. It was distinctly hostile. And almost the only reason this extraordinary idea took flight was Elizabeth Cary Agassiz. By birth a daughter of Boston's merchant aristocracy, by marriage a Harvard faculty wife (and a famous one; she was the widow of Louis Agassiz), as well as known to have been very much the famous Swiss scientist's colleague and partner in many of his

OPPOSITE: *Longfellow House, Radcliffe Yard*

Massachusetts Hall and First Church

learned activities, Agassiz was also on her own account the founder of a
girls school, altogether a formidably serious woman gifted also with considerable social skills. No one was surprised when she was elected
Radcliffe's first president in 1882, though she was sixty years of age in an
era when that was very much the period of old age and retirement. She was
a young sixty, not an old sixty, and she inspired everyone, particularly
President Eliot, who though he was conflicted about higher education for
women, saw well enough where Agassiz's apparently very modest idea of
hiring Harvard faculty to teach women would lead: "If Harvard College
takes up the education of women," said Eliot, "is there any reason to suppose that it will ever renounce it?"

      The genius of the idea of Radcliffe was in its sweet reasonableness.
Agassiz was no crusader for co-education at Harvard; she only proposed to
hire Harvard faculty so as to provide higher education for women who were
to be segregated at some distance from Harvard Yard for that education.
Underpaid professors could be expected to approve. Radcliffe was, so to
speak, to be a college without a faculty of its own. But that it should have
access to Harvard's faculty! It was, Agassiz felt, "the one thing that would
make the Annex unique." Thus Radcliffe's first president would say, tactfully
but truthfully—in her commencement address of 1896: "The true builders of
Radcliffe have been and are the Harvard professors. . . . They represent its
true wealth and strength." A master stroke, though even then it took tortur-
ous negotiation to work out the details. Harvard, for instance, would not at
the time even discuss granting degrees to women. Agassiz on the other hand

refused in turn to settle for anything like what she called a Radcliffe "ladies degree." On the other hand she had no recourse to newspaper reporters. Nor was she aggressive. Only persistent and unyielding, determined as she put it to make "the governing boards of Harvard our allies." And in the end the stalemate was broken by the breathtakingly simple though novel idea of Radcliffe granting the degrees, but with Harvard serving as "visitor" by the terms of Radcliffe's charter, certifying those degrees as the equivalent to Harvard's own. It was, wrote Agassiz, "a distinction without a difference." And not only bachelors and masters degrees were at issue. Agassiz's genius for demanding nothing and getting everything extended even to the college's name. Out of several choices Agassiz it was, according to David McCord, who suggested the college be named after Ann Radcliffe, later Lady Mowlson, in the seventeenth-century the first woman—among the very first of either gender—to give money *to Harvard*. Such statecraft.

And it continued in the work of Agassiz's successors. For instance, Radcliffe's first full time president, Ada Louise Comstock, who struggled to keep Radcliffe and Harvard on the same page even after Radcliffe had achieved sufficient repute, to become entirely independent (a thing more than one Harvard leader hoped for!) negotiated with President Conant in 1943 something called "coordinate education." Conant's famous remark that, as a result of the agreement, "Harvard is not coeducational in any respect except in point of fact" more or less tells the story. More than two decades later, Harvard having assumed full responsibility for graduate women in

Harkness Commons

Fairchild Hall

1963 and fourteen years later for undergraduate women, Faye Levine, writing in the first (1965) Harvard/Radcliffe Yearbook, would say pretty much the same thing: "Being at Radcliffe means nothing more than being a girl at Harvard," wrote Levine, the first woman executive editor of the *Crimson*, adding: "It is a tricky business since everyone knows that there are no girls at Harvard." Shades of Elizabeth Agassiz, whose spirit surely hovered over Harvard's 1970 commencement, the first held jointly with Radcliffe. In 1971–72 co-educational residence began, and since 1975 undergraduate admission has been gender blind. And in the fullness of time Radcliffe College just passed away. All that is left is the genius of Agassiz's idea, now fully realized (and if that isn't statecraft of the highest order I don't know what is), and Harvard's Radcliffe Institute of Advanced Studies. The tenth of Harvard's graduate schools, this institute is intended to be "a scholarly community where individuals pursue advanced work across a wide range of academic disciplines, professions, and creative arts." This writ reflects Radcliffe's increasing interest over the years in graduate studies, marked by the founding by Radcliffe President Mary Ingraham Bunting of what is today the Bunting Fellowship program and the establishment in 1992 of the Graduate Consortium in Women's Studies linking six Boston-area institutions of higher learning. Finally, though it is true that Radcliffe College is no more and that today Harvard College *is* coeducational in theory as in fact, the Radcliffe Institute's mandate also extends to "sustain[ing] a strong, continuing commitment to the study of women, gender and society." Thus the resolution of the Harvard/Radcliffe issue—involving the long and gradual development of a policy that would come to terms with the eventual necessity of gender blind admission to Harvard College—was a long time coming. Indeed, it simmered for nearly two decades during the administration of President Bok, achieving a certain equilibrium with the Harvard/Radcliffe agreement of 1971, which though it did establish fully co-educational residence at Harvard was widely referred to for years as the "non merger," it left so much at issue. Finally, the matter was resolved by Bok's successor, Neil L. Rudenstine, who in 1991 was elected Harvard's twenty-seventh president.

A Princeton man, and a Rhodes Scholar at Oxford, Rudenstine earned his doctorate at Harvard in Renaissance literature; thereafter he taught both at Harvard and Princeton, rising at the latter to become university provost. Scarcely was he inaugurated at Harvard before events plunged him into every possible ramification of diversity, which was to be a focus of his leadership. Rudenstine began the complete rejuvenation of the African Studies Department, which under Henry Louis Gates, Jr., would achieve great distinction. The new president, himself part Italian and part Jewish, also dealt sensitively with tensions between black and Jewish students. Similarly, when the commencement appearance of General Colin Powell raised the controversial issue of gays in the military, Rudenstine brokered a dignified compromise that welcomed Powell commencement morning but included the first (and very affirming) presidential speech to Harvard's Gay and Lesbian Caucus at the Faculty Club commencement night. No one, accordingly, was surprised when during his presidency the number of women among Harvard's senior faculty more than doubled. Diversity was hardly the new president's only concern. Of key importance has been his attempt to try and bring Harvard's ten rather balkanized graduate schools into a greater unity. Thus he led in the early 1990's an unprecedented cross-faculty academic planning process, followed by the first university-wide fundraising campaign. A historic success, netting more than 2.6 billion dollars from nearly 175,000 alumni and friends, it powerfully enabled not least both student and faculty diversity. No achievement was more important in this area than the final Harvard/Radcliffe merger, creating a high profile interdisciplinary research institute that, given Radcliffe's endowment, was at once of national significance. At a dinner on September 26, 1999, at the last meeting of Radcliffe's trustees, Rudenstine, presented with Radcliffe's 1894 charter, declared that Radcliffe's transformation into "one of just a few major institutions of advanced study in the country" would in turn endow Harvard with a new distinction. By that 1999 dinner women had already lived in Harvard Yard for over a quarter century, marked in 1997 by the Bradstreet Gate built across from Memorial Hall.

84. Fay House *1806, 1870; A.W. Longfellow, remodeling and additions, 1890*

If Louis Agassiz's great monument at Harvard was University Museum (see Walk Eight), Elizabeth Cary Agassiz's was Radcliffe College. It was enough for one couple! And it was characteristic of the symmetry that runs through Harvard/Radcliffe. There being Harvard Yard, there was also, for instance, Radcliffe Yard. Nor was that the end of it. Fay House, which stands just to the right of the Gray Gate from Garden Street, Radcliffe's first official building, purchased 1885, had already (which was a part of the point of buying it surely) a venerable Harvard history. A Federal mansion of 1806, a relic from President Kirkland's day, Edward Everett had lived there before it passed to the Fay family in 1835. Longfellow often visited there (once, according to David McCord, he stayed in order to "shell peas"). In 1836 Samuel Gilman (who had married a Fay sister) wrote "Fair Harvard" in Fay House's northeast bedroom, still Harvard's song today. All there was for years to Radcliffe, Fay House is also evocative of Gertrude Stein's time here in 1893–98. The College's foremost alumna (except perhaps for Helen Keller), Stein who studied history, philosophy, and psychology, graduating magna cum laude, was even then absolutely indifferent to convention. She was also very much the individual, describing a Corot in Boston's Museum of Fine Arts in the most arresting way: "It looked like the evening star; it looked as Tannhauser felt and more than that one could feel how it looked and so there was no bother." Doubtless the same instincts account for why later she bought the first two Cubist pictures Picasso painted. No one ever thought that at Radcliffe, where she was a part of a small circle of earnest students, but her appearance, as unconventional as her mind, did not go unnoticed. Big, heavy set, extremely mannish, her hair very short at a time such was not the fashion, Stein invariably wore black, her distinctly large figure un-corseted, her appearance a bit untidy. Her hero was William James, with whom she conducted psychological experiments, and it was in connection with her studies with him that Stein's first published work, "Normal Motor Automatism," appeared in the *Harvard Psychological Review* in September 1896.

So many ghosts. Grace Tucker recalled as a student in the 1920s knocking "on the great walnut doors of the Dean's room, Mrs. Agassiz's parlor," in Fay House. "It was such a beautiful room, rich in architectural beauty and old New England furnishings, richer still in the atmosphere and traditions of the old Fay House. I always fixed my gaze on the lovely portrait of Mrs. Agassiz over the mantle, awaiting the moment when [Dean] Irwin would raise her bent head from close contemplation of the papers on her desk....Her admonitions were kindly, her decisions firm and immutable." Earnest days. Wise heads. And by then that splendor of architectural detail was not Federal but Victorian. Although still today the original swelling brick bays of the 1809 facade survive on Garden Street, most of Fay House as now

Fay House

configured and added to reflects a remodeling of 1890 by A. W. Longfellow, whose firm alone is responsible for the third floor throughout and the large addition to the south. Sensitive to the original late Georgian design of the house, and doubtless alert also to the seminal design across the common the year before of Charles McKim's Johnston Gate, where as we've noted McKim introduced the Colonial Revival aesthetic to Harvard, Longfellow (the architect as we've seen of several Harvard buildings) was always in the early days Radcliffe's architect of choice. To some extent this was because of the patronage of Elizabeth Agassiz, whose house he had designed, but probably more importantly because Alice Mary Longfellow, the daughter of the poet and herself active in Radcliffe's affairs, was his cousin. Of course there was hardly any possibility of a woman architect; such postgraduate professional training was only just beginning to be opened to women like Eleanor Raymond (see Walk Two). Indeed women made their way in the arts in those days with scarcely greater ease than in any other profession. (Consider Anne Whitney's heroic efforts to overcome opposition to her sculpture of Charles Summer in Harvard Square; see Walk Two). Another woman intent on such a vocation did, however, play a significant artistic role in Radcliffe Yard's architectural development: Sarah Wyman Whitman (she of spectacular stained glass at Memorial Hall). A Boston painter and a master as it turned out of Art Nouveau book cover design (for Houghton Mifflin mostly), she had studied in Paris under Thomas Couture and also under William Morris Hunt. Whitman worked closely with Longfellow (with whom she was a member of Boston's Society of Arts and Crafts) on the interior design of all his buildings at Radcliffe. More important, she was also an advisor to Charles McKim.

85. Murray Research Center *McKim, Mead & White, 1897*

Given McKim's role in creating in Harvard Yard the iconic "Harvard brick" image still dominant today, it was only natural that Radcliffe should seek him out. To be more Harvard than Harvard was always part of the strategy Elizabeth Agassiz and her cohort pursued earnestly and with success. Agassiz's insistence that Radcliffe Yard be located across Cambridge Common in sight of Harvard Yard was characteristic. Thus when in 1887 she was able to get hold of enough lots to begin the development of Radcliffe Yard (a process that finally required the assembling of eighteen lots over a thirty-year period), the first building to be erected was a design of McKim's—the late Georgian style dark red brick gymnasium, today the Murray Research Center and Radcliffe Dance Center. McKim was also asked at the same time to do a Radcliffe master plan. (The symmetries even extended to the gymnasium's donor, Harriet Lawrence Hemenway; her husband had been the donor of Harvard's gym of the same name.) Perhaps, too, here was an example of those laissez-faire days from which came much good, for Hemenway may have specified the architect. All that is known is that according to Leland Roth, the leading McKim scholar, Whitman in February of 1897 got in touch with McKim in aid not just of a gymnasium but of an overall master plan of a proposed Radcliffe Yard, a plan McKim suggested focus on a new library. How at ease Whitman and McKim were on the subject, and that they were clearly allies, is clear in McKim's writing to her: "Some day, *after dinner*, and when you are not harassed by the outside world," he wrote, "please turn to Raphael's 'Marriage of the Virgin' and let me know if the little temple in the background . . . does not appeal to your imagination as an appropriate theme for a library for a Radcliffe girl." Alas, the gymnasium was to be McKim's only Radcliffe work. But it established in the wake of antique Fay House Radcliffe's future design concept.

86. Agassiz House and the Arthur and Elizabeth Schlesinger Library on the History of Women in America

Agassiz House *A. W. Longfellow, 1904*
Schlesinger Library *Winslow & Bigelow, 1907*

The library finally built here, today perhaps the greatest repository of its kind in the world, is not, however, of any note architecturally. The Schlesinger Library (as it is today called) was the work of Winslow and Bigelow, a run of the mill Boston firm. More interesting by far is Agassiz House. The work in 1904 of A. W. Longfellow, it is the centerpiece of the octagonal climax of Radcliffe Yard. And this climax discloses how influential McKim's master plan

modest old New England clapboard house, looking by no means out of place, but somehow rooting everything and bringing everything down to earth. Thus the two old houses still in Radcliffe Yard—survivors, both, of many grand master plans gone, happily, awry—are examples of how the smallest thing, in Larry Woiwode's words, "may suddenly crack open and pitch its author into the past." Harvard is full of such moments, and this being New England, it is nearly always old clapboard houses (professors' widows can sometimes yet be seen in their gardens) that nestle unexpectedly next to great colonnaded facades, the way Wadsworth House in Harvard Yard appears suddenly around the corner, stubbornly, wonderfully, pitching one into not just the past, but many pasts—in Wadsworth's case George Washington's in the eighteenth century, as much Henry Adams' in the nineteenth century, or David McCord's in the twentieth. But what is an important episode in old Harvard Yard stands out in Radcliffe Yard, so much newer and so much more intimate, as key. For Radcliffe Yard, looked at purely architecturally, has need of such graces. I agree with Bainbridge Bunting that "any of the red brick academic buildings here can be duplicated on many American campuses." The ensemble as a whole works wonderfully. And it is Bunting who points out how "the gray clapboard Federal houses . . . impart an atmosphere so essentially of New England and Cambridge that no replacement, however imposing, could take their place."

Curiously, the architecture of each of the three sides of Radcliffe Yard reflects just the three environments that open out to each side of that Yard, which has become historically a kind of triangular hub. First, the Jeffersonian axiality of Agassiz House and its flanking buildings on the Yard's north side leads (by way of either the Agassiz Gate of 1916 or the Mary Coes Gate of 1913 between Fay House and the old gym) four blocks up Garden Street to what was once Radcliffe's grand quadrangle of dorms, today forming Harvard's three "Quad Houses." Second, the small early nineteenth-century clapboard houses on the yard's west (southwest) side give on—via the Gilman Gate this time—to the more domestic scale of Brattle Street and a walk of perhaps half an hour from the old Radcliffe President's House opposite Radcliffe Yard to Elmwood, today the residence of the president of the university. Third, the institutional brick but informally arrayed buildings on a theme of Harvard Yard on the south (southwest) side of Radcliffe Yard mark Appian Way, the beginning of the realm of the Graduate School of Education, the campus of which brings our long circuit back to Harvard Square. Each environment is worthy of close inspection.

89. First Church (Congregational), the "Quad Houses," and Observatory Hill

First Church (Congregational) *Abel Martin, 1870*

Currier House *Harrison & Abramovitz, 1965*

Cabot House

> *Elwell & Blackwell, Briggs Hall, 1923; Kilham & Hopkins, Barnard Hall, 1932; Whitman Hall (1912); A. W. Longfellow (Bertram Hall, 1901, Eliot Hall, 1906); Ames & Dodge (Cabot Hall, 1937)*

Pforzheimer House *Maginnis & Walsh, 1947–1957*

Hilles Library *Harrison & Abramovitz, 1965*

University Observatory *Isaiah Rogers, 1843–1851*

Kittredge Hall *William Mowll, 1909–1915*

Asa Gray House (No. 88 Garden Street) *Ithiel Town, 1810*

Symmetry again. As the First Church in its Unitarian incarnation stands guard over Harvard Yard, and was until the 1870s the scene of Harvard's commencement, so the First Church in its orthodox or Congregational incarnation (though in a Victorian building) stands guard over Radcliffe Yard, at the corner of Garden Street and Mason Street, where it was the scene of many a Radcliffe baccalaureate. The design of Abel Martin, it is a handsome enough Victorian pile. Alas, Radcliffe was not able to buy any of the land nearby on this or the other side of Radcliffe Yard. Agassiz had hoped to annex Appian Way, but was forced to look for property further afield, in the event at Phillips Field, four blocks up Garden Street.

Briggs Hall of Cabot House and Moors Hall of Pforzheimer House

Hilles Library

Acquired in 1900, this large tract was in 1902 laid out by architect Guy Lowell in an axially aligned plan on rather a grand scale. Lowell, however, was no Bulfinch. The amplitude and graciousness of the setting encouraged a harmonious ensemble nonetheless, if not an inspired one. First was best. Bertram Hall of 1901, with elegant terraces and living rooms and dining rooms and bedrooms with fireplaces and window seats, and its mate, Grace Eliot Hall of 1906, both by Longfellow, are the centerpieces of Cabot House today, which was established in 1970. Likewise Pforzheimer House, founded in 1961, consists of three brick dorms of 1947–1957 by Maginnis and Walsh, Comstock Hall, Holmes Hall, and Moors Hall with its pilastered frontispiece and cupola, the quad's finale at its northern end. The pride and joy of these northernmost Houses is the newest of all Harvard's Houses, Currier House, established in 1970 and consisting of four halls: Bingham, Daniels, Gilbert, and Tuchman. Purpose-built from the ground up, Currier is the work of Harrison and Abramovitz, who brought a new architectural distinction to the Radcliffe Quad when they designed Hilles Library in 1965. Intended as a joint library for all three Houses, it is a splendid building. As Robert Bell Rettig has pointed out, "Hilles appears formal and monumental, but formality breaks down inside into a series of intimate book alcoves and study spaces." It is surrounded by delightful terracing of a kind that old Radcliffe President Briggs, who once described the Radcliffe campus as "composed chiefly of a few back yards and an undersized apple tree," would surely approve of. Perhaps David McCord said it best when he wrote that "all these structures are comfortable to leaf or vine; the grass improves from year to year." He was not joking. The spacious greensward of the Quad is like nothing else in Cambridge. So are some of the stories told here of this or that hall. In Eliot, for instance, "there was a student room on the first floor that had a window opening onto the back terrace," according to one reminiscence. "The window was covered by a heavy metal grating, but this could be unlocked from the inside in case of fire—or to allow ingress and egress after hours. Occasionally it was opened to admit a midnight guest. This room was much in demand by adventurous and independent young women; one of its occupants during my time later worked for a brief period as a high-priced call girl, while another became an English duchess."

Across from Radcliffe Quad and worth mentioning because its domed centerpiece was designed by Isaiah Rogers in 1844–51—but not dwelling on because it is so hedged in by later and entirely utilitarian buildings—is the Harvard Observatory, atop Observatory Hill. Also nearby is Kittredge Hall, named for George Lyman Kittredge, the home of Harvard University Press, the display room of which is in the Holyoke Center arcade in Harvard Square. Most interesting of all is the Asa Gray House, named after the distinguished seventeenth-century Harvard botanist; this building was originally the garden house of the old Harvard Botanic Garden, long since closed (though many of the original trees and landscape features survive amid later buildings). Now at No. 88 Garden Street, this house was moved from the site of Kittredge Hall. Erected in 1810, this very elaborate Federal domicile is the first building known to have been designed by Ithiel Town, just after his studies with Asher Benjamin in Boston. Later Town became a leading architect in New York.

90. Greenleaf House and Cronkhite Graduate Center to Brattle Street and Elmwood

Greenleaf House (76 Brattle) *1859*

Loeb Drama Center *Hugh Stubbins Associates, 1959*

Cronkhite Graduate Center *Perry, Shaw, Hepburn, Kehoe and Dean, 1956, 1960*

Stoughton House (90 Brattle Street) *Henry Hobson Richardson, 1883*

Philip Johnson House (9 Ash Street) *Philip Johnson, 1941*

Vassall House (94 Brattle Street) *circa 1650, circa 1746, 1870*

Episcopal Divinity School *Ware and Van Brunt, chapel and quad, 1868*

Nabokov House (8 Craigie Circle) *A. W. Longfellow, 1892 (Winthrop Hall)*

Vassall-Craigie-Longfellow House (105 Brattle Street)
        1759 (attributed to Peter Harrison)

Thorp House (115 Brattle Street) *Longfellow, Alden and Harlow, 1887*

9M	Youth Fours Men	8:57 AM	Unofficial	GO!
9W	Youth Fours Women	9:11 AM	In Progress	GO!
10M	Grand Master Singles Men	9:34 AM	Coming Up	GO!
10W	Grand Master Singles Women	9:51 AM	Coming Up	GO!
11M	Youth 8 Men	10:14 AM	Coming Up	GO!
11W	Youth 8 Women	10:34 AM	Coming Up	GO!
12M	Masters 4 Men	11:02 AM	Coming Up	GO!
12W	Masters 4 Women	11:16 AM	Coming Up	GO!
13M	Senior Master Singles Men	11:35 AM	Coming Up	GO!
13W	Senior Master Singles Women	11:52 AM	Coming Up	GO!
14M	Master 8 Men	12:12 PM	Coming Up	GO!
14W	Master 8 Women	12:27 PM	Coming Up	GO!
15M	Master Singles Men	12:45 PM	Coming Up	GO!
15W	Master Singles Women	12:52 PM	Coming Up	GO!
16M	Ltwt 4 Men	1:11 PM	Coming Up	GO!
16W	Ltwt 4 Women	1:20 PM	Coming Up	GO!
17M	Ltwt Singles Men	1:36 PM	Coming Up	GO!
17W	Ltwt Singles Women	1:46 PM	Coming Up	GO!
18M	Ltwt 8 Men	2:06 PM	Coming Up	GO!
18W	Ltwt 8 Women	2:16 PM	Coming Up	GO!
19M	Champ 2 Men	2:34 PM	Coming Up	GO!
19W	Champ 2 Women	2:45 PM	Coming Up	GO!
20M	Champ 4 Men	3:08 PM	Coming Up	GO!
20W	Champ 4 Women	3:21 PM	Coming Up	GO!
21M	Champ 8 Men	3:45 PM	Coming Up	GO!

HEAD OF THE CHARLES

ORDER OF EVENTS

OCTOBER 19-20

2002

Event	Division	Start Time	Status
		SATURDAY, OCTOBER 19, 2002	
1M	Club 8 Men	12:00 PM	Adjusted GO!
1W	Club 8 Women	12:18 PM	Adjusted GO!
2M	Club 4 Men	12:45 PM	Adjusted GO!
2W	Club 4 Women	1:07 PM	Adjusted GO!
3M	Club Singles Men	1:38 PM	Adjusted GO!
3W	Club Singles Women	1:54 PM	Adjusted GO!
4M	Master 2 Men	2:17 PM	Adjusted GO!
4W	Master 2 Women	2:29 PM	Adjusted GO!
5M	Collegiate Eight Men	2:53 PM	Adjusted GO!
5W	Collegiate Eight Women	3:06 PM	Adjusted GO!
6M	Champ Singles Men	3:24 PM	Adjusted GO!
6W	Champ Singles Women	3:34 PM	Adjusted GO!
		SUNDAY, OCTOBER 20, 2002	
7M	Sr. Veteran Singles Men	8:00 AM	Unofficial GO!
8M	Veteran Singles Men	8:19 AM	Unofficial GO!
7W	Sr. Veteren Singles Women	8:34 AM	Unofficial GO!

Robert Frost House (35 Brewster) *William and John H. Besarick*
Baker House (195 Brattle Street) *H. Langford Warren, 1895*
Bartlett House (165 Brattle Street) *1873*
Elmwood (33 Elmwood Avenue) *1767*

Leaving Radcliffe Yard, not from the north by Agassiz House, but by the
Gilman Gate to the west beside the Buckingham House, discloses at once
what is surely one of the most famous streetscapes in America—Brattle
Street—Tory Row. For more than three centuries, to pass, as Alison Lurie
put it, from the "pale spring green [of Radcliffe Yard to] the lilac-overhung
walks and gray eighteenth-century or Victorian Gothic houses on Brattle,"
has been a prospect that has enchanted. Across the street Greenleaf House,
the old Radcliffe's president's house catches the eye. A robustly modeled
and detailed Victorian pile of 1859, once the home of Mary Longfellow
Greenleaf, the poet's sister, it contrasts sharply with the Loeb Drama Center
to its left, designed for the Harvard/Radcliffe Dramatic Club in 1959. A handsome contemporary design, it is the work of Hugh Stubbins, a Boston architect of national repute who, in fact, built a house for himself and his family
not far from here (and doubtless for that reason was the more sensitive to
Brattle Street's more domestic scale). Unlike the Carpenter Center, the other
half of Harvard's aggressive move in the 1960s to annex studio and performance art to the curriculum, the Loeb pleased even die-hard Brattle Street
traditionalists; Stubbins' modern but straightforward and uncontroversial
design, built mostly in brick, was rescued from complete boredom by a
beautiful serpentine wall and terrace to the north overlooking the presi-

Loeb Drama Center

dent's house garden and by an ingenious use of hanging metal screens on the facade—which are especially effective as something like a marquee at night. More interesting within, the Loeb has, in fact, been called the world's most flexible theater. The principal auditorium, or Mainstage, can be converted into three configurations—standard proscenium architectural with stadium-type seating, the Elizabethan or Shakespearean form of half in-the-round, or the full theater in-the-round—all in minutes by a single controlling device. The Loeb today is still the home of Harvard/Radcliffe Drama, but also of the nationally famous American Repertory Theater directed by Robert Brustein.

Equally a contrast with the old president's house, but for quite another reason, is the Cronkhite Graduate Center on the other side of Greenleaf House. The pride and joy of the Radcliffe Graduate School when built, and intended somewhat to ameliorate the isolated, lonely graduate school experience, the building represents Georgian traditionalism's last shallow gasp before modernism conquered all at Harvard. Its most interesting feature, moreover, is its garden, which can be reached by an inconspicuous path to the right of the president' house. It is named for Helen Keller, who along with Gertrude Stein is probably Radcliffe's most famous alumna, and the first woman to be given an honorary degree by Harvard, in 1955. The garden's rich fragrances—Keller's favorites, lemon verbena, rose geranium, and heliotrope—as well as its burbling fountain make it possible to enjoy for both sighted and unsighted. The fountain, a stone pedestal form, is flanked by two plaques, one lettered conventionally, the other in Braille: "In Memory of Anne Sullivan, Teacher Extraordinary—who beginning with the word water, opened to the girl Helen Keller the world of sight and sound through touch. Beloved companion through Radcliffe College, 1900–1904."

To venture up Brattle Street from this point could be dangerous to our focus here, so many and various are the landmarks to be found in this quarter. As Brattle Street winds for one delightful block after another, only those houses with particular reference to Harvard architecture can properly be touched on here. Immediately, at the corner of Ash Street there is one of H. H. Richardson's masterworks, the Stoughton House, 90 Brattle Street, built by him for the mother of the historian John Fiske in 1883. Just a little way down Ash at No. 9 is the Philip Johnson House of 1941; built when that architect was a student at the Design School, it is a provocative forerunner of the Glass House of later years. Back on Brattle the Vassall House at No. 94 is the first of several ancient houses in the area, built originally (though since altered) ca. 1650, when Harvard was very young. Beyond that is the picturesque Gothic Revival stone campus of the Episcopal Divinity School, some of it also designed by A. W. Longfellow in the 1890s (just before his major work in Radcliffe Yard), but more the work in the 1860s and '70s of Ware and Van Brunt. Only a few minutes walk away is the most famous house in America north of the White House in

Elmwood

Washington, D.C., and east of Frank Lloyd Wright's Falling Water in Pittsburgh: the Vassall-Craigie-Longfellow House. So much a shrine is this house it has annexed its own block-long park setting—Longfellow Park—which runs down to the Charles River and the Longfellow Memorial, the work in bronze of sculptor Daniel Chester French. Longfellow first came to this house—already famous as George Washington's residence at the start of the Revolution—when he began to teach at Harvard, later buying it, and he lived here through all the days of his glory from 1837 until his death in 1882, attracting to it such exotic visitors as Oscar Wilde. The house itself, one of the great mansions of "Tory Row," has been endlessly copied and look-alikes at this point can probably be found in every state in the union. Today it is a museum, operated by the National Park Service.

Every other house in this quarter has some significance, indeed, very often layers of significance. At 35 Brewster Street, just up Riedesel Avenue, off Brattle beyond the Vassall-Craigie-Longfellow House, consider, for instance, the house of Robert Frost, a student at Harvard from 1897 to 1899, later the Norton Professor in 1936, and very much Longfellow's successor in the twentieth century as America's characteristic poet. Another poet, Robert Lowell, once wrote, "I walked by his house on Brewster Street in Cambridge. Its narrow gray wood was a town cousin of the farmhouses he wrote about.... It was a traveler from the last century that had inconspicuously drifted over the custom's border of time.... The lights were out that night; they are out for good now, but I can easily remember the barish rooms, the miscellaneous gold-lettered old classics, the Georgian poets, the Catullus by his bedside.... And the stool drawn up to his visitor's chair so that he could ramble and listen." Frost moved here in 1941. Also just off Brattle, up Craigie Street at No. 8 Craigie Circle, is Vladimir Nabokov's old house. Back on Brattle, at No. 195, is George Baker's (see Walk Two), designed by H. Landford Warren, founder of Harvard's Architecture School. Nearby at No. 165 is John Bartlett's, he of "Bartlett's Quotations." Finally at No. 33 Elmwood Avenue is the residence of Harvard's president today, Elmwood.

Elmwood stops time the way an aria does an opera, and does so similarly, usually giving rise to surprisingly intense feeling. A later owner cautioned once that though it was "a pleasant old house," living there posed risks: "It will make you a frightful conservative before you know it. It was born a Tory and will die so. Don't get used to it." And in this seduction architecture plays a key role, for this is a house the eye, and the mind's eye too, fastens on. Though it is a bit of a box—tall, high shouldered, gaunt even—it is beautiful enough in its New England eighteenth-century way, commodious, stately, regal even, and in this a link to Harvard's most ancient days and thus as seemly a home for its president as could be found outside the Yard. Tory-born indeed, it is also Puritan plainspoken in mien, enacting in one design the royalist-patriot debate we saw in eighteenth-century Harvard Yard. Echoes of this debate—Elmwood's oldest aria if you will—have even been sometimes heard in modern times. In her mid-twentieth-century reminiscence of the house, Esther Lowell Cunningham recounted how during the American Revolution the house was used as a hospital and how this gave rise to her and her siblings wondering:

> who the people were that pricked their names on the attic door. There was "Daniel," for one. . . . The door opened on the attic stairs, and the names were made with three-cornered pricks. I was told the soldiers used the point of a bayonet. Sometimes when I awoke in the middle of the night and heard the winter storm howling outside, the wind roaring down the great chimneys, and the oaken beams in the attic above me cracking and groaning with the cold, I thought, as I lay shivering, that the ghosts of the soldiers were stumbling about over my head, "Daniel," perhaps, among them.

There ought to be more ghosts than Daniel at Elmwood, though reliable testimony is naturally slight. Built in 1767 as the seat of Lieutenant Governor Thomas Oliver, the last of the royal deputies, it was in the eighteenth century a place of vice-regal pomp; here, surely, was the last place, for the last time, the King's health was drunk within the orbit of Harvard College. Yet Elmwood was in the same era a place of violence and riot, the kind that comes by night with flaring torches, mob-borne, intent on Oliver's resignation from the Royal Council. Not long after, he went into exile in England where—because like so many Tories he was a patriot, albeit a moderate who lost control of the situation—he pined for America the rest of his life. If any shade haunts Elmwood Oliver does.

Fascinating the way architecture nearly always survives one regime into another, often as a kind of stage set. In the new republic there was still need for governors, and for Elmwood. It later became the residence of Governor Elbridge Gerry (he of gerrymandering—oh well, so much for republican virtue), and it is a nice question whether or no Gerry is a sufficiently respectable shade for already so august a house. There is no question at all about the star of Elmwood's third act, however, though the poet will be allowed no arias, being James Russell Lowell of Victorian fame, whose verse is no longer much admired. He himself, however, still attracts; his now more famous modern poet cousin, Robert Lowell, used to tell of passing the house of his by then long dead kinsman (as Elmwood famously was in the nineteenth century) as an undergraduate in the 1950s: "Easy to imagine his bohemian velvet jacket, but hard to enter the life and wonder what conversation I might have had with the grizzling poet." Still the young modern could write of the fast fading Victorian not only that he was among those "pedestaled for oblivion" but that he "env[ied] his strenuous grace," so certifying Lowell certainly as a proper shade for Elmwood. As too would be Elmwood's early twentieth-century owner, A. Kingsley Porter, who presided over Elmwood's fourth act with memorable brilliance. Harvard's most celebrated medievalist in his day, Porter and his wife led a scintillating intellectual and social circle centered on Elmwood, shadowed always, however, by the threat of scandal, for Porter was gay. In an age when President Lowell, according to Richard Norton Smith, told another homosexual professor that Lowell's solution to the problem would be suicide, it was Porter's solution too. So much history. So many secrets. Elmwood, I sometimes think, is Harvard's attic. Like an opera, beautiful but heartless.

91. Graduate School of Education Campus

Larsen Hall *Caudill, Rowlett, and Scott, 1964*
10 Appian Way *1855*
Gutman Library *Benjamin Thompson Association, 1969*
Read House *ca. 1772*
Nichols House *Oliver Hastings, builder, 1827*
Farwell Place houses

The southern boundary of Radcliffe Yard is Appian Way, where Radcliffe began in 1879. Laid out in 1810, this romantically named street also sheltered (at age ten in 1940–41) the poet John Berryman, who would later appropriately write a long twentieth-century poem inspired by Anne Bradstreet, the Harvard Square poet of the seventeenth century (see Walk Two). It is a very porous boundary, for the campus of the Graduate School of Education, which begins on Appian Way, has encompassed both sides of the street since the teachers bought Longfellow Hall from Radcliffe. Both campuses, indeed, leak into each other all along Appian and in ways both ideological and architectural. For example, the School of Education (which not only trains teachers but the primary function of which is to conduct advanced research in the field of education itself) was the first of Harvard's graduate schools to admit women as degree candidates. Note also the way the Education School's landmark Larson Hall of 1964, draws its inspiration for the brilliant abstraction of its roofline from the chimney/vents of Georgian Revival Bryerly Hall in Radcliffe Yard. Despite this contextual deference, Larsen Hall, like so many modern landmarks at Harvard, is much joked about (called "neo-Aztec," for instance) by its detractors, though it is one of the handsomest of Harvard's post–World War II buildings.

The School of Education, relatively speaking one of Harvard's newest graduate schools (founded in 1920), boasts a campus which is among the most historically interesting architecturally, and though among the smallest in the university, is also among the most charming. This is true not only because its individual structures, both ancient and modern, are of high quality. It is also true because, uniquely among all the university's campuses, Harvard has contrived from scratch a campus where newly designed structures and older structures moved from other places have been knit together imaginatively so as to set off each other and create a varied and stimulating urban environment. The historic buildings are genuinely historic and the modern buildings are frankly modern, not decorator reproductions. As one plunges from Appian Way past the Gutman Library entrance plaza into the campus's heart, it's a delightful walk.

On the left, the last original structure standing on Appian Way, No. 10, an 1855 Greek Revival house, prepares one for the delightful surprise further along and further in. As one penetrates further and further, Ben

Gutman Library

Read House

Thompson's superb Gutman Library of 1972 is at once screen and shield to the busy urban scene of lower Brattle Street, its broad expanses of glass continually inviting the eye into the library's daily life. Behold, there is suddenly a lovely brick paved and grassy cul-de-sac hard by the library's east flank, where two historic old houses, which once stood where Gutman Library now is, have been superbly sited. To the left is the small yellow clapboard two-story Read House of ca. 1772, now the home of the Native American Program, which rejoices in one of the architectural gems of Harvard: a superb, boldly scaled Palladian doorway, copied from one of the best known eighteenth-century pattern books, Batty Langley's *City and Country Builder* of 1740. Built by James Read, a patriot rather than a Tory, and thus a simpler house than many on Tory Row (where it was formerly No. 55 Brattle) the Read House is the more stunning an ornament of this tranquil cul-de-sac for the other old house set at right angles to it, the Nichols House. Formerly No. 63 Brattle, this later house is now the Educational Technology Center. A bit awkwardly, but charmingly, in its provincial way, the two bays to either side of the Nichols House entrance swell into a large front porch that runs straight across this gray clapboarded house's front, its principal ornament a series of Tuscan columns. It is all so much a time capsule—the more so for being a contrived one—there may be no more tranquil place at Harvard. And to walk past the eighteenth-century Reed House and around behind the Nichols House is to emerge into an early nineteenth-century actual historic landscape as it grew up in time—Farwell Place. A narrow, quiet street time seems to have quite left alone, Farwell Place leads to the back of Christ Church of 1760 and the Old Burying Ground of 1635, where we started this peregrination nearly four centuries ago.

Schools of Medicine, Public Health, and Dental Medicine, and Arnold Arboretum

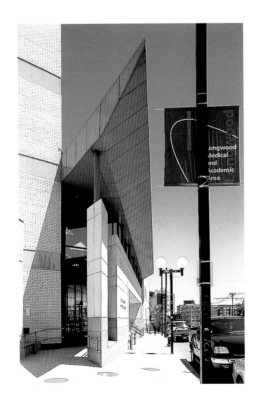

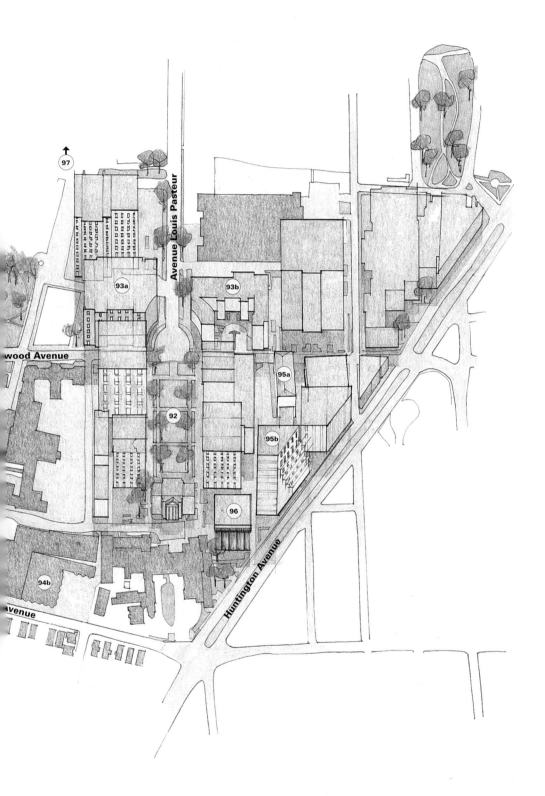

Longwood Campus and Jamaica Plain

Harvard Teaching Hospitals

The rather exotic name of Harvard's medical campus—Longwood, after Napoleon's home in exile on the island of St. Helena—highlights the fact that the community of Old Cambridge, though it now extends some way to the south, east, and north around Harvard Square, is only one, albeit the most venerable and historic, of five Greater Boston neighborhoods with which, architecturally and otherwise, Harvard interfaces intimately. The other four are Mid-Cambridge, the early nineteenth-century upper middle class suburban community to the west of Harvard Square, already dealt with here; Allston, a farming village by 1900 become working class suburb (named after the painter and Harvard graduate, Washington Allston), and Longwood and Jamaica Plain, two fashionable mid-century railroad suburbs. All four are part of larger municipal and county jurisdictions today, and none has its own political identity (though some did in the nineteenth century), but each still has a distinctive cultural and social identity that contributes importantly to Harvard's built environment. In Longwood's case that identity is highly aristocratic, David Sears' original estate of that name having been laid out in 1848 for him by one of the designers of Mount Auburn Cemetery (itself the design prototype of the bucolic American Victorian suburb) as a particularly elegant suburban subdivision. Together with the adjoining Cottage Farm area, perhaps Boston's first picturesque romantic suburb, Longwood in the 1840s featured a Gothic Revival architectural aesthetic and a curvilinear tree shaded landscape aesthetic (not unlike that of the New Yard then developing around Gore Hall), an aesthetic contemporaneous with (and rivaling) the more famous Llewellyn Park in New Jersey, often called America's first nineteenth-century romantic suburb.

Quite a few of Harvard's architects whose work has already been touched on here lived in or around Longwood as it developed, including H. H. Richardson himself. And for the same reasons as the architects, doctors were also drawn to the area, attracted by its highly patrician tone (set by such amenities as the still extant Longwood Cricket Club of 1877) and the artful design of the area's subdivisions, somewhat inspired by the English country town of Colchester, the Sears ancestral seat. Not surprisingly the extension of Back Bay Boston, called the Fenway, an increasingly institutional area which adjoined Longwood (the two areas knit together by Frederic Law Olmsted's Boston Park System), also experienced enormous growth, cresting in the early twentieth-century with the erection of the Gardner Museum, Boston Symphony Hall, Horticultural Hall, the Museum of Fine Arts, the Boston Opera House, and (in particularly close proximity to Longwood) Harvard's medical school, its first affiliated hospitals in the area, and ultimately two more Harvard graduate schools, those of dental medicine and public health. Not altogether by accident, one imagines, in time the name Longwood came to be used for both the original suburban residential area and that part of the immediate adjoining institutional area of the Fenway dominated by Harvard medicine. However, the residential amenities of the original Longwood, though the fact of them facilitated the move greatly, did not spark the Medical School's decision to settle there in the first place. (Nor was the present location the only one considered; another site was where MIT now stands.) What has always been most vital to the medical school from the beginning is the necessity of integrated teaching hospital facilities, the reason the school abandoned Harvard Yard in the first place.

Astonishingly, the entire history of the medical school from the eighteenth to the twentieth centuries—and this says much about Harvard's history and its intimate links to the great Boston families—can be best told through the history of just one such family. In 1781 the first medical instruction given at Harvard was by 29-year-old John Warren, the head of the army hospital at Boston and brother of Joseph Warren, the patriot who sent Paul Revere on his storied ride and then went on to fight and die at the battle of Bunker Hill. And it was the same John Warren, in 1782 when the Medical School was founded, who became its first professor. Similarly, it was his son, John Collins Warren, who later held the same professorship, who started (with James Jackson) the *New England Journal of Medicine and Surgery*, and who founded in 1821 the Massachusetts General Hospital at the foot of Beacon Hill, where that now world-renowned hospital is still located, and to which the medical school promptly relocated. Indeed, it was John Collins Warren who famously performed the historic surgical operation in which ether was used as an anesthetic, an event the effects of which (whether it was the first or actually the second such use of ether) were epochal in the history of medicine. The architectural setting of that operation should not be missed by any visitor to Harvard, not only because the Bulfinch Pavilion (first built in 1818–23 and altered 1844), as it is now called, is very much the spiritual home of Harvard Medicine, but because it ranks with University Hall as Harvard's first great architecture. Indeed, the Massachusetts General building is a version of one of Bulfinch's early designs for University Hall—while it would not have looked at all well in Harvard Yard, it is arguably one of Bulfinch's masterworks. The building, though it has been lengthened, is very beautiful, and the historic Ether Dome itself, site of the operation, is generally, though not always, accessible to visitors, and is still in use today.

To resume our history of the Warren family, it was John Collins Warren's son, of the same name, also a professor of surgery at Harvard, who in the early twentieth century raised most of the funds for the Medical School's final move from Beacon Hill to Longwood—sparked in the first place by how dazzled Harvard then was by new hospital facilities at Johns Hopkins in Baltimore. All appointments at Hopkins were in the hands of the medical school faculty (as they were not absolutely then at the Mass General), and Harvard determined to have such a hospital, a hospital to which, as President Eliot put it in 1907 (alluding tactfully to the key underlying issue), the sort of doctors Harvard was seeking would be attracted, doctors who would put the emphasis not only on teaching, but on "medical and surgical progress," for example, research. (Thus in its Medical School dedication issue the *Boston Medical and Surgical Journal* editorialized on "The Need of a Hospital for the Harvard Medical School.") Canny New Englanders, the Harvard Corporation, rather than taking immediate responsibility for such a new hospital, encouraged a group of Boston businessmen (led by that indefatigable doer of good deeds, Henry Lee Higginson) to secure sufficient land, one half of which having been secured for the medical school, the other was sold mostly to the trustees of another Boston millionaire, Peter Bent Brigham—with whom, David McCord documents, an agreement was reached *before* the medical School's move on the erection of a university hospital named after Brigham. It was an inspired alliance. The Brigham trustees brought to the table some 5.3 million dollars, in those days almost one quarter Harvard University's total endowment. Meanwhile, a group of New York and Boston donors gave the medical school buildings, led by J. P. Morgan, whose initial gift of one million dollars was announced by Eliot at the 1901 commencement.

The unity thus established between medical school and teaching hospital, a hospital the appointments to which are made by the medical school's dean, himself appointed by Harvard's president, has proved enduring. Indeed, it quickly enough encompassed another hospital, Children's— today, perhaps, the foremost pediatric hospital in the world—the trustees of which bought from the university the remaining part of the original medical school land. At the dedication of Children's, the three speakers were Boston's Mayor, Harvard's president, and the medical school's dean—lest there by any doubt that Children's too was to be a "university hospital." That was in 1914, the year after the Brigham opened. In later years "an Umbilical Bridge" (McCord's term) connected the two hospitals. Indeed, the only problematic element of the new medical campus, which has grown over the years to compass now also the Beth Israel Deaconess Medical Center and several smaller institutions like the Dana Farber Cancer Institute, was that a certain rivalry was set up in Harvard medicine, particularly between the old campus and the new, between the "Mass General" and new "Peter Bent." So much the better perhaps. That the ties within Harvard medicine remain strong between the two flagship hospitals has never been in doubt. Oglesby Paul, the distinguished medical historian, reports that President Conant was urged to combine them in the 1950s, though they are, of course, located at either end of the in-town area. It was perhaps inevitable. In 1993 they finally joined forces to form Partner's Healthcare.

92. Harvard Medical School

Shepley, Rutan & Coolidge, 1906;
Ellenzweig Associates, Tosteson Center remodeling, 1987

When Charles Eliot stepped down from Harvard's presidency, an honorary degree citation in 1909 described his impact on medical education this way: "not in buildings alone, but also in the instruction and research within its walls he found the Harvard Medical School brick and left it marble." Especially on the architectural side the community was not unappreciative; Avenue Louis Pasteur, which the city gratefully laid out to lead the medical school's great white marble court—215 feet wide, 514 feet long—is Boston's grandest axial street plan. Within the court itself five buildings around it culminate in the heroic, four-story Ionic portico of Building A, itself centered on a huge columned multi-storied central space, originally the Warren Anatomical Museum, now the offices of the dean and of the medical school's central administration. A fragment, so to speak, of the great white city of the 1893 Chicago World's Fair, this is "Imperial Harvard" at its most imperial, befitting a medical school that pulls no punches in describing itself in the various literature of the medical area as "the world's preeminent institution in medical education and research," presiding over a campus that is called with equal hauteur "a complex network of clinical and preclinical departments, laboratories and affiliated hospitals [with] a faculty of almost 3000 and a student body of over 800 men and women."

The great court itself remains largely as it was built, and though very formal it has proved very flexible. For instance, the marble block nearest Longwood Avenue on the court's west side was beautifully remodeled in 1987 to become the Tosteson Medical Education Center, the headquarters of five academic societies that serve as the organizational framework of medical education here. Modeled closely after the structure of the Harvard Houses that President Lowell extrapolated in the 1920s and 1930s from the Oxbridge/Harvard collegiate model, these five "societies" were a dramatic innovation of the 1980s, featuring senior faculty as "masters," and tutorial teaching. Equally dramatic was the architectural expression of the new structure by Ellenzweig Associates. Using the building's original marble exterior at its back as an interior, a marvelous glass-domed infill Commons area was created to serve as the centerpiece of five "nodes," one for each society, the central commons all the while sustaining a very interactive environment where the idea is that humanistic dialogue should keep good company with increasingly high-tech programs. In fact, in an unusually dramatic and effective use of Harvard's own history four of these programs are named after great figures from the Medical School's past: for example, Oliver Wendell Holmes, Sr. A good example of the way in which the seemingly extreme polarities between

Harvard Medical School

Harvard College, the Medical School, and the Law School even a century or more ago could be bridged by one Boston family, the Holmeses have been as important as the Warrens in Harvard's history. The role of the College in Holmes, Jr.'s formation and his dominating eminence in the history of American law has already arisen here. At the Medical School an important part of its history and architecture celebrates Holmes, Sr., himself a notable graduate of the College and the son of a pastor of Cambridge's First Church, who even in the face of his son's achievements remains a key figure; not only as a well known man of letters and as the author of the still highly regarded "Autocrat of the Breakfast Table," but for a much less widely read book (to put it mildly) of 1843, titled *The Contagiousness of Puerperal Fever*, a book M. R. Small has in fact called "the first important contribution to medical research by an American physician." Holmes Sr., professor of anatomy, was Dean of Harvard Medical School in from 1847 to 1853.

The element of the design expression of all this that works best is the way the informal, lively commons area is no less so for the parade of busts of Harvard worthies and medical educators that dominates the scene. The pedagogical purpose is obvious. Less so, but all the more effective for that, is the way a form, the marble bust, a form now thought stuffy and certainly no longer artistically very lively, is used without irony in a very modern, communicative, almost interactive way—all the more so given the Medical School's classical white marble aesthetic.

93. Vanderbilt Hall and the Old Boston Lying-In Hospital Building

Vanderbilt Hall *Coolidge, Shepley, Bulfinch & Abbott, 1927*
Lying-In Hospital Building *Coolidge and Shattuck, 1923*

Forming a graceful semi-circle at the head of Avenue Louis Pasteur at the main entrance to the medical school's great court are these two buildings, among the finest in the Longwood medical area, though the once very great elegance of each has been compromised. To the west the old Lying-In Hospital is of such quality its designer was singled out back in the 1920s by G. H. Edgell, in his *American Architecture Today* as having "attained something of the modernist expression that we associate with the work of [Louis] Sullivan and [Frank Lloyd] Wright"—high praise indeed—though Edgell knew his Boston well enough to add the disclaimer that said designer "would probably deny, indignantly and correctly, that he had any such aim." Still, the design was not only modern on the outside. Even then hospitals were notoriously needy of as much flexibility as possible as they grew. Consequently, the interior walls of this building were designed as nearly as possible entirely as movable partitions. It seems in the long run to have availed little, however, considering the horrible additions with which this building, now a part of Brigham and Women's, is burdened. At Vanderbilt Hall, on the other hand, on the other side of Avenue Louis Pasteur, a center originally for student social life, it is the interior that has suffered through remodeling, particularly its handsome pilastered dining hall, a victim of the more informal pattern today of student life and the need for more office space. Only one end survives and that to little but memorial point. The exterior of this handsome old building is, however, happily as elegant as ever.

94. Children's and Brigham and Women's Hospitals and the Medical Area Power Plant

Old Peter Bent Brigham Hospital Court *Codman and Despradelle, 1911*
Hunnewell Building of Children's Hospital *Shepley, Rutan and Coolidge, 1913*
Children's Hospital Medical Center Garage *The Architects Collaborative, 1964*
Medical Area Power Plant *Benjamin Thompson Associates, 1979*

The medical school and its teaching hospitals today present the visitor with an enormous complex that is not very understandable. Indeed, the discontinuity between the distinction of Longwood's medicine and the blandness shading to ugliness and chaos of so much of its architectural expression is troubling. All that can be said usefully here is that a few buildings do stand out. Among these are the Old Peter Bent Brigham Buildings, the heart now of Brigham and

Bulfinch Pavilion, Massachusetts General Hospital

Women's Hospital. Originally inspired by Florence Nightingale's dictates about fresh air and open pavilions (thus many wards of the original hospital were duly "fitted up with pergolas, sunrooms and verandahs"), the Brigham's architecture rises directly across Shattuck Street from the Medical School's main building. And the Brigham's entrance court, centered on its temple-front main building, of brick and terracotta most graciously allied, is for all its charm monumental enough—modeled as it is on the Parthenon. Chronology as well as architectural heft mislead here, however. The two great classical courts of medical school and teaching hospital where they back on to each other yield all the advantage to the Medical School; that is of marble, the hospital of brick; as the Medical School is of 1906, the hospital of seven years later. But as we know now the Medical School was only built here *after* Harvard had agreed with the Brigham trustees on their joint venture.

On the Longwood Avenue side of the medical school stands the original building of Children's Hospital: the Hunnewell Building, designed by Shepley Rutan and Coolidge in 1913. Of interest as an early example of the use of "concrete conglomerate ... with no attempt to make it an artificial stone," as the architects put it, the visitor will observe that at some point the temptation to dissemble proved too much, after all, and the facade has subsequently been scored off to suggest stone masonry." Originally, there were two graceful circular iron staircases on either side of the first floor entrance, ascending to the colonnaded porch. Imperial Harvard is not the attraction here, however; Children's Medical Center's architectural distinction today comes from the masterfully conceived, poured-in-concrete therapeutic and research complex of 1962–71 planned by The Architects Collaborative. TAC designed several components of the complex, most notably the dramatically cantilevered Children's Hospital Garage of 1964, TAC's John C. Harkness the partner in charge. Also of interest is the Medical Area Power Plant by one-time TAC principal, Ben Thompson. Especially on this campus, the lofty cylindrical tower and boldly scaled circular rooftop vents of this building stand out conspicuously, as much of a landmark as Longwood has.

95. Schools of Dental Medicine and Public Health

Harvard Dental School *Shepley, Rutan & Coolidge, 1909*
Francois-Xavier Bagnoud Center for Health and Human Rights
   Shepley, Bulfinch, Richardson & Abbott, remodeling, 1996

Two other of Harvard's ten graduate schools are located on the Longwood campus. The oldest by far is Harvard's Dental School, founded in 1867; the first anywhere established in close affiliation with a medical school, the dental school also lived for a considerable time in the shadow of the Massachusetts General Hospital. The school, based originally a No. 54 Anderson Street on Beacon Hill, followed the medical school to Longwood. Progressive in its goal "to place stronger emphasis on the biological basis of oral medicine," the dental program provides for first and second year students to attend joint classes with medical students. The Dental School's

Harvard Dental School

Bagnoud Center

home, a quite nondescript building (not destined, one imagines, for long life), is nonetheless approached by an elaborate exterior stone staircase of extraordinary pomp. Very different is the architectural image of the School of Public Health, the seven-story keel-shaped Bagnoud Center, of highly polished granite, glass, and concrete—which may be said to represent the architectural coming of age of the youngest of the three Harvard professional schools on the Longwood campus. Though young—the school's origins date only to 1909 and in its present form it was not founded until 1922—the Harvard School of Public Health has long been at the forefront of disease prevention worldwide, since Alice Hamilton, the first woman professor in the entire university, undertook pioneering studies for the school of lead and mercury poisoning. Indeed, for twenty-seven years, from 1962 to 1989, five successive Harvard School of Public Health alumni have had the stewardship of the U.S. Centers for Disease Control and Prevention.

96. Countway Library

Hugh Stubbins, 1959; Shepley, Bulfinch, Richardson & Abbott, remodeling, 1999

By any measure the finest architecture on Harvard's Longwood medical campus, the Countway Library was very adroitly inserted immediately between the medical school and Brigham and Women's Hospital to the west and the Schools of Public Health and Dental Medicine to the east, set in a series of plazas that begin to tie together these four pillars of Harvard Medicine in an area that often seems disordered if grand. The building defers to its august classical surroundings in its symmetrical form and its limestone facing—and in the view of one scholar it rather improves upon them! ("The gentle reforming of the classical proportions of the earlier Medical School campus persists so forcibly in [Stubbins'] Modern building, that it both maintains a strong identity and becomes a part of its context.") Best of all there is evident a sure-footed abstract classicism about Countway, which brilliantly picks up on the grand (but not brilliant!) classicism of the medical school's great court. This reflects the skill one always senses in the work of the Countway's architect, Hugh Stubbins, Boston's star architect and TAC's chief rival in that era, best known for his Federal Reserve tower in Boston and his City Corp tower in New York. Gropius' colleague as a professor for many years at Harvard's Graduate School of Design (where he taught Paul

Countway Library

Rudolph, Philip Johnson, Robert Geddes, Araldo Cossulta, and Henry Cobb
among others), the independent-minded Stubbins was, however, much
more influenced in the 1950s by Alvar Aalto and the Scandinavian school.
This influence is particularly evident in Stubbins' dramatically curvilinear
Congress Hall of 1957 in Berlin. Indeed, throughout this period he was forever coming in second to Saarinen in one job interview after another: "That
is why my success at the Countway … was so important to me," Stubbins
later recalled, "because Saarinen had been interviewed earlier and had recommended that it be put underground." Later, in Harvard Yard, in 1973, as
we've seen, Stubbins followed that course with his Pusey Library, but in 1965
Stubbins, the chair then of Boston mayor John Collins' Design Committee,
was much under the influence of Kallmann and McKinnell's design of the
Boston City Hall. That landmark, one of the great American buildings of the
twentieth century, though it has not always had a good effect on its legion of
admirers (remember the addition to Harvard's Music Building), here animated Stubbins to a work of great distinction, particularly in the play of mass
and scale and volume and void on the exterior. Dominated by a deep top-
heavy City Hall–type cornice, the Countway's facades are mostly windowless
in appearance, containing volumes of inward-facing reading alcoves with
largely unseen side windows to hold down glare. Brutalist in style, the effect,
if it is very classical, is also very modern—an example of the most sophisticated contextualism rather than the usually kindergarten contextualism of so
many subsequent architects of more historicist leanings. Stubbins, an architect deeply imbued with the New England aesthetic that was born in the Folk

Gothic and early Georgian work of the eighteenth century showed here that it could inform modernism as well.

The reason for the seemingly windowless exterior becomes evident at once inside this entirely inward-facing building. A central skylit court is surrounded by open stacks and perimeter walls of study alcoves, while in the court's center a dramatic curved staircase (recently extended up another floor) fills the space for all the world like the grand stair of an opera house. To either side large mural-like paintings herald the two great glories of Harvard Medicine: to the left the first public demonstration of the use of anesthesia at the MGH; to the right the first successful human kidney transplant at the Brigham by Nobel laureate Joseph E. Murray. Again, holy ground.

97. The Arnold Arboretum

Arboretum Landscape
> *Frederick Law Olmsted, landscape architect, in collaboration with*
> *Charles Sprague Sargent, 1872–1882*

Hunnewell Building *A. W. Longfellow, 1891–1893*
Main and Side Gates *A. W. Longfellow, 1898–1899*
Entryway and Pond Culverts *John C. Olmsted, circa 1899*

History never did anything more strangely appropriate in Boston's architectural and topographical development than to wrap the chaotic architecture of Harvard's medical campus—which Donald Lyndon, after all, has described as "rather like a jungle populated by large, exotic and unrelated species"—with an extensive green belt of some of the most serene works of Frederick Law Olmsted, the first and certainly the foremost landscape architect of the nineteenth century. Two parks, each part of Boston's so called "emerald necklace," enfold the area all along its west, north and east boundaries—the Back Bay Fens and the Riverway. And it is hardly less strange historically or topographically that they should connect Harvard's two most disparate quarters, the chaos of its medical center, Longwood, with the serenity of its horticultural center, the Arnold Arboretum, where there is architecture of some interest but landscape architecture of international renown.

Today the Arnold Arboretum is one of the great tree and plant museums and horticultural research centers of the world, and the oldest in the country. It takes its name from a rich New Bedford, Massachusetts, merchant and dedicated amateur horticulturist, James Arnold, who bequeathed a sum to Harvard in 1868 for just such an arboretum. Harvard ultimately acquiesced and located the new arboretum in the Jamaica Plain section of the then rather rural Town of West Roxbury, on farmland previously left to

Harvard by another ardent tree lover, Benjamin Bussey, a Boston silver-smith and Revolutionary War veteran whose own goals were more for Harvard establishing a school of agriculture. In the event the school (called the Bussey Institute), like the Lawrence Scientific School, seemed never to catch hold. But the Bussey farm—famous for its beautiful woods (haunted by Margaret Fuller during a stay here in 1839–42)—proved a perfect site for the arboretum, and in 1872 Harvard appointed Charles Sprague Sargent, the Professor of Horticulture at the Bussey Institute, the first director. An inspired choice, Sargent, though he had little money (the Arnold bequest was modest), had great vision. He and Olmsted, both of whom lived quite close to Richardson nearby, and often plotted plans together, talked President Eliot into deeding the arboretum to the core municipality of Greater Boston, the small central City of Boston, which in its brief (and mostly unsuccessful) late nineteenth-century attempt to coax its surround-ing suburbs into union had annexed the Arboretum's home community, the Town of West Roxbury, as well as the adjoining City of Roxbury. The core city, in return for being able to incorporate the Arboretum into the public park system it was also then attempting to assemble (more successfully in the case of parks than suburbs) accepted ownership and agreed to bear the cost of maintaining the park, leasing it back to Harvard for development of its tree and plant museum for a thousand years—for one dollar. Sargent's idea, though it was controversial (both the Harvard Corporation and the Boston City Council were wary and had to be talked into it), proved fructify-ing. Olmsted by Sprague's report came on board almost at once; in 1873 Sprague, writing to Professor Benjamin Robinson, a Harvard botanist, reported: "Olmsted immediately grasped the idea that an arboretum where the public could see varied plantings of rare and exotic trees and shrubs skillfully selected, artistically arranged and grown under scientific oversight, would not only be an appropriate feature in the park system, but," Sprague concluded, "might well become its culminating attraction."

For Harvard, where architecture has always meant only buildings (unlike, say, Princeton, whose character derives as much perhaps from its landscape architecture) the result was exceptional. According to Cynthia Zaitzevsky, the leading Olmsted scholar of her generation, Olmsted's "emer-ald necklace" of Boston parks, itself a masterwork of international stature— "acclaimed," she rightly contends, "as a cultural achievement comparable to its contemporaries, the Museum of Fine Arts and the Boston Symphony"—does, indeed, today achieve a very real culmination in Harvard's arboretum, which now "retains more of the character and land-scape effect of Olmsted's design than any other part of the Boston park sys-tem." That fact is all the more significant, however, because the arboretum was by far the most challenging part of that system to achieve, its design concept requiring that it be both scientific museum and public park. The

didactic purpose (trees grouped by family and genus, for example) had to be disclosed itself in logical sequence along roadways, which, on the other hand, Olmsted had also to design as naturalistic, indeed, romantic responses fitted to the existing topography and to his overall aesthetic of a rural New England landscape. Yet it was just in "blending the scientific and the picturesque [that] Sargent and Olmsted were brilliantly successful," Zaitzevsky concludes. In which success architecture of stone and mortar also figured. Alas, the splendid Roxbury pudding stone Bussey Institute of 1870 by Peabody and Stearns has been destroyed. But the arboretum's other original late nineteenth-century landmark, the Hunnewell Building, still stands. It was given by yet another avid horticulturist, Hollis Hunnewell (he of the many terraced and gorgeous gardens of "Wellesley," the family's estate in the Boston suburb since named, like the college, after the estate), as an all purpose administration, library, museum, and herbarium building. Designed in 1891–93 by A. W. Longfellow, who also designed the attached herbarium wing in 1912, it is very Richardsonian, evocative of Sever Hall in its proportions; the building's battered walls and robust geometry, hardly picturesque in the usual way, certainly not in silhouette, nonetheless contribute to an overall effect that is very romantic. So do Longfellow's arboretum gates. Also of interest is the boulder culvert at the entryway to the park. Like the culvert of the nearby pond, it was designed by John C. Olmsted, nephew and partner of the master. A final footnote: it was Frederick Law Olmsted's son, Frederick Jr., who created at President Eliot's request the country's first landscape architecture curriculum for Harvard in 1900. Named professor in that field at Harvard in 1902, in the same year, Frederick Jr., already landscape architect to the Boston Metropolitan Park Commission and a founder of the American Society of Landscape Architects, was asked by President Theodore Roosevelt to undertake the redesign of the center of the nation's capital.

OPPOSITE: *Hunnewell Building*

Kennedy School of Government, Harvard Stadium, Soldiers Field, and School of Business

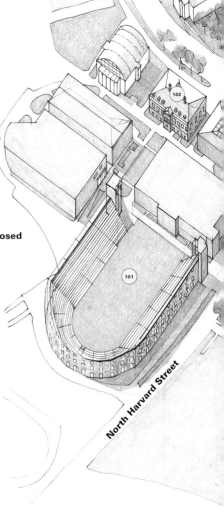

Allston Campus and Cambridge South

Cowley Monastery Church

98. John Fitzgerald Kennedy Presidential Library Site and Park and Cowley Monastery Church

Proposed JFK Library *I. M. Pei, 1974*
JFK Park *Carol R. Johnson & Associates, 1985*
Cowley Monastery Church *Ralph Adams Cram, 1936*

Like Sherlock Holmes' dog—the one that did *not* bark in the night—the most significant architecture here *isn't* here at all, was in fact never built. And the JFK Park now laid out in its place is small consolation. Look instead at the Old Cambridge riverfront to either side of JFK Park. Massive, densely packed, intensely developed blocks of housing—whether neo-Tudor apartment blocks or neo-Georgian college dormitories—crowd right up to Memorial Drive without any open space at all except for rather tight but wonderfully elegant courtyards that are entirely ornamental (meant to be seen as one goes in and out, not used for sitting, sunbathing, sports or whatever). The result is a brilliant cityscape, at once densely urban and quietly ruminative, sidewalks that encourage, for example, the sort of quiet and privacy one wants in heavily built-up city residential areas. JFK Park, on the other hand, is anti-urban in the extreme. An attempt, indeed, to suburbanize the city, it is a large, amorphous, undefined greensward that encourages an intensive and noisy usage; while the park is too big to exclude sports, its memorial fountain (naive hope) is often the haunt of splashing kids and skateboarders. This memorial aspect, hardly successful, is all that is left of the commission for the presidential library that launched the career of one of the world's foremost architects—I. M. Pei—but launched him somewhere else, distinctly a tragedy for Harvard. Today the magnificent glass pyramid that was the centerpiece of Pei's brilliant library design scintillates not on the banks of the Charles, alas, but in Paris, in the great court of the Louvre. Notice particularly the Cowley Fathers Monastery Chapel, which adjoins the park—of all the churches in Harvard's immediate orbit the most memorable and one of the last works of America's greatest twentieth-century church architect, Ralph Adams Cram. The rather conventional exterior does not begin to convey the power and majesty of the church's interior, a traditional place of refuge and support for many at Harvard over the years, as Jill Ker Conway, for example, recounts in her autobiography.

KENNEDY SCHOOL OF GOVERNMENT AND SCHOOL OF BUSINESS

99. Belfer Center and Littauer Center

Architectural Resources Cambridge, 1977, 1982

Belfer Center

What survived the Kennedy Library fiasco was the Kennedy School. President Bok's visionary transformation in the 1960s and '70s of Harvard's rather lackluster School of Public Administration into the dynamic and high profile John F. Kennedy School of Government was one of the most timely and idealistic responses of Harvard in our time to the needs of contemporary life in America. It ended up embodied, however, by architecture that ranges from embarrassing (the buildings facing the Charles Hotel) to moderately interesting (the corner buildings on Eliot Street at JFK Street, the Belfer Center). One of the smallest and poorest of Harvard's graduate schools, with no faculty of its own, the School of Public Administration, established in 1936, was headquartered in the old Littauer Center in the North Yard from 1939 to 1978. Like the Lawrence Scientific School or the Bussey Institute it must be accounted one of Harvard's failures. By the 1960s, however, interest shifted from public administration to public policy, from management of bureaucracies to analytic studies in government. And this inspired President Bok, joining forces with the Kennedy family, to virtually refound the school in 1966, galvanizing the newly renamed school with the establishment of the Institute of Politics. Conceived by Professor Richard Neustadt as the place where (independent) scholarship met politics, the institute offers classes, sponsors visiting fellows, and published the *Harvard Political Review*. The school itself meanwhile today has over 700 full-time students in several masters and doctoral programs. The idea impresses. The architecture doesn't.

100. Weld and Newell Boathouses, Larz Anderson Bridge and the Newell Gate

Weld Boathouse *Peabody & Stearns, 1906*
Newell Boathouse *Peabody & Stearns, 1899*
Larz Anderson Bridge *Wheelwright, Haven & Hoyt, 1900*
Newell Gate *H. Langford Warren, 1897–1900*

Is it coincidence that politics, sports, and business (the subjects of this Walk) have come to roost within sight of each other beside Harvard College (see Walk 12) at the intersection of John F. Kennedy Street and the Charles River? Sports came first, in the post–Civil War era when, in fact, the subject

Weld Boathouse

of athletics much vexed the Harvard community. Even the Phi Beta Kappa speaker in 1893, MIT economist Francis Walker, took the subject as his theme, contrasting the pre–Civil War college hero—he of "towering forehead," "pale" complexion and too many "moods" and "literary" interests, with post–Civil War men of action. In fact, even before the war interest in sport quickened noticeably at Harvard. In rowing, for instance, the first Harvard-Yale race occurred in 1852, and it is that sport that is celebrated by the Weld Boathouse of 1906 (today the home of the women's crews) and its earlier fellow on the opposite bank, Newell Boathouse of 1900 (now the domain of the men). Both buildings in their dignity and elegance seem to evoke the early spirit of those days, when competitiveness was somewhat tempered by the old gentlemanly code of sportsmanship, which an Oxford rowing coach recruited by Harvard defined rather nicely as "strength without aggression, confidence without self-assertion, cheerfulness without ostentation, and endurance to the end." But it was really not tempered very much at all where it really mattered—football.

Harvard, which had greatly influenced the development of the American form of the game since its first game with McGill (under Rugby rules) in 1874, had by the 1880s begun to almost obsess on beating Yale. In that decade and in the '90s, Harvard managed to lose all but two games to its rival in New Haven. Even Henry Adams, no jock he, was distressed; writing to a contemporary, he complained: "You must have put real genius into discovering how not to win." A crisis of manhood portended, though in truth it was a simple definition of manhood that focused on football victories, as the guardians of amateur athletics and good sportsmanship above all kept pointing out. Of this point of view President Eliot himself (a celebrated Harvard rower as an undergraduate) was increasingly in the 1890s the champion; his opponent another president, the chief rough rider himself and a fierce advocate of violent sport, Theodore Roosevelt. At Harvard "there were no battlefields in sight," dryly recounts Kim Townsend, who analyses the moment in his perceptive *Manhood at Harvard*. But, beginning in 1890, there was—Soldiers Field! The successor to all those old playing fields by then being built over north of the yard, Soldiers Field remains today the site of Harvard's playing fields, approached by the Larz Anderson Bridge that crosses the Charles just next to the Weld Boathouse.

In that splendid bridge one sees a distinctive architectural mode originally adopted for Harvard athletic facilities, a mode characterized by the distinctive use of concrete-wall fields dressed with red brick decorative trim, also evident in the architecture of Weld Boathouse, which was the design of Robert Peabody, who had been captain of crew in his own student days. The design of Weld has extraordinarily robust detail, including a flamboyantly modeled ships' prow at the cornice over the main door. This is true as well of the bridge, designed in 1912 by another Harvard graduate who became an architect, Edmund Wheelwright, he of the Lampoon Castle. Already the designer of the Longfellow Bridge, by far Boston's most magnificent such structure, Wheelwright endowed the Anderson Bridge not only with the concrete and brick decorative scheme, but with extraordinary and, indeed, fully sculptural ornamental gilded mantlings, detail as flamboyant but infinitely more stylish than that of the boathouse. This mantling surmounts the entrance piers at both ends of the bridge and was once partnered by gilded street lamps, which ought to be restored. (In fact, the whole bridge stands in need of restoration—rather surprising considering how eagerly such issues have been taken up by preservationist activists in and around the Kennedy Library site.) The mantling was modeled by no less than Johannes Kirchmayer, one of the leading American architectural sculptors of the period. Its richness is perhaps

Weld Boathouse and Weeks Bridge

Weld Boathouse

explained by the design concept of the structure: "May this bridge," declares a bronze plaque on the Cambridge side, "connecting the College Yard and playing fields of Harvard, be an ever present reminder to students passing over it of loyalty to country and Alma Mater."

Given that design concept it is not surprisingly the bridge's concrete and brick palette, so obviously derived from the earlier Weld Boathouse on the Cambridge side of the river, is echoed as well by the first architectural feature encountered once across the bridge and on the Allston side—the Newell Gate, the centerpiece of the ornamental fence that surrounds the College's playing fields. In his study of the subject already referred to, noting President Eliot's and the faculty's determination to keep Harvard's athletic program uncorrupted (the teams were not allowed to play professionals, for example, or to have professional coaches), Townsend writes: "The metaphorical fence that these men erected around the 'amateur' and gentlemanly play of the undergraduates took physical form when they had the athletic fields enclosed—in order, they said, to 'protect the grounds and exclude objectionable persons.'"

101. Harvard Stadium *Charles McKim and George Bruno de Gersdorff, 1902*

In a word—a masterwork: "functionally almost perfect, structurally innovative and aesthetically advanced"—so Bainbridge Bunting wrote and it is hardly possible to argue with his analysis: "The largest ferro-concrete structure in the world...The U-shaped stadium was shorter and wider than a Roman circus and yet, unlike a Greek amphitheater, was artificially formed through raised seating of reinforced concrete. The elegance and power of the resulting building, opened in 1903, proved conclusively the aesthetic viability of massive ferro concrete—the material that Frank Lloyd Wright would use two years later at Unity Temple in Chicago." (Mostly built in 1902–1903, the colonnade that surmounts the structure, originally a promenade, was not completed until 1910.) The chief architect, who contrived the stadium's proportions and its inspired siting –open end to the river and the college beyond—was Charles McKim. First used for the Yale game in 1903,

Harvard Stadium

the stadium was built courtesy of the princely donation of 100,000 dollars from the Class of 1879—a gift that began the practice of landmark twenty-fifth reunion gifts. Young Franklin Roosevelt, meanwhile, in the stands for the Yale game that year with cousin Eleanor, would propose to her the next day. Also in attendance the first year was Harvard's most famous twentieth-century designer, R. Buckminster Fuller, only eight years old when the stadium opened. He recalled 80 years later "the smell of its new concrete," comparing it to "the smell of the new concrete in the...subway" to down-town Park Street from Harvard Square, which had opened nine years later. It was, wrote Fuller, "the typical environmental smell at the portals of a new age into which we all were entering."

The grandeur of the huge new stadium surely did much to tilt the decision for football at Harvard, a decision still up in the air when the stadium opened in 1903, and one in which President Eliot and President Roosevelt went head to head at a conference among Harvard's, Yale's and Princeton's coaches—such was the gravity of the event—held at the White House! Indeed, after a season of vicious play and brutal injuries an over-seers committee had demanded either the reform of the game or its aboli-tion at Harvard. In response, the Harvard Graduates' Athletic Association formed a committee under the leadership of John Reid (Harvard's first paid football coach; the barriers *were* falling), which proposed nineteen new rules—most notably the introduction of the forward pass, made necessary by the fact that the gridiron in Harvard Stadium could not be widened except at enormous cost. Fearful that Harvard (setting an example many might follow) might otherwise ban the game, the newly formed collegiate athletic association adopted all Harvard rules. Narrowly, over Eliot's objection, the governing boards voted to continue football, which, indeed, then entered a golden era at Harvard under Coach Percy Haughton—the most famous football coach in Harvard's history. During Haughton's tenure from 1908 to 1917 Harvard finally began to dominate Yale in the sport. The Haughton Memorial on the north side of the roadway surrounding Soldiers Field features two bas-reliefs by R. Tait McKenzie. The larger relief depicts Harvard's legendary head football coach in a characteristic pose, crouching at the sidelines; the smaller, side relief shows a group of players just after Haughton—a notable punter—has kicked the ball. It should also be noted that the Stadium's classical pomp has many times proved irresistible to Harvard drama types. As early as in 1906 Aeschylus' *Agamemnon* and as recently as in 1983 Euripudes' *Bacchal* have been staged here.

102. Dillon Field House *Coolidge, Shepley, Bulfinch & Abbott, 1931*

Harvard Hall. University Hall. Memorial Hall. Emerson Hall. Widener Library. All of these buildings have been advanced variously here as the heart and soul of Harvard. For the athlete it would seem Harvard Stadium, by contrast, would be the logical choice. But for the Harvard author who most conspicuously celebrated the jock ethos it was Dillon Field House. "Widener is only the brains of Harvard," Eric Segal (he of *Love Story*) has written: "To

Bright Hockey Center, Newell Boat House, Dillon Field House, and Murr Center

me, its heart lies across the Charles River—in Dillon Field House." A graceful structure of 1931 whose cupola is, in fact, notably reminiscent of Harvard Hall's, it must be said that architecturally, Dillon, in abandoning the concrete and brick palette for a more conventional all brick facade, disappoints architecturally. For all that it is a nice enough building, the last built here of much architectural distinction in what since World War II has become a huge athletic area. Today Harvard fields nearly sixty varsity and junior varsity teams, including what might be called the Eliot-Roosevelt compromise, Ivy League football, about which there is no longer much controversy! As to that, perhaps the last word should go to Santayana. He had in the end comparatively few good things to say of Harvard, or, indeed, of America, when you think of it. But in "Philosophy on the Bleachers," he allowed as how "seated there in the stands, watching some well-conceived contest like our foot-ball, the whole soul is stirred by a spectacle that represents the basis of life." He had seen what even Eliot had not.

103. Harvard Way and Morgan Hall *McKim, Mead & White, 1926*

Business School, Harvard Way

Harvard Way, a veritable enfilade of arching trees to each side of a gracious Georgian Revival street; it is the most beautiful avenue at Harvard. Bar none. The last thing in the world it evokes is business. Instead, one all but expects to hear the soft bump of tennis balls. But on second thought (for if you listen carefully enough there *are* tennis balls), one feels soon enough in Harvard Way's sylvan perfection and realized ideal the sovereign power of money. This is Harvard's Business School.

Business came to roost here next to sport and politics by no prearranged plan and only after a long and none too promising pre-history beginning in 1908 in odd corners of University Hall and Widener Library. Like Law and Medicine, Business, born in Harvard Yard, was simply too big an idea to be long content there in the shadow of the college. Not that the Business School's pedigree is wanting; "The idea which ultimately resulted in the first graduate school of administration in America was conceived as early as 1885 by president Charles W. Eliot," according to official recounting. However, Morison noted much more specifically in 1934 that the B-School began (long before the Kennedy School was ever imagined), as an "inconspicuous appendage for Professor A. C. Coolidge's project for a School of Political Science," and was subsequently made a separate school in 1908 as a result of the business panic of the year before; "The economic tail," quoth Harvard's historian, "was lopped off behind the ears of the political dog." Somewhere between Eliot's idea and Coolidge's, in an age when business was increasingly of greater and greater importance, came the not unrelated idea, according to Theodore White, that in the wake of "the Spanish American War...a few public spirited alumni decided that the United States, for its new empire, needed a colonial school of administration to match Britain's imperial and colonial civil service." However public spirited the impulse, as Morison also points out, the new school "met with strong opposition on the assumption that it was to be a mere school of successful money-making; and," he continues, presumably with a perfectly straight face, "although that motive has not been absent from the students' minds, the object of [the first] Dean [Edwin] Gay and his staff was to create a practice, a profession, and an ethic of business management. Unlike business schools in most American universities, it was open only to college graduates."

None of this convinced the late George Apley in John P. Marquand's novel of that name; he always looked away when driving along the river by that "most damnable example of materialism," as he called this magnificent campus. Built in 1925–27, it was given by George F. Baker, a New York banker, but Baker had been talked into it by a Boston bishop, of all people, Episcopal bishop William Lawrence. At the campus' 1927 dedication much was made of the B-School's purpose as above all the formulation of high ethical standards for American business. Who even today is to pronounce, historically, on all this? Wending one's way up Harvard Way past Morgan Hall (that's J. Pierpont Morgan, of course, Baker's longtime friend and associate), there does, however, come to mind in this beautiful tree-shaded way the reflection in the 1930s of no less than the philosopher Alfred North Whitehead, whose son taught at the Business School. He believed that the B-School's dean of the time was "one of a group of businessmen and educators [who had] gone far to avert the disaster of an American social revolution." That was the fear engendered, of course, by the Great Depression, which descended upon America only three years after this new campus was dedicated. The lush architecture, the flora and the fauna, all of it, must have embarrassed more and more as that depression deepened. For, architecturally, it is never entirely clear how to take the B-School. Is it like the television in the reproduction Colonial keeping cupboard? At first glance the B-School seems more like the embodiment of Plato's academy, or a curious sort of New England Versailles or Schonnbrun. The older neo-Georgian parts of the B-School, where brick and stucco "houses" alternate with handsome arched connecting gates, can be

Harvard Business School

quite charming, and because one thinks of business as less apt to encourage thoughtful walks than, say, history or philosophy, the obviously high
priority given here to aesthetics rather startles. Aesthetes may or may not
like it, but I think Jane Jacobs knew: "The aesthetic sense in general is far
more utilitarian in our lives than we give it credit for," Jacobs has written.
"It is not a frill. It may be very essential to our survival.... Aesthetic sense
may be awfully important in maintaining our whole ability to create."

Notwithstanding all that, when the smoke cleared after World War
II the B-School's subsequent development showed only too well that its
high-minded goals would need to be vigilantly guarded as against what
might be called the mentality of the bottom line. President Bok found this
out in the late 1970s, and one has to reach back to Eliot's renewal of the
Medical and Law Schools in the late nineteenth century to match the effect
of Bok's dramatic intervention into the life of the Business School in 1978 in
his annual report (made public the following year in full). Harvard's president raised urgent questions about the Business School's values and
lifestyle, questions which according to *Fortune* magazine left "the ethical
quality of its instruction open to doubt." That same year *The Wall Street
Journal* (just prior to Bok's report being made public) raised its own questions about the Business School, emphasizing the whole matter of its culture of truth-telling (or not!). Bok, for all his informal modern ways very
much a severe, patrician Yankee in that department (one who drove his own
Volkswagen and looked askance at the limousines and corporate jets of the
business world—and whose wife, moreover, Sissela Bok, taught ethics at
the medical school and authored a book entitled *Lying*), acted decisively. A

shake-up at the Business School included the president's appointment of a new dean, and more than one person that year must have remembered all the old controversies about the Business School's founding seventy years earlier. However difficult to maintain, the B-School's ideals have endured, and its repute is on the whole rather enviable. Being first—and it is only fair to say this earliest major graduate business school in the country all but invented the MBA degree, to say nothing of the case-study method of studying business—has posed risks. The Business School has long been one of Harvard's Big Three professional schools, along with Law and Medicine. Even today there are many who would question whether or not business is a profession in the sense law and medicine are, to say nothing of divinity or education. But it is perhaps just Harvard's vocation to engage issues of that sort, for it would be naive to suggest business is only about private gain, an idea the Puritans who founded Harvard would themselves have given the lie too.

104. The Great Court and the Baker Library
McKim, Mead and White, 1926

The Business School's original architecture reflects many of these historical tensions—and never more so than at the school's heart, in the Great Court, which opens grandly to the river, flanked to each side by generous inter-locking buildings in a complex of extraordinary amplitude, resembling, indeed, nothing so much as Sir Christopher Wren's Royal Hospital at Greenwich. Less splendid, to be sure, but more focused: instead of the somewhat anti-climatic Queen's House at Greenwich, at the Business School there is Baker Library. Endowed with a conspicuous colonnade and cupola as well as ornamental mantling in the pediment, it dominates the scene thoroughly. Yet the really dominating aspect is the campus across the river. Standing in the Great Court you may hear the bell hung in the central gilded cupola of the Baker Library—brought from old Harvard Hall rather as medieval clerics might have brought a saint's relics—to endow the B-School with some memory of the Old Yard, the land of its beginnings across the river. Even if you don't happen to hear the bell, the court offers (it is Harvard's most spectacular vista) a view of the Cambridge riverfront that makes the connection with old Harvard even more strikingly. One thinks of Peter Cohen's observation, in his "The Gospel according to Harvard Business School," that "'across the river' is a threat...[a place of] daydreamers...self-righteous idealists....And, although they never admit it, across the river for many [B-School students...means] Harvard Yard. The realization," Cohen concludes, "that we, as graduate students...are kind of stepsons of this prestigious family." Yet that feeling of being a step-

Baker Library

son is common to all graduate students in all fields who go to college at one place and to graduate school at another. And did not the B-School itself begin life as one of those daydreams of Harvard Yard, daydreams by idealists like President Eliot?

What a daydream! The design of the Business School in the early 1920s confronted Harvard with the challenge of creating an academic community then that was "larger than the whole university was fifty years ago," in the contemporary words of G. H. Edgell, who interestingly analyzed the proposals of the six architects who were invited to participate in the final competition. Edgell emphasized the work of four designers: Coolidge, Shepley, Bulfinch & Abbott, who echoed the series of formal but independently sited front-facing open courts of their freshmen dormitories on the opposite Cambridge riverfront; Perry, Shaw and Hepburn, whose plan, wrote Edgell, "avoided the symmetry and formality we associate with French design, [because the designer felt] it out of harmony with the [informal] traditions of Harvard architecture"; Guy Lowell, whose proposal was symmetrical and formal but was disposed informally, in fact, diagonally, its central court on axis with a main gate facing the Larz Anderson Bridge; and McKim, Mead and White (which is to say their successor firm, all these principals having then died or retired), whose plan Edgell described as "a formal group...with radial lines from the river, a vista of the main access leading to the library." All the proposals were Georgian Revival in style. No deliberations were ever published, but the winning design, McKim, Mead and White's, albeit a bit thin in feeling, is conspicuous for the successful way it seeks reconciliation at

Harvard between the two really quite divergent architectural traditions that emerged in the late nineteenth and early twentieth centuries.

Consider. The rather cold classicism of the medical school makes no apology for the way its pomp seemingly repudiates the Old Yard. Nor does the parade of limestone columns of the Law School. But the architecture of the Business School (somewhat in the tradition of Widener Library— red brick, after all, because it's *in* the Yard), is distinctly making an overture. In just the way Bulfinch in the early nineteenth-century, at University Hall particularly, sought to reconcile the architectural expression of Harvard's warring eighteenth-century aesthetics—elegant vice-regal and plainspoken patriot—and Richardson in Sever Hall the Georgian and Victorian traditions, so in the early twentieth century the design of the Business School seeks to reconcile the pomps of "imperial Harvard" with the old red brick boxes of Harvard Yard, by that time so infinitely venerable and gracious. In its size, symmetry, and colonnaded central library, the Business School Great Court is recognizably Imperial Harvard. But in its library's gold-domed cupola and heraldic pedimental mantling (after the fashion of Holden Chapel), and above all in the way the Great Court eschews marble for brick, imperial classicism for the more domestic Georgian classicism, the Business School also defers to the eighteenth-century Old Yard. Withal, some of its passages (the alternation of stucco and brick, for instance) are undoubtedly charming. The reconciliation is a success. "A great many haughty windows framed in red brick" was Peter Cohen's reaction. Brilliant architectural criticism. For all the Great Court's deference to the Old Yard, one would never in any sense at all say that about Harvard Yard.

105. Kresge and Burden Halls, Soldiers Field Apartments, Chapel, Shad Hall and Spangler Center

Kresge Hall *Perry, Dean & Hepburn, 1953*
Burden Hall *Philip Johnson, 1968*
Soldiers Field Apartments *Benjamin Thompson, 1974*
Class of 1959 Chapel *Moshe Safdie, 1992*
Shad Hall *Kallmann, McKinnell and Wood, 1985*
Spangler Center *Robert A. M. Stern, 2000*

The Business School's post–World War II architecture is less interesting. At the end of Harvard Way Kresge Hall of 1953 is pale, expiring neo-Georgian. Diagonally across the street is the unrelieved dark red brick cubistic mass, Burden Hall, by Philip Johnson of fifteen years later; as at Ben Thompson's adjoining Soldiers Field Apartments of 1974, the new dawn of the modern

TOP, LEFT AND RIGHT: *Shad Hall*
BOTTOM: *Class of 1959 Chapel*

movement is very evident, but not inspiring. Another decade and closer to our own time, a block further south, stand three structures of the 1980s and '90s along Gordon Drive. These carry the tale forward, as the Business School in the 1980s began to turn away from the river and in upon itself, just the way (though from streets usually) Harvard has ever developed. The master planner for this development was Moshe Safdie, who also designed the first of these three structures we meet, the controversial Class of 1959 Chapel. Variously monster or masterpiece according to your point of view, the chapel sports an interior whose colors are controlled by computer-assisted prisms, the work of artist Charles Ross. The second of three structures, scheduled for completion in 2000, is the Spangler Center by Robert A. M Stern. Lastly there is Shad Hall of 1985 by Kallmann, McKinnell and

Wood. The oldest of these three examples of contemporary design, Shad has intrigued critics as disclosing KMW's propensity for unexpected but elegant forms. Critic Elizabeth Padjem has called attention to the way the splendid steel lintel of the entrance bay is "supported by a single column with an outrageous gilded capital [also steel], a 'gilded fist' that the architects thought was an appropriately muscular metaphor for an athletic building on a campus where cupolas display 'gilded crania.'"

106. Graduate Student Housing and Proposed Harvard Museum of Modern Art

Graduate Student Housing *Machado & Silvetti, 2000*
Proposed Museum *Renzo Piano, 2000*

Graduate Student Housing

As this book was going to press two exciting new projects—the most important architecture at Harvard in decades—have been announced as projected to stand at either end of the Western Avenue Bridge. On the Allston side graduate student housing is being designed by Machado and Silvetti, Boston's leading architects today, best known perhaps for their spectacular parking garage at Princeton and their work at the Getty Museum in Malibu in Los Angeles. Wonderfully, they throw the upper floors across the full width of the open end of their great court, which remains a gallant response to those other courts opposite but, by that one stroke, becomes something new in courtyards—if you will, something wonderful. Notice, too, the way the brick of the courtyard turns the corner, bleeding into the side facade. The project proposed for the Allston side of the bridge is a museum of modern art for Harvard's collection. The design is still in the conceptual stages. However, too much cannot be expected from the commissioned architect, Renzo Piano. Nor does Boston have any cultural need greater than for this exciting new project.

Coolidge Residential Colleges

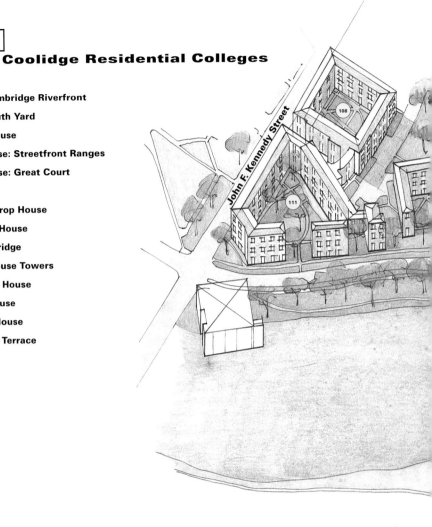

Allston Campus and Cambridge South

107. The Old Cambridge Riverfront and the South Yard

Harvard's finale. Nowhere in American higher education is there a more majestic Georgian Revival panorama than these riverfront residential colleges, an ensemble that is arguably Charles Coolidge's masterwork. They are popularly called the River Houses. Harvard when it subdivided in 1930 preferred "House" to "College" for reasons of antiquity and sentiment. The long cherished nickname of the first Harvard College building of 1638 had been "the House," even as it is still at Oxford the nickname of perhaps the grandest college, Christ Church. Similarly, English Cambridge's oldest college is Peterhouse. Harvard's decision was in my view, however, a mistake, and one that Yale, simultaneously endowed with a college system by the same donor, did not repeat. "House" is too vague, easily confused with many similar sounding but quite different things—fraternity houses, dormitories, and historic homes—to take just three examples common in academe. Thus perhaps the leading House of Harvard's original seven (named after President Lowell and his family), has, historically, been known to insist on "college" after its name; on the front cover of old issues of the House magazine, *The Lowellian*, for example, where COLLEGIUM LOVELLENSE is blazoned proudly. Significantly, Lowell himself first used the word college, writing in 1929 that "Harvard University is about to develop . . . self-contained colleges or schools, which we call Houses."

That was the president's description of a project funded by the largest gift by far in Harvard's history to that time, a project the *Boston*

Lowell House and Charles River

Transcript pronounced "one of the most radical innovations ever under-taken by American higher education." President Conant, Lowell's successor, declared in 1936: "the fundamental principles of this educational system of ours were determined by the adoption of the General Examination and the Tutorial System on the one hand, and the establishment of the House Plan on the other." And it was the resolution of problems at Harvard, which first surfaced here in Walk Four along the Gold Coast to old "Apthorp College." Indeed, residential colleges were considered at Harvard in 1871 and again in 1895—and in the early 1900s at Princeton, where Woodrow Wilson led perhaps the most influential campaign for such a subdivision. It was the obvious solution for any college growing uncontrollably and increasingly swamped by the different values—academic and social—of the universities developing around them in the late nineteenth century. In 1926, Yale was actually offered the funds for residential colleges by Edward Harkness, a Yale alumnus, but was unable to act on the matter. President Lowell's plan succeeded first. Because it was funded by the same donor, tired of waiting for Yale, the witticism that Lowell had realized Princeton's idea with Yale's money at Harvard is very nearly the truth.

Yet Lowell's commitment to the idea was long-standing and more carefully thought out, rooted in concerns both social and scholastic. During the last decade of Eliot's presidency, Lowell was a founder of the History and Literature Committee, which offered the first tutorial—one on one teaching—at Harvard. Abbott Lawrence Lowell also was the central figure in the early 1900s debate as to whether Harvard should allow students more and more to fend for themselves in Cambridge boarding and apartment houses, thus encouraging many barriers of class and ethnic segregation. Lowell asserted, in a speech in 1907, that "what we want is a group of colleges, each of which will be national and democratic." Two years later he was president, and history seemed to conspire with him. Alumni, working through area realtors, had been buying up riverfront property—mostly modest wooden houses and tenements—made newly attractive as a result of the damming of the Charles River, and Lowell eventually had over seven acres available for the first stage of his plan: riverfront dormitory halls origi-nally used only for housing freshmen, which as he admitted later, in 1926, were conceived "with a view to building upon them a set of colleges." Indeed, housing freshmen separately (in the Old Yard ultimately) was for Lowell a prerequisite to subdividing into colleges, an answer to what he perceived as the greatest problem posed by his project. "If men, on coming to Harvard, entered the college they preferred," wrote Lowell, "all the boys from Groton, for example, would want to go in together." Nor could Harvard in those days force the issue, lest it alienate alumni and lose appli-cants. Lowell's eventual solution was inspired. Freshmen would be assigned democratically the first year—a pill Lowell thought would be easy

Leverett House towers

enough to swallow, because the second, after a year of new and widening friendships, they would be allowed to apply to any of the new colleges. (Today, to protect diversity on all levels, sophomores are also assigned randomly to the Houses themselves; there is no longer any element of choice, on the part of the student or the House.) "The common freshman year," wrote Lowell, "[would be] the only means...for overcoming a primary and fatal difficulty to the plan of colleges."

With the physical nucleus of the future Houses—the riverfront dormitories—in place, Lowell also turned to the scholastic goals the Houses were to promote—not as a substitute for courses, but as a corrective to their limitations. Lowell's policy of "concentration and distribution" went into effect in 1914; in 1917 the general examination followed, the great symbol of his determination that the Harvard undergraduate degree represent more than merely passing courses. As each department was won over, Lowell's next domino fell—to prepare students for generals, there must be tutors. In this way he created the teaching staffs of the future Houses. It was a masterly plan. Lowell disarmed opposition at each step with the quite truthful claim that the latest reform was only the logical outcome of the one before it. Few caught on until the actual division into colleges—the "capping stone" of the tutorial system, Lowell called it—was announced in 1929. As *The New York Times* pointodly observed then of the Houses, "outwardly the pattern of the teaching system of Harvard is not changed. This change was accomplished several years ago." But with the Houses it achieved maturity. And if the "capping stone" had been a long time in coming, it was for good reason. When H. I. Brock entitled his article in *The New York Times* on the Houses "Dividing the Invisible Harvard College," Lowell wrote Brock to say what "an excellent title" it was. But few could face the fact that, in all but name, Harvard College had died. Indeed, the matricidal aspect of establishing what amounted to successor colleges explains Lowell's caution, why he had had to look outside Harvard, significantly, for the necessary funding. An application for one college was made to a foundation in 1926, but failed. It was Harkness, finally, who came to Lowell's aid.

More than one legend has grown up around their first meeting. Most picturesque is Lucius Beebe's, in his *Boston and the Boston Legend*:

> Without appointment, [Harkness] presented his card to [Lowell's] chief secretary. The president had but remotely heard of Mr. Harkness, but a hurried investigation of the files of the Boston Herald brought back the magic telephoned words "Standard Oil" and "millions," and Mr. Harkness was shown in with suitable noises.... [Harkness] ventured to inquire what was [Lowell's] guess of the gift he had offered the uninterested men of Yale. [Lowell] opened a drawer, consulted a sheaf of papers, and announced the

cost would be $11,500,000 plus or minus.... [Lowell] explained that he himself had long dreamed of just such a house plan.... Mr. Harkness knew the hand of fate when he saw it and presented Harvard, then and there, with $11,500,000 plus or minus.

It was not, of course, so simple. Wrote Lowell's biographer, Henry Yeomans, of the necessary—and fractious—faculty meetings: "Only the men closest to [the president] at the time knew the feeling of uncertainty beneath his apparent confidence." Professor Julian Coolidge brought the matter to a head by putting the question directly to the president on the floor of the faculty. "Does this," he asked, "commit the faculty to the whole scheme of dividing up into colleges?" Lowell replied, "It does not commit the faculty to anything to which they do not wish to commit themselves, but I will say frankly that that is my object." (Coolidge would be the first Master of Lowell House.) "Lowell pushed hard," according to Yeomans, "so hard that some members thought the plan had been railroaded through," but there was not one dissenting vote. It was the climax of Lowell's presidency and of the modern history of Harvard College, which having struggled in the seventeenth century to achieve the standards of an Oxbridge college, now in the twentieth, after begetting a great university, was resolved now to reinvent for itself the original collegiate model. It was an achievement for Lowell's college that raised it finally to the level of Eliot's university. And it was a very close thing. As Morison pointed out, tutorial was not well enough established for Lowell to have founded the Houses until about 1926. But five or six years later it probably would have been too late. Lowell retired in 1933 at age 76, and his suc-

Malkes Athletic Center

Eliot House, with Malkin Center and Kirland House in foreground

cessor's priorities were altogether different. Even if Conant had been willing, it is hard to imagine Harvard undertaking such a project during the Great Depression. A few years either way, and the House Plan would most likely have proved impossible.

Architecture was key in Lowell's whole concept of residential colleges, and he sought of the architects nothing less along the river than the most beautiful collegiate architecture in the country, an ensemble that would have to be beautiful front and back. "Front" in this case meant not street facing but river facing, while "back" (hardly back in the usual sense) meant what was to be called the South Yard, which most of the new colleges would surround in the way a richer and more established seventeenth- and eighteenth-century Harvard College would have surrounded the Old Yard if Harvard's meager colonial resources had allowed something more lively and elaborate (as post-Victorians saw it; hence the Georgian Revival!) than the simple brick rectangles of the seventeenth and eighteenth centuries. And the view from the Malkin Athletic Center, built on the north side of the South Yard as a joint athletic facility for all the new Houses, discloses how well Charles Coolidge and his colleagues succeeded against all odds. (Harvard could buy up the land, but was limited by Old Cambridge's ancient street pattern). Indeed, much of the distinction of the complex of Houses around the South Yard and along the Cambridge bank of the Charles arises from the way the architects massed Classical Georgian forms in very un-classical, even medieval configurations. The view from the Malkin discloses this very clearly. Four of the original residential colleges— Kirkland House and Eliot House to the east, Winthrop House straight ahead, and Lowell House to the left, compose together brilliantly—a high church eighteenth-century style Harvard Yard, as it were. For while President Lowell cheerfully acknowledged—no problem in Anglophile Boston—his debt to Oxbridge (which reciprocated; various of its colleges presenting gifts to mark the House's opening), *the English college Lowell most admired, after all, was seventeenth-century Harvard College*. It is true that Lowell studied the modern state of the British model carefully, but he warned that "mere imitation" of Oxbridge would be fatal. If he had a low opinion of the American system of courses without small residential colleges and tutors, at the same time he also thought that Oxbridge lacked "the courses which give the [American] undergraduate an opportunity to come into close contact…with a number of professors.…" And in the most critical constituents of his plan—the attempt to bring faculty and students together in "the collegiate way" on a daily basis, Lowell was by no means emulating the customs of the Oxbridge residential college as they had developed by his day. Nor did Harvard's president, who was determined not to end up with rich Houses and poor Houses, for example, attempt to replicate the self-governing and self-financing aspect of the Oxbridge colleges, whose customs in those respects had given rise to major reforms at both Oxford and Cambridge in the 1920s. In addressing both his scholastic and social goals, President Lowell was using old forms historically common to Oxbridge and Harvard to create a new combination that answered Harvard's needs, not Oxbridge's, and in the twentieth, not the seventeenth century.

108. Kirkland House

Smith Halls *Shepley, Rutan & Coolidge, 1913*
Bryan Hall and Master's Lodgings *Coolidge, Shepley, Bulfinch & Abbott, 1931*
John Hicks House *1760*

The new Houses made their point crystal clear by the way not just elements of eighteenth-century motifs were included, but through the reuse of original eighteenth-century fabric, including several whole buildings. The Rev. Mr. Apthorp's "Episcopal palace," for example (see Walk Three) became the Master's Lodgings of Adams House. Similarly, at Kirkland House. Although Kirkland's main quad was formed by Smith Hall, one of Lowell's first freshman dormitories, to it was added by Coolidge in 1931 a most charming smaller court, around which stand a new dormitory, Byran Hall, the Master's Lodgings, and the Kirkland Library, this last an eighteenth-century house, which stood once where the Malkin Center now is and was moved here when the small court was built. Not just this dwelling's venerable architecture, but also its history, compels attention. Built in 1760 by John Hicks, a fierce patriot and a Revolutionary War soldier killed in a skirmish with British soldiers the day after the Battle of Lexington Green, this old clapboard house was later used during the Revolution by patriot General Israel Putnam as his headquarters. Not only is there just this very American aspect to the building's history but there is a specifically Harvard connection as well, for both of John Hicks' two sons attended Harvard in the eighteenth century, something President Lowell and his architect doubtless picked up on at once. Its annexation to Kirkland House reveals the flair and imagination both client and designer showed in the original design concept of the River Houses. There was from the first—still is—something about them that excited the imagination.

109. Lowell House: Streetfront Ranges

Holyoke Street, Holyoke Place and Mill Street Ranges

Coolidge, Shepley, Bulfinch & Abbott, 1930

Lowell House, tower and pediment

The emphasis on things American (and Harvard) as opposed to British (and Oxbridge) extends also to purely architectural aspects throughout the River Houses, and to new work as well as recycled work. Witness the great heraldic pediments, gorgeously detailed, of the Holyoke Place and Mill Street Ranges of Lowell House— clearly inspired by eighteenth-century Holden Chapel in the Old Yard. Above all there is Lowell House's entrance tower, obviously modeled on that of Independence Hall in Philadelphia, an American icon of the period eclipsed only perhaps by Mount Vernon. Note too that while for the casual observer it has long been smart to prefer the *original* in Philadelphia to the *reproduction* at Harvard, the truth is that though one may admire Independence Hall for many reasons, the originality of its steeple is not one of them—the Philadelphia steeple having been itself closely modeled on that of St. Magnus the Martyr in London. Moreover the Cambridge tower may be better than the Philadelphia tower. Consider. The easiest way to design "blown-up" Georgian (Lowell House is much bigger than Independence Hall) is to multiply details—a route fatal to the chaste, restrained quality of American Georgian. Yet of the two towers, Lowell's is simpler and more grandly conceived. Moreover, there is another dimension to Lowell's tower: the sound that comes from this very American form is very *un*American, in fact, distinctly Russian, the result of the donor having saved a chime of bells from a Russian monastery that the newly triumphant Soviets of those days were upon the point of melting down, as part of their policy of silencing all Russian church bells, which they did for most of the twentieth century. "Cacophonous and at the same time hypnotic," as James Billington put it in *The Icon and the Axe*, Russian bells or zvon, which are not arranged chromatically the western fashion, yield a peculiar but mesmerizing sound: "a 4/4-time blend of dirge, railroad-crossing clangor and shattering wine goblet," in the apt words of Michael Wines. And the result is "a disharmonious sweetness that assails the ears, and, once inside, makes a beeline for the heart." True. There would be no mistaking Lowell House's Russian bells for anything likely ever heard from the belfry of Independence Hall.

110. Lowell House: Great Court

Coolidge, Shepley, Bulfinch & Abbott, 1930

In its Great Court especially one sees that this is the centerpiece of the River Houses. Only the Princeton Graduate College of 1912 can rival Lowell House as the masterpiece of the residential college building type in America. It was acclaimed within a year or two of its opening, when the Boston Society of Architects awarded it the J. Harleston Parker Gold Medal for the outstanding design built that year in Greater Boston. Bainbridge Bunting and Robert Nylander fairly gush in their Old Cambridge volume about "the masterful way the massing of the buildings on different sides of the quadrangle is varied." Walter Muir Whitehill called Lowell house in 1980 "a masterpiece of creative eclecticism." They are all right. Indeed it is a measure of what distinguished design this is that Lowell House discloses so well President Lowell's idea of the House. Little understood because the residential college is so rare a building type in America today, the critical component of Lowell's philosophy is that it be a self-contained community—best exemplified by Andrew Hollein's experience of the early 1960s, that Harvard for him "shrank to a few hundred living around a courtyard with two apple trees and an elm." He went on to recall that "those doors around the courtyard ... led me to a library, a friend, a squash game, a dinner," all within the House. Thus the building type gathers architecturally around an entirely introverted central court, the more enclosed the better. The point of entry and departure is the gate house, surmounted at Lowell by its lofty bell tower, with the porter's (at Harvard, the superintendent's) lodge at the entrance the separation between "outside" and "inside." The great court within, where the president of the university installs a new master and where, after commencement, the master presents the degrees (signed by the master as well as by Harvard's president and the Dean of the Faculty of Arts and Sciences) to the House's graduating class, is overlooked near the gatehouse by the lodgings of the senior, or head, tutor. This is because the senior tutor, today the academic dean of a House, has historically always been responsible for internal discipline. These lodgings also illustrate President Lowell's efforts to make the Houses attractive to the faculty. Lucius Beebe admiringly described a senior tutor's rooms in 1930: "The whole suite is finished in the mellow brown of natural wood.... Both study and living room have fireplaces flanked by bookshelves in arched recesses behind glass. Morning sun to one side, afternoon sun to the other." Such amenities to a lesser extent are also found in tutors' and students' lodgings all around the court, originally single suites (study, bedroom, bath) and doubles (study, two bedrooms, bath). The numerous entry

OPPOSITE: *Lowell House, small court*

doors proclaim the shunning of the long institutional corridor in favor of the traditional staircase, with suites opening off each landing. Lowell felt that the corridors did not encourage study, and since originally the rents decreased as one mounted to the top floors, he thought stairways would "avoid the association of men by floors, which means more or less by amount of rent." Each entry was thus a social cross-section of the house, student-faculty distribution (and discipline) insured by locating tutors' studies on the ground floor. Furthermore, as expressive as the entry doors are the myriad chimneys; nearly all studies, including those for students, have wood-burning fireplaces. Nine different mantelpiece designs were used in an effort to vary the suites as much as possible, amenities that are often misunderstood. Lowell, a very austere Yankee in his tastes, never squandered money; he was concerned instead with encouraging students to think and study, and fireplaces in this value system were not frills. As John Brubacher and Willis Rudy point out in their *Higher Education in Transition*, those who doubted that the Houses would be emulated elsewhere thought the problem was not cost but a basic "anti-intellectualism ... reflected in the fact that most student residences in America showed no appreciation of the necessary conditions of intellectual work. Students were herded together two, three or four in one set of rooms ... forced to do all their studying [elsewhere]...." The contrasting values represented by the Houses (at least as originally designed!) can be keenly felt in every entry—and especially in the overall labyrinthine quality, often mistaken for bad design, that characterizes them. Yet this is village design after all. Things are apt to be, as Beebe remarked of the Lowell senior tutor's suite, "agreeably difficult of access," for privacy, no less than quiet, is critical to intellectual work.

Also worth noting in the Court is the library range. Given the aggressively secular nature of Harvard by 1930, if one does not expect a chapel, neither does one expect a library, Lowell being two blocks from one of the world's largest. The House libraries, endowed with upwards of seven thousand books and such agreeable features as leather armchairs, Oriental rugs, and good paintings, were conceived as open-shelf libraries, geared to the tutorial program, and intended to encourage students to read widely beyond their course assignments under their tutors' guidance. Similarly arts facilities were provided; there is a music room in Lowell's bell tower, which commands a delightful view of the Charles (the grand piano had to be hoisted into it). Lowell House also has squash courts. The president explained to Harkness at their first meeting that truly collegiate sport, open to all, was an important part of the kind of life he was trying to restore through the Houses, and from the beginning, the Houses have competed in many sports with each other and with the Yale colleges. Finally, across the court, one sees the historic three-part nucleus of the residential college—the master's lodgings, the senior common room, and the great hall, where the

Lowell House, dining room and tower

community takes its meals. This sequence, the basis of the plans of all the Houses where these facilities were newly built, derives from the medieval Cambridge college, which for the most part related these elements similarly. Indeed, to walk into the Lowell dining hall is to duplicate in plan the experience of a student at Harvard in the seventeenth century, right down to the bulletin boards in the entrance or "screens" passage (in the 1660s, the buttery wall), where notices are posted. Through this sequence the nature and function of the residential college is expressed as exactly as the sequence of sanctuary, choir, and nave discloses the function of a church.

The role of a master of a residential college has perhaps never been better defined than in this charge to the magister of a medieval college at Cambridge: "To give his most earnest attention to all matters, spiritual and temporal, within or without, remotely or nearly concerning the House . . . and manfully to defend the rights of the House, that so the scholars might peacefully and diligently pursue their studies." Thus the splendors of Lowell's master's lodgings. The original senior common room, the gathering place for senior (i.e., faculty) members of a college, is next to the master's lodgings, reflecting the relation of tutors to the master, who appoints them. And the fact that the senior common room connects the master's lodgings with the great hall reflects the position of the tutors in the life of the house—midway between the master and his students. In the great hall itself, furthermore, the "houseplace" where master, tutors, and students gather daily for meals and where plays, and other activities take place, the role of the master and faculty is again expressed; the senior common room, at the master's end of the hall, opens onto the traditional dais with its high table, from which the master presides on great occasions over his or her house. At the other end of the hall, the junior, or students' common room, entirely under undergraduate control, and a traditional gathering place for plays and readings and musical events today, completes this eloquent sequence. The hierarchy is not what one expects. The master's house is beautiful, and the senior common room more elegantly detailed than the junior, but traditionally primacy has been ceded to the great hall, an understanding of which is key to understanding the residential college. Lowell's great hall was endowed with a suite of chandeliers worthy of a palace, not because Harvard was a rich man's college or because there was money to throw away; but because in each House the Hall is the modern successor to that ancient Hall of Harvard's first House, the Old College in Harvard Yard of 1638. And as such *these House dining halls are Harvard's most important classroom*. (The chandeliers in Lowell's Hall are designed in the same style, by the way, as those of Bulfinch's principal room in University Hall, the design of which inspired the Lowell Dining Hall.)

The best recent explication of the role of the Hall in a Harvard House comes from another alumni reminiscence, Toby Marotta's from the 1950s: "There were lots of opportunities to get to know a lot of different people. I remember that as one of the things I really liked about the dining hall. It was this grand wood-paneled room with high windows and a lot of space. As you'd get your food, you could look around and decide whom you were going to sit with, what kind of conversation you might have, who looked like they were in a good mood, whether you were going to sit alone or join someone who was sitting alone or sit with a group. Three times a day there was this wonderful opportunity."

Lowell House opened in the fall of 1930 and on September 29th Edward Harkness and President Lowell celebrated the establishment of Harvard's new Houses with the master and tutors of Lowell House, holding high table on the dais in the great hall for the first time. Guests included the British ambassador and the governor of Massachusetts. A splendid and historic occasion, it raised for many the whole question of the nature and style of revived collegiate life. The *Crimson* labeled high table "one of the most forced institutions ever established at Harvard." Actually, though it had lapsed like so many of Harvard's collegiate traditions, high table as we've seen was an ancient tradition at Harvard, one that had survived even the American Revolution. Moreover, *The New York Times* reported that there were half a dozen undergraduates on the dais, and that they went into the senior common room and "had coffee with the guests and dons afterwards." The fact that Harvard's Houses were a modern adaptation of ancient Oxbridge/Harvard collegiate tradition was never clearer, for John Hancock met no students at the high table in Harvard Hall in the eighteenth century, nor does any Oxbridge don today. Rather, the idea was to put an old tradition to new uses, much as at Princeton's Graduate College, where every student in rotation was invited to dine with the master at his table. Without surrendering the benefits of drawing twenty or more students, tutors, and guests together into a small, self-contained group, Lowell House's first master, Professor Julien Coolidge, by having the group dine conspicuously and splendidly at high table "in hall," seized upon the central aspect of Lowell's idea of the House by dramatically illustrating faculty-student interaction in a highly visible way. The mealtime give-and-take of teachers and students, the nucleus of House life, was now what high table was to be about.

111. Eliot House *Coolidge, Shepley, Bulfinch & Abbott, 1930*

The third of the Houses that surround the South Yard is by far the largest and, while by no means Lowell's equal for beauty of mass and proportion and detail, is hardly less interesting architecturally. Or less splendid! In Eliot's magnificent great hall the design module of its paneling is taken from the dimensions of the full-length portrait by John Singer Sargent of President Eliot that is the Hall's chief ornament, while its richly modeled golden Baroque-style chandeliers are as apt to this more baronial oak-paneled Hall as Lowell's crystal chandeliers are to its lighter and more elegant design. Indeed such is the magnificence of Eliot's Hall that George Homans once declared: "One ought to eat only venison, drink only champagne in the

Eliot House

Eliot House, the rivergate

Eliot dining room." This robust feeling extends to the exterior, even to the elephant heads (Eliot's crest) of the pediments in the Great Court. There are none of Lowell House's chaste Federalisms here. Whereas Lowell is of varying and brighter shades of red brick with jointing of nearly white mortar, at Eliot the brick is very much darker, with jointing of pinkish-gray mortar. But while not as lyrical as Lowell, Eliot—which instead of Lowell's beautifully rectangular lot is hemmed in by an uneven, elongated polygonal lot—is a tour de force of ingenious design. The classic residential college sequence, for example, of Master's Lodgings, Senior Common Room (SCR), Great Hall (with high table dais at the SCR end), and Junior Common Room at the Hall's other end is the basis also of Eliot's plan. But at Eliot this sequence is more complicated, spread out over three courtyards. The Hall and JCR adjoin the Great Court, the SCR and the Master's Lodgings adjoin the smaller Master's Court, overlooking which is also the Society of Fellows dining room and also the Senior Tutors lodgings, some rooms of which also overlook the Great Court at the House's main entrance. Moreover, there is a third court, the Forecourt, from which the main entrance passageway penetrates this sequence between the SCR and the Hall dais.

Eliot House, because its first senior tutor was F. O. Matthiessen, a brilliant young scholar in the 1930s who virtually created the field of American literature (previously a footnote to English literature), also got off with a bang, in its case early establishing itself as a prodigious intellectual center, a repute greatly bolstered by having T.S. Eliot himself as a resident don in its early period when the poet was Charles Eliot Norton professor. This association, just the kind of fructifying experience the Houses were built for, sparked Matthiessen's book about Eliot, perhaps the first truly distinguished scholarship to emerge from any House senior common room. Eliot House, indeed, has remained notable in this respect. In Dante Della-Terza's essay of 1983, "Fridays at Eliot House," the Babbitt Professor of Comparative Literature writes: "Entering the Senior Common Room, I receive each time the impression of the intense iconic interacting of a highly relevant intellectual past with a productive present.... The portrait of a student who did well, T. S. Eliot, looks thoughtfully toward... F. O. Matthiessen, [a]... great scholar and teacher." Such was the importance of Eliot's SCR,

Della-Terza concludes, it became to him "a sanctuary for our [its members'] interior liberty." And very much as well a resource to students who did well! (The other side of the life of a SCR, which exists ideally as much for students as for dons, was never touched on more eloquently than by Theodore White: "[my tutor] approached me as if he were an apprentice Pygmalion.... He yearned that I do well. It was not only that I was invited to my first tea party... learning to balance a tea cup properly... it was his absolute devotion to forcing my mind to think that speeded the change in me.") Carried to the level of the mastership, it was at Eliot House too that one of the two of Harvard's greatest masters long reigned—John Finley. (The other was Eliot Perkins at Lowell, both in the post–World War II period). Many times it has been mooted, though abandoned for reasons of privacy infringement, that a book should be published of Finley's letters of recommendation and nominations for fellowships and such. It was not for nothing that Eliot House can brag it had more Rhodes Scholars one year than any other college in the United States.

112. John Winthrop House

Standish and Gore Halls *Shepley, Rutan and Coolidge, 1913*
Master's Lodgings *Coolidge, Shepley, Bulfinch & Abbott, 1930*

Winthrop House connects the South Yard with the river, and its sense of refinement and amplitude is such that one can sympathize with those (very often graduate students, who are not always well treated at Harvard) who grow, perhaps, in the face of the Houses a tad resentful; a senior Harvard dean in a recent book referred to the Houses as "very fancy dormitories," singling out "notions of student lifestyle that included maids, suites, waitresses, menu selection and tablecloths" without ever addressing Lowell's serious purposes and the point made earlier about counteracting American anti-intellectualism as much with a fireplace in every study as a don in every entry.

LEFT: *Winthrop House/Gore Hall*
RIGHT: *Leverett and Winthrop Houses*

Winthrop House has for long made good use of both. Spread out among three magnificent courts opening to the river (one of them, Gore Hall, inspired by Sir Christopher Wren's work at Hampton Court Palace in the late seventeenth century, when Harvard was still struggling in its first wooden wilderness college), this House always arrests any walker by the river. Similarly, its history will interest anyone who wishes to explore the background of the House Plan. President Lowell, more a creature of his own era than many realize, was keenly alert to William James' theories of behaviorism, as Richard Norton Smith points out, adding that "out of [Lowell's] desire to avert [academic] departmental isolation had come the House plan."

It was at Winthrop, for example, that the sons of Joseph Kennedy first ran into a House tutor named John Kenneth Galbraith—fateful meeting; Galbraith would become J. F. K.'s future Ambassador to India and close advisor generally. It was also at Winthrop that young Kennedy wrote his senior thesis—"Why England Slept." History is layered here. Winthrop House bears, after all, one of the great names of Boston's Puritan Age. And one wonders if the Kennedy boys knew that the favorite haunt of their parents when courting was opposite this magnificent riverfront? "In the late afternoon sunlight one of [Joe and Rose's] favorite rambles took them [along] the opposite bank of the winding Charles River...with a stirring vista of Harvard before them." Those intricate wrought-iron traceries of gates, by the way, are the work of two famous American artists, the foremost in that medium in the twentieth century, Samuel Yellin of Philadelphia and Frank Koralewski of Boson's Krasser studio.

Does all this sound a tad dated vanilla? Factor in the recollections of J. Anthony Lukas about "visits to the black jazz clubs of the South End...where Charlie Parker, Billie Holliday, Billy Eckstine...were known to play [and to] Scollay Square, Boston's historic honky-tonk quarter, which catered to...traveling salesmen, sailors...and, of course, hard-boiled Harvard sophomores....My guide assured me that no liberal education was complete without at least one visit to the [Old] Howard [burlesque theater]. More memorable was a visit to one of Scollay Square's penny arcades, where I played my first game of pinball....A few months later...the *Crimson* installed a machine." All of which, mind, was the initiation of Lukas into "the sophisticated ambiance of Winthrop House's B-entry."

Weeks Bridge *McKim, Mead & White, 1926*
McKinlock Hall *Coolidge, Shepley, Bulfinch & Abbott, 1925*
Hall Range and Master's Lodgings *Coolidge, Shepley, Bulfinch & Abbott, 1930*

The fifth of the new Houses, just beyond Winthrop, is best seen entirely from the river, where the Great Court of McKinlock Hall, Leverett's oldest dormitory, may perhaps claim to be the grandest of all the riverfront courts by virtue of its own annexed, so to speak, bridge: the graceful, almost lyrical Weeks footbridge by McKim, Mead and White thrown across the river at this point. A bridge, moreover, that leads many lives; it not only carries steam pipes as well as walkers from one side of the river to the other, it is the locale on starlit summer evenings of the Tango Club of Boston. It is also a perfect vantage point to take in the whole architectural panorama of the Coolidge residential colleges, the original conception that moved Lucien Price to write: "[The Houses] shed a glamour about the life of learning." Added Price: "There is imagination in them." Which one sees here. But since World War II the idea of the House has been more and more of a struggle to maintain. An example is Leverett House's Great Hall. Either a trapezoid or a trapezium, depending on who you believe—a problem the architects overcame by an optical illusion (the difference in width between the two ends of the Leverett Hall is made inconspicuous by almost imperceptible variations in detail)—Leverett's elegant dining hall met the same post-war fate as all the House

LEFT: *Weeks Bridge and Lowell House*
RIGHT: *Leverett House, McKinlock Hall*

dining halls. There was immense overcrowding in Hall as in rooms, and wait-ress service was abandoned in favor of cafeteria lines. Worst of all china was abandoned (each house originally had its own) and plastic mess trays intro-duced! ("Designed by Gropius to make food look like nuts and bolts," in Anne Fadimen's apt phrase.) It was a mercy President Lowell did not live to see it. Indeed, the story is told of Evelyn Waugh visiting a friend in Eliot House, and both men making only a "rapid progress through the Hall, peering at the con-tents of the plastic trays and exclaiming in crisp English voices: "How revolt-ing! How depraved! How sick-making." No one disagreed. Today, if there is not usually china, there are at least dishes. The mess trays are no more.

114. Leverett House Towers and Quincy House

Leverett House Towers and House Library
Shepley, Bulfinch, Richardson & Abbott, 1958
Quincy House *Shepley, Bulfinch, Richardson & Abbott, 1958*

Quincy House

Leverett Towers, the first post–Lowell-era House architecture, designed in a modern idiom by the same firm who had designed the Georgian Houses and Harvard's first high-rise building any-where, are not very successful. Nicely sited in a sunken court, the House Library is quite a pleasant free-standing pavilion, but the twin twelve-story tow-ers, with their rather prominently mod-eled elevations and odd rooflines (giant in and out baskets, David McCord called them) are intrusions on Charlesbank Harvard it is hard to for-give. Quincy House on the other hand, though bland, is more successful, transitional in feeling and not altogether timidly so, for the dormitory wing elevations are in their way really very expressive—small casements mark bedrooms; large plate glass windows (every third floor) mark sitting rooms; the tutors suites on the ground floor are set along terraces with semi-private gardens, and the Master's Lodgings is the penthouse. The House Library and the Hall are lower attached pavilions. Mather Hall of 1930, originally part of Leverett House, helps the court greatly, and although somewhat more open in feeling, and certainly more modern, there is about Quincy the same intro-verted sense one gets through the River Houses.

115. Dunster House *Coolidge, Shepley, Bulfinch & Abbott, 1930*

Dunster House

An extraordinary piece of architecture, Dunster is a kind of epitome of all the Coolidge residential colleges. As an institution, it should be said, Dunster's deliberate and pronounced differences from Lowell House are notable, largely because of the influence of the two founding masters. At Dunster it is the House Library, not the Hall, that is given the place of honor. Dunster also was planned to be more "democratic"; in its Hall there is no dais. Instead, at the master's end of the Hall there is the "Master's Door," which connects directly to his lodgings, a rather forced "Americanism," perhaps, intended as rejoinder to Lowell House's suppos-edly "Anglophile" high table dais, but certainly original and effective. Both common rooms also adjoin each other beside the hall, not designated "senior" and "junior" and both open to students and faculty in either case, a custom also followed originally at Adams House. But notwithstanding these architectural expressions of Dunster's own character, Coolidge's

Dunster House, with Leverett House towers at left and Mather House tower at right

Dunster House

design is notable for its unusual, indeed, inspired use of sources. Firstly, Dunster's tower—an exception in that it is a paraphrase of a British not an American source (Wren's Tom Tower at Oxford's Christ Church)—is unusual in that while the source is Gothic, Dunster's tower is classical. Yet the cupola is as essentially classic a form as the tower is a Gothic form; and as Wren classicized the tower so admirably (in his London church steeples, from which derive so many of New England's), it ought not to surprise anyone that he was sufficiently intrigued with such things to Gothicize a cupola—or that Harvard's architect at Dunster, Hugh Shepley, should then turn the thing around and classicize Wren's Gothic cupola. There is a long and honorable history of such transpositions. At Dunster old fabric also was used; the glowing pine paneling of the Hall dates from the early nineteenth century. But even more interesting, Dunster's triangular lot, which would have unnerved most architects, was instead the point of departure for a triangular plan of set-backs that is then brilliantly picked up in the river facades by great triangular pediments and a vigorous set-back massing. Ingeniously designed to admit more light and afford better river views, this massing is derived from 1930s skyscraper design. If a line is drawn from the top of the tower to the pediments at each end of the house, then continued to the ground and along the foundation, Dunster appears as a triangle laid flat and then stood on end. It is a bravura performance.

116. Mather House and Peabody Terrace

Mather House *Shepley, Bulfinch, Richardson & Abbott, 1968*
Peabody Terrace *Sert, Jackson & Gourley, 1963*

Two contemporary works side by side, and it is Peabody Terrace that at once
stands out. Unique on the Cambridge side of the river in being graduate student housing for married couples, Peabody is a modernist masterpiece worthy of comparison with Harvard's more storied brick neo-Georgian riverfront
courts. Moreover, William J. R. Curtis, the eminent architectural historian,
has observed that at Peabody Terrace architect José Luis Sert also achieved
something of a shotgun marriage between high style collegiate architecture
in whatever idiom and the ubiquitous vernacular tenement architecture of
the Boston area, one cluster of which backs onto Peabody Terrace. Wrote
Curtis: "[Sert's work at Peabody Terrace is an] extension [of Le Corbusier's]
utopian vision of an alternative city...modulated, rendered less absolute
and wedded with a pre-existing context. Motifs of Corbu-like streets-in-the-
air are fused with Harvard's iconic Georgian grads and Boston's vernacular
tenement tradition of 'three deckers' with their ubiquitous porch railings,
one above the other, reflected in Peabody Terrace's grill-like treatments of
fenestration." Add irregular massing, textured facades, silver-gray concrete
and primary colors and Sert's distinctive style emerges. Moreover, Sert, on a
much larger scale, in the design of Peabody Terrace helped knit together the
two sides of the Charles in the way his Boston University Law School tower
down river and on the Charles' opposite bank responds in its design language to Harvard's towers at Peabody Terrace.

  In comparison, Mather House is not so arresting in and of itself but
is of particular importance to our theme in this walk as virtually the only
effort at Harvard to translate the typology of the residential college into high
rise architecture. And in that more limited context it succeeds. Lowell's idea
of the House does survive, though barely, the compromise of abandoning
the traditional entry system and piling up student suites, floor after floor, in
a skyscraper—justified as this is in some sense by the dramatic river views
undergraduates enjoy (indeed, at a fraction of the cost of adults in any of
the river's comparable residential towers). The trapezoidal court is handsome and throughout the design of Mather reddish brown pre-cast concrete
contrasts nicely with white poured concrete and both with the dark brick of
the Fire Escape Tower, the Master's Lodgings, and the Hall, the interior of
which is starkly beautiful. But Mather's excellence is best disclosed by walking across the street back to Dunster House, with which Mather shares
more than a kitchen. For unlike Leverett Towers—the first and not very successful attempt on the river at modernist House architecture—Mather is
very much meant to be seen in conjunction with the older neo-Georgian
residential colleges and specifically with Dunster, both of which play off

each other very well. Jean Paul Carlhian, SBRA's lead architect for Mather, was in his day a gifted designer and much respected the work of Henry Shepley and, above all, Charles Coolidge, the master to whom Harvard owes its riverfront residential colleges. Handsome as Mather is, it is content to defer, and defer it should, to Dunster, which is so much more than handsome, surpassed not even perhaps by Lowell House in its masterful form. Dunster fuses the neo-Georgian collegiate mode not just with eighteenth-century English-American sources like Holden Chapel, but also with twentieth-century sources like big-city set-back skyscrapers. In this sense the most constructive comparison here shifts from Mather House and Dunster to Peabody Terrace and Dunster—also in view from this riverfront perspective—for Dunster and Peabody are in a league of their own here, alike masterpieces of powerfully synthetic but original architecture.

I am reminded of Leonard Barkan's study, in his *Unearthing the Past*, of the work of Michelangelo and another Renaissance sculptor, less gifted and more typical (because more imitative), Bacio Bandinelli. In that study Barkan points to a key distinction. Observing how even "Vasari approve[d of Bandinelli's] practice of [a kind] of imitation that keeps the viewer aware of the gaps between an ancient original and a modern work," Barkan saw in Michelangelo's oeuvre, however, something else very different—that at the highest level of creativity "the histories of revival are composed in a fugue of glorious antiquity, great genius and originality produced by passionate engagement with the past." The result, Barkan argues, is an "art that collapses or substitutes for historical time," or, as he puts it elsewhere in the same study, art that "telescopes history." The River Houses exactly! Musing between the South Yard and the river, Allston on its other side (where to both sides of the Business School and the Stadium so much of Harvard's future architecture must lie), this perspective of Barkan's about art and historical time—a theme of this book—is very pertinent to Harvard on the eve of its fifth century. For in and of itself the university (at over 50,000 students, faculty and staff) is now considerably bigger than many Boston neighborhoods and even whole suburban towns. Harvard is today, in fact, the second largest non-governmental employer in the Boston area, the nation's seventh largest metropolis, inevitably prompting at the end of these walks a brief meditation on the university's future development. Is there any limit to Harvard's growth?

It seems only prudent to ask. *Yet that is one of those questions no generation can honorably or reasonably ask of the next one.* And never is the reason why clearer than along the riverfront, where—100 years or so ago now—Harvard grew so suddenly and dramatically in the period between 1912 and 1930, and in a way we'd now find highly controversial, displacing whole blocks of neighboring residents. But it was a growth spurt both Harvard and Old Cambridge survived very well indeed. Moreover, it was a development, however huge, by which Harvard was able to renew some of

Peabody Terrace

its most ancient ideals, ideals formed in the 1600s in that tiny street-facing open court off today's Massachusetts Avenue, of which only the original seventeenth-century footprint and eighteenth-century Massachusetts Hall now survive, ideals re-established here along the river at a vastly greater scale than even President Kirkland or Charles Bulfinch could have imagined.

Another lesson, one more narrowly architectural, also arises here. President Lowell's idea of the House, after a quick flash of architectural genius on the part of Charles Coolidge, quickly exhausted the capacities of its original built embodiment. One has only to look at the pallid neo-Georgian of the 1940s and '50s to see this. (Harvard has really no equivalent to the architecturally distinguished Yale residential colleges of the 1960s by Eero Saarinen.) And from our perspective, when architecture has meanwhile undergone a revolution—or two or three—Harvard architecture can be seen to be today at a critical point. Witness the words of Ada Louis Huxtable in her *The Unreal America* about the situation in the twenty-first century:

> Every premise about the art of building and the nature of the environment is being re-examined and overturned or restated in some drastically revised form. An era of unrestricted exploration has followed modernism's rigid limits and postmodernism's partying with the past.
>
> What these architects are doing, in a sense, is reinventing architecture. They are stretching the limits of the art.... It is a not-so-gentle revolution.... Unlike the modernist revolution [of the 1900–1930 period], this radical work does not build its strengths by breaking with the past but, more like the Renaissance, transforms its sources through a brilliant synthesis, with far-reaching influence and effect.

So the circle is rounded after all, and in its affinity for the Renaissance way of creativity even the most radical of the architecture of the early twenty-first century has its revivalist aspect. But that is on an infinitely more sophisticated level than the ubiquitous, safe, red-brick and white-trim, neo-Bulfinch historicist infill that seems to tempt some still at Harvard. Poet Robert Lowell pointed out some time ago the trouble with this. Observing that he had the "sinking feeling" that around Boston the citizen was more and more coming to adopt the attitude of "a tourist, a caretaker, and not the householder," and that increasingly men and women "live in New England as the Venetian now lives in Venice," Lowell put his finger on the crux of the matter: "The old," he wrote, "is beginning to have the air of a chain of perfectly restored eighteenth-century Treadway Inns." I think of the child pointing excitedly to Mount Vernon on the Potomac cruise: "Look, mother, a Howard Johnson's." By endlessly copying and mimicking the antique we endanger the real thing, *which ultimately disappears*. Some few artists—Michelangelo is not the only example; Charles Coolidge is another more modest case in point—transcend the problem, often in an age of transition easing the passage for us all. But the masters of the New England aesthetic in architecture today are all modernist, architects like Peter Forbes, Thompson and Rose, Schwartz/Silver and Leers, Weinzapfel. Designers of larger and, indeed, international focus, whose work also comes to mind in a context at once global and regional are Tadao Ando (the Boston and Japanese aesthetics have a long recognized historic affinity), Renzo Piano, Alvaro Siza, Norman Foster, and I. M. Pei (so like TAC is that firm's Puritan-like geometrical sensibility), and Rafael Moneo and Machado and Silvetti, in both cases firms with strong Harvard connections.

Today, Harvard must reach toward the work of men and women like this, which is not to exclude perhaps riskier choices: Frank Gehry—hope rises—was given an honorary degree by Harvard in 2000; Rem Koolhaus surveys Allston. More immediately, however, one awaits Machado & Silvetti's graduate student dormitory and, at the other end of the Western Avenue Bridge, Renzo Piano's design for the projected new museum of modern art, a "MOMA" Harvard and Boston alike have needed for so long. Adjoining it is a majestic old power station (Sheaff and Jaastad, 1901), the preservation of which in connection with the new museum of modern art in a way similar to what has recently been done at the Tate in London suggests even more striking possibilities. In fact, all along Charlesbank the eye sweeps expectantly along the horizon, dreaming the twenty-first century dreams of Harvard in the metropolis of the future. It will all be very new. But it is an old story here. Seamus Heaney's words come at once to mind: "A Spirit Stirs/John Harvard Walks the Yard/The Books stand open/And the Gates Unbarred."

Bibliography

Amory, Cleveland. *The Proper Bostonians.* New York: E. P. Dutton, 1947.

Bailyn, Bernard and Fleming, Donald, et al. *Glimpses of the Harvard Past.* Cambridge, MA: Harvard University Press, 1986.

Bentinck-Smith, William. *The Harvard Book.* Cambridge, MA: Harvard University Press, 1982.

Brown, Walter. *Harvard Yard in the Golden Age.* New York: A. A. Wyn, 1948.

Bunting, Bainbridge, and Margaret Henderson Floyd. *Harvard: An Architectural History.* Cambridge, MA: Harvard University Press, 1985.

Bunting, Bainbridge and Robert H. Nylander. *Old Cambridge.* Vol. 5. *A Survey of Architectural History in Cambridge.* Cambridge, MA: Cambridge Historical Commission, 1973.

Cannell, Michal. *I. M. Pei.* New York: Carol Southern, 1995.

Carlock, Marty. *A Guide to Public Art in Greater Boston.* Boston: Harvard Common Press, 1993.

Curtis, William J. R. *LeCorbusier: Ideas and Forms.* London: Phaidon, 1986.

Dober, Richard P. *Campus Architecture.* New York: McGraw-Hill, 1996.

Dubois, Diana. *My Harvard, My Yale.* New York: Random House, 1982.

Edgell, G. H. *American Architecture Today.* New York: Scribners, 1928.

Floyd, Margaret Henderson. *Architectural Education and Boston.* Boston: Boston Architectural Center, 1989.

Harvard University Handbook. Cambridge, MA: Harvard University Press, 1936.

Harvard University, Bricks and Mortar. Cambridge, MA: Harvard University, 1949.

Hayes, Bartlett. *Hugh Stubbins*. New York: Pilgrim Press, 1983.

Heaney, Seamus, foreword. *Dimitri Hadzi*. New York: Hudson Hills, 1996.

Huxtable, Ada Louise. *The Unreal America*. New York: New Press, 1997.

Isaacs, Reginald. *Gropius*. Boston: Little, Brown, 1981.

Kirker, Harold. *The Architecture of Charles Bulfinch*. Cambridge, MA: Harvard University Press, 1969.

Kirstein, Lincoln. *Mosaic*. New York: Favrar, Straus & Giroux, 1994.

Kohn, Wendy, ed. *Moshe Safdie*. London: Academy, 1996.

Kreiger, Alex. *The Architecture of Kallmann, McKinnell and Wood*. Cambridge, MA: Graduate School of Design, 1988.

Lant, Jeffrey L. *Our Harvard*. New York: Taplinger, 1982.

Mailer, Norman. "Mr. Maugham's Party" in *First Flowering*, Richard M. Smoley, ed. Reading, PA: Addison-Wesley, 1977.

McCord, David. *In Sight of Sever*. Cambridge, MA.: Harvard University Press, 1963.

David Mitchinson, ed. *Celebrating Moore*. Berkeley, CA: University of California Press, 1998.

Morison, Samuel Eliot. *Three Centuries of Harvard*. Cambridge, MA.: Harvard University Press, 1936.

O'Gorman, James. *Living Architecture*. New York: Simon & Schuster, 1997.

Rettig, Robert Bell. *Guide to Cambridge Architecture*. Cambridge, MA: M.I.T. Press, 1969.

Roth, Leland. *McKim, Mead & White, Architects*. New York: Harper & Row, 1983.

Santayana, George. *Persons and Places*. New York: Scribners, 1944.

Sekler, Eduard F., and William Curtis. *LeCorbusier at Work*. Cambridge, MA: Harvard University Press, 1978.

Shand-Tucci, Douglass. "Charlesbank Harvard." *Harvard Magazine*. Nov–Dec 1980.

Shand-Tucci, Douglass. "Does the Spire of Old North Church Belong in Harvard Yard?" *Harvard Magazine*. Nov–Dec 1982.

Smith, Richard Norton. *The Harvard Century*. Cambridge, MA: Harvard University Press, 1986.

Stirling, James et al. *James Stirling*. London: Thames & Hudson, 1994.

Turner, Paul V. *Campus*. Cambridge, MA: M.I.T. Press, 1984.

Ulrich, Laurel Thatcher. "Harvard's Womanless History." *Harvard Magazine*. Nov–Dec 1999: 51–59.

Updike, John, foreword. *The Harvard Lampoon Centennial Celebration*. Martin Kaplan, ed. Cambridge, MA: The Lampoon, 1973.

Weller, George. *Not to Eat, Not for Love*. New York: Harrison Smith and Robert Haas, 1933.

White, Theodore. *In Search of History*. New York: Harper & Row, 1978.

Whitehill, Walter Muir. "Noble, Neglected Memorial Hall." *Harvard Bulletin* 74 (1972).

———. *Boston in the Age of John Fitzgerald Kennedy*. Norman, OK: University of Oklahoma Press, 1966.